the Word

ENCOUNTERING THE LIVING WORD OF GOD, JESUS CHRIST

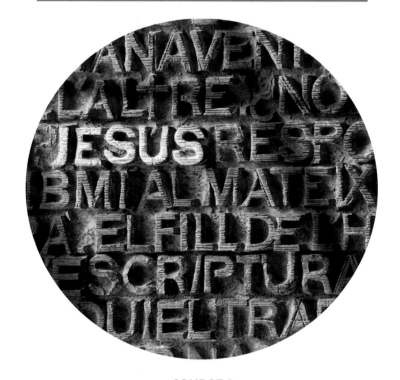

COURSE I

The Revelation of **Jesus Christ** in Scripture

OurSundayVisitor

Curriculum Division

hs.osvcurriculum.com

The Subcommittee on the Catechism, United States Conference of Catholic Bishops, has found this catechetical text, *The Word*, copyright 2011, to be in conformity with the *Catechism of the Catholic Church*.

Nihil Obstat
Rev. Dr. S. R. Olds, S.Th.D.
Censor Librorum, Diocese of Orlando

Imprimatur
✠ Most Rev. John Noonan
Bishop of Orlando
June 2, 2011

The Imprimatur is an official declaration that a book or pamphlet is free of doctrinal or moral error. No implication is contained therein that anyone who granted the Imprimatur agrees with the contents, opinions, or statements expressed.

Write:
Our Sunday Visitor Curriculum Division
Our Sunday Visitor, Inc.
200 Noll Plaza
Huntington, Indiana 46750

Our Sunday Visitor High School Series is a registered trademark of Our Sunday Visitor Curriculum Division, Our Sunday Visitor, 200 Noll Plaza, Huntington, Indiana 46750.

For permission to reprint copyrighted material, grateful acknowledgement is made to the following sources:

Our Sunday Visitor Curriculum Division gratefully acknowledges the contributions of students from Saint Elizabeth Academy in St. Louis, Missouri; Saint Piux X High School in Houston, Texas; and Archbishop Chapelle High School in Metairie, Louisiana.

The Scripture quotations contained herein are from the *New Revised Standard Version Bible: Catholic Edition* copyright© 1993 and 1989 by the Division of Christian Education of the National Council of the Churches of Christ in the U.S.A. Used by permission. All rights reserved.

Excerpts from Vatican Council II documents are from "Vatican Council II: Constitutions, Decrees, Declarations" edited by Austin Flannery, O.P., copyright© 1996, Costello Publishing Company Inc., Northport, NY, and are used by permission of the publisher. All rights reserved.

Catechism excerpts are taken from the *Catechism of the Catholic Church,* second edition, for use in the United States of America, copyright© 1994 and 1997, United States Catholic Conference – Libreria Editrice Vaticana.

Excerpts from the English translation of *The Liturgy of the Hours* copyright© 1974, International Committee on English in the Liturgy, Inc. All rights reserved.

"There's a Great Camp Meeting" from *American Negro Songs* by John W. Work, 1998, Dover Publications. Reproduced with permission from Dover Publications, Inc.

"Oh God of All Children" from *Guide My Feet* by Marian Wright Edelman. Copyright© 1995 by Beacon Press. Reproduced with permission of Beacon Press in the format Textbook via Copyright Clearance Center.

Prayers for a Planetary Pilgrim by Edward M Hays, © 1989, 2008. Adapted and excerpted with permission of the publisher, Forest of Peace, an imprint of Ave Maria Press ©, Inc., Notre Dame, Indiana 46556. www.forestofpeace.com

"The Lord Is My Light" © 2004, Angus McDonnell. Published by spiritandsong.com ©, 5536 NE Hassalo, Portland, OR 97213. All rights reserved. Used with permission.

"Here I am, Lord" Text and Music © 1981, OCP. 5536 NE Hassalo, Portland, OR 97213. All rights reserved. Used with permission.

The Word High School Student Edition
Item Number: CU1509
ISBN: 978-0-15-902414-0

1 2 3 4 5 6 7 8 9 10 015016 15 14 13 12 11
Webcrafters, Inc., Madison, WI, USA; July 2011; Job# 92346

CONTENTS

PRIMARY SOURCES

FEATURES

This is a private reflection that will give you a way to keep track of your spiritual journey, your discoveries along the way, your aspirations, truths, and goals.

GO TO THE SOURCE

Often the textbook will discuss Scripture, but sometimes we will send you directly to the Bible with this feature. You may be analyzing the passage, discussing it, breaking it open, and applying it to your life.

PRIMARY SOURCES

This feature will take you directly to a source that is not the Bible such as Church documents, the Catechism, historical writings, or hs.osvcurriculum.com to help you process the information.

Catholic LIFE

Here you will find stories about people and organizations in the Catholic Church who have modeled discipleship.

THINKING THEOLOGICALLY

This feature will help you talk about your understanding of the nature of God using contemporary insights and experiences.

Spiritual Practices in the Life of DISCIPLESHIP

These are specific behaviors that when done over time, help open us up to God's grace, and at the same time, help make us instruments of God's grace.

Faith Culture

Historical, geographical, and/or cultural background may include maps, photos of architecture, or scenes from history or other cultures to give you a better appreciation for a time, place, or culture that you have read about.

GLOBAL PERSPECTIVES

This feature includes statistics, connections, and other information to step outside your own world. The information will usually bring global awareness to a subject such as the environment and the use of resources.

EXPRESSIONS OF FAITH

This feature focuses on symbols, rites, seasons, and devotions of the Catholic faith. It introduces or reacquaints you with the rich fabric, layers, and expressions of Catholicism and may answer, why do Catholics do the things that they do.

Going Moral

These are designed to involve you in the process of making moral decisions by presenting real-life moral dilemma based on something in the chapter.

JUSTICE AND DISCIPLESHIP

These features will delve into Catholic Social Teaching and will serve as a reminder that those who accept Jesus' message to follow him are called his disciples.

HONORING THE BODY

These features explore body-related topics based on a series of talks by Pope John Paul II called Theology of the Body. The topics include sexuality and health-related issues for all of us made in the image and likeness of God.

Who are the people in this photo following?

Who made the invitation to "follow me"?

CHAPTER **1**

Follow Me

Go to the student site at
hs.osvcurriculum.com

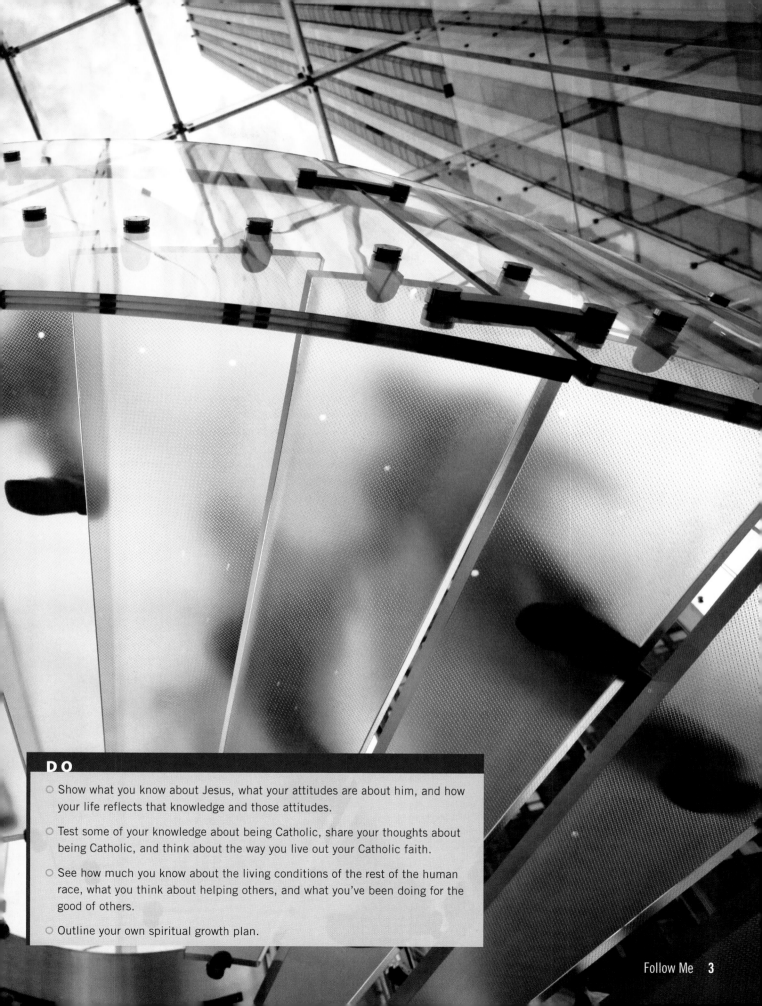

DO

- Show what you know about Jesus, what your attitudes are about him, and how your life reflects that knowledge and those attitudes.

- Test some of your knowledge about being Catholic, share your thoughts about being Catholic, and think about the way you live out your Catholic faith.

- See how much you know about the living conditions of the rest of the human race, what you think about helping others, and what you've been doing for the good of others.

- Outline your own spiritual growth plan.

High school religion will be your hardest subject because it may change the way you live your life. Sure, chemistry is tough. Learning a foreign language takes a lot of effort. Science and history require you to master a ton of facts. Math is challenging. English requires discipline.

Religion, however, asks you to apply everything you learn to the way you live. It requires you to be unselfish, to develop a life of prayer, to examine your decisions, to ask for forgiveness, to go to Mass on Sundays, to receive the Sacraments, and to nurture your soul. It insists that you love your enemies, feed the hungry, turn the other cheek, obey the Commandments, form and inform your conscience, study the ways of God, and be a member of the Church.

And follow The One.

Nothing is more satisfying than living your faith.

Faith feeds your spiritual hunger, gives you strength to hang on when times are tough and comfort in times of sadness, opens your heart to love, improves your relationships, enlightens you when you lose your way, and brings you inner peace. Living your religion makes eternal happiness possible when your current life ends.

So when it comes to faith and religion: What do you know? Where do you stand? What do you do? What's your plan? Here's your chance to figure it out.

WHAT ABOUT YOU?

Discipleship . . .

How do we experience the glory of God?
What characteristics define us as the Body of Christ?
What does it mean to be a disciple of Jesus?
How do we judge whether we are doing enough as disciples?

As Catholics, we profess that we believe in one Lord, Jesus Christ, but how many of us would actually call ourselves disciples? Being a believer is one thing. Being a disciple is another. A believer can accept important religious concepts to be true, but a disciple goes further. The disciple studies those concepts and makes a commitment to them. The disciple allows those beliefs to shape the way he or she lives.

> *If you continue in my word, you are truly my disciples; and you will know the truth, and the truth will make you free.*
>
> —John 8:31-32

A disciple is someone who studies the ways of a teacher and follows them.

In sports, for example, coaches sometimes talk of being a disciple of a former mentor who taught them a certain style of play or emphasized certain aspects of the game. Musicians and actors say the same thing about someone in their field whom they studied and emulated.

In your religion courses, you are being called to consider Jesus' invitation to "Follow me." The bishops of the United States want you to have an opportunity to start a fresh and complete study of Jesus' teachings and the effects his teachings can have on your life every step along the way.

> *We need . . . concrete ways by which the demands, excitement, and adventure of being a disciple of Jesus Christ can be personally experienced by adolescents—where they tax and test their resources and where they stretch their present capacities and skills to the limits. Young people need to have a true opportunity for exploring what discipleship ultimately involves.*
>
> —USCCB, *Renewing the Vision*

We will begin with a series of surveys. Answer the questions honestly and to the best of your ability, but be patient with yourself if you struggle with some of them. Only you—not your teachers, fellow students, or anyone else—will know which surveys are yours.

These surveys serve two purposes:

- to give you a better sense of your religious knowledge, attitudes, and behaviors, and
- to give your teacher a better sense of where your whole class is at to begin with.

You already believe. Now consider discipleship. Only God knows where it may lead you.

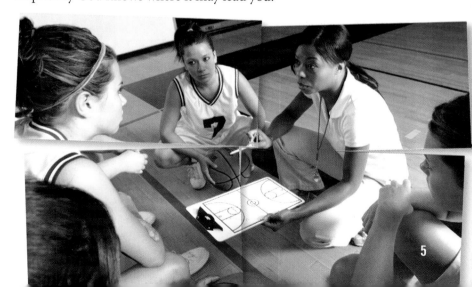

When it comes to Jesus: What do you know?

1. When was Jesus born (approximately)?

_____

2. In what city?

_____

3. What was his nationality?

_____

4. Who was his family's famous ancestor?

_____

5. What term do we use for the way Mary became pregnant and gave birth?

_____

6. What word do we use to describe that the Son of God became man?

_____

7. What was Jesus' mission?

_____

_____

8. What did he say was the Greatest Commandment?

_____

_____

9. What was the Transfiguration?

_____

_____

10. To what does the Paschal Mystery refer?

_____

_____

11. To what does the Resurrection refer?

_____

_____

12. What did Jesus institute at the Last Supper?

_____

_____

13. Which books in the Bible focus on Jesus' life and teachings?

_____

_____

14. Describe two of his parables.

_____

_____

15. Describe two of his miracles.

_____

_____

16. Write down one of his sayings that you have never understood.

_____

_____

17. Put these events in chronological order by placing 1 through 10 next to each:

_____ Agony in the Garden

_____ Teaching in the Temple

_____ Sermon on the Mount

_____ Resurrection

_____ Flight into Egypt

_____ Crucifixion

_____ Temptation in the Desert

_____ Pentecost

_____ Baptism by John the Baptist

_____ Ascension

When it comes to Jesus: Where do you stand?

How much do you agree with each of the following:

☐Very little   ☐Somewhat   ☐Quite a bit   ☐Very much

1. I have a spiritual relationship with Jesus.
☐Very little   ☐Somewhat   ☐Quite a bit   ☐Very much

2. Discipleship appeals to me.
☐Very little   ☐Somewhat   ☐Quite a bit   ☐Very much

3. I have experienced my sins forgiven.
☐Very little   ☐Somewhat   ☐Quite a bit   ☐Very much

4. Jesus' teachings can make the world a better place.
☐Very little   ☐Somewhat   ☐Quite a bit   ☐Very much

5. I consider Jesus to be the Lord and Savior.
☐Very little   ☐Somewhat   ☐Quite a bit   ☐Very much

6. My relationship with Jesus is important to me.
☐ Very little ☐ Somewhat ☐ Quite a bit ☐ Very much

7. I'm interested in learning more about Jesus and his teachings.
☐ Very little ☐ Somewhat ☐ Quite a bit ☐ Very much

8. I'm interested in strengthening my relationship with him.
☐ Very little ☐ Somewhat ☐ Quite a bit ☐ Very much

When it comes to Jesus: What do you do?

1. I pray to Jesus.
☐ Not at all ☐ Some ☐ Quite a bit ☐ Very much

2. I read the Bible.
☐ Not at all ☐ Some ☐ Quite a bit ☐ Very much

3. I'm on the path of discipleship.
☐ Not at all ☐ Some ☐ Quite a bit ☐ Very much

4. I consider Jesus' teachings when making decisions about how to act.
☐ Not at all ☐ Some ☐ Quite a bit ☐ Very much

5. I place my trust in him.
☐ Not at all ☐ Some ☐ Quite a bit ☐ Very much

6. My relationship with Jesus influences the way I live.
☐ Not at all ☐ Some ☐ Quite a bit ☐ Very much

7. I have discussions about his teachings.
☐ Not at all ☐ Some ☐ Quite a bit ☐ Very much

8. I think about what he would want me to do.
☐ Not at all ☐ Some ☐ Quite a bit ☐ Very much

9. I feel close to Jesus.
☐ Not at all ☐ Some ☐ Quite a bit ☐ Very much

10. He brings me inner peace.
☐ Not at all ☐ Some ☐ Quite a bit ☐ Very much

11. I seek him.
☐ Not at all ☐ Some ☐ Quite a bit ☐ Very much

12. I can tell when Jesus is speaking to me.
☐ Not at all ☐ Some ☐ Quite a bit ☐ Very much

13. I choose my closest friends based on how seriously they try to follow Jesus' ways.
☐ Not at all ☐ Some ☐ Quite a bit ☐ Very much

14. Jesus' teachings influence how I decide if something is right or wrong.
☐ Not at all ☐ Some ☐ Quite a bit ☐ Very much

15. My relationship with Jesus affects the music I choose to listen to.
☐ Not at all ☐ Some ☐ Quite a bit ☐ Very much

Within the Body of Christ . . .

As Catholics, we travel the journey that Jesus asked his disciples to follow. We do it as a community of believers. Jesus made it clear that discipleship was not something to be lived on one's own in a "me and Jesus" relationship. He established the Church based on the rock of Saint Peter and the Apostles, and entrusted to them the Good News of salvation, his mission, and saving work. In every generation, their successors, the Pope and Bishops in union with him, continue to lead the Church and, inspired by the Holy Spirit, hand on the faith of the Apostles until Christ returns in glory.

With Peter as their first universal leader, the Bible says "they devoted themselves to the apostles' teaching and fellowship, to the breaking of bread and the prayers" (Acts 2:42). The "breaking of bread" and

East Timorese girls hold candles during a Mass prayer

"the prayers" refers to the celebration of the Eucharist. In so doing, the Apostles and disciples followed Jesus' command to "do this in memory of me." Catholicism traces its roots to Peter and the Apostles. It is a historical fact.

> *And I tell you, you are Peter, and on this rock I will build my church, and the gates of Hades will not prevail against it. I will give you the keys of the kingdom of heaven, and whatever you bind on earth will be bound in heaven, and whatever you loose on earth will be loosed in heaven.*
>
> —Matthew 16:18-19

The Catholic Church preserves the special gifts given to Peter, the Apostles, and the disciples. These make us who we are and are at the center of our Catholic identity. Catholics base their faith and beliefs on Jesus' revelation of the Trinity, his founding of the Church, the Sacraments, Scripture and Tradition, and other gifts listed below. We root our Catholic belief in the Paschal Mystery—Jesus' Passion, death, Resurrection, and Ascension.

The gifts given by Jesus to the Church are described here in terms of "special characteristics." Taken together, they form the core of Catholic belief and practice. In a sense, they make us Catholic. These characteristics are consistent in Catholic Tradition from the time of the Apostles. They have not and will not change, no matter what's happening in society and the world. In every generation the Church passes them on to the next and teaches why they are important to understanding ourselves and our calling in life.

As we mature in faith, we better understand our Catholic identity, that is, what it means to be Catholic. Our faith is a way of life that is meant to permeate everything we do. In religion courses over the next several years, we'll study in detail these characteristics of Catholicism. We'll probe into the Church's teachings about them, and experience first-hand how each one enriches our faith.

1. The Church is Trinitarian.

The great mystery of the Trinity—God the Father, God the Son, and God the Holy Spirit—permeates every aspect of Catholic belief, practice, and worship. Our understanding of the Trinity is part of everything Catholics believe and do, including how we worship and pray. The Trinity is a unity of three equal, yet distinct, Persons, possessing the same divine nature. The Trinity is a divine community, from which all loving human communities take their origin. The communal nature of the Catholic Church is based in the Trinity.

The Trinity is the central mystery of our faith. Trinitarian belief roots who Catholics are, what we believe, how we pray, and what we teach. The Church administers the Sacraments using the Trinitarian formula. In the Rite of Baptism, for example, the bishop, priest, or deacon baptizes in the name of the Father, and of the Son, and of the Holy Spirit. The priest invokes the Trinity in the Eucharistic Liturgy, the Sacraments, and the Divine Office. Catholics begin and end their prayers with the Sign of the Cross, a reminder of our Baptism and the Trinity.

Every time the Church celebrates the Eucharist, we remember the reality of Trinitarian love, witnessed in Jesus' eternal sacrifice, which he offered to the Father through the Holy Spirit. In the Eucharist, we receive Jesus, really present, Body and Blood, soul and divinity. Church members are united to Christ and one another. Together we form the Mystical Body of Christ.

2. The Church is Christ-Centered.

The Catholic faith centers on Jesus Christ, ". . . the eternal Son of God made man" (*Cathechism of the Catholic Church*, 423). Jesus is the Alpha and the Omega, the beginning and end of all things. Jesus is the heart and center of the Catholic faith. He is the way, the truth, and the life. He reveals deep mysteries of the Triune God, heads the Church, shows us the moral path to salvation, and gives us the Sacraments as means to salvation. He teaches us about his Father and sends the Holy Spirit to be with us always.

Because of his great love, Jesus died on the cross for our sins and rose from the dead. He left us a perpetual reminder of his sacrifice in the Mass, when he is present among us, Body and Blood, soul and divinity. Jesus invites us into an intimate relationship of friendship with him, encourages us to praise the Triune God, and tells us to ask God for help in our needs. He promises eternal life to his faithful followers.

3. The Church is a community.

Jesus gifted us with the love that the three Persons in the Trinity share with each other. He founded his Church on the divine love that the Trinity has for humankind. United in the Holy Spirit, this Pilgrim People lives in the world, as Jesus did, but aspires for a more fulfilling happiness than this world provides.

The Church anticipates Jesus' coming again and our eternal reward in Heaven.

The Trinity, a communion of love, shares divine grace through the Church. The Church gives us the age-old teachings and practices that keep us on the right path. These are Jesus' gifts to us. Indeed, Catholicism is lived out in community, following Jesus' way and inspired by the Holy Spirit that praises and honors the Father in appreciation for what we received.

Catholics on Earth are united in faith and love with the saints in Heaven and the souls in Purgatory. We call this the "Communion of Saints." Every Sunday at Mass, we pray in the Creed that we "believe in the communion of saints." After Mass, some Catholics remain and pray the Rosary before a statue of a saint. Someone in your family might have a prayer table at home with a picture of a deceased loved one and a candle. Because we on Earth are united with the saints in Heaven and the souls in Purgatory, we ask all our friends to pray for us—those living on Earth, those being purified in Purgatory, and those rejoicing forever in Heaven.

4. The Church is sacramental.
Jesus is the fundamental Sacrament and most fully reveals God to us. The Catholic Church is a sacramental people. She carries on Christ's work on Earth and communicates his message and way of life through her teaching, social ministries, and liturgy. The seven Sacraments of the Catholic Church continue to celebrate Jesus' Paschal Mystery, each one celebrating a special aspect of this Mystery. The Sacraments are holy signs of God's desire to be one with us. For example, Baptism gives us the new life of grace, as we are reborn as sons and daughters of God. Matrimony reflects God's desire to share his love in the love that a husband and wife have for each other. Every Sacrament celebrates God's love and invites us into a special relationship with Jesus through the Sacrament celebrated.

Sacramental belief is fundamental to who we are and what we do as Catholics. The Sacraments help us fulfill our spiritual needs and draw us into relationship with Christ and one another. Instituted by Christ to give us grace, the seven Sacraments are outward signs of this grace. They use rituals and symbols reflecting the holy presence of the divine.

As concrete actions rooted in the things that we use daily (water, bread, wine), Sacraments do two things: they point beyond themselves to something else—a sacred reality—and they bring about what they signify by making that reality present—new life, healing, forgiveness, membership, and so on. We know that Sacraments point to something else, but often we forget that they bring about or effect what they signify. For example, the Anointing of the Sick brings about spiritual and sometimes physical healing.

Catholic sacramentality goes beyond the seven Sacraments. Rooted in them, we celebrate other sacred signs of God's love, called *sacramentals*. They bear a certain resemblance to the Sacraments, but are given to us by the Church, not Christ. Catholics walk into a Catholic Church, dip their hand into "holy water," and make the Sign of the Cross. We genuflect or bow to Jesus, present in the tabernacle, before entering the pew and kneeling down. Some Catholics focus on the life-sized crucifix hanging above the altar. During Advent, we see a wreath with four candles at the front of the church. During Easter, we see a large, white Paschal candle near the altar. If we attend a Baptism, we see oils and water. Catholics use colors, symbols, and actions that speak to us in ways that don't require words.

5. The Church is Eucharistic.
The root meaning of *eucharist* in Greek means "thanksgiving." Our thanksgiving rests in the great sacrifice that Jesus offered for us on the cross, which we celebrate in the Eucharist.

As a sacramental community, Catholics root everything in the Eucharist. All the other Sacraments lead to it and flow from it. The

Eucharist is the source and summit of our lives. Catholics also call the celebration of the Eucharist "the Mass." The Eucharist is not simply a symbolic reminder of Jesus' sacrifice. Christ is present in this celebration in special ways. He is present in the community gathered together, in the Word proclaimed, in the person of the priest-celebrant, and most especially in the consecrated Eucharistic species, Jesus' Body and Blood.

By "Real Presence" we mean that the Eucharist is the real presence of Christ, whole and entire, under the appearances of bread and wine. While a memorial of Jesus' sacrifice on the cross, the Eucharist is more than just that. It is Christ's real presence.

In a wide sense, Catholics realize that we can be "eucharist" to each other when we share God's love with others. Since God dwells within us, we give thanks for the blessings we received by sharing our gifts with our brothers and sisters.

6. The Church is Biblically-Based.

The *Catechism* says, ". . . the Church has always venerated the Scriptures as she venerates the Lord's Body. . . . In Sacred Scripture, the Church constantly finds her nourishment and her strength, for she welcomes it not as a human word, 'but as what it really is, the word of God'" (CCC, 103-104). These words indicate the importance of Scripture for Catholics.

The early Church saw the Old Testament as containing the revelation of God's plan of salvation for humankind. They recognized the unity of this plan in the Old and New Testaments, studied the prophecies of a coming Messiah, and showed how Jesus fulfilled them. New Testament writers wrote down faithfully the teachings of Jesus and interpreted the Old Testament in light of his death and Resurrection (see CCC, 129).

New Testament writers, under the inspiration of the Holy Spirit, testified to the faith of the early Christian community. The New Testament must be interpreted in light of this faith, passed down to us in the Church's Tradition. Scripture and Sacred Tradition are bound closely together, as two distinct modes of transmitting God's Revelation.

Catholics cherish the Scripture, read it, and use it in their prayers. The Church's Liturgy of the Hours and the Sacraments, and especially the Mass, contain readings from both New and Old Testaments. The Church encourages Catholics to read and study the Scriptures as key sources of spiritual nourishment and growth.

7. The Church is one.

There are four marks of the Church, that is, essential identifying characteristics by which she is known—one, holy, catholic, and apostolic. The descriptions that follow, like all the summaries in this section, are overviews to give the general sense of each.

"The Church is one because of her source: 'the highest exemplar and source of this mystery is the unity, in the Trinity of Persons, of one God, the Father and the Son in the Holy Spirit'" (CCC, 813).

"The Church is one *because of her 'soul:'* 'It is the Holy Spirit, dwelling in those who believe and pervading and ruling over the entire Church, who brings about that wonderful communion of the faithful and joins them together so intimately in Christ that he is the principle of the Church's unity'" (CCC, 813).

The Church is one body in Christ, in faith, in the Sacraments, and in hope (see CCC, 866). The Church is formed and united through the work of the Holy Spirit and under the leadership of the bishops united with the bishop of Rome, the Pope.

8. The Church is holy.

"The Church . . . is . . . holy. This is because Christ, the Son of God, who with the Father and the Spirit is hailed as 'alone holy,' loved the Church as his Bride, giving himself up for her so as to sanctify her. . . . The Church, then, is 'the holy People of God. . . .'" (CCC, 823).

The Church is made holy because of her union with Christ; in turn, she makes others holy. She disseminates through her ministries the graces won by Jesus on the cross that make us holy. The Church, then, is holy in her members.

9. The Church is catholic (universal).

The Church is catholic in two ways. "First, the Church is catholic because Christ is present in her. . . . Secondly, the Church is catholic because she has been sent out by Christ on a mission to the whole of the human race" (CCC, 830-831).

Jesus dwells in the Catholic Church. Through his Holy Spirit he energized the Church to live and act in his name. The Church is for all people, everywhere. We are called to share the Good News by what we say and how we act. The Church's missionary work continues today, as the Holy Spirit guides her to go "to the ends of the earth" to preach, baptize, and minister in Jesus' name.

Wherever we go, Catholics profess the same beliefs and celebrate the same Sacraments, under the leadership of the Pope and bishops. When at Mass, no matter where we are, we can recognize it as the same Mass as the one in our parish. Its style, language, or music may differ, but it is the same Mass, because Jesus himself again offers his eternal sacrifice to the Father, through the ministry of the priest.

Catholicism accepts people from every place and walk of life. If we want to attend Mass every day, welcome to the Catholic Church. If we want to pray the Rosary, this is a great Catholic blessing. If we want to study the Bible, the Church encourages it on all levels. If we want to serve the poor, this is a prime commitment of the Catholic Church. The Church unites diverse spiritual practices, interests, devotions, and practices under the essential teachings of our faith.

10. The Church is apostolic.

The Church is founded and built on Peter and the twelve Apostles. After his Ascension, Jesus led the Church through Peter and the other Apostles. When they died, his leadership continued through their successors, namely the Pope and the bishops acting in union with him. Pope Benedict XVI succeeded Blessed Pope John Paul II, who succeeded Pope John Paul I, who succeeded Pope Paul VI, who succeeded Pope John XXIII. This line of Popes can be traced historically all the way back to Saint Peter, the first Pope.

The Catholic community is apostolic because we can trace our roots back to Peter and the Apostles and those who came after them. We are a Church led and united by the Pope and bishops, and ministered to by the ordained ministry of bishops, priests, and deacons.

Pope Benedict XVI at an outdoor rally in Yonkers, N.Y.

Consecrated brothers and sisters and the laity exercise other important kinds of leadership. Lay ministry today has a big impact on the Catholic Church in the United States. There are lay and consecrated religious diocesan chancellors, canon lawyers, pastoral administrators, pastoral team members, liturgists, musicians, catechists, servers, readers, and others.

National Catholic organizations, social agencies, hospitals, diocesan staffs, pastoral councils, finance councils, youth organizations, and more help to bring Jesus' message to all people. Catholicism has a clear leadership and organizational structure to which many different Church ministries contribute and share in the Church mission.

11. The Church advocates justice for all.

Many Catholic organizations serve those in need. Catholic Charities provides direct aid to people in need as a result of various circumstances or natural disasters. Catholic Relief Services works around the world as an advocate for change, empowering people to overcome such things as poverty and armed conflict. Bishops lead national discussions about stopping the nuclear arms race and opposing abortion and euthanasia. They speak out on matters of social justice. The Church encourages her members to perform works of mercy by reaching out to the needy in our midst. She also advocates acts of social justice that challenge unjust social structures that keep people impoverished.

The Catholic Church emphasizes seven principles of social justice. The principles are: 1) the life and dignity of the human person; 2) the rights and responsibilities of the human person; 3) participation in family and community; 4) option for the poor and vulnerable; 5) the dignity of work and the rights of workers; 6) the solidarity of the human family; and 7) care for all of God's creation.

12. The Church has a positive view of creation, the world, and human nature.

The Original Sin of Adam and Eve wounded creation. We are born into a flawed and imperfect world. Catholics believe that this world is not totally corrupt. God is very much present, and we recognize his presence in creation's beauty, truth, and love. We are made in the image of God and enter life with both goodness and imperfection.

To be saved, we need God's grace won by Jesus' death on the cross. As we reflect on our true meaning on Earth, we rely on our faith and reason to know more about God and our eternal destiny. Through faith and reason we probe more deeply into the world and human nature. In so doing, we discover how the Spirit is leading us.

For Catholics, faith and reason are partners. Catholicism fully accepts the Bible as God's word and welcomes ongoing biblical study and discussion. Often new insights come by using our reason to probe into the mysteries revealed in Scripture.

Catholics have always affirmed the importance of both faith and reason. Both are central to us and interconnected. Although we can come to certain knowledge of God's existence through reason alone, knowledge of the divine mysteries requires both faith and reason.

This is what is needed . . . a Church which will know how to invite and welcome the person who seeks a purpose for which to commit his/her whole existence; a Church that is not afraid to require much after having given much; which does not fear asking from young people the effort of a noble adventure, such as following the Gospel.

—Blessed Pope John Paul II

When it comes to being Catholic: What do you know?

1. Name the seven Sacraments of the Church.

2. Which are the Sacraments of Initiation?

3. Who is the Pope now?

4. Who's your bishop?

5. What do we celebrate on Pentecost?

6. What's Transubstantiation?

7. What's the Immaculate Conception?

8. To what does the Triduum refer?

9. What's the Trinity?

10. When does the Church teach that life begins?

11. Where's the Church's official headquarters?

12. Name the marks of the Church.

13. What are the catacombs?

14. What was the Reformation?

15. What does Palm Sunday celebrate?

16. Which book in the Bible tells us about the early Church?

17. Name the modern Council that renewed the Church.

18. What Church season consists of forty days of fasting?

19. What does Confirmation signify?

20. What is Genesis?

21. What does Easter celebrate?

22. Name the Ten Commandments.

23. What is the prayer Jesus taught us?

24. Which famous Catholic saint and theologian wrote *Summa Theologica*?

25. Which Catholic confronted King Henry VIII about his extramarital affairs?

26. On what feast day do we celebrate Mary's great love for the Mexican people?

27. Who was the first and so far only Catholic president?

28. Muslims, Christians, and Jews all share the same ancestor. Who is it?

29. What do we say together at Mass that summarizes our Catholic beliefs?

When it comes to being Catholic: Where do you stand?

How much do you agree with each of the following:
☐ Very little   ☐ Somewhat   ☐ Quite a bit   ☐ Very much

1. Being Catholic is important to me.
   ☐ Very little   ☐ Somewhat   ☐ Quite a bit   ☐ Very much

2. I plan on staying Catholic as an adult.
   ☐ Very little   ☐ Somewhat   ☐ Quite a bit   ☐ Very much

3. I'm interested in learning more about Jesus and the Catholic Church.
   ☐ Very little   ☐ Somewhat   ☐ Quite a bit   ☐ Very much

4. My parish is welcoming.
   ☐ Very little   ☐ Somewhat   ☐ Quite a bit   ☐ Very much

5. I'm interested in going on a retreat.
   ☐ Very little   ☐ Somewhat   ☐ Quite a bit   ☐ Very much

6. I'm comfortable discussing Catholic teachings and practices.
   ☐ Very little   ☐ Somewhat   ☐ Quite a bit   ☐ Very much

7. Going to Mass is important to me.
   ☐ Very little   ☐ Somewhat   ☐ Quite a bit   ☐ Very much

8. Being part of a parish is important to me.
   ☐ Very little   ☐ Somewhat   ☐ Quite a bit   ☐ Very much

9. Being Catholic has brought me inner peace.
   ☐ Very little   ☐ Somewhat   ☐ Quite a bit   ☐ Very much

10. Being Catholic has given me direction.
    ☐ Very little   ☐ Somewhat   ☐ Quite a bit   ☐ Very much

11. Being Catholic helps me grow closer to God.
    ☐ Very little   ☐ Somewhat   ☐ Quite a bit   ☐ Very much

12. Catholicism has a lot to offer people.
    ☐ Very little   ☐ Somewhat   ☐ Quite a bit   ☐ Very much

13. I would like to be a better Catholic.
    ☐ Very little   ☐ Somewhat   ☐ Quite a bit   ☐ Very much

When it comes to being Catholic: What do you do?

How true are the following statements about you?
☐ Not at all   ☐ Some   ☐ Quite a bit   ☐ Very much

1. I consider the teaching of the Church when determining what's right and wrong.
   ☐ Not at all   ☐ Some   ☐ Quite a bit   ☐ Very much

2. I participate in Mass on Sunday.
   ☐ Not at all   ☐ Some   ☐ Quite a bit   ☐ Very much

3. I talk about Catholic things to my family and/or friends.
   ☐ Not at all   ☐ Some   ☐ Quite a bit   ☐ Very much

4. My family takes being Catholic seriously.
   ☐ Not at all   ☐ Some   ☐ Quite a bit   ☐ Very much

5. During Lent, I fast or do something that I don't ordinarily do the rest of the year.
   ☐ Not at all   ☐ Some   ☐ Quite a bit   ☐ Very much

6. I've memorized and use a Catholic prayer.
   ☐ Not at all   ☐ Some   ☐ Quite a bit   ☐ Very much

7. I take part in my parish.
   ☐ Not at all   ☐ Some   ☐ Quite a bit   ☐ Very much

8. I regularly receive the Sacrament of Penance and Reconciliation.
   ☐ Not at all   ☐ Some   ☐ Quite a bit   ☐ Very much

9. My Catholic faith affects my life.
   ☐ Not at all   ☐ Some   ☐ Quite a bit   ☐ Very much

10. I've been on retreats.
    ☐ Not at all   ☐ Some   ☐ Quite a bit   ☐ Very much

11. I attend a Catholic youth group.
    ☐ Not at all   ☐ Some   ☐ Quite a bit   ☐ Very much

12. I've checked out Catholic topics online.
    ☐ Not at all   ☐ Some   ☐ Quite a bit   ☐ Very much

13. I try to practice my faith.
    ☐ Not at all   ☐ Some   ☐ Quite a bit   ☐ Very much

14. I chose this high school because it's Catholic.
    ☐ Not at all   ☐ Some   ☐ Quite a bit   ☐ Very much

15. I've been spiritually moved by some prayer experiences and liturgies.
    ☐ Not at all   ☐ Some   ☐ Quite a bit   ☐ Very much

For the Glory of God . . .

The fullness of joy is to behold God in everything.

—Saint Catherine of Genoa

God created the heavens and Earth out of his love and goodness. From that we have always realized a basic truth: "The world was made for the glory of God" (CCC, 293). God didn't create everything to give himself more glory. Instead, it was to show his glory; to communicate it.

Jesus sought to glorify the Father. "I will do whatever you ask in my name, so that the Father may be glorified in the Son" (John 14:13). You may recall the biblical account of the Transfiguration. At that time, if only for a moment, Jesus showed that he shared his Father's glory. As a divine Person who took on our human nature, Jesus also revealed that he would enter his glory through the cross.

This sacrifice by Jesus was also for the glory of God. He did this to sanctify or purify us from our sins. The Church, the people of God, were joined to Jesus through his act of self-giving. In turn, Jesus endowed us with the gift of the Holy Spirit, again for the glory of God. We, then, are the "holy People of God" (CCC, 823).

All this was done so that we could experience God's glory. As we learn in Ephesians 1:5, we are the Father's adopted children through Jesus Christ. There is nothing we can do to deserve this grace, this gift from God, but once we realize that he has given us this free gift of his Son, we become his children. This is our purpose. This is God's vision. "For 'the glory of God is man fully alive'" (CCC, 294). The *Catechism* helps us imagine what it will be like for those of us who see God.

The ultimate purpose of creation is that God "who is the creator of all things may at last become 'all in all', thus simultaneously assuring his own glory and our beatitude."[1]

—CCC, 294

Our own ultimate happiness will be the result of creation and God's plan of salvation through Jesus. "Man, and through him all creation, is destined for the glory of God" (CCC, 353).

It's important to keep in mind that God did not create all this to benefit himself in any way as some would have us believe. The *Catholic Encyclopedia* points out that God needs nothing, and he does not need help in carrying out his will. In discussing the topic of God's glory, the online *Encyclopedia* also reminds us that every individual thing God has created contains some part of his "infinite perfection. Each reflects in fixed limitation something of His nature and attributes." The inanimate objects of his creation, the mountains, the air, the planets, and vast solar systems for example, cannot give glory to God as we can. We understand the written Scripture and the Tradition handed down. We can accept and use what we learn from God's Revelation, and we praise God for these things. Our praise, however, is not simply our words or understanding. It is what we hold in our hearts and will. Our recognition of God's glory

REFLECT ❯❯ Think about how you reflect God's glory in your life. Compose a short prayer to ask the Father's help in becoming more like him.

drives our behavior in obedience to his will and in serving him and others.

We know that power or knowledge gives us new responsibilities in life. But in our gift of intelligence and free will from God, and in accepting our spirituality, we have a duty to return God's glory by living our lives as he calls us to do. The more perfectly we do that, the more perfectly we reflect God's glory.

When it comes to the glory of God: Where do you stand and what do you do?

How true are the following statements about you?
☐ Not at all   ☐ Some   ☐ Quite a bit   ☐ Very much

1. I know what the glory of God is.
☐ Not at all   ☐ Some   ☐ Quite a bit   ☐ Very much

2. I follow Jesus' example to glorify God.
☐ Not at all   ☐ Some   ☐ Quite a bit   ☐ Very much

3. I can tell you how I glorify God.
☐ Not at all   ☐ Some   ☐ Quite a bit   ☐ Very much

4. I recognize the glory of God in creation.
☐ Not at all   ☐ Some   ☐ Quite a bit   ☐ Very much

5. I know the holy people of God.
☐ Not at all   ☐ Some   ☐ Quite a bit   ☐ Very much

6. I know my purpose as a child of God.
☐ Not at all   ☐ Some   ☐ Quite a bit   ☐ Very much

7. I realize that I reflect part of God's infinite perfection.
☐ Not at all   ☐ Some   ☐ Quite a bit   ☐ Very much

8. I see God's glory in the people around me.
☐ Not at all   ☐ Some   ☐ Quite a bit   ☐ Very much

9. I know that obeying and serving God gives him glory.
☐ Not at all   ☐ Some   ☐ Quite a bit   ☐ Very much

10. I return God's glory through the way I live my life.
☐ Not at all   ☐ Some   ☐ Quite a bit   ☐ Very much

. . . and the Good of the World

Jesus gave us the bottom line about what's expected of his disciples. He told us exactly how each of us will be judged in the end. In Jesus' description of the final judgment in the Gospel according to Matthew, we also see the error of being religious without following through with loving and compassionate actions.

What does it mean to be a good person? Many would say it means trying not to hurt anyone. Some would say it means respecting and accepting all people, regardless of the color of their skin, their style of clothes, or the music they listen to. Many would say "being a good person" means being honest and patient with others.

All of these things are part of what it means to be a morally good person. But it's more than just one or the other. It involves the decisions we make and the actions that lead from them—decisions about the place we give God and the Church in our lives, the way we choose to spend our time, the people or things we allow to influence us, the way we think about and treat others, whether we are open to God's grace and live as he intended.

Being morally good is about *being* and *doing*, about answering God's call to holiness through prayer, the sacraments, and living by the Commandments and Beatitudes; through studying Scripture and following Christ's example in our daily lives, through learning what the Church teaches and why, and applying that understanding to the choices we make and the actions that flow from them. When we answer the call to holiness, in our being and our doing, we can grow closer to God—Father, Son, and Holy Spirit—and in holiness.

So how do we know if what we are doing is morally good? Three elements determine the morality of a human action: The object, which characterizes the action in and of itself. The intention, which is the immediate end or purpose the person intends to achieve through the action. The circumstances, which surround the action.

For an act to be morally good, all three—the object, intention, and circumstance—must be good. A person's conscience can make a right judgment on the morality of an act based on reason and God's law. Or it can make an erroneous judgment that is contrary to reason and the law. A well-formed conscience makes judgments based on reason, and is upright and truthful. And we must diligently inform our conscience so that it is well-formed, through studying the wisdom of Scripture and Church teaching, frequent prayer and the counsel of wise moral people we trust (see CCC, 1796, 1798, 1799, 1757, 1760).

The world has always needed people who are willing to direct their lives toward helping others. Jesus told us it would be this way until the end of time. Discipleship is a call to act as Jesus did, serving someone and something other than yourself.

GO TO **THE SOURCE**

Jesus tells us that he will sit on a throne of glory and judge the nations of the world.

Read Matthew 25:31-46.

○ Using what you have read from Matthew 25, finish this sentence: "We are expected to . . ."

When it comes to the good of the world: Where do you stand?

How much do you agree with each of the following:
☐Very little ☐Somewhat ☐Quite a bit ☐Very much

1. Combating world hunger is important to me.
   ☐Very little ☐Somewhat ☐Quite a bit ☐Very much

2. Sacrificing for others in need should be a normal expectation for all.
   ☐Very little ☐Somewhat ☐Quite a bit ☐Very much

3. I'm interested in learning more about the needs of others.
   ☐Very little ☐Somewhat ☐Quite a bit ☐Very much

4. The world is not in a hopeless situation.
   ☐Very little ☐Somewhat ☐Quite a bit ☐Very much

5. We can solve the world's inequities.
   ☐Very little ☐Somewhat ☐Quite a bit ☐Very much

6. I believe that we who have resources must share with those who don't.
   ☐Very little ☐Somewhat ☐Quite a bit ☐Very much

7. There are local people and situations that need real help.
   ☐Very little ☐Somewhat ☐Quite a bit ☐Very much

8. This information about poverty makes me want to do something to help.
   ☐Very little ☐Somewhat ☐Quite a bit ☐Very much

9. Poverty makes me wonder about God.
   ☐Very little ☐Somewhat ☐Quite a bit ☐Very much

10. I want to help out but don't know how.
    ☐Very little ☐Somewhat ☐Quite a bit ☐Very much

When it comes to the good of the world: What do you do?

How true are the following statements about you?
☐Not at all ☐Some ☐Quite a bit ☐Very much

1. I actively seek to help others.
   ☐Not at all ☐Some ☐Quite a bit ☐Very much

2. People would say that I'm a giving person.
   ☐Not at all ☐Some ☐Quite a bit ☐Very much

3. I pay attention to what's lacking in the world.
   ☐Not at all ☐Some ☐Quite a bit ☐Very much

4. Noticing others in need comes easy for me.
   ☐Not at all ☐Some ☐Quite a bit ☐Very much

5. I help out without being asked.
   ☐Not at all ☐Some ☐Quite a bit ☐Very much

6. I volunteer for service opportunities.
   ☐Not at all ☐Some ☐Quite a bit ☐Very much

7. I've stood up (for) when something wasn't fair to another person or group.
   ☐Not at all ☐Some ☐Quite a bit ☐Very much

8. I've confronted racist jokes, false rumors, etc.
   ☐Not at all ☐Some ☐Quite a bit ☐Very much

9. I've made sacrifices for something or someone other than myself.
   ☐Not at all ☐Some ☐Quite a bit ☐Very much

10. I've donated to a worthy cause.
    ☐Not at all ☐Some ☐Quite a bit ☐Very much

11. I pray for others.
    ☐Not at all ☐Some ☐Quite a bit ☐Very much

12. I reach out to those who are usually excluded.
    ☐Not at all ☐Some ☐Quite a bit ☐Very much

13. I comfort the sorrowful.
    ☐Not at all ☐Some ☐Quite a bit ☐Very much

14. I share what I have with those who need it.
    ☐Not at all ☐Some ☐Quite a bit ☐Very much

15. I encourage the discouraged.
    ☐Not at all ☐Some ☐Quite a bit ☐Very much

16. I root for others.
    ☐Not at all ☐Some ☐Quite a bit ☐Very much

17. I celebrate with those who are happy over something.
    ☐Not at all ☐Some ☐Quite a bit ☐Very much

18. I apologize when I hurt someone's feelings or ignore a chance to help them.
    ☐Not at all ☐Some ☐Quite a bit ☐Very much

It's Your Call

What do you want to work on? It's your call.

Spiritually speaking, this course will continually ask you to mark down what is helpful to you. Every time you see the *My Faith* feature, for example, you will have a chance to make some notes, do some serious thinking, and keep moving forward the way you want to go.

It's your call, but that call is coming from God. The voice of God the Father is calling you to live a life as he intended. It is the call of the Holy Spirit, speaking to your inner wishes and fears. And it is the call of Jesus, saying, "Follow Me."

Let this course keep you in touch with the voice of God. Use this course to take you away from all the noises that make God's voice hard to hear. It's your call.

Based on what I already know about myself, and based on the spiritual invitation to Discipleship . . . within the Body of Christ . . . for the glory of God and the good of the world.

I would like to gain more knowledge about:

I'd like to develop more . . .
  appreciation/respect for:
  gratitude for:
  openness about:

I need to re-think some of my actions and decisions regarding:

I'd like to follow up on some of my spiritual interests, such as:

Beginning My Spiritual Growth Plan

Go to the student site at
hs.osvcurriculum.com

PRAYER

Opening Prayer

Dear Jesus,
We are your disciples.
We want to take your message everywhere
in the world.

You knew us before we were conceived.
We have known you since our earliest memories.
Now we are seeing you through new eyes.
We are your disciples.

But we are sometimes afraid, Lord.
Maybe afraid of what our friends might think.
Maybe afraid that that we don't trust enough.
Maybe afraid to let go.

We know that when we are close to you our fears
subside.
We are glorified in your presence.

Lord, you set the example for us.
You have given us new life.
We are ready to bear your cross.
We are your disciples.

But sometimes we are also anxious, Lord.
We worry about grades.
We worry about each other.
We try to go it alone.

We know that when we do your will our worries
melt away.
We are glorified in your presence.

Lord, you died for our sins.
You arose to new life and are with the Father.
Through the Holy Spirit, we are closer to you.
We are your disciples.

Yet, sometimes, we don't understand, Lord.
The world is confusing.
Why can't life be easier?
What is our role?

We know that as we become better disciples
our understanding will increase.
We are glorified in your presence.

Please ease our fear.
Please relieve our anxiety.
Please help us to understand.
But always, it is your will we desire.
Help us to be like you and be close to us on
our journey in your love.
Amen.

Closing Prayer

God our Father,
Through your Son and Holy Spirit we will not be
afraid to carry your loving message to all the places
our life journey will take us. With your help we will
work to overcome the anxiety that interrupts our
life of discipleship. We will continue to try to
understand our place in the world. Our place is
where you want us to go. Surround us with your
love and guide us with your gentle hand.
We pray in your holy name.
Amen.

What can we tell about
the faith of these people?
What does that say about how we
encounter God?

CHAPTER **2**

Called to
Know God

Go to the student site at
hs.osvcurriculum.com

DO

○ Explain some ways God's Revelation is made known to us.

○ Explore five "proofs" of God's existence.

○ Delve into the mystery of God.

○ Examine how theologians and mystics have come to know about God.

○ Learn about how God calls and we respond in prayer.

○ Consider the role of discipleship on the spiritual path.

○ Study how God is also revealed in the natural world.

DEFINE

Trinity	Council of Nicea
wisdom	Nicene Creed
reason	theology
Divine Revelation	logic
faith	objective
discipleship	subjective
doctrine	mysticism
dogma	contemplative prayer

Read these scenarios.

A high school student studying biology says: "Studying the human birth process convinced me that there is a God. The mother's body 'automatically' starts producing some new stuff just so she can nurture the baby. Afterward the process just automatically stops. It's too perfect, too complicated to be designed by accident. It had to be invented by someone like God."

A soldier says: "War is hell. Literally. Guys brutally trying to kill each other. It's ruthless. It's the last place on Earth that you'd expect to see God. But there is something really powerful—holy, really—when you witness someone sacrifice his or her life for another person or for the people of that country. On both sides. Whenever I saw it, I felt like I saw true love. Am I making any sense?"

Breaking news reports a massive earthquake in Haiti killing more than 100,000 people. After watching the report, a high school sophomore stands up and heads to the fridge saying: "I don't get it. How can God, who's supposed to be so loving and all, bring this on 100,000 innocent people?"

HOW DO YOU RESPOND?

Where Are You?			
Choose the response that best reflects where you are right now.			
How strongly do you believe in God?	☐ Quite a bit	☐ Somewhat	☐ A little	☐ Not at all
How much do you know about God?	☐ Quite a bit	☐ Somewhat	☐ A little	☐ Not at all
How often do you pray?	☐ Almost daily	☐ Weekly	☐ On occasion	☐ Not at all
How much does your faith shape your decisions?	☐ Quite a bit	☐ Somewhat	☐ A little	☐ Not at all
Where do you most often meet God?	☐ At Mass	☐ In thoughts	☐ In nature	☐ Not at all

Longing for God

How can we know him?

What's God like?

Does it make a difference what a person believes?

Does God exist apart from us or within us?

What does he expect from us?

People have asked these kinds of questions for thousands of years. Signs of this search for God span history, from prehistoric cave paintings to medieval cathedrals to today when many people explore different types of spirituality. We can't escape the fact that people long for God. They long to know God and to understand more about him. In many ways, this longing reflects the desire to really know who we are and why we are here. This yearning for God is part of what it means to be human. It comes from God, who has known us since the beginning of time, before we even existed. We are religious by our human nature.

As he awaited his fate with the lions in the Roman Colosseum, Saint Ignatius of Antioch spoke of his longing for God. "Him I seek, who died for us: him I desire, who rose again for our sake." The *Catechism of the Catholic Church* points out that the desire for God is written on the human heart (see CCC, 27). We were made to be with God. The sincere desire for God is a gift from God himself. It prompts us not only to seek the one true God, but also to do what is good and reject evil. We seek him because in him we are complete. In him, we find true happiness.

Humans desire to know and love God because he calls each of us to grow close to him. God continually sustains our lives and invites us into relationship with him. Thus we can say that we are religious by vocation. The word *vocation* means one's calling or purpose in life. God calls us beyond ourselves to friendship with him, to become his adopted children and to live a loving life.

God wants to be part of our lives, but how can we really know him? The Holy Spirit moves us to know Jesus and grow close to him. Jesus makes it clear that if we know him, we know the one who sent him. "No one has ever seen God. It is God the only Son, who is close to the Father's heart, who has made him known" (John 1:18).

This course focuses on coming to know God—Father, Son, and Holy Spirit—through Jesus in Scripture. The bottom line is that we know God because he makes it possible. Each Person of the **Trinity** relates to us in different ways so that we can come to the ultimate truths. It is through Jesus, the only Son of God the Father, that God's plan for us is fully revealed. It is this gift of knowledge about God that draws us into relationship with him and fulfills our longing for him.

While many people might think of vocation as something that characterizes adult life, each person is called to believe in and follow Christ at one's Baptism. This baptismal call is one to become Christlike. No matter our age or state in life, we live out our baptismal call by serving God and working with the gifts and talents God has given us. Our ultimate vocation, our destiny, the whole purpose of life, is union with God.

Trinity the mystery of one God in three divine Persons: Father, Son, and Holy Spirit

Young man praying at a National Catholic Youth Conference

> When I was a child, I spoke like
> a child,
> I thought like a child, I
> reasoned like a child; when I
> became an adult,
> I put an end to childish ways.
>
> 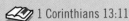 1 Corinthians 13:11

Discuss
- What image of God did you have when you were really young—for example, when you made your First Communion?
- What image of God do you have now?
- What do you think caused the change?

In Silence and In Noise

Longing for God leads us to want to *understand* God. Silence can be part of both longing and wanting to understand. Life is noisy. Silence can help us "go inside" ourselves to reflect. Sometimes we reflect on the big questions, such as who God is or in what direction we're going. We have a tendency to take some things for granted when we get too busy—things like all the good that comes from God, our family and friends, and our natural longing for God. They may get pushed away or buried underneath all our other tasks, interests, relationships, and expectations.

Saint Catherine of Siena once said, "God is closer to us than water is to a fish." A revealing proverb helps explain this: Even though they were swimming in water, the fish thought they were thirsty. Like those fish, we are "swimming" in God's presence. God is so close that we sometimes take him for granted, just as we might our friends and family or even breathing clean air. But God is with us always, even when we don't acknowledge him. The Acts of the Apostles explains that in God we live and move and have our being (see Acts 17:28).

Before he began his mission of salvation, much of Jesus' life seems to have consisted of silence. Only the account of Jesus in the Temple when he was twelve years old breaks that silence (see Luke 2:39-52). In that one story, we get a peek at the mystery of Jesus' mission and his understanding that he is the Son of God (see CCC, 534). "Did you not know that I must be in my Father's house?" (Luke 2:49).

wisdom a spiritual gift that makes it possible for someone to know about the purpose and plan of God; one of the seven gifts of the Holy Spirit

reason the ability to think, decide, and form conclusions in a logical way

Click off the television. Log off the computer. Turn down the music. Set your cell phone ringer to off. Enter into that silence. Allow yourself to wonder. Saints throughout the ages say that if you go deep enough, God will find you in that silence, and you will answer.

> *Come on now, get away from your worldly occupations for a while, escape from your tumultuous thoughts. Lay aside your burdensome cares and put off your laborious exertions. Give yourself over to God for a little while, and rest for a while in Him. Enter into the cell of your mind, shut out everything except God and whatever helps you to seek Him once the door is shut. Speak now, my heart, and say to God, "I seek your face; your face, Lord, I seek."*
>
> —Saint Anselm of Canterbury c.1033–1109

Let's be clear. We can and do experience God in the busyness of our lives. That includes the technology that makes up a big part of our daily routines. Whether it's through silence, private prayer, the Sacraments, Church teachings, nature, or one another, there are many ways to come to know God. All of these are ways to gain **wisdom**, a spiritual gift that makes it possible for someone to know about the purpose and plan of God (see CCC, Glossary). We can reflect on God in the silence as well as in the "noise" that characterizes our modern lives.

The Mystery of God

We can't go too far into a study of our Catholic faith without exploring the mystery of God. The ancient Israelite journey of faith is actually where Christianity, and our search for wisdom, begins. Christianity has its roots in the Jewish faith and was also influenced by Greek culture at the time. Greeks were known for philosophy, which involves a rational investigation of truths and principles. The word *philosophy* literally means "love of wisdom." Using that wisdom, Greek philosophers believed human beings are capable of arriving at truth using **reason**, our ability to think or decide in a logical way. Since that time, philosophers have tried, but struggled, to understand God.

In fact, during the Middle Ages, the greatest religious scholars applied rational thinking to the question of God's existence. They concluded that the existence of God makes more sense than the opposite.

The scholars found that we human beings can "think our way" to an affirmation that God exists. Like those scholars, we realize God's existence today using what the *Catechism* calls "the natural light of human reason" (CCC, 47). However, no matter how hard we try to understand and describe God, "Our human words always fall short of the mystery of God" (CCC, 42).

Recall Which culture influenced the early development of Christian philosophy?

Infer What does the phrase "make room for wisdom" mean?

God Is Love

Have you ever thought that as our faith grows, so does our desire to understand the mystery of God? Believing is a particularly human thing to do, made possible through the grace of God. Think about it. We believe in people all the time. We might show up early at school because our algebra teacher promised to be there to answer questions. If our parents promise to pick us up after the dance, we trust that they will be parked outside when it's over.

There is a certain amount of love that drives people to make those kinds of commitments to one another. That love builds our relationships, like those we enjoy with our family and friends. The closer we are, the more we care about what's happening in each other's lives.

Throughout history, thinkers and scholars have tried to discuss God in philosophical ways. But this chapter and this course explain what Scripture makes known to us about the mystery of God: God is truth, God is light, and God is love. While we can get a sense of God's love, we can never know it fully. We do know that God's love is beyond any experience we have of love. Out of love, the Father sent his only Son to us, to become man and to sacrifice his life in order that we may have eternal life.

REFLECT

How can you come to know more and share more about God in your use of electronic communication, with things like computers, MP3 players, cell phones, TV, and video games?

What are some ways you can reduce the "noise" and make more room for wisdom to enter into your life?

>> **Describe a recent insight you have had about God, or what it was like when you deliberately sought wisdom by reflecting on something spiritual.**

Thus we say love is a gift from God, the greatest mystery of all. But as Pope Benedict XVI said in his first encyclical, or official letter to the Church, the meaning of love has been diluted. The encyclical is titled *Deus Caritas Est,* or "God Is Love." Why did the Holy Father choose the theme of love? Here's an explanation he gave in a 2006 speech:

"The cosmic excursion in which Dante, in his 'Divine Comedy,' wishes to involve the reader, ends in front of the perennial Light that is God himself, before that Light which is at the same time 'the love that moves the sun and the other stars.' Light and love are . . . the primordial creative powers that move the universe.

"If these words in Dante's 'Paradiso' betray the thought of Aristotle, who saw in the eros [physical attraction] the power that moves the world, Dante nevertheless perceives something completely new and inconceivable for the Greek philosopher . . . this God has a human face and . . . heart.

HONORING THE BODY

"Do you not know that your body is a temple of the Holy Spirit within you, which you have from God, and that you are not your own? ... Therefore glorify God in your body."

—(1 Corinthians 6:19-20)

One Body

IN THIS CHAPTER we are dealing with things like how we can come to know God and why he wants to be in relationship with us. God tells us he is love, and we know that we've been created in his image. You could say we were made to "be love," to know his love, to show love, to share love.

What about sex? What if two people really love each other? Is it morally wrong to have sex before marriage? If it feels right, how can it be wrong? Many of us have had questions like these. Later courses provide an in-depth study of the moral teachings of Jesus and the Church, but these questions can't wait. We face moral decisions every day. We form our consciences as we learn more about who God is, what he has made known about himself, and what difference that makes for how we live.

Sex in itself is good when used according to God's designs. When it is not, sexual actions are morally wrong and sinful. Used properly, it definitely means something significant. God intended for the sexual aspects of our bodies to be a way for two people to say: "We love each other enough to become one," and "We love each other enough to create and care for the life of another." When we don't honor what sex truthfully means, we lie and damage ourselves, others, and our relationship with God.

> The fact that they become one flesh is a powerful bond established by the Creator. Through it they discover their own humanity, both in its original unity, and in the duality of a mysterious mutual attraction.
>
> —Blessed Pope John Paul II, *Theology of the Body*, 10:2

You've heard the phrase adapted from Genesis 2:4, "two become one." We know *that* is what physically happens in sexual intercourse, but we're selling ourselves short if we think that's *all* that happens.

The *Catholic Theology of the Body* explains that sexual intercourse is God's way of letting two people signify that they have become one—*physically, emotionally, and spiritually*. This union involves a total gift of self between two married spouses—mutually given and received in love—and the openness to the gift of life that they are called to share in. Sexual intercourse says, "I give my whole self to you," and we cannot say that in an authentic way if we haven't given our whole selves in marriage.

This intense message is communicated with the body, in the body, through the body—it's a bodily language. The body was designed by God to be truthful. Look at our bodily reactions, like sweating when we're nervous. Have you ever tried to suppress laughter when you find something hysterically funny? How do you think lie detectors work? When we lie and when we laugh, the body reacts.

What would it take for you to open yourself up to someone and be totally vulnerable—like emotionally naked—with your whole life? In God's design and vision, through sex, the body communicates that two people become one physically, emotionally, and spiritually, with exactly that level of vulnerability and openness. What does it take to get there? It takes the reliability and trustworthiness of the sacramental commitment of marriage.

But some people do have sex outside of marriage. Sometimes they say they "really love each other," and other times love has nothing to do with it. They give into temptation.

We have to remember that the Holy Spirit will help us avoid temptation. Calling on the Holy Spirit when we are tempted gives us strength. God promises we will not be tested beyond what we can handle. "He will also provide the way out so that you may be able to endure it" (1 Corinthians 10:13).

One such temptation is recreational sex, or sex without commitment. Recreational sex involves two people knowingly tossing aside any pretense of commitment. "Friends with Benefits" is really an attempt to isolate the pleasurable side effects from bodily communication. In order for people to use their own bodies (and other people's) like that, the body has to cut off honest communication. And just like in the rest of life, the longer and deeper this damage goes, the longer it takes for the body to begin to heal this trust.

With relational sex, the man and woman are somewhere on the spectrum of commitment: they are more than friends, but not married. So the body knows it can *kind of* trust and be vulnerable, but not really. Even if the relationship progresses to marriage, the trust has been damaged. Instead of becoming more open, the body learns to be guarded. Why does this matter? Because in non-marital sex, people disrespect the image of God within, damage their body's ability to truthfully communicate, and derail discipleship.

Committed sex takes place as a blessing in the permanency of marriage. Here, as husband and wife, "two become one," honoring the body's communication with love. Here, vulnerability and openness are pursued and protected with the reliability of commitment. Real, true, mature love respects and honors the body.

>> List your top five questions or comments on this topic.

Think of your three favorite books, movies, or television shows. In what ways do they provide positive examples of respecting and honoring the body? How about negative examples?

Do you find the *Catholic Theology of the Body* to be different from mainstream abstinence programs? Explain your answer.

List
○ Make a comprehensive list of the people who love you.
○ What conclusions can you make about the people on your list?
○ What conclusions can you make about yourself from the list?

"Today, the word 'love' is so spoiled, worn out and abused that one almost fears to pronounce it.

And yet, it is a fundamental word, an expression of the primordial reality. We cannot simply abandon it, but we must take it up again, purify it and bring it to its original splendor so that it can illumine [shed light on] our life and guide it on the right path."

Love is the force behind God's creation of the universe, Pope Benedict explained. Out of love God made the world and all that's in it. Out of love he made himself known to our first parents and subsequent generations. Out of love God remained faithful, as his creation did not. Out of love God protected and challenged his people. He acted on his love. He gave of himself, knowing that the return could not live up to the gift. The Pope said the best example of love is Jesus, our God who took on a human face and possessed a human heart.

Jesus' life demonstrated how every form of love involves giving ourselves to others, first and most fundamentally to God. Today, very often love is reduced to common biological terms, but the "right path" the Pope refers to involves loving with body *and* soul. How can we love by giving ourselves to others, sacrificing and having compassion as Jesus did? What does that look like in terms of how we treat our parents and family members, our friends, those we see every day but don't know personally? We might not be able to fully understand "God is Love," but we don't have to in order to experience it and respond to it.

Recall What does *Deus Caritas Est* mean?

Analyze Give two examples of the truth of that statement.

QUICK REVIEW

1a. Summarize Give two examples of ways in which humans express a longing for God.

b. Analyze How do you think people misuse the word "love"?

2a. Explain How can silence help connect us to God?

b. Recall What famed literary work does Pope Benedict XVI refer to in his first encyclical?

c. Support What are some of the ways a person grows in his or her relationship with God?

Listen and Discuss With a partner, take turns completing these statements. Listen carefully to each other, and ask clarifying questions if necessary.

○ I relate to what Saint Anselm says about giving "yourself over to God for a little while" when I . . .

○ In my life right now, I see God most clearly in . . .

○ In order to experience God, I can . . .

○ One question I still have about the material in this section is . . .

Pray Compose a short prayer that puts your yearning for God into words.

SELF-ASSESS

Which statement best reflects where you are now?

☐ I'm confident enough about the material in this section to be able to explain it to someone else.

☐ I have a good grasp of the material in this section, but I could use more review.

☐ I'm lost. I need help catching up before moving on.

Meeting God

Think about what your friendships are like. Usually, the more you make yourself known to someone, and the more the other person lets you know him or her, the closer you are.

Something similar happens with God. The more opportunities you have to come to know him better, the closer you can become. And the more you tell God about what's on your mind and in your heart, the closer the friendship. The relationship, the sharing, always starts with God, but it's a two-way street.

We meet God in different ways because he comes to us in different ways. Some are natural. Throughout the Church's history, many have discussed faith in connection to an awareness of nature. Those would include the author of the Book of Genesis, the psalmists, Saint Francis of Assisi, and Saint Thomas Aquinas. The natural world of creation is the foundation of all God's works.

You are great, O Lord, and greatly to be praised; great is Your power, and of Your wisdom there is no end. . . . You have formed us for Yourself, and our hearts are restless till they find rest in You.

—Saint Augustine of Hippo, *Confessions*

By the streams the birds of the air have their habitation; they sing among the branches. From your lofty abode you water the mountains; the earth is satisfied with the fruit of your work.

—Psalm 104:12-13

Using our God-given abilities—such as reason and conscience—we can come to know something of God through the created world, especially in humans, who are made in God's image. When we listen to our conscience, we can see that God is present and active in our world and in our lives. By human reason, we can be certain that God does exist. The chart in this section addresses some of these ways of knowing God.

However, throughout history, God has made himself known to humans through actions and events, through love and goodness, through patience and constant forgiveness. We call this communication **Divine Revelation**, God making known his mystery and plan of redemption in ways we could never know by ourselves. And this communication is shared with us through two related, but distinct, ways—Scripture and Tradition, which are referenced in the accompanying chart and discussed in depth in Chapter 3.

Divine Revelation God's communication of himself, by which he makes known the mystery of his divine plan, a gift of self-communication which is realized by words and deed over time, and most fully by sending us his own divine Son, Jesus Christ (CCC, Glossary)

Knowing God	
BY NATURAL WAYS	**THROUGH DIVINE REVELATION**
These are ways we can come to know God through our own seeking:	These are ways God helps us comprehend truths we couldn't know without his help:
The world around us. We can use our human curiosity and thinking skills to recognize signs of God's presence in creation.	**Sacred Scripture (the Bible).** The Sacred Scriptures are God's inspired word, the written record of God's Revelation in history. Scripture tells the story of God's relationship with his People, starting with the Israelites, the sending of his Son—who is the heart and center of Sacred Scripture's unity, and through the early stages of the Church.
The human person. We can use our human experience of relationships to get a sense of what it means to know and love God and to be known and loved by him.	**Sacred (Apostolic) Tradition.** Tradition refers to the living transmission, under the inspiration of the Holy Spirit, of the message of the Gospel in the Church. The Holy Spirit guides the Church in her knowledge of God as revealed in the Scriptures, in reflecting on what knowing God requires of us, and in forming doctrine rooted in that relationship.
The experience of our ancestors in faith. We can learn from the various ways people throughout history have come to know God, especially the experience of Israel as recounted in the Old Testament.	
The understanding of the Church. Throughout history, bishops and popes, priests and religious theologians and teachers have reflected on who God is and how we come to know him.	

faith believing in God and all that he has revealed; faith is both a gift from God made possible by accepting and submitting to grace and a free, human choice

As the chart shows, God and his plan for our salvation are disclosed through nature and Divine Revelation. His plan is revealed over time. He spoke to our first parents, promised to send a redeemer after their Fall, and offered them a covenant. God selected Abraham to serve as father of many nations. Gradually, God formed his own People—the People of Israel. In time, God sent his greatest gift—his own Son, Jesus Christ. Through Jesus, we are introduced to the central and most important mystery of our faith: God is Trinity—Father, Son, and Holy Spirit. These key aspects of God's Revelation are part of what we call salvation history. Through Divine Revelation, we are able to know God, to respond to him, and to love him more than we could through any of our own natural abilities.

Identify What do we mean when we say God is Trinity?

Reflect What are some natural ways in which God has made himself known to you?

Responding to God

Earlier we noted that the hunger for God urges us to search for him. God's Revelation of who he is and his plan for us calls for us to respond. That response is **faith**—believing in God and what he has made known through words and deeds. Faith involves accepting God's Revelation and submitting one's whole self—mind and will—to God.

Faith—like hope and charity—is a theological virtue. The word *theological* means

REFLECT

"Question the beauty of the earth, question the beauty of the sea, question the beauty of the air distending and diffusing itself, question the beauty of the sky . . . question all of these realities. All respond: 'See, we are beautiful.' Their beauty is a profession. These beauties are subject to change. Who made them if not the Beautiful One [Pulcher] who is not subject to change?"[2] (CCC, 32)

>> **Write a paragraph in response to this quotation from Saint Augustine citing a time where you experienced God in the beauty of creation.**

In the Bible, we read about people saying "yes" to God. Read both of these accounts: The Command to Sacrifice Isaac, Genesis 22:1-19; The Birth of Jesus Foretold, Luke 1:26-38.

1. What risks did Abraham and Mary accept by saying "yes"? Why were they willing to do so?

2. In what ways do young people take risks to share and respond to their faith today?

"concerning God." They are called the theological virtues because they come from God, are directed toward him, and reflect his presence in our lives. The word *virtue* means "a good habit or response." Virtues are good moral and spiritual habits that help us make good moral decisions, avoid sin, strengthen character, and perform good deeds.

Faith involves giving the best of ourselves to God who *first reveals himself* to us. Faith actually begins with God. It is saying "yes" to the invitation that God offers us to follow his ways. It connects with our deepest human desire to better understand God. Guided by the Holy Spirit, our continual "yes" to God's invitation strengthens our friendship with him and can lead to life with him forever.

God's invitation isn't abstract or other-worldly. His invitation comes through Scripture and Tradition, and most especially in Jesus Christ. Our response to faith in Jesus Christ leads to **discipleship**, that is, a life rooted in Jesus, supported by the Church, and lived out in community.

In discussing the theological virtue of faith, the *Catechism* said this about being a disciple:

> *The disciple of Christ must not only keep the faith and live on it, but also profess it, confidently bear witness to it, and spread it. . . . Service of and witness to the faith are necessary for salvation.*
>
> —CCC, 1816

discipleship accepting Jesus as our Lord and Savior and following him by studying and putting his ways into practice

PRIMARY SOURCES

" The Holy Spirit gives us the strength and courage to respond to God's word. Read the following passage and discover how when we are hearing the word in the right way, we are called to respond.

Go to the student site at **hs.osvcurriculum.com**

The Holy Spirit works within us to allow what we read to have an effect on us and to gradually change us. Reading the Bible with the Spirit of God will not allow us to remain neutral. If God is truly communicating with us, then we must respond in some way. Sometimes it may be toward a deeper relationship with God in prayer. At other times, our response might be to change our actions in relationship to other people. Other passages might challenge us to act in an area of Christian life that we had neglected before.

Introduction to the Bible by Stephen J. Binz, page 14

>> **How have you been prompted by the Holy Spirit to respond to God's word?**

What part of Christian life would you like to work on?

Discipleship means *believing* and *living* a life based upon our belief. Discipleship is about responding to Jesus' call in the many areas of our lives. It's about our priorities, the place Christ and the Church occupy in our lives, and the choices we make. Discipleship is about our personal connection and commitment to God, an openness to the Holy Spirit acting in our lives, and a desire to worship God through the Sacraments, in our prayer lives, and in the challenging moments of our lives. It's about what we say, how we act, and with whom we spend time. Discipleship involves the sacrifices we willingly make to follow Jesus and his example (see CCC, 520).

Jesus told us to do as he did, to love as he loved. We saw how Jesus loved. He loved the Father above all things. In his healing actions and challenging but comforting words, he loved. He gave of himself beyond expectation, really beyond understanding. In doing so, he made the Father's love, which he himself receives, known. So, as his disciples, when we love, in some ways we make known Jesus' love, which he has willing given to us. This is what the virtue of charity, also called love, is about, what the love between the Father, Son, and Holy Spirit makes possible.

Tell What do we mean when we refer to discipleship?

Elaborate Why do we describe faith as a response?

Seeing the Connection

Let's take a look at what it means to respond to God's invitation, to be open to the Holy Spirit's movement in our lives. You may already be familiar with the event from the Gospel according to Luke about a man struggling to get a glimpse of Jesus. The crowd around Jesus was thick, and the man was short. The Go to the Source box on this page gives you some background and questions for reading the passage in Luke.

Through his approach to Zacchaeus, Jesus gives a glimpse into a central theme in his mission: the Kingdom of God. We will detail this more later, but Jesus preached of a Kingdom that is not a geographical place or an earthly, political authority. The Kingdom is God's rule and reign in our lives and in our world. We read in Scripture that "the kingdom of God is . . . righteousness and peace and joy in the Holy Spirit" (Romans 14:17).

GO TO THE SOURCE

Let's look at a story that illustrates how Jesus and people connect. Tax collectors won't win popularity contests in any society, but they were particularly despised during Jesus' time. In Jesus' day, they were Jews who collected taxes from fellow Jews to give to their oppressors, the Romans.

Read about Zacchaeus the tax collector in Luke 19:1-10, then compare and contrast that story with Matthew 21:28-32 and Luke 18:9-14.

1. Why do you think the Gospel writer specifically chose to describe the conversion of a tax collector in this incident?

2. What risks did Zacchaeus take to respond to Jesus' invitation, and how do you think his actions changed him?

3. What does this story tell us about Jesus?

4. To tell this story today, who might replace the tax collector to make the same point?

Giving THANKS

Giving thanks in this case is not about a turkey dinner in late November. And it's not just about saying thanks for the blessings God has given you. At its core, the spiritual practice of giving thanks is about observing.

The practice of giving thanks is a discipline that requires you to recognize the good things in life, both small and large, and to acknowledge them as gifts from God.

When you practice giving thanks, you strengthen your spirituality, because it develops in you an attitude of gratitude. Gratitude is a virtue, and the more you practice it, the more likely you are to feel thankful and express it.

The practice of giving thanks consists of two steps: **See It, Say Something.**

The first step might be the hardest. Most of us have no problem saying thank you when we are given something we need. But everyday life is noisy. We get busy. Daily life can be stressful, complicated, or boring. So it's kind of easy to miss the blessings God gives us, including those he gives us through others.

Jesus told us to "have eyes to see" (see Mark 8:18). In order to practice giving thanks, we first have to get better at noticing the many forms of God's protection, love, and guidance.

Then Say Something.

Thank God for showing you something, giving you everything, and sparing you from most things. Thank God for your life, the place you sleep, the place you learn, the food you eat, the beauty of the season, the chance to pursue your interests . . . the list is endless.

Thank the person who acted kindly. Say something to the teacher or coach who went the extra mile. Thank the parent who once again helped you out.

Many believe that giving thanks is the most important spiritual practice of all. If you *intentionally make it a habit,* it will affect how you look at your life, the quality of your relationships with others, and the depth of your friendship with God.

> **Share a time when you gave thanks to God.**
>
> **What might giving thanks to someone do for the relationship you have with him or her?**
>
> **Why say thanks to strangers you may never see again?**
>
> **Name someone who deserves your thanks right now.**

Witness of Faith

SAINT FRANCIS OF ASSISI (1182-1226)

Saint Francis of Assisi led what many would call one of the best examples of a life of discipleship. Francis was born in Assisi in central Italy and was baptized Giovanni, or John. His name was later changed to Francesco, or Francis, probably because of his father's extensive trade with the country of France.

Francis' father was a wealthy cloth merchant, and as a young boy, Francis lived a privileged life because of his family's wealth. However, a series of life-altering experiences—being a prisoner of war, becoming ill, and encountering a leper—led him to a conversion experience.

At church one day, Francis experienced a call from God to repair the Church. Misunderstanding the call, Francis removed and sold goods from his father's warehouse to finance the renovation of the church building, known as San Damiano Church in Assisi. When brought to trial for his theft, Francis publicly disrobed and returned his clothes to his father, understanding at last that he was called to reform God's Church.

Francis no longer worried about what he wore or ate, and he focused on following Jesus' example of trusting God would provide for him. Francis was frequently seen begging for food in the streets, visiting the sick in hospitals, preaching a message of peace and purity, and caring for those neglected by others. Francis lived a simple life, and he was not afraid to work with people, in the fields, and among the animals.

In 1210, Francis' community journeyed to Rome to seek the approval of Pope Innocent III for its religious rule and order. In an age of wealth, Francis favored the poor; in an age of crusades and war, he stood for nonviolence and peace; in an age when women needed support, he helped form a religious community for women, the Order of Saint Clare.

Francis spent a great deal of time out of doors as a result of his chosen lifestyle of poverty. A passage from Scripture that inspired him was "Consider the lilies of the field, how they grow; they neither toil nor spin, yet I tell you, even Solomon in all his glory was not clothed like one of these" (Matthew 6:28-29).

Saint Francis of Assisi was a man who had a profound love for God's creatures. In art, he is often depicted with arms outstretched preaching to the birds and beasts of the forest. Francis regarded all creation as his family.

Think About It Why do you think it was difficult for Francis to understand God's call to rebuild his Church?
Why do you think the Scripture passage from Matthew was such an inspiration for Francis?
How has God provided for your needs in life?

Go to the student site at
hs.osvcurriculum.com

And from Zaccheaus's response, we get a sense of discipleship and living for the Kingdom. When we enter into a relationship with Jesus, we have to continually examine how we live. This is what it's like for anyone who wants to be a disciple of Jesus. We believe and then act on that belief. Never by ourselves, even if we are physically alone in that moment. The Church helps us. The Holy Spirit strengthens and guides us. Faith-filled people in our everyday lives and our saints model it for us.

Identify In the Spiritual Practices feature, what are the two steps to giving thanks?

Analyze With his words, Zacchaeus indicates that he is determined to be not just one who believes in Jesus, but a disciple of Jesus. Millions of people—for two thousand years—have found meeting Jesus worth going out on a limb for. Why?

REFLECT

Listen! I am standing at the door, knocking; if you hear my voice and open the door, I will come in to you and eat with you, and you with me (Revelation 3:20).

>> **How does Jesus "knock on the door" of your life these days?**

SECTION 2 REVIEW

QUICK REVIEW

1a. Name What term describes God's disclosing his plan of redemption in ways we could never know ourselves?

b. Explain What does it mean when we say faith actually begins with God?

c. Analyze Why does Saint Augustine refer to our hearts as "restless"?

2a. Recall What did Jesus promise would happen if we approach faith more seriously?

b. Explain What are two ways through which people come to know God?

c. Analyze If we say only God can fulfill our yearning for joy and peace, then why do people pursue so many other means?

ACT

Create a profile of a favorite saint who *believed* then *acted*.

Answer these questions:

○ Why does this saint inspire you?

○ How did he or she live and *act* as a *response* to God's love?

SELF-ASSESS

Which statement best reflects where you are now?

☐ I'm confident enough about the material in this section to be able to explain it to someone else.

☐ I have a good grasp of the material in this section, but I could use more review.

☐ I'm lost. I need help catching up before moving on.

Talking about God

For the Catholic faith to grow as it has for thousands of years, spreading across continents and cultures, the Holy Spirit had to guide people in their belief and sustain them in their uncertainty. Believing in God and responding to him requires our whole selves, mind, heart, and head. We can and do accept fundamental teachings of the faith without fully understanding them. But we also seek to figure out as best we can what they mean so we can talk about God and to God with increased understanding. And the Church helps us do just that. She has since the very beginning and continues to do so today.

Early Church leaders spent a lot of time seeking an accurate understanding of the nature of God and putting those understandings into words. They read Scripture, studied, debated, prayed, and called on the Holy Spirit for guidance in forming an accurate presentation of fundamental Christian beliefs.

When discussing faith and Church teachings, two terms often come up: *doctrine* and *dogma*. **Doctrine** is a broader term. It refers to general Church teachings, for instance, the Church's teaching on certain aspects of social justice. Doctrine, referring to the Church's teachings, is reflected in the contents of the *Catechism*. But the *Catechism* contains both dogmas (defined Church teaching) and doctrine (general Church teaching). We have to assent to both dogmas and doctrines.

Dogma is a more specific term. It refers to the truths of Revelation that have been defined by the Church as "*de fide*" and must be held by all Catholics. Over the centuries, not a great number of these have been defined. The divinity and humanity of Christ and the three Persons in the Trinity are dogmas. Dogmas are the fundamental teachings of the Church that come into existence because a doctrine was denied.

For example, the Eucharist was a doctrine until the 13th century, when heretics denied the Real Presence. The ecumenical council of Lateran IV made this a dogma of Transubstantiation. An ecumenical council is a meeting of the world's bishops, usually called by the Pope, to exercise their shared authority over the universal Church. To sum up, all dogmas are Church teachings, but not all Church teachings are dogmas. Both are part of our faith commitment as members of the Church.

Important bishops and popes from the first eight centuries of the Church, are known as "the Fathers of the Church." These bishops and popes clarified and passed down Catholic doctrines and dogmas. We've already quoted one of them in this chapter: Saint Augustine. Women also contributed to Christian philosophical and theological thought at this time. For instance, one of the Church Fathers refers to Saint Macrina (c.330–380) simply as "the Teacher." Along with her brother, Saint Basil, Macrina began monasteries for women and men.

The first of the Church Fathers was Saint Athanasius (c.297–373). He served as Bishop of Alexandria in Egypt, one of the world's main centers of learning at the time. He suffered for his efforts, and spent fifteen years in exile when rival bishops who held heretical teachings about Jesus gained control of the city.

Athanasius faced his first banishment in 325 because he refused to receive a man named Arius back into communion with the Church. Arius backed an idea called Arianism—the belief that Jesus was not of the same substance as God. Arianism was later declared a heresy, but not before political decisions forced Athanasius out again in 341, this time to Rome for three years. Athanasius spent much of his life defending Jesus' divine nature as the Son of God.

doctrine general Church teachings

dogma fundamental truths of Revelation that have been defined by the Church as "*de fide*" and must be held by all Catholics

Established more than three hundred years before the birth of Christ, Nicea is located on the eastern shore of Lake Iznik in northwestern Turkey.

○ Nicea is now known as Iznik. In 325, the Church's first ecumenical council took place in the town center.

○ The council upheld Jesus' divinity and condemned Arianism, which said Jesus was "from another substance" than that of the Father (CCC, 465).

○ Nicea/Iznik is well known for its colorful pottery and well-preserved monuments that represent the Roman, Byzantine, and Ottoman ages.

○ Turkey is a secular republic with a majority Sunni Muslim population.

Faith & Culture

 Go to the student site at **hs.osvcurriculum.com**

Council of Nicea first ecumenical council held in the year 325 in modern-day Turkey

Nicene Creed profession of Catholic faith, which came from the first ecumenical Councils of Nicea and Constantinople

In the year 325, Athanasius and about three hundred other bishops took part in the **Council of Nicea**. An ecumenical council is a meeting of the world's bishops, usually called by the Pope, to exercise their shared authority over the universal Church. A second meeting was held in 381 at the Council of Constantinople. The **Nicene Creed** stems from these two ecumenical councils. It is a summary of the main doctrines of the faith, and in it we profess our belief in the Triune God—Father, Son, and Holy Spirit. The Nicene Creed continues to be proclaimed at Mass every Sunday throughout the world. We owe thanks to Church Fathers such as Saint Athanasius for explaining that Jesus is the true God and true man, the only Son of the Father.

Throughout his life Athanasius spoke about the union of divine and human natures in the one Person of Jesus Christ. Athanasius explained that God created human beings in his image to share life with him. Human beings lost sight of God, but the Father never stopped loving them. He sent his only Son, who took on human flesh to teach us the ways to salvation, save us from the power of sin, and reestablish our friendship with the Father. Then, in the ultimate act of self-giving, the death and Resurrection of Jesus restored human beings to life with God and brought about ultimate victory over sin and death.

Understanding Jesus as the Word of God who became man to save us and restore us to eternal life is the vital part of the Good News. We celebrate this in a special way during the Christmas and Easter seasons. We grow to better appreciate this Good News when we read the Bible, participate in Mass and the other Sacraments, and focus on Jesus in prayer.

Restate What is the difference between doctrine and dogma?

Explain For what reason did Saint Athanasius suffer?

Explain
○ Choose three statements from the Nicene Creed: one that you really connect with, one that you want to understand better, and one that would choose to explain to a younger person. Talk about each.

Faith and Reason

The word **theology** literally means "the study of God" or "the word about God." Theology moves the discussion of truth seeking beyond what human reason alone can achieve. Saint Anselm (A.D. 1033–1109) described theology as "faith seeking understanding." In a 2002 address to the Pontifical Academy of Theology, Pope John Paul II called theology a journey with Jesus, under the guidance of the Holy Spirit, whose mission is to help Christians understand the Good News of the Gospel and bring it to the world.

Catholicism has always considered faith and reason to be partners. Many of the greatest theologians and philosophers, such as Saint Thomas Aquinas, understood this relationship. Aquinas argued that what we learn from our own reasoning and from faith comes from God.

Aquinas laid the foundation for applying science and logic to the question of God's existence. **Logic** is defined as a specific method of forming an argument or conclusion. Anyone who searches for God can find certain ways to know him. Today we often refer to these as paths or pathways to God. Traditionally they have been known as *proofs of God's existence*, but not like proofs in biology or chemistry class. These proofs for God form "converging and convincing arguments," which help people to feel certain about the truth (CCC, 31–33).

Aquinas and other theologians pointed out that God's existence cannot be known without using reason, and everything we do know about God is limited by human constraints. Still, if we start not with God himself, but with the beings he created, we can see that something caused us to exist. The chart on the next page describes what Aquinas called his five ways or arguments to show the existence of God.

Choose

As a class, post signs around the classroom that each display one of Aquinas' five arguments for the existence of God (see chart, next page).

○ Choose which argument best describes your opinion about God and stand by that sign.

○ List at least two reasons why you chose that sign. Be prepared to explain your reasons.

○ What do these reasons say about your relationship with God?

theology the study of God or of religious faith and practice. Saint Augustine described it as "reasoning or concerning the deity" (*City of God* VIII, i)

logic specific method of forming an argument or a conclusion through the use of reason

Aquinas' Ways or Arguments for the Existence of God

1 **Immovable Mover** Everyone agrees that things move in our universe. Bowling balls roll down lanes, cars drive down highways, rivers flow from high to low points, planets revolve around their suns, and galaxies expand. At one point, these objects were at rest. Nothing can move by itself. Someone or something started them in motion. The sequence of motion does not go on forever, so something is the first mover that does not need to move. This immovable mover or unmoved mover is God.

2 **First Cause (Uncaused Cause)** Nothing can be the cause of itself or bring itself into existence, because it would need to exist before itself. This is impossible. When something happens, there is a series of causes that make it happen. For example, every person needs previous people to exist. Something had to be the first cause. If the previous cause didn't exist, then neither would its result. There exists then a first cause or the uncaused cause. We call this uncaused first cause God.

3 **Argument from Necessary Being** Everything in the universe exists for a limited time. Here Aquinas argues that if all things can either exist or not exist, then at some point in the past nothing existed. If at some point nothing existed, then nothing would exist now, because you can't get something from nothing. Since people and things exist today, then at least one being exists of its own necessity. Nothing brought this being into existence, and it causes the existence of everything else. We call this necessary being God.

4 **The Moral Argument (Perfect Being)** This way argues that there are different degrees of perfection, like goodness and truth, among the things of the universe. For example, some people behave better than others. There has to be some perfect being that is the highest degree of goodness and from which all good things flow. Aquinas uses fire to illustrate this argument. The closer items get to a fire the hotter they become. In the same way, the closer we get to the perfect being that creates goodness in the world, the better we become. The most perfect being that causes the goodness and perfection of all things is God.

5 **Argument from Design** Natural things that lack reason operate according to a plan and move toward a goal. They do not do so by chance, but because of a purpose. There is an order to how a seed becomes a tree, but the seed knows nothing about how to go about it. Aquinas used the example of an arrow guided by the archer and flying toward a target as its goal. For natural things to reach their goal, they need guidance from an intelligent being or designer. There exists then an intelligent designer who orders all things according to a plan. We call the intelligent designer God.

Debate
Whether God exists remains a hot topic that surfaces in the media from time to time. There is an old axiom: "For those who doubt, no proof is satisfactory; for those who believe, no proof is necessary."

Open this up for debate: Which half of the axiom adequately reflects today's culture?

Another topic to debate: What amount of proof will satisfy someone who denies God's existence?

THINKING THEOLOGICALLY

Lex Orandi, Lex Credendi is an ancient theological phrase that means, "the Church believes as she prays." This means the prayer of the Church holds the beliefs of the Church.

Read this second century Christian prayer from the Didache (DEE•duh•kay):

As the piece [of bread] was scattered over the hills and then was brought together and made one, so let your Church be brought together from the ends of the earth into your Kingdom. For yours is the glory and the power through Jesus Christ forever.

>> In the Nicene Creed we profess belief in the "one, holy, catholic and apostolic Church." We call these the four essential, distinguishing marks of the Church. Which mark of the Church does this prayer express?

Lex orandi, lex credendi can be used to help you understand your own beliefs. Write out your favorite prayer. What does this prayer show about your beliefs in God?

Blessed Pope John Paul II used the word *harmony* to describe this relationship. The teachings of faith can be better understood with the help of reason. And, in searching for the truth about God, reason and faith work together.

In his encyclical *Fides et Ratio,* or "Faith and Reason," the Pope said faith has no need to fear reason. He pointed out that Aquinas helped reconcile the distance between faith and reason, between the secular world of science and the Gospel. In other words, the Church does not negate the world, and science should not ignore faith.

Explain Why aren't faith and reason considered opposites?

Infer What is a limitation of relying only on human reason to know God?

Two Approaches

Modern theologians sometimes distinguish two ways to speak about God. A person can arrive at the truth about God through both subjective and objective approaches.

For example: Professional journalists covering a news story do their best to remain **objective**, or not be influenced by personal thoughts. They don't allow their personal opinions to influence the story.

Bloggers, columnists, or commentators may take the opposite, or **subjective**, approach, often filtering what happened through their own experiences and reflection. What they write or say may be one hundred percent their own opinions.

objective not influenced by personal feelings or opinions when considering or representing facts

subjective an attitude or viewpoint arising from personal background, experience, bias, or reflection

Some theologians, for example, feel that the classical "proofs" for God's existence are too objective, meaning too divorced from actual human experience.

Other people dismiss faith entirely, saying it is too subjective and comes only from individual experiences and feelings. Either approach can discover signs of God's existence, but both have their limits. During his 2008 visit to the United States, Pope Benedict XVI said faith is not limited to personal experiences alone. God's Revelation gives each generation the chance to find the ultimate truth for themselves. God tells us about himself, most fully through Jesus Christ.

Still, as Romans 5:5 explains: "God's love has been poured into our hearts through the Holy Spirit." Both objective and subjective approaches allow us to know and proclaim the hope of Christ.

Define Would a blogger filter news from an objective or subjective approach?

Contrast Explain the difference between an objective approach and a subjective approach to learning about God.

Discuss

In small groups, talk about which approach—objective or subjective—appeals more to you. Be prepared to explain your answer.

SECTION 3 REVIEW

QUICK REVIEW

1a. Recall Who was Athanasius?

b. Elaborate How did the Church Fathers help people understand and speak about their faith?

c. Analyze Why do you think professing our faith in the words of the Nicene Creed is part of the Mass? What is the significance of the gesture we use when reciting it?

2a. Recall Aquinas set the tone for applying science and logic to the question of what?

b. Summarize What evidence did Aquinas' first proof, the argument from motion, give for the existence of God?

c. Analyze Why do you think people feel the need to prove (or disprove) the existence of God?

ACT

Design an image, such as a screensaver, T-shirt graphic, or logo that illustrates one of Aquinas' five ways of demonstrating God's existence.

SELF-ASSESS

Which statement best reflects where you are now?

☐ I'm confident enough about the material in this section to be able to explain it to someone else.

☐ I have a good grasp of the material in this section, but I could use more review.

☐ I'm lost. I need help catching up before moving on.

Relating to God

Thomas Aquinas once said that all of the time speculating about the nature of God could not compare to one moment spent in prayer. Perhaps we can easily grasp what he meant. Wouldn't we trade hours of talk about love for one moment of actually experiencing love? It's hard to get excited about a God described as "uncaused cause" and "unmoved mover."

God first calls to us by creating us and telling us about himself. Prayer begins with God. We respond by sharing with God our gratitude, questions, needs, problems, and concerns for others—the deepest parts of who we are. Prayer involves our whole being—our minds, hearts, souls.

We pray in different ways, for different reasons. When we thank God or express our deepest concerns—really, any time we pray—we grow closer to him. We grow stronger as disciples. And when we pray, the Holy Spirit enables us and is with us. Pope Benedict XVI, in his encyclical *Spe Salvi,* or "On Christian Hope," calls prayer the most important lesson in learning to hope.

> *"When no one listens to me any more, God still listens to me. When I can no longer talk to anyone or call upon anyone, I can always talk to God."*
>
> —Pope Benedict XVI, *Spe Salvi* #32

Personal prayer is an encounter between ourselves and God. When we cannot find the right words to say, Pope Benedict suggests the prayers of the Church, the saints, and the liturgy. This "intermingling" of personal and public prayer is how we communicate with God, how we become open to him, and how we prepare to serve others. It is how we strengthen ourselves with hope. Then, Pope Benedict says, we will become "ministers of hope for others."

Traditional Prayer Forms

Part of the grace that comes to us from the Holy Spirit prompts us to pray in these traditional ways.

1 **Prayer of blessing:** We ask for God's blessing in this basic Christian prayer. God's gift and our acceptance of it is an encounter between God and us. We bless ourselves, others, and objects with the Sign of the Cross, a reminder of our Baptism.

2 **Prayer of petition:** We are not afraid to ask God for something we need, such as help with our relationships or with the decisions we face.

3 **Prayer of intercession:** We ask God to bless or help others, maybe someone sick or even those who have hurt us. The Prayer of the Faithful at Mass is a good example.

4 **Prayer of thanksgiving:** We acknowledge our gratitude for what God has done for us. A common example is thanking God for the food we eat.

5 **Prayer of praise:** We give God glory for being God, separate from anything specific he has done for us. An example here is the "Glory to God" prayer in the Mass.

EARLY Monastic Life

Early Christian life was characterized by dedication to God. Early Christians prayed, fasted, and gave to the poor, but did this while living with their families. Around the year A.D. 270, some people decided that the best way for them to really know Christ was to live a simple life alone, meditating on Scripture and praying. These men became known as hermits or monks, and women were nuns.

Saint Anthony of Egypt (250–355) is the first known monk. His life was one of prayer and self-sacrifice. Saint Athanasius, in a biography of Saint Anthony, writes that Anthony lived the words of the Gospel: "Go, sell what you own, and give the money to the poor, and you will have treasure in heaven . . ." (Mark 10:21). Saint Anthony lived in the desert in a mountainside cave in what is Libya today. Many imitated his life and wanted to live a similar lifestyle. Saint Anthony, known as first of the "desert fathers," established a rule for them to follow. The monks lived a simple life, doing manual labor to earn money for the poor and to support themselves.

In Egypt, **Saint Pachomius** (292–348) started the first monastery in A.D. 320 on the banks of the Nile River and is credited with writing the first communal rule for monks. The monks lived a life of silence and wore a habit of coarse white linen with a hood that kept them from seeing one another at meals. Before his death, Saint Pachomius had founded nine monasteries for men and two for women.

In the East, **Saint Basil the Great** (329–379) founded the first monastery in Asia Minor in Pontus on the southern coast of the Black Sea. His monastic rule, which focused on community life, liturgical prayer, and manual labor, has been the most lasting of those in the East. His sister, Saint Macrina, founded communities of nuns in the same area.

↗ Go to the student site at **hs.osvcurriculum.com**

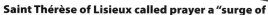
All four Gospels identify Jesus as a man of deep prayer. Prayer accompanied the major events in his ministry. The Gospels, for example, record Jesus' prayer as he considered what would happen when he was handed over.

"Then he withdrew from them about a stone's throw, knelt down, and prayed. 'Father, if you are willing, remove this cup from me; yet, not my will but yours be done'" (Luke 22:41-42).

Jesus' words echo those he taught us in the Lord's Prayer: "Thy will be done." Prayer puts us in touch with God's plan for us. Prayer connects us to God's love.

> *"The Creator, who is so great, so wise, has doubtless hidden secrets in all created things, and we can benefit from knowing them. . . . I believe that in each smallest creature, though it be but a tiny ant, are more wonders than we can comprehend. . . . I discover secrets within us which often fill me with astonishment: How many more must there be that are unknown to me! O my Lord and my God! How stupendous is your grandeur! . . . How great are your mysteries! . . ."*
>
> —Saint Teresa of Ávila (1515–1582), in *Sacred Voices,* edited by Mary Ford-Grabowsky

Intimate Union

Catholicism has a rich history of people who have had overwhelming experiences of God's love. They sensed God's presence and met him at many different times and points in their lives. They remind us that, "God calls us all to this intimate union with him" (CCC, 2014).

Mysticism refers to this intense experience of union with God. Mystics often speak of their relationship with God in terms of intimacy and love.

Mystics encounter Jesus in a deeply personal, intimate way. Their lives are characterized by intense, silent prayer that grows through love and adoration of God's goodness. Known as **contemplative prayer**, it is "the simple expression of the mystery of prayer. It is a gaze of faith fixed on Jesus, an attentiveness to the Word of God, a silent love" (CCC, 2724).

Mystics are not just in convents and monasteries, unknown to most of us. They are all around us, often without us even knowing it.

Recall How many Gospels identify Jesus as someone of deep prayer?

Explain What did Thomas Aquinas mean when he said all of his time speculating about the nature of God was not worth one moment spent in prayer?

mysticism an intense experience or direct communication of love of and union with God

contemplative prayer a solemn, silent expression of prayer that focuses on Jesus and the word of God

MY FAITH

Use this space to build your own faith portfolio.

Make some private notes about your spiritual growth.

Keep track of your own faith journey.

Reflect on where God might be speaking to you right now.

Mark the spiritual commitments, questions, and actions that are important to you.

At the end of the course, you will be asked to summarize some of what you have come to understand and appreciate.

The theologians, mystics, and philosophers all tell us about God yearning for us. What do you think God desires for you? Describe your longing for God today.

Spiritual growth combines "turning upward" to God, "turning inward" to our deepest spiritual voice and feelings, and "turning outward" to what's going on with friends, family, and the rest of the world. Where would you say that you put your spiritual attention most often— "upward," "inward," or "outward"?

Which of these three dimensions do you think God is asking you to give more attention to? How can you respond? Or are you already on it?

What have you learned about God from books? From nature? From your family or other people? At Mass?

What have you learned about God by heart? What knowledge of God is now part of your soul and goes with you wherever you go?

Consider these questions thoughtfully and write your personal thoughts in the space provided.

Go to the student site at
hs.osvcurriculum.com

Discipleship . . . within the Body of Christ . . . for the glory of God and the good of the world

Paul the Philosopher and Mystic

Paul plays a pivotal role in the earliest days of the Church. Although he is not one of the first followers of Jesus, through the grace of God, he is transformed from being one who persecutes Christians into being their greatest advocate. His transformation is described in the Acts of the Apostles as no less than being blind and having his sight restored.

He takes on the philosophers and argues that the wise recognize the one, true living God; only fools miss this truth. In a letter to Christians in Rome he writes that: "Ever since the creation of the world his eternal power and divine nature, invisible though they are, have been understood and seen through the things he has made" (Romans 1:20). In other words, there is no conflict between the truth we discover through observing the world around us (creation) and the truth we find in Scripture. Both are, in a sense, the word of the Creator.

In those words to the early Church, Paul urges us all to make ourselves new in Christ. We might think Paul means we should change our behavior, but as Pope Benedict XVI points out, he is talking about something deeper. Paul says what must become new is our way of thinking. "This surprises us," Pope Benedict said in a homily closing the Pauline Year. "Renewal must go the very core. Our way of looking at the world, of understanding reality all our thought must change from its foundations." Normally our thinking is limited to "possession, well-being, influence, success, fame," but Saint Paul is talking about something more profound. What we must do, Paul says, is let go of ourselves and learn what God wants. God's will then becomes our will. "We must learn to share in the thinking and the will of Jesus Christ," Pope Benedict said in June 2009. "It is then that we will be new people in whom a new world emerges."

Saint Paul makes his way to the great centers of Greek and Roman thought such as Ephesus and Athens, making the case for belief in Christ as perfectly compatible with the best that philosophy has to offer.

Saint Paul

He is a great example for bringing the mind and heart together. He also has a deep, loving relationship with Christ such as the mystics have. He expresses this experience in what amounts to a love poem:

Who will separate us from the love of Christ?
Will hardship, or distress, or persecution, or
famine, or nakedness, or peril, or sword? . . .
No, in all these things we are more than
conquerors through him who loved us.
For I am convinced that neither death, nor
life, nor angels, nor rulers, nor things present,
nor things to come, nor powers, nor height,
nor depth, nor anything else in all creation,
will be able to separate us from the love
of God in Christ Jesus our Lord.

—Romans 8:35, 37-39

Write

Paul writes two of his letters to the Christian Church in Corinth. In the first Letter to the Corinthians, he offers a description of true love that has become a classic statement on love.

○ Read Paul's hymn to love, I Corinthians Chapter 13.

○ Quietly pray for a moment, trying to center yourself on Christ. Then write the hymn in your own words, or write your own poetic description of what Christian love entails.

Famous Mystics

Teresa of Ávila is in good company among many mystics who enlighten and encourage us in our prayer. Among them are Saint Hildegard of Bingen (1098–1179), Saint Thérèse of Lisieux (1873–1897), and Thomas Merton (1915–1968).

Blessed Hildegard von Bingen composed a wide body of written material from visions received through what she called the voice from Heaven. She was a twelfth-century poet, composer, naturalist, healer, theologian, prophet, preacher, and founder of convents.

Blessed Hildegard von Bingen

Known as Saint Hildegard, she was the tenth child born to a noble family in Bermersheim, in what is now Germany. At eight, she was sent to a Benedictine convent where she learned how to read and write. Hildegard's spirituality grew and other parents sent their daughters to the Benedictine convent at Disibodenberg.

Perhaps Hildegard's best-known work is *Scivias*, in which she lists visions such as the following and then interprets them.

> *I saw a great mountain the color of iron, and enthroned on it One of such glory that it blinded my sight. On each side of him there extended a soft shadow, like a wing of wondrous breadth and length. Before him, at the foot of the mountain, stood an image full of eyes on all sides, in which, because of those eyes, I could discern no human form. In front of this image stood another, a child wearing a tunic of subdued color but white shoes, upon whose head such glory descended from the One enthroned upon that mountain that I could not look at its face.*

—Hildegard of Bingen, *Scivias*

Report

Write a report on one of the following modern mystics:

○ Charles de Foucauld, Barbara Hallensleben, or Jacques Fesch.

○ Describe the experience of God revealed by the mystic you studied.

Thomas Merton lived life intensely, the good and the bad of it, through his college years. Then he felt drawn to the Catholic Church and to the monastic life. He entered the Trappist order of monks at the Abbey of Gethsemani in Kentucky. At first he saw living as a monk as a way to get away from the superficialities of life. In time he came to see that the life of prayer, manual labor, and silence helped him appreciate all of life more deeply. He describes an experience he had one day when he went into town.

> *In the center of the shopping district, I was suddenly overwhelmed with the realization that I loved all those people, that they were mine and I theirs, that we could not be alien to one another even though we were total strangers. It was like waking from a dream of separateness, of spurious self-isolation in a special world, the world of renunciation and supposed holiness. The whole illusion of a separate holy existence is a dream.*

—Thomas Merton, *Conjectures of a Guilty Bystander*

Thomas Merton

Saint Thérèse of Lisieux, who came to be known as "the little flower," was a French girl of fifteen when she entered the Carmelite religious order. At the request of her superiors, she began writing about her life, and we are blessed with an honest report of what this sensitive young woman was going through until her death by tuberculosis at the age of twenty-four. Her relationship with Jesus was always intense but never easy. At times she felt rejected or cast aside.

Following is her account of an incident when she experienced intense love for Jesus. She said the experience was like those described frequently by the saints, but which happened to her just once and lasted for only a moment.

Thérèse of Lisieux

Discuss

○ What's the strongest characteristic of Christian mysticism?

○ There is a difference between knowing *about* someone and actually *knowing* someone. Apply this distinction to a relationship with God.

> *I was commencing the Stations of the Cross in the choir that day when, suddenly, I felt that I had been wounded by a dart of fire so ardent that death must be near. I have no words to describe it; it was as though an invisible hand had plunged me into fire. And such fire! Yet at the same time, what sweetness! I was burning up with love and was convinced that to withstand such an onslaught of love for one minute, nay for even one second more, was impossible. Death must surely ensue.*
>
> —*Prayers and Meditations of Thérèse of Lisieux,*
> Cindy Cavnar, ed.

Although Thérèse spent much of her brief life in a monastery, she became one of the most popular saints of all time. In a sense she offered a pathway to everyday mysticism for modern Catholics, which she called "the little way." She advocated doing "random acts of kindness" before that phrase became popular. She said that if we performed daily tasks with a spirit of love, they would express the love of Jesus in us and through us.

Tell Describe the relationship between Jesus and Saint Thérèse of Lisieux.

Contrast How are Christian mystics different from the way popular culture presents "mystics"?

Pilgrim's Journey

> *We are pilgrims progressing from time to eternity, and our goal is the Father himself. He constantly calls us beyond what is familiar and comfortable to new paths of faith and trust. As we draw nearer, he sometimes seems to draw away, but only because he is a mysterious God whose thoughts are not our thoughts, whose ways are not our ways. Like Abraham, we must go forward, not knowing where we are being led. Like Abraham, and Jesus after him, we must constantly turn toward the Father, who is faithful, and trust him. Moment by moment, if we respond to the Father's love, he will bring us unerringly, through Jesus, to himself.*
>
> —Blessed Pope John Paul II, *Homily in Canberra, Australia, November 24, 1986, #5*

That is how Blessed Pope John Paul II described our journey to God as he spoke during a 1986 trip to the South Pacific. So, pilgrim, does it sound a little scary when the Pope says things like "not knowing where we are being led"? But that is the point. We are being led. We are being called by the one who created us. God wants to be close to us and for us to take him places. What could that mean?

PRIMARY SOURCES

"The Canticle of Brother Sun" is attributed to Saint Francis of Assisi, who had a close relationship with nature and with God. The poem, which is sometimes sung during liturgies, praises God for the sun, moon, stars, water, and Earth. Here is one stanza:

➚ Go to the student site at **hs.osvcurriculum.com**

}

Be praised my Lord, through all your creatures, especially through my lord Brother Sun, who brings the day; and you give light through him. And he is beautiful and radiant in all his splendor! Of you, Most High, he bears the likeness.

>> **Read the entire "Canticle of Brother Sun" provided by your teacher.**

What does it say when someone refers to natural things in human terms, such as brother and sister?

Where is the one place on Earth where you feel close to God's creation? Write a paragraph describing that place.

especially of noble beings, and knowledge of happiness and misery in the next li

---

SECTION 4 REVIEW

QUICK REVIEW

1a. Recall Name the traditional types of prayer.

b. Explain What does it mean to say Jesus was someone of "deep prayer"?

c. Evaluate Why does Pope Benedict XVI say that prayer is important in learning to hope?

2a. Identify What is mysticism?

b. Infer How does life in a convent or monastery differ from your own life?

c. Evaluate At this point in your life, where can you say God is leading you in terms of your response to faith?

ACT

Analyze how much time you spend in prayer and identify when you might be able to find more opportunities to talk with God.

SELF-ASSESS

Which statement best reflects where you are now?

☐ I'm confident enough about the material in this section to be able to explain it to someone else.

☐ I have a good grasp of the material in this section, but I could use more review.

☐ I'm lost. I need help catching up before moving on.

PRAYER

Leader:
O God, you are my God, for you I long.

All:
For you my soul is thirsting. Your love is better than life. My lips will
speak your praise.

Reader 1:
Our spirit hungers for your love, O divine Maker of hearts,
For the taste of your joy and the aroma of your peace.
May this time of prayer fill us with the whisper of your presence,
And let us feel the touch of your hand upon our hearts.
We long, God, for the depths of your love, to know your quiet constancy,
the feast of your friendship that feeds us without end.
We pray that you will awaken us to your presence Lord.
We ask this through Christ, our Lord. Amen.

(Adapted from Edward Hays,
Prayers for a Planetary Pilgrim, p. 172)

Reader 2:
As the deer longs for streams of water, so my soul longs for you, O God.
My being thirsts for God, the living God. When can I go and see the face
of God? My tears have been my food day and night, as they ask daily,
"Where is your God?" Those times I recall as I pour out my soul, when I
went in procession with the crowd, I went with them to the house of God,
amid loud cries of thanksgiving, with the multitude keeping festival. Why
are you downcast, my soul; why do you groan within me? Wait for God,
whom I shall praise again, my savior and my God (see Psalm 42:1-6).

Closing (All):
God, our Father, we know that you long to be close to us.
Help us to recognize your presence in our lives and make us aware of our never-ending
need for you. Help us to celebrate your love, even on days when you feel distant to us.
Send us the Holy Spirit to remind us that you are never far away and that nothing can
separate us from the power of your love.
We ask this through Christ, our Lord. Amen.

Discussion
Reflect on your own yearnings for God. How have they evolved or changed
over the years?

CHAPTER 2 REVIEW

TERMS

Use each of the following terms in a sentence that shows you know what the term means. You may include more than one term in a sentence.

wisdom	Council of Nicea
reason	Nicene Creed
Divine Revelation	theology
Trinity	logic
faith	objective
discipleship	subjective
doctrine	mysticism
dogma	contemplative prayer

PEOPLE

Identify the person who best fits each description.

1. Spanish mystic who clearly saw love as the way to God.

2. Brother and sister saints who founded monasteries for women and men.

3. Twelfth-century mystic and composer whose music is still popular.

4. Church Father who defended Jesus' divine nature as the Son of God.

5. North African bishop who wrote about his lifelong yearning for God.

6. American mystic who found deep meaning in monastic life.

7. Medieval thinker who summarized five ways for demonstrating God's existence.

8. Great missionary and writer of letters to early Church communities.

9. Young French saint who advocated performing "random acts of kindness."

UNDERSTANDING

Answer each question and complete each exercise.

SECTION 1

1. **Explain** *Deus Caritas Est*—How is this true?

2. **Explain** What does it mean when we say we are "swimming" in God's presence?

3. **Elaborate** Why do surveys about belief in God often include questions about belief in Heaven and Hell?

4. **Synthesize** What were the consequences of believing in God for Saint Ignatius in the second century? Why do you think people's belief in God continues in spite of—or even becomes stronger because of—the risk of persecution and death?

SECTION 2

5. **Identify** Name two ways God is known to us, and give an example of each.

6. **Explain** How do we know about the Trinity, or God in three Persons?

7. **Explain** Faith is a response to what?

8. **Analyze** What was Jesus showing us about the Kingdom of God through his interaction with Zacchaeus?

SECTION 3

9. **Recall** What did Saint Thomas Aquinas apply to the question of God's existence?

10. **Articulate** Compose a paragraph explaining the reason(s) you believe in God or indicate "the proofs" of God's existence that make sense to you. Then identify one of Aquinas's proofs that comes closest to your own thinking and explain why.

11. **Recall** Who were the Church Fathers, and what role did they play in helping Christians know and talk about God?

12. **Summarize** Why do we owe thanks to the Church Fathers such as Saint Athanasius?

13. **Identify** What is contemplative prayer?

14. **Evaluate** Why would Saint Hildegard's music and other works be popular today?

15. **Analyze** Why do Christian mystics often use the language of human love and intimacy to describe their relationships with God?

16. **Infer** Why does Pope John Paul II say we are "pilgrims processing from time to eternity"?

CONNECTING

Visual This photo shows light streaming into a cathedral.

What symbols of spiritual longings can you infer from the design of churches and cathedrals like this one?

Question After working through this chapter, what advice would you give someone who wants to know God better? In what ways have you personally come to know God better after working through this chapter?

Imagine Picture in your mind what it would be like if mystics and philosophers like Thomas Aquinas or Teresa of Ávila had a social media page today, and used it to promote their way of knowing God. Think about a specific person from this chapter and answer these questions:

○ How might this person describe himself or herself in two or three sentences?

○ What popular songs or movies might this person recommend that express views about God?

○ What famous people today might choose to sign up as this person's "friends" on social media?

Challenge You are texting when your friend asks a question:

> **Friend:** Can you go to the beach Sunday?
>
> **You:** Sorry, I have to read at Mass.
>
> **Friend:** Can't someone else do it?
>
> **You:** No, I'm scheduled.
>
> **Friend:** Why do you have to go to church at all?
>
> **You:** It's important.
>
> **Friend:** How do you even know God exists?

○ What is your next reply?

○ Continue the conversation, anticipating at least two more questions your friend might ask and how you would answer. Use information from the chapter to answer your friend.

SELF-ASSESS

On Your Own Make a list of the most important things you learned from this chapter. Select three things that represent your growth in understanding as you worked through this chapter. Write a paragraph explaining your three selections.

With a Partner List what you found most helpful or interesting in this chapter, as well as any other questions that have surfaced.

CHAPTER **3**

Bible Background

DO

- Identify what you already know about the Bible.

- Understand what we mean by God's Revelation.

- Describe a time when God may have been speaking to you.

- Examine the relationship between Scripture and Tradition.

- Recognize how the Bible inspires God's People.

- Learn what it takes to correctly understand God's word in the Bible.

- Find out about and use historical-critical approaches to Scripture.

- Know the structure of the Bible and how it came to be.

DEFINE

Magisterium	genre	deutero-canonical
Tradition	metaphor	books
Deposit of Faith	apocalyptic	oral tradition
biblical inspiration	New Testament	Gospels
biblical inerrancy	Old Testament	synoptic Gospels
historical-critical	Septuagint	Epistles
approach	canon of Scripture	Acts of the Apostles
literary criticism	Palestinian Canon	Book of Revelation

Go to the student site at
hs.osvcurriculum.com

Read these scenarios.

In a van riding home from the basketball tournament, the talk turns to religion. A friend says: "My cousins believe that the Bible is one hundred percent true. Totally. No questions. Adam and Eve ate the apple. Jonah got swallowed by a whale. Moses parted the Red Sea—just like in the movie."

But another friend says: "A whale can't swallow a human. It's not scientifically possible. And there's no such thing as a talking snake."

"Makes no difference to my cousins. To them, the Bible's totally true. They just say 'Believe it.'"

The Book of Revelation describes a heavenly war that takes place between good and evil with monstrous beasts, flying horses, and the devil wearing the number 666. Is this what the end will be like?

Movies and books come out about newly discovered Gospels, secret biblical codes, and complex cover-ups regarding hidden and controversial Bible stories and facts. Some of these imply that there were politics involved in writing the Bible and in some Church declarations.

HOW DO YOU RESPOND?

Where Are You?				
Choose the response that best reflects where you are right now.				
How much do you know about what's in the Bible?	☐ A lot	☐ Quite a bit	☐ A little	☐ Not much
How often do you read the Bible?	☐ A lot	☐ Quite a bit	☐ A little	☐ Not much
How often do you pray with the Bible?	☐ A lot	☐ Quite a bit	☐ A little	☐ Not much
How much do you think the Bible can help you?	☐ A lot	☐ Quite a bit	☐ A little	☐ Not much
How many Bible stories do you know?	☐ A lot	☐ Quite a few	☐ A few	☐ Not many

The Word of God

How can we know God?

What's God like?

Does it make a difference what a person believes?

What does God expect from us?

When you listen to music on the Internet, a pop-up window sometimes displays background information about the artist. Maybe it says something about how the band formed or how the singer came up with the title of the song.

This chapter does something similar, but on a much larger scale. It provides a guide to the Bible. This background information can help you become a more thoughtful and faithful reader of Scripture. The goal is not simply to learn *about* Scripture, but to learn *from* Scripture. Ultimately it's about getting to know Jesus better, understanding more about God the Father's desire to share himself with us, and opening ourselves to seeing the Holy Spirit's action in our lives and the world.

Some people can pick up a Bible, open it, read a passage, and have their lives transformed. Saint Augustine, whom you read about in the second chapter, writes about such a life-changing experience. The Bible passage he read talked about adopting the ways of Jesus Christ and ignoring the desires of the flesh—for example, being lazy, gambling, eating too much, sexual desires—that can distract people from following Christ. Augustine was moved by the passage and dramatically changed his lifestyle.

A sophomore at Saint Elizabeth Academy in St. Louis, Missouri, recently wrote that her life was transformed after randomly reading Exodus Chapter 20, which includes the Ten Commandments. "This chapter really changed my life because it teaches me how God . . . wants me to live on this Earth," the sophomore wrote. "The Bible has become my best friend now, and by doing this I think I am helping myself, but I am also helping my friends . . . because they see that my way of living is now different from theirs so they decided to make some new changes as well."

We can have similar experiences with Scripture if we are open to it. However, we can all benefit from understanding more about this Book of books. As you work through this chapter, keep these questions in mind:

- Just as having background on a song helps me experience music better, how does background information enhance what I take from the Bible?

- How much of this information is different from what I already know about Scripture?

- How will knowing this information help me grow to know and follow Jesus better?

GO TO THE SOURCE

The Scripture passage that led Saint Augustine to turn his life around and follow Christ was Romans 13:13-14.

1. Look up the passage, then research Augustine's early life. Why do you think this passage spoke so strongly to him?

2. Think of a Scripture passage that you need to hear a lot, that stays with you, that you cannot forget. What is it, and why this passage? How does it apply to your life? What might the Holy Spirit be telling you?

Scripture *and* Tradition

Early on, the Holy Spirit guided the Church Magisterium to accept the Jewish Torah as the first five books of Scripture, sorted out the rest of the books of the Old Testament, and identified which writings were to be included in the New Testament. The term **Magisterium** refers to the living, teaching office of the Church. The Magisterium—that is, the bishops in communion with the Pope (the Bishop of Rome)—is alone responsible for interpreting the word of God, whether in Scripture or in Tradition.

Notice that the word "Tradition" is capitalized. **Tradition** in this sense is defined as the living transmission of the Gospel message in the Church (see *Catechism of the Catholic Church*, 78). We hear God's word and are guided by the Holy Spirit through *both* Sacred Scripture and Tradition. Sometimes we call it Sacred Tradition or Holy Tradition. This stresses the work of the Holy Spirit in the passing on of faith.

In a broad sense, tradition means "that which is handed on." Your local parish, for example, may have a tradition every May of holding a procession and crowning a statue of Mary with flowers. The May Crowning is a wonderful tradition, but it should be classified as "tradition" with a lower-case t.

Tradition and Scripture are bound together and come from one common source, the one sacred **Deposit of Faith**. Both Scripture and Tradition are God's Revelation to us, and they have equal and essential roles in the Church. They must be honored equally (see CCC, 80 and 82).

However, Tradition is also distinct from Sacred Scripture, encompassing the apostolic preaching and teachings that the Church defined as doctrines after the time of the Apostles. Through Tradition, the Church, in her doctrine, life, and worship, perpetuates and transmits all that she is and believes (see CCC, 77-78).

So it is through this Tradition that the Church first handed on the Gospel message and later determined which materials would be included in Sacred Scripture (the Bible). The early Church began with verbally telling and retelling the Gospel stories, along with passing along and reading aloud the letters of early Christian leaders, such as those from Saints Peter and Paul.

The Holy Spirit was actively guiding those early Christians, even during that stage of oral tradition. We will cover this more later in the chapter. This spoken word was important because after Pentecost, the Apostles began to tell others what Jesus had said and done, with a fuller understanding provided by the Holy Spirit (see CCC, 96 and 126). In doing so, the Apostles passed on the Gospel message Jesus had entrusted to them. This is why Tradition is often called Apostolic Tradition.

Tradition is not restricted to the Holy Spirit's role in *the past*. It refers to the *constant* passing down of the Gospel message, which continues in the Church today. The prayers and the Creeds that we profess are the same as they were long ago, but the Holy Spirit helps us to understand, proclaim, and live by them today.

Until the 1960s, for example, Mass was celebrated in Latin as it had been for centuries. Now we can use local languages to celebrate Mass. This change was part of the renewal brought about by Vatican Council II, which we will discuss later, but which took place under the guidance of the Holy Spirit.

Magisterium the official teaching office of the Church—the bishops in communion with the Pope—that interprets Scripture and Tradition and ensures faithfulness to the teachings of the Apostles

Tradition the living transmission, under the inspiration of the Holy Spirit, of the message of the Gospel in the Church (see *Catechism*, Glossary)

Deposit of Faith the heritage of faith contained in Sacred Scripture and Tradition, handed on in the Church from the time of the Apostles, from which the Magisterium draws all that it proposes for belief as being divinely revealed (see *Catechism*, Glossary)

THE Book OF Kells

The Book of Kells contains the four Gospels and explanations about them. It was written for use in public worship and is considered to be the finest surviving decorated manuscript produced in medieval Europe.

Columban monks probably wrote it around the year A.D. 800 on the Isle of Iona, Scotland, to honor Saint Columba. During that time, the Vikings raided monasteries, searching for manuscripts because of the precious jewels that decorated them. The book was moved to Kells, Ireland, sometime in the ninth century to keep it from being found. Later the Church took it for safekeeping during the Protestant Reformation. It was given to Trinity College in Dublin, Ireland, in the seventeenth century, and it has been preserved there ever since. It has been on display in the college library since the nineteenth century. Two volumes can be seen: one opened to a decorated page and another to one to two pages of script. In 2009, for example, the decorated page on display was from the Gospel according to Luke and showed the body of Jesus being placed in the tomb. The text pages are from the Gospel according to John. In it Jesus says:

> "I am the light of the world. Whoever follows me will never walk in darkness but will have the light of life."
>
> John 8:12

The book is written on vellum (a fine-grained unsplit calfskin prepared especially for writing on). It contains Latin text in a writing style that includes elaborate script similar to calligraphy, with large, richly colored initial letters accompanied by magnificent decoration. In fact, many pages are only decorative and are made with as many as ten different colors, some of which were created with expensive European dyes. These pages contain portraits of Mary, the Gospel writers, and scenes from the Bible and nature. The detail on some pages is so intricate that designs can only be seen with a magnifying glass.

Christ Enthroned

The Long Room of the Old Library at Trinity College, Dublin, Ireland

Scripture & Tradition

The significant relationship between Scripture and Tradition can be summed up in the following points:

1. Christians in the first century did not yet possess a written New Testament. Instead they relied on oral tradition that the Apostles shared from Jesus' own teachings and example, in addition to what they came to understand from the Holy Spirit. Through this process, we came to the written contents of the New Testament (see CCC, 83).

2. The work of the Holy Spirit is contained in the "written word" (Scripture) and continues in the Church today (Tradition).

3. Scripture and Tradition, under the inspiration of the Holy Spirit, are preserved and handed on as the sole deposit of the Word of God under the leadership of the Magisterium, namely the Pope and the bishops in union with him as the successors of the Apostles.

4. Scripture and Tradition have a common divine source and serve a common purpose, namely to proclaim and promote the Word of God.

5. Scripture provides a record of the beliefs and practices of the early Church. Scripture and Tradition are bound together.

6. Tradition always remains equal and faithful to the Word of God revealed in Scripture.

The Church constantly seeks guidance from Scripture in order to be faithful to its inspired message. Sacred Scripture is integral to every celebration of the Sacraments, which are part of Tradition and how we celebrate and passs on our faith. The prayers we pray during the Eucharist and other Sacraments help us apply God's word to our lives. The *Catechism* is a classic example of Tradition. It relies heavily on Scripture, as have the popes, bishops, and theologians quoted and recorded in its pages. It contains numerous references to Scripture. When you consider Scripture and Tradition, you can't have one without the other.

Through the Magisterium, the Church helps her members as they approach Scripture and try to learn from it. "'The task of giving an authentic interpretation of the Word of God, whether in its written form or in the form of Tradition, has been entrusted to the living, teaching office of the Church alone. Its authority in this matter is exercised in the name of Jesus Christ'[3] This means that the task of interpretation has been entrusted to the bishops in communion with the successor of Peter, the Bishop of Rome" (CCC, 85).

Through Tradition, the Church helps us understand and connect God's word revealed in the Scripture to our lives. For example, bishops write pastoral letters guiding and instructing Catholics in their dioceses. In papal encyclicals the Pope teaches Catholics everywhere about important issues of faith and morals. Church Council Documents are also part of the Tradition of the Church. These documents are the records of the decisions made during ecumenical councils—gatherings of the world's bishops called by the Pope to teach and guide the Church, like the Second Vatican Council previously mentioned.

Identify What is the Magisterium?

Restate What is the one common source from which Scripture and Tradition flow?

Inspired Words of God

High school seniors often get to choose a quote to go with their yearbook picture. ("A wasted day is one when I don't laugh." "Old friends are the best friends." "Good music will get you through.") Some search for a saying they find inspiring, meaningful, or descriptive of their hopes and dreams. Others choose a line that is funny or irreverent, but that choice says something about them as well. If all such sayings in a yearbook were gathered into a booklet, could that collection of sayings be considered a "holy" book—at least for that particular graduating class?

Imagine you are feeling down or stressed about some things in your life. Then you hear a song with some words that make you feel better. It provides just the right message you needed at that moment. Could that song lyric have been a gift from an inspired "deejay in the sky?" Remember when you saw a movie or read a book that spoke to you in a special way? You could call that movie or book "inspiring."

Biblical inspiration is much more than what's described above, but those ideas get us thinking about important things. The Holy Spirit does indeed touch us in many ways. Wisdom can come to us in a variety of ways. Biblical inspiration, however, is the gift of the Holy Spirit that assisted the human authors in the writing of biblical books. God inspired the writers, who used their own abilities and different literary styles to communicate his word. Because of this divine inspiration, God is the author of Sacred Scripture, acting in and through the human authors. Because of this, Scripture teaches faithfully, without error, the saving truth that God wants us to know about himself and his plan for all people (see CCC, 105-106).

This inspiration means that the Bible contains truth provided to us by God. So, when Scripture is proclaimed during Mass, the reader concludes by saying, "The word of the Lord," and we respond, "Thanks be to God." During the reading of the Gospel, we

Share
Describe a time when you felt that the Holy Spirit found a way to speak to you or pointed you in the right direction. How was that message delivered? What impact did it have on your connection to God? Describe it to two different people and then listen to their stories.

stand because we are hearing in particular about God's Word in Jesus. The Bible is the only source for the readings in the liturgy and the sacraments because Scripture is the inspired Word of God.

Human authors composed these writings at different times, but always under the guidance of the Holy Spirit. As we read through the Bible, we will find God's message presented in a variety of ways. However, the message is ultimately one and the same. From beginning to end, Scripture tells us about God, whom we ultimately meet in Jesus Christ.

Sometimes people might misunderstand what inspiration means when applied to Scripture. It doesn't mean that God was

biblical inspiration the gift of the Holy Spirit which assisted human authors in the writing of biblical books and which assured that the writing teaches without error God's saving truth

The four Gospels each begin differently because they were not written for the same audiences or at the same time, but they all reveal the same Good News of Jesus.

Read the following passages and compare and contrast how each Gospel begins:

○ Mark 1:1-15

○ Matthew, Chapters 1–2

○ Luke, Chapters 1–2

○ John 1:1-18

biblical inerrancy the teaching that the Bible presents faithfully and without error the truths that God revealed for our salvation

whispering in the ear of a human author who then wrote down what God said without thinking. This "human word processor" image doesn't explain biblical inspiration. Inspiration means that God speaks *through* human authors. For biblical writers, the inspiration of God renders the author capable of writing with divine authority, but the author is still responsible for writing elements such as style, language, and artistic point of view.

Define How does the Church define biblical inspiration?

Conclude How does biblical inspiration give the Bible its special quality?

Explain

Put this statement in your own words: God is the author of Scripture, but at the same time, it was indeed written by human authors.

Nothing but the Truth

The inspired books teach the truth. "Since therefore all that the inspired authors or sacred writers affirm should be regarded as affirmed by the Holy Spirit, we must acknowledge that the books of Scripture firmly, faithfully, and without error teach that truth which God, for the sake of our salvation, wished to see confided to the Sacred Scriptures"[4] (CCC, 107).

The truth that we are talking about here is *religious* truth, or the deeper meaning that God intended to reveal to us in a particular way. In this case, that way is through Scripture. We read Scripture with an understanding of religious truth.

As noted in the previous *Catechism* quotation, we can go to Scripture with complete confidence that it conveys truth "firmly, faithfully, and without error." God has given to us the truth we find in Sacred Scripture "for the sake of our salvation." We use the term **biblical inerrancy** to explain that the truth found in the Bible is "without error." The phrase applies to the truths necessary for our salvation, but not to some historical or scientific statements. We will have more coverage of biblical inerrancy in later chapters.

We know that God communicates his message to us in the Bible. We can't really know all that God has to say through the words of Scripture. However, learning about the writings themselves can help us understand what God wants us to know about himself, ourselves, and his plan for us. While the Bible is without error, a person's understanding of what a passage in the Bible means *can* be *with error*. So it is the role of the Magisterium to interpret Scripture. The Church has also given us guidelines on "searching the Scriptures" to help us understand them better and to ensure that our understanding and application are more closely aligned with God's message. The next section in this chapter discusses information we need to know when reading Scripture.

Name What term refers to the Bible as written "without error"?

Summarize From where does our "complete confidence" in the Bible come?

Read and Compare

Read these four passages from the New Testament, then describe what message you believe God is conveying in each. Then compare your thoughts to the interpretations from Church Tradition provided by your teacher.

○ Isaiah 40:11 (Like a shepherd)

○ Matthew 11:25-27 (Praise of the Father)

○ Mark 8:34-35 (Take up your cross)

○ John 13:4-11 (Washing of the feet)

PRIMARY SOURCES

Biblical Inspiration }

Just as Jesus was true God and true man, the Bible is divine and also human. "Indeed the words of God, expressed in the words of men, are in every way like human language, just as the Word of the eternal Father, when he took on himself the flesh of human weakness, became like men" (*Dogmatic Constitution on Divine Revelation*, 13). The following excerpt discusses how God guided humans in the writing of Scripture.

➚ Go to the student site at
hs.osvcurriculum.com

"A text that God had miraculously dictated to humans from on high might be easier to believe than a word written by human beings over many centuries. In the same way, a God who descended to earth amidst spectacular wonders might be easier to believe than a God who came in human flesh, living in poverty and suffering. When we listen to the word of God in Scripture, we must realize the full humanity of that word. Jesus is the Word made flesh; the Bible is the Word of God in human words. We will not understand the Scriptures completely if we undervalue either their full divinity or their full humanity.

"We can better appreciate this incarnational understanding of Scripture if we think about how God inspired its human authors. He guided them so that they communicated the truth he wanted to entrust to the Bible. But while guiding them, he did not violate their freedom: he did not prevent them from expressing their own individual personalities and viewpoints. God gave these human authors understanding, insight, wisdom, and the impulse to write but left them free to think, to choose, and to express ideas in their own unique way."

—*Conversing with God in Scripture* by Stephen J. Binz

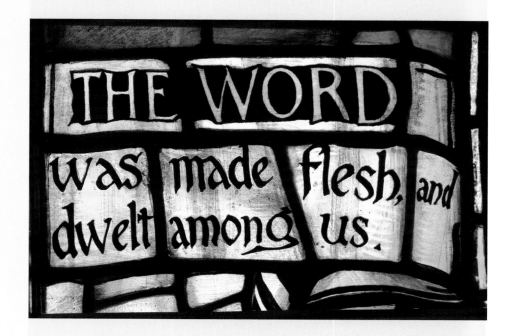

>> **Describe why the words of the Bible are both divine and human.**

How does this excerpt help you to understand the Incarnation?

SECTION 1 REVIEW

QUICK REVIEW

1a. Contrast Describe the difference between learning *about* Scripture and learning *from* Scripture.

b. Recall Who guides the Church through Scripture and Tradition?

c. Contrast What is the difference between Tradition and tradition?

2a. Explain Can Tradition replace Scripture? Why or why not?

b. Analyze How did God's inspiration work to produce the Bible?

c. Recall How can you be more assured that interpretations of Scripture are without error?

3a. Recall Which Bible statements are guaranteed by biblical inerrancy?

b. Analyze Can personal interpretations of the Bible be erroneous? Why or why not?

c. Describe How does biblical inspiration work?

Listen and Discuss With a partner, complete these statements:

○ The Bible is important to me because . . .

○ The Bible is important to the Church because . . .

Pray Compose a short prayer of thanks for Sacred Scripture.

SELF-ASSESS

Which statement best reflects where you are now?

☐ I'm confident enough about the material in this section to be able to explain it to someone else.

☐ I have a good grasp of the material in this section, but I could use more review.

☐ I'm lost. I need help catching up before moving on.

Importance of History and Culture

"Cubs Maul Cardinals." "St. Francis defeats Cardinal Newman." Suppose someone a thousand years from now reads these headlines from today's sports websites. If unfamiliar with our current news reporting styles, the future reader might get a very different understanding of the headlines from the one intended. Even though each headline tells us the truth, they are not literally true. No little bears attacked a bunch of red birds as a group of spectators watched. Francis, the saint from Assisi, didn't actually battle with the nineteenth century Cardinal Newman. The headlines are simply written in a way that reflects the language of our time.

In the same way, the human authors of the Bible used types of writing and other sources of information that reflected their time. They adapted stories and images from area cultures to make their points about God. Therefore, the more we know about how people wrote, thought, and expressed themselves in biblical times, the better we can understand what they meant. The term commonly used for this approach to Scripture is the **historical-critical approach**.

In order to discover the sacred authors' *intention, the reader must take into account the conditions of their time and culture, the literary genres in use at that time, and the modes of feeling, speaking, and narrating then current. "For the fact is that truth is differently presented and expressed in the various types of historical writing, in prophetical and poetical texts, and in other forms of literary expression."*[5]

—CCC, 110

Some explanation of the terms "history" and "critical" is needed. The word "critical" here refers to looking at the meaning of the text, not *criticizing* it. And we all know what history is, don't we? Everything that has already happened is history. Historical writing simply tells us about the past, right?

Actually, modern historians point out that there is always some degree of interpretation and selection when writing about the past. For instance, someone might write about what happened last weekend in a number of ways.

- One version: My older brother picked me up early from the party. We didn't talk much on the ride home.

- Another version: My brother picked me up early from the party. He seemed like he really wanted to tell me something. At home, all our relatives were there because my brother had just found out about the scholarship to college he was hoping for, and he wanted me to celebrate with him.

historical-critical approach
analyzing a biblical text to try to learn the sources that influenced it, how people thought and expressed themselves at the time, and what the text meant to the audience for which it was written

Exegesis is a Greek word that means, "to draw out." It is defined as analyzing specific passages of Scripture from different perspectives in order to discover the meaning. A historical-critical approach to the Bible asks the same questions about Scripture that we would ask of other writings if we wanted to understand them better.

What are some questions we could ask about a piece of writing that would help us understand it better? Apply those questions to this passage from the Old Testament: 2 Chronicles 1:1-13.

What type of writing would help you better understand Scripture?

Discuss the following statement: The historical-critical approach gets at the truth of the Bible better because it uncovers the deeper meaning of the Scripture rather than just using a literal interpretation.

Which one of these versions is "history" and which one is "interpretation"? In fact, both are selective accounts of the same events. The first account appears to be a "just the facts" account of a ride home, but isn't the second account actually more truthful? We could add other accounts—say, from the perspective of the older brother or of whoever was waiting for the boys at home. The historical-critical approach attempts to see how historical facts and interpretation are combined in any part of the Bible.

The Bible does contain much historical writing. A king named David ruled Israel around 1000 B.C., for example. The Bible, however, includes a number of stories about David. Why these stories? Why not others? That's where divine inspiration comes in. What does God want us to learn from these stories? What are the biblical writers prompted to share to present more than a "just-the-facts" account of David? In their

eyes, he is a great king, a charismatic figure, the savior of his people. Perhaps they felt compelled to express David's joy and gratitude toward his God. For instance, one story describes a scantily dressed King David singing and dancing through the streets of Jerusalem as the Ark of the Covenant makes its way through the city. His wife is scandalized by his behavior, but it demonstrates David's unbounded joy in the Lord (see 2 Samuel 6:14-16).

List What three things does the *Catechism of the Catholic Church* say the reader of Scripture needs to discover about the sacred author's intention?

Conclude Finish this statement: The more we know about how people wrote, thought, and expressed themselves in biblical times . . .

History and Storytelling

You might be comfortable with the notion that all history is interpreted and a matter of perspective. However, we do know that some stories in the Bible have no basis in history. Here we need to make some distinctions.

1. Some biblical writings express the inspired truth in non-historical ways. That is, they are closer to the short stories we read in English class than to what we read in history class. Large portions of the Book of Jonah include this kind of writing.

Draw

Choose one event and draw separate pictures of both scriptural accounts:

1. The birth of Jesus: Matthew 1:18-25 and Luke 2:1-20
2. The Last Supper: Mark 14:12-25 and Luke 22:7-23
3. The Resurrection: Mark 16:1-8 and John 20:1-10

○ How do we benefit from having different accounts of the same event?

○ Does one account appeal to you more than another? Why? What might that say about how you relate to Jesus or what the Father might want you to reflect on at this point in your life?

2. Even when they wrote about histori-cal events, the biblical writers seemed to mix together facts, interpretation, and popular stories. They didn't have a "fact checker" for their writing, as that wouldn't really be necessary for getting across the message that God wanted us to hear. At times they combined differ-ent events to make one coherent story. The Sermon on the Mount in Matthew Chapter 5 is a collection of multiple teachings from various times, but it's crafted with a beginning and an end to imply that Jesus gave this sermon all at one time. Other times they told a story in a way to get across some moral message, such as the Parable of the Mustard Seed in Matthew 13:31-32, Mark 4:30-32, and Luke 13:18-19.

On the other hand, the Bible contains much that is historically accurate. By reading it, we learn a lot of historical information about people who lived three thousand years ago. However, the authors wrapped the history and the message in many different packages. So remember what the *Catechism* tells us: Whatever form the packaging takes, inside it is truth *inspired by the Holy Spirit* meant *for our salvation* (see CCC, 106-107).

Recall What book is mentioned as not being purely historical?

Elaborate What do we mean by using the word "packaging" in talking about Scripture?

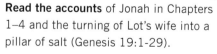

GO TO THE SOURCE

Read the accounts of Jonah in Chapters 1–4 and the turning of Lot's wife into a pillar of salt (Genesis 19:1-29).

After each, answer this question:

○ What truth is God conveying through the biblical author?

Literary Criticism

The word *criticism* usually implies a nega-tive comment, such as "Those clothes look ridiculous on you." **Literary criticism**, how-ever, refers to analyzing writings to get a better sense of their possible meanings. Applied to the Bible, literary criticism tries to understand a part of Scripture as a par-ticular type of literature, such as poetry.

We know we can't read poetry, fiction, and newspapers the same way. The Bible contains many different **genres**, or types, of writing. Sometimes they are separated from other genres. For instance, the Book of Psalms is a collection of 150 songs. The Book of Proverbs is a collection of wise say-ings. Both are also wisdom books.

The Bible also makes frequent use of **metaphor**. Even though most of us don't live near sheep today, the metaphor "the Lord is my shepherd" (Psalm 23:1) still speaks to us of God's vigilance in looking out for us. Metaphors invite us to apply biblical images to our lives today.

literary criticism analyzing writing in terms of the literary form in which it is written

genre type of writing, such as history, parable, or poetry

metaphor a figure of speech comparing two things that are unlike but have certain similarities. The metaphor uses a concrete word to refer to something else to indicate a resemblance, for example, "God is my rock."

Discuss

1. Name types of media you have seen used in documentary films—for example, music, interviews, reenactments, commentary. Explain the difference between using media to bring out the truth and using it to distort the truth. Give examples of each.

2. Think of one event that is important to your school. If five different students, teachers, or school workers filmed a documentary of that event, how might their films differ?

3. Explain how your discussion of documentary films can help you understand the difference between "the facts" and "interpretation" in reading Scripture.

Biblical Genres

Here are some of the genres of writing found in the Old Testament. Read portions of the books or stories listed and find an example of each genre. Explain why it meets the criteria of that genre.

poetry/song—Book of Psalms, Song of Solomon, Lamentations, Exodus 15, Job	**folk legend**—Noah and the Ark
proverb—Book of Proverbs, Ecclesiastes	**sermon**—in many books of the prophets
law—end of Exodus, Leviticus, Deuteronomy	**prayer**—2 Chronicles 6:12-42
origin stories—creation accounts, Adam and Eve	**epic**—the story of Moses
historical narrative—Joshua, Judges, 1 and 2 Samuel, 1 and 2 Kings, 1 and 2 Maccabees	**oracle** (foretelling the future)—Numbers 23-24
prophecy—in books named after the prophets	**benediction** (blessing)—Genesis 1:28
apocalyptic (prophecy of end times)—Daniel	**malediction** (curse)—Genesis 9:24-27

Parables are short symbolic stories that convey a hidden truth or meaning. They are found mostly in the New Testament, but there are examples in the Old Testament as well. One Old Testament example is The Song of the Unfruitful Vineyard that begins Chapter 5 in the Book of Isaiah.

Another type of writing found in limited use in both the Old and New Testaments is **apocalyptic**. A well-known work of apocalyptic writing is the last book of the Bible, Revelation. Through the use of rich imagery, it describes a battle between good and evil, with the promise that even though we are in dark times now, in the end good will prevail. It is similar to some fantasy literature, such as *The Lord of the Rings* and *The Chronicles of Narnia*.

apocalyptic Greek for "unveiling," a type of writing, often prophetic, that uses symbolic imagery to depict future events, often as a triumph of good over evil

Name What are three genres used by biblical authors?

Explain For what purpose is metaphor used in the Bible?

Faith & Culture

Millions have read *The Lord of the Rings* by J.R.R. Tolkien, but not everybody knows he was Catholic.

- Tolkien's faith and expertise in languages shaped his novels, and he referred to *The Lord of the Rings* as a "Catholic myth." In fact, Tolkien used their common love of myth to convince fellow Oxford University professor C.S. Lewis to return to Christianity.

- In an interview about the friendship between Tolkien and Lewis, biographer Colin Duriez explains: "The Gospels had all the qualities of great human storytelling. But they portrayed a true event—God the storyteller entered his own story, in the flesh, and brought a joyous conclusion from a tragic situation."

- For Tolkien and Lewis, the satisfaction they took from great literary works affirmed the greatest story of truth, the life of Jesus. Lewis' faith influenced his own fiction, including *The Chronicles of Narnia*.

C.S. Lewis

J.R.R. Tolkien

Catholic Voices

THE CHURCH HAS ENJOYED a rich history and culture that tells her story through the ages. Let's look at three people who didn't just learn about Scripture, but learned *from* Scripture. They modeled their lives on the Word of God and became examples of disciples for us all. Three of the greatest voices from the history of the Catholic Church are found in Saint Ignatius of Loyola, Saint Joan of Arc, and Saint Francis Xavier.

Saint Ignatius of Loyola (1491–1556)

Saint Ignatius was born at the Castle of Loyola in Guipúzcoa, Spain. He became a page, and then a soldier in the Spanish Army fighting against the French. After suffering a serious leg injury, he spent a year recuperating. During that time he read the lives of the saints, and decided to become a saint himself.

He lived a life of extreme poverty and self-denial. He devised a system of spiritual exercises, which he hoped would help people encounter Christ on a personal level.

His education included eleven years in various universities. A group of young men gathered around him. Together they traveled to Rome and presented themselves to the Pope. The Pope saw this group as an antidote to the Protestants, who were rejecting Church leadership. In 1540, the Pope designated Ignatius' group to be a new society—the Society of Jesus, or the Jesuits.

Ignatius founded the Gregorian University in Rome and a college in Germany designed to train priests. Within twenty-five years, more than one thousand Jesuits ran one hundred colleges in Europe and the Americas. Their rigorous program of study included the Ignatian program of spiritual exercises, and created an educated group of Catholics who could challenge the best Protestant minds of the time.

He was canonized in 1622.

Saint Joan of Arc (1412–1431)

The patroness of soldiers and of France, Saint Joan of Arc was born in the village of Domrémy, near the province of Lorraine. She is said to have heard the voices of Saint Michael, Saint Catherine of Alexandria, and Saint Margaret of Antioch, which told her to go to the King of France to help him reconquer his kingdom. At that time the English king was after the French throne.

Saint Joan was only seventeen when she told the King of England to withdraw his troops from French soil. She was given a small army with which she defeated the English at Orléans on May 8, 1429. Due to her military successes, King Charles VII chose her to enter Rheims on July 17, 1429. Joan was by his side when he was crowned.

In 1430 she was captured by the Burgundians and sold to the English. She was imprisoned, tried by an ecclesiastical court, and condemned to death as a heretic. She was burned at the stake at Rouen on May 30, 1431. At her death, she asked for a crucifix, which she held up until she died. Her body was thrown into the River Seine. She was later exonerated of all guilt, canonized in 1920 by Pope Benedict XV, and called Saint Joan of Arc, the Maid of Orleans and patroness of France.

Saint Francis Xavier (1506–1552)

Saint Francis Xavier was born in the family castle of Xavier, near Pamplona, Spain. While studying at the University of Paris, he met Ignatius Loyola. He joined with him and in 1534 became one of the seven who founded the Society of Jesus (the Jesuits).

He was ordained in 1537, went to Rome, and in 1540 was ordered with another Jesuit to minister in the Far East as the first Jesuit missionaries. When he arrived in India in 1542, he discovered that the Indian converts knew very little about Christian beliefs. He wrote basic prayers and the Creed in simple rhymes that were easy for the new converts to remember and recite. Indian children would follow him around and recite the Lord's Prayer and other prayers with him. Through him, Catholicism gained a firm foothold in India, Japan, and Southeast Asia.

Pope Pius X declared Francis Xavier patron saint of Christian missions. He is also known as "the Apostle to India" and as "the Apostle to Japan." He was canonized with Saint Ignatius of Loyola in 1622 by Pope Gregory XV, and is one of the patron saints of India, Borneo, and Japan.

Find more faith profiles of the saints, see the appendix at the back of this text.

"Do you not know that your body is a temple of the Holy Spirit within you, which you have from God, and that you are not your own? ... Therefore glorify God in your body."

—(1 Corinthians 6:19–20)

No Body

THE OLD TESTAMENT origin story of Adam and Eve tells about creation and what is often known as The Fall. In this account, we see Adam and Eve struggling with limits, and yielding to the temptation to go beyond those limits. We all struggle with limits and *rationalizations*, or making excuses to justify behavior and test limits.

It seems like any trouble we find ourselves in has to do with crossing a line. Yet for all our struggles, we constantly want to know what the limits are: How late can I stay out? What can I get away with? How fast can I drive without getting pulled over? And one favorite topic to rationalize seems to be sex: how far is too far?

When it comes to sex, because we're talking about people and the relationships between them, rationalizing about limits misses the point.

In this field, so profoundly and essentially human and personal, one must before all else look toward the human being as a person, toward the subject who decides about himself or herself, and not toward the "means" that turn him into an "object" (of manipulations) and "depersonalize" him. What is at stake here is an authentically "humanistic" meaning of the development and progress of human civilization.

—Blessed Pope John Paul II, *Theology of the Body*, 129:2

In our bodily communication, in our relationships with one another and God, limits are not about rationalizing: "What can I get away with," but rather reasoning: "What do I need to eliminate so I can live and love more fully?" Instead of "How far is too far?" maybe the better question is, "How can I best express my love and affection for another, while respecting and honoring the image of God within?"

Let's be specific about "How far is too far?" A reasonable answer would be the moment we go from respecting the human dignity within us and others to using the body simply as a means for pleasure. The author of *Love, Dating and Sex,* George Eager, defines going too far as when: either person's hands start roaming; either starts to remove clothing; you are doing something you wouldn't do around someone you respect; you are arousing genital feelings; or you are arousing feelings that make it difficult to make intelligent decisions (USCBB.org, *Sex, Love and Character: A Message to Young People*, Thomas Lickona, Ph.D.). The moment our bodily communication becomes self-centered or dishonors commitments, we have gone too far.

Part of the problem is that when we rationalize "how far is too far," we can slip into thinking that "if everyone's OK with it," then there's nothing to worry about. That's like saying, "So long as I give you permission, it's OK to disrespect me and treat me like an object." No body and nobody should be disrespected. Ever.

By creating us as men and women, God gives each of us personal dignity, which we should acknowledge and accept. The need to respect ourselves and others applies not only to the honest bodily activity of sexual intercourse, but also to everything from kissing to how we dance with one another.

Think about the meaning that is communicated when couples kiss. In what circumstances would this be inappropriate and disrespectful? Well, if one (or both) of the people were already in a committed relationship with someone else, there is a reasonable cause for concern. It comes back to respect.

We know that married spouses become one in sex, but there are a whole lot of levels of physical expression between kissing and sexual intercourse. There are certainly physical expressions of affection, appropriate to the circumstances of the relationship, which honor the image of God within. However, rationalizing an "everything but" attitude incorrectly sets the limit at sexual intercourse and sees all other sexual activity as fair game. The issue here is that the body is being used rather than respected, which undermines vulnerability and genuine communication.

And then there's dancing. You know the type of dancing that teachers, administrators, and parents all object to. Lots of conversations between student government and faculty focus on what certain dances may or may not be "suggesting." But the bottom line is that some dance styles do not honor the image of God within. Rather, the bodies involved are being used as a means for pleasure, attention, excitement, power, and control.

How far is too far? Manipulating and using one another is too far. No body deserves that.

Your body, your very self deserves love and respect, because you are created in the image and likeness of God.

>> Do you know someone who really tries to honor the image of God within others? What lessons do you take from their example?

What are some ways in which our culture focuses only on limits when it comes to the topic of our bodies? What are the disadvantages of this?

In what ways do you respect and honor the image of God in others? In yourself?

Identify one way in which you can better practice honoring the image of God in others or within yourself.

SECTION 2 REVIEW

QUICK REVIEW

1a. Recall What is the historical-critical approach to the Bible based on?

b. Analyze Is it possible to write without interpreting events? Why or why not?

c. Explain How is historical criticism used to examine Scripture?

2a. Define What is *exegesis*?

b. Recall How important was historical accuracy to the writers of the Bible?

3a. Define What is literary criticism, and how is it used to interpret the Bible?

b. Explain How do metaphors enrich the Bible?

ACT

Select your favorite genre and read a Bible selection in that genre. Compare and contrast the Bible selection with other reading you have done in that genre.

SELF-ASSESS

Which statement best reflects where you are now?

☐ I'm confident enough about the material in this section to be able to explain it to someone else.

☐ I have a good grasp of the material in this section, but I could use more review.

☐ I'm lost. I need help catching up before moving on.

The Old Testament at a Glance

The Old and New Testaments each contain a collection of separate books. Twenty-seven books make up what all Christians—Catholics, Orthodox, and Protestants—call the **New Testament**. The Catholic **Old Testament** contains forty-six books, which is seven more than most Protestant Bibles include. Why the difference between what Catholics and Protestants consider the books of the Old Testament? To answer that question, we need to understand some Jewish history, particularly regarding the living situation of Jews in the few centuries before Jesus.

Jesus spent all of his adult life living in Israel. At the time, however, more Jews lived in cities and towns outside of Israel. They lived throughout the Roman Empire and were known as diaspora Jews. It wasn't as if they chose to live in the suburbs. Centuries before the time of Jesus, the Israelites were exiled from Israel for almost fifty years. Many chose not to return for a variety of reasons when the exile ended.

The diaspora Jews tended to be more comfortable speaking Greek, which was the common language in most parts of the Roman Empire. They also lived differently from their sisters and brothers in Israel. For example, Alexandria in Egypt was a center of learning for centuries before Jesus' time. As these Jews studied their past and gathered for worship, they felt a need to have their Hebrew Scriptures translated into the "common language" with which they were familiar—Greek.

Legend has it that seventy-two scholars in Alexandria began the task. Thus, their translation is known as the **Septuagint**, a Latin word that means "seventy." This translation of the Hebrew Scriptures was complete and in common use among Jews outside Israel about one hundred years before the birth of Jesus.

Tell How many books are included in a Catholic Bible?

Explain Why did Jews want to translate their Scriptures into Greek?

Modern day Alexandria, Egypt

Two Slightly Different Canons

Before the time of Jesus, all Israelites agreed on what were the major books of Hebrew Scriptures. However, a few of the more recent, minor writings were accepted as Scripture by some Israelites but rejected by others. The scholars who oversaw and approved the Septuagint included seven books and parts of two others in their canon that were not in the Hebrew version.

The Greek Septuagint was used by New Testament writers and early Christians. Because it was so widely used from the very beginning, in time, the Church officially accepted the additional writings included in the Septuagint as the canon of the Old Testament. The term for the officially recognized collection of inspired books of the Bible is the **canon of Scripture**. Canon refers to a standard of measurement, just as an inch, a foot, and a yard designate standard lengths.

As early as A.D. 160, we had a list of the books that make up both the Old and New Testaments. By the fourth century, Christians in the West almost universally recognized the forty-six books found in the Septuagint and the twenty-seven books that now make up the New Testament as the canon. We find a list of the books of the Bible as we have them today in the official pronouncements of three gatherings of local bishops in North Africa—the Council of Hippo (A.D. 393) and two councils held at Carthage (A.D. 397 and A.D. 419). Saint Augustine of Hippo, mentioned earlier in this chapter, oversaw the workings of these local councils.

These local—as opposed to ecumenical, or universal—councils had to deal with heresies, or beliefs and opinions contrary to the faith, that were strong in the area where each meeting was held. For that reason, it was particularly important to spell out clear Christian teachings about various aspects of Church life, including the makeup of Sacred Scripture. The Catholic Church did just that at these and other councils.

Why were the Gospel according to Thomas and other letters written to early Christian communities not included in the canon? Quite simply, the canon only includes texts that are *divinely inspired*. The Catholic Church took very seriously the responsibility of discerning, under the guidance of the Holy Spirit, which texts were inspired by God. We know that some of these writings did not include the fullness of Jesus' life and teaching, perhaps because the author did not like what happened to him. Some of these writings did not address beliefs such as the Incarnation, suffering, death, and/or Resurrection of Jesus. In 1546, at the Council of Trent, the Catholic Church officially designated the writings of the Septuagint, along with all the books of the New Testament, as Sacred Scripture, thus setting the canon.

Recall What is the earliest date for which we have a list of books that make up the Old and New Testaments?

Explain Why did the Church officially include the Septuagint as the canon of the Old Testament?

canon of Scripture the list of writings officially recognized and accepted by the Catholic Church as inspired books of Sacred Scripture

The Books of the Old Testament

Here is a list of the books of the Old Testament according to the Catholic canon. Jews divide these writings into three groups: the Torah (first five books), the Nevi'im (prophets), and the Ketuvim (writings). Books marked with an asterisk are not included in the Protestant canon.

PENTATEUCH	HISTORICAL	WISDOM AND POETRY	PROPHECY
Genesis	Joshua	Job	Isaiah
Exodus	Judges	Psalms	Jeremiah
Leviticus	Ruth	Proverbs	Lamentations
Numbers	First Samuel	Ecclesiastes	Baruch*
Deuteronomy	Second Samuel	Song of Solomon	Ezekiel
	First Kings	(or Song of Songs)	Daniel *
	Second Kings	Wisdom*	(a few sections)
	First Chronicles	Sirach*	Hosea
	Second Chronicles	(or Ecclesiasticus)	Joel
	Ezra		Amos
	Nehemiah		Obadiah
	Tobit*		Jonah
	Judith*		Micah
	Esther*		Nahum
	(a few sections)		Habakkuk
	First Maccabees*		Zephaniah
	Second Maccabees*		Haggai
			Zechariah
			Malachi

SOURCE: The New Revised Standard Version Catholic Edition

Scripture passages in this textbook are from the New Revised Standard Version Catholic Edition.

The Palestinian Canon

While Jews outside of Israel used the Greek Septuagint, first century Jews within Israel used what we refer to as the **Palestinian Canon**. At the end of the first century A.D., a group of Jewish rabbis designated this Hebrew language Palestinian Canon as their canon, leaving out those additional writings included in the Septuagint.

Christians, on the other hand, considered the Septuagint as the Scripture that comprised the Old Testament. Around four hundred years after the birth of Jesus, when Saint Jerome was given the task of translating the Bible into Latin, he used the Septuagint as the basis of his translation. His Latin translation, called the Vulgate, served as the standard Bible until the time of the Protestant Reformation in the sixteenth century. Some early Protestants realized that there was the Palestinian Canon of the Hebrew Bible that did not include all the books found in the Septuagint. They believed that this canon was older and represented the original Hebrew Scriptures. Thus, they included only its writings in their version of the Old Testament.

Protestant Bibles leave out the nine writings (seven books and two sections of other books) in the Septuagint. These disputed writings, not in the Palestinian Canon, are called **deutero-canonical books** by Catholics and "apocryphal books" by Protestants.

Describe Why do Jews today not include all the books contained in the Septuagint in their sacred Scriptures?

Infer How long did Saint Jerome's Latin translation serve as the standard Bible?

Palestinian Canon the books of Hebrew Scripture often used in Israel (Palestine) at the time of Jesus and declared the official Jewish Scriptures by rabbis around A.D. 100

deutero-canonical books Catholic expression referring to those writings included in the Septuagint (Greek Old Testament) not found in the Palestinian canon of the Hebrew Bible; literally, "second canon"

Old Testament Origins

You may have an English teacher who wants a first draft of a paper before you submit the final copy. After reading over your draft, your teacher may suggest you create a new, stronger beginning, and that you make a series of changes throughout the paper to demonstrate more clearly the point you are trying to make. The Bible itself shows signs of reworking of material. Many Scripture scholars agree that the books of the Old Testament underwent several editorial phases.

Biblical writings came from prior **oral tradition**. Oral tradition refers to stories and sayings handed down by word of mouth before writing became commonplace. For a nomadic people such as the Israelites, handing on stories orally was particularly important. Carrying large scrolls through the desert wouldn't have made much sense even if writing had been developed at the time. Studies indicate that pre-literate peoples possessed a great capacity to remember stories verbatim. Handing down stories, songs, poems, and proverbs was a sacred trust. Individuals who specialized in memorizing and reciting them were often held in great respect.

The oldest portions of the Bible were written around 900 B.C.; most of the remaining portions of the Hebrew Bible were written by 500 B.C. The very beginning of the Bible—the seven-day account of creation—was likely added by the last authors/editors of the Hebrew Bible. Genesis contains two different accounts of creation—the description of the world created in seven days and the creation story centered around Adam and Eve in the garden. Most scholars agree that the Garden of Eden story is the older account. They would also agree that we need to get a fuller grasp on what God was telling us about himself, the world, and the role and importance of humans in creation and his plan.

Catholics have had Saint Jerome's translation of the Bible since the early 600s. It was known as the Vulgate and was used for more than one thousand years. In 1546, the Council of Trent named it the only authentic Latin version of the Bible. The English version is known as the Douay-Rheims Bible, named after the two French cities where it was published in the sixteenth and seventeenth centuries. English Bishop Richard Challoner revised that version starting in 1749. Then in 1943, Pope Pius XII urged Catholic biblical scholars to research original Greek and Hebrew texts in newer translations.

The Confraternity of Christian Doctrine (CCD) in the U.S. undertook the translation of Scripture from original languages as a response to Vatican II principles for Scripture's liturgical use. The goal was for a translation that was appropriate for liturgical use, individual reading, and study. This translation, the New American Bible (NAB), was first published in 1970. Revisions of parts of the translation took place in 1986 and 1991.

oral tradition stories, poems, songs, and proverbs that are passed down verbally from one generation to another without being fixed in written form

MY FAITH

Use this space to build your own faith portfolio.

Make some private notes about your own spiritual growth.

Keep track of your own faith journey— where are you when it comes to relying on the Father? What about Jesus is most inspiring? How aware are you of the Spirit's action?

Mark the spiritual commitments, questions, and actions that are important to you.

Spiritual Growth Plan

Life's pretty busy these days. So what can you do to take a more *organized* approach to your spiritual growth this year? Here are a few ideas to help you begin to sketch out your own Spiritual Growth Plan. Pick one or two and write them in the provided space.

- ○ Read the Bible once a week.
- ○ Take five minutes in a quiet place, opening yourself to the Spirit of God.
- ○ Add at least one daily Mass to your week.
- ○ Write down how you see God in others and in different events.
- ○ Practice Giving Thanks (see Chapter 2).
- ○ Establish a daily prayer routine.
- ○ Completely read one of the Gospels in thirty days.
- ○ Put at least five songs that have a spiritual message on your personal playlist.

At the end of this course, you'll be expected to describe some of what you did to nurture your spiritual growth and whether or not the plan worked for you.

Go to the student site at
hs.osvcurriculum.com

Discipleship . . . within the Body of Christ . . . for the glory of God and the good of the world

In 2011 the New American Bible, Revised Edition (NABRE) was first released. It is the result of almost 20 years of work by nearly 100 scholars and theologians, including bishops, revisers, and editors.

Along with the NAB and NABRE, a few other translations of the Bible are approved by the U.S. Catholic Bishops for Catholic use. Among those is the New Revised Standard Version-Catholic Edition, 1991, the translation used in this course.

In 1604, British King James I brought together the leaders of the Church of England, who had joined Martin Luther. Those gathered wanted to translate the Latin and Greek versions of the Bible available to them into the language of the people—in this case, English. At least five English translations were already available, but they were deemed inadequate. Forty-seven of the best British biblical scholars worked on the new translation until it was published in 1611. It was called "the Authorized Version" or simply "the King James Bible."

It quickly became the most popular English language version for Anglicans and other Protestants. It remained so until the middle of the twentieth century.

Recall When was the earliest part of the Old Testament written down?

Infer What affect did the nomadic lifestyle of the Israelites have on Scripture?

SECTION 3 REVIEW

REVIEW

1a. Define What is the Septuagint?

b. Contrast What is the difference between the Old Testament and the New Testament?

c. Infer Why do you think the New Testament writers used the Septuagint?

2a. Recall What is the canon of Scripture?

b. Analyze Why would the contents of Sacred Scripture need to be officially adopted by the Church at a council?

c. Differentiate What is the difference between the Septuagint and the Palestinian Canon?

3a. Tell How did oral tradition contribute to the Bible?

b. Explain Why was the King James Version of the Bible so popular?

Listen and Discuss With some partners, discuss this question.

○ What do the different efforts to work on the Bible help you understand about its importance through history?

SELF-ASSESS

Which statement best reflects where you are now?

☐ I'm confident enough about the material in this section to be able to explain it to someone else.

☐ I have a good grasp of the material in this section, but I could use more review.

☐ I'm lost. I need help catching up before moving on.

The New Testament at a Glance

Gospels the Good News—the message of God's mercy and love, his Kingdom, and salvation revealed in Jesus. In particular, the four accounts of the life, teaching, death, and Resurrection of Jesus contained in the New Testament are the Gospels according to Matthew, Mark, Luke and John.

Synoptic Gospels the Gospels according to Matthew, Mark, and Luke insofar as they display much similarity. Synoptic means "similar" or "to see together"

The introduction to the New Testament provided here is likely a refresher of what you've learned before. It introduces the books of the New Testament.

The New Testament is a much more compact set of writings than the Old Testament. Its books were written over a period of fifty years or so, in roughly the second half of the first century (A.D. 50–100).

At the center of the New Testament are the four **Gospels**: "The *Gospels* are the heart of all the Scriptures 'because they are our principal source for the life and teaching of the Incarnate Word, our Savior'"[6] (CCC, 125). We say the Gospels are at the center because their focus is on Jesus Christ, the Son of God who is true God, and true man.

The four Gospels are named for Matthew, Mark, Luke, and John. Matthew, Mark, and Luke are known as the **Synoptic Gospels** because large amounts of each are common to all three. They follow a similar outline or synopsis. All but sixty-eight of the verses in Mark, for example, can also be found in Matthew and Luke. Each of the Gospels provides a unique point of view on Jesus while presenting fundamental truths that are essential to our faith and our understanding of God the Father, his Son Jesus, and the Holy Spirit. The personality and perspective of each Gospel's author do come through, but the concern of the early Church was: Does this Gospel accurately reveal the life and message of Jesus? The answer to that question by the early Church was a definite yes.

Compare

Using one of the Scripture references listed below, compare the ways the same story is told in the various Gospels. Make a note regarding any differences. If your Bible has footnotes, then it will provide cross-references that tell you where the same story can be found in other Gospels. The list below will help you find an event in one Gospel.

○ Infancy Narrative: Matthew 1:18—2:12
○ Jesus teaching in the Temple: Luke 2:41-52
○ The Parable of the Rich Young Man: Matthew 19:16-30
○ Last Supper: Luke 22:14-23
○ Agony in the garden: Mark 14:32-42
○ Betrayal by Judas: Matthew 26:47-56
○ Peter's denial: Mark 14:66-72
○ The crucifixion: Matthew 27:32-44
○ Jesus commissions the disciples: Luke 24:44-49

"The Word of God, which is the power of God for salvation to everyone who has faith, is set forth and displays its power in a most wonderful way in the writings of the New Testament"[7] which hand on the ultimate truth of God's Revelation. Their central object is Jesus Christ, God's incarnate Son: his acts, teachings, Passion and glorification, and his Church's beginnings under the Spirit's guidance.[8]

—CCC, 124

The four Gospels make up the heart of the New Testament, but most of the New Testament is actually made up of Letters, also known as **Epistles**.

Saint Paul wrote the earliest of these Letters. In fact, his Letters were written before the Gospels and are the *oldest* writings of the New Testament. Thirteen Letters in the New Testament are attributed to Saint Paul. For one of those Letters, however, we are not sure who wrote it. We only know to whom it is addressed: "the Letter to the Hebrews."

Other New Testament Letters are attributed to authors named Peter (two Letters), James, Jude, and John (three Letters). However, we cannot say with any certainty who actually

Memorize

○ In a Bible find the page that lists the books of the New Testament in order. With one or two partners, take turns testing each other until you have memorized the books of the New Testament in order. Hint: Memorize the order of the first seven to eight books. Then memorize the order of the next eight or so. Do this until you have all of them memorized.

○ After that, take the "find a book" test by opening the New Testament to any page. Have a partner call out the name of a book and see how quickly you can determine whether to turn pages forward or backward based on how well you have memorized the order.

The Twenty-Seven Books of the New Testament

Gospels
Matthew, Mark, Luke (synoptic Gospels)
John

History
The Acts of the Apostles

Pauline and Other Letters

Romans	1 Thessalonians
1 Corinthians	2 Thessalonians
2 Corinthians	1 Timothy
Galatians	2 Timothy
Ephesians	Titus
Philippians	Philemon
Colossians	Hebrews

Catholic Letters*

James	1 John
1 Peter	2 John
2 Peter	3 John
Jude	

Apocalypse
Book of Revelation

* These Letters are often called "catholic Letters" because unlike Paul's Letters, which are addressed to specific churches, these Letters are catholic, or "universal," because they were written for the entire Church.

wrote these other Letters. They were either written by an Apostle or by someone associated with one of the Apostles. In fact, an important criterion for all the writings that make up the New Testament is that early on they were seen as directly connected to the Apostles in some way. But no matter who the human authors may have been, we know God inspired and guided them, and is therefore the divine author of all the books of the Bible.

Describe Why are the Gospels called the heart of all the Scriptures?

Explain What fact helped identify which writings would be included in the New Testament?

Acts and Revelation

Two other books complete the New Testament canon: the Acts of the Apostles and the Book of Revelation.

The **Acts of the Apostles** tells of events that took place in the early days of the Church. It centers mostly on the activity of Saint Paul, who traveled far and wide spreading the Good News of Jesus, frequently getting into trouble with authorities for doing so. The Acts of the Apostles was apparently written by the same author who wrote the Gospel according to Luke. Both books are addressed to "Theophilus," which may be either the name of a person or an honorary title, literally meaning "beloved of God." The Acts of the Apostles gives us a sense of the unifying and life-giving power of the

Epistles the twenty-one Letters included in the New Testament

Acts of the Apostles New Testament book that gives an account of events in the early Church

Holy Spirit, whom Jesus poured out upon his Church to build her up. In this book, we get a glimpse of the love and commitment of the early Christians, the impact the message of Jesus and their witness had on others, and the struggles they endured in spreading the Good News of Jesus.

Book of Revelation last book of the Bible; an account of highly symbolic visions of the future of the Church and the end times

The **Book of Revelation** was discussed briefly earlier in this chapter. It is addressed to someone named John, so it also bears the title "The Revelation to John." It is written in a style found in some Old Testament writings, most notably the Book of Daniel. This style, known as apocalyptic, is a type of writing that uses symbolic imagery to depict imagined future events, often as a triumph of good over evil.

Scripture scholars have discovered that this type of writing was popular in Jewish circles from around 200 B.C. to A.D. 200. The Book of Revelation is filled with symbolism often couched in visions that the author has experienced. For instance, Revelation 5:6 speaks of a lamb with seven horns and seven eyes that is slain. Chances are, this refers to Jesus, who is called a lamb led to slaughter elsewhere in Scripture. The number seven is symbolic of "fullness" and "completeness." Horns likely refer to Christ's power and eyes likely refer to wisdom.

The Book of Revelation in some ways can be considered a bookend to the Bible, along with Genesis. Genesis begins with creation. The last vision in Revelation describes "a new heaven and a new earth" (Revelation 21:1)—that is, the "new creation" ushered in by Jesus. It concludes with the plea: "Come, Lord Jesus! The grace of the Lord Jesus be with all the saints. Amen" (Revelation 22:20-21).

Identify Which Gospel may have been written by the same author of the Acts of the Apostles?

Elaborate What makes the Book of Revelation a unique work among sacred Scripture?

Research
Look up the topic of apocalyptic literature.

○ Explain in your own words how the Book of Revelation fits this type of literature.

○ Give two examples from Revelation that back up your answer.

Create
○ Make a timeline using all the pertinent dates from this chapter.

○ What surprised you most about the timeline?

○ What is the most important entry on your timeline?

➔ Go to the student site at **hs.osvcurriculum.com**

The Importance of Reading Scripture
God's truth in Scripture comes in many different genres—stories from the distant past, metaphorical images, laws and teaching, prophecies, poetry, and songs. His truth is conveyed through multiple means. In Scripture, God chooses to reveal his message to us through human authors who were influenced by particular times and places. Although these writers worked long ago, we know that they conveyed some very important things that God wanted us to know about him and our relationship with him.

The Bible may seem complicated at times, requiring focused attention and some hard work on our part. But for thousands of years it has served as a lifeline to God in Christ Jesus. Fortunately we have the Holy Spirit to help us. Ultimately, all the writings that make up the Bible, the Old and New Testaments, point to the Son of God who took on flesh and blood to reveal God fully and faithfully—Jesus Christ. And we have Church Tradition handed down by the Magisterium from the time of the Apostles to guide us as we seek to understand and apply the Bible's message.

A Contemporary Ancient Practice

Word Made Flesh, Donald Jackson, 2002, *The Saint John's Bible*, Hill Museum & Manuscript Library, Order of Saint Benedict, Collegeville, Minnesota, USA, Scripture quotations are from the New Revised Standard Version of the Bible, Catholic Edition, Copyright 1993, 1989 National Council of the Churches of Christ in the United States of America. Used by permission. All rights reserved.

AFTER THE COLLAPSE OF THE ROMAN EMPIRE in the fifth century, a time often referred to as the Dark Ages, monastic communities played an important role in preserving education in Western civilization. These communities of prayer and work dedicated to the service of God became centers of scholarship and producers of ancient manuscripts. Part of their religious vocation included copying ancient texts in scriptoria rooms. Among the texts copied were sacred writings of the Church, including the Bible. This practice grew into an art form of illuminated texts. Large, lavish volumes were produced, but the invention of moveable type and the printing press replaced the illuminated Bibles in the fifteenth century.

Five hundred years later, the monks at the Benedictine Abbey of Saint John's in Collegeville, Minnesota, commissioned the production of a new illuminated manuscript Bible. This historical work is called *The Saint John's Bible*. When completed, *The Saint John's Bible* will be written and illustrated entirely by hand. Six professional scribes have worked on the new Bible in a scriptorium in Monmouth, Wales, under the direction of renowned calligrapher Donald Jackson. As the project's website points out, *The Saint John's Bible* is a work of art and a work of theology. The team of artists in Wales has worked with a team of monks and biblical scholars at Saint John's in Minnesota to join the ancient techniques of calligraphy and illumination together with the scripturally Benedictine spirituality.

The 1,000 pages or so of manuscript are a blend of modern technology and ancient craftsmanship. The book has been produced following the same standards that the medieval monks used. This time, however, computers were used to size the type and define line breaks for each page as well as to guide the layout of pages. Computers were also used to determine the placement of the one hundred sixty illuminations found in the seven volumes of *The Saint John's Bible*. In addition to quill pens and handmade inks, the scribes worked with hand-ground pigments on calfskin vellum pages just as their ancient predecessors would have. Gold and silver leaf was used to gild the pages.

>> **What kind of scribe would you have been?**

Describe the patience you think it would take to hand copy the entire Bible. Do you or someone you know have patience like that?

Describe the Bible or Bibles that you and your family have at home.

Pursuing a Fair Wage

As a college student at Notre Dame University and a participant in the college's Center for Social Concerns, Brigitte Gynther saw firsthand the severe working and living conditions of Florida farmworkers. She organized fellow students to encourage the university's involvement with Interfaith Action of Southwest Florida.

Gynther eventually became the coordinator of Interfaith Action of Southwest Florida. She was also the recipient of the 2009 Cardinal Bernardin New Leadership Award from the United States Conference of Catholic Bishops for her role in supporting and empowering farmworkers from the Coalition of Immokalee Workers.

Gynther has helped farmworkers pursue fair wages and improve working conditions. She has played a key role in mobilizing Catholic and other faith communities to convince some of the largest restaurant chains and grocery stores in the United States to pay tomato workers an extra penny-per-pound picked. Gynther has also led efforts against human trafficking and worker slavery as well as played an influential role in the development of the national Campaign for Fair Food movement. She relies on Catholic Social Teaching to guide her work.

"Catholic social teaching lifts up right relationships, working together in respect," Gynther said. She sees her work as building a bridge so that Florida farmworkers and people from other backgrounds can build relationships. She wants people to see the root causes of problems faced by farmworkers, and that people can do something about it.

Bishop Roger P. Morin is chairman of the USCCB Subcommittee on the Catholic Campaign for Human Development. He commends Gynther and her work.

"Brigitte's commitment to standing with the Immokalee [Florida] workers is a powerful illustration of CCHD's work to empower low-income people to address the root causes of poverty in their communities," he said in a news release. "Her support for the farmworkers' struggle to ensure that human dignity and basic rights are protected is an illustration of the Gospel call for the faithful to stand in solidarity with those who are vulnerable" (see Luke 4:18-20).

The Cardinal Bernardin New Leadership Award is given to 18- to 30-year-old Catholics who take a lead in battling poverty and injustice in the United States with community-based solutions. Its namesake, the late Cardinal Joseph Bernardin, was the former archbishop of Chicago and a prominent advocate for those who were poor and in lower income brackets, wanting to bridge barriers based on ethnicity, economics, and social class.

Think About It How does the work of Brigitte Gynther serve God?
In what way might her work impact your life?
How do you stand in solidarity with the most vulnerable people where you live?

QUICK REVIEW

1a. Recall How long did it take to write the New Testament?

b. Conclude Which was written over a shorter span of time, the New Testament or the Old Testament?

c. Name Who is considered the author of many of the Letters in the New Testament? What is another name for the Letters?

2a. Recall Which of the four Gospels are called synoptic?

b. Explain What was an important criterion for a writing to be included in the New Testament?

c. Identify Which two books in the New Testament are neither Gospels nor Letters?

3a. Name Whose struggles and accomplishments are included mainly in the Acts of the Apostles?

b. Infer Why is it useful to read the Acts of the Apostles today?

c. Recount What is the difference between the type of writing in Revelation and in the rest of the New Testament?

ACT

On your own, choose two passages from any of Paul's Epistles that mean something to you.

○ Rewrite each one in your own words.

○ Then, for each one, add at least two or three more sentences that connect it to some specific aspects of life today.

○ Share your work with others in small groups.

Pray Select a passage from one of the Synoptic Gospels and then compose a short prayer relating that passage to your own life.

SELF-ASSESS

Which statement best reflects where you are now?

☐ I'm confident enough about the material in this section to be able to explain it to someone else.

☐ I have a good grasp of the material in this section, but I could use more review.

☐ I'm lost. I need help catching up before moving on.

PRAYER

The Prayer Practice of Lectio Divina (Divine Reading)

- Choose a Scripture passage: the Gospel of the day, a psalm, or a parable.

- Quietly sit in silence for a moment or two, to clear your mind of any distractions.

- Read the passage.

- Quietly sit in silence for a moment.

- Reread the passage. As you do, listen carefully for a word that speaks to you. Just one word.

- Reflect on the chosen word, quietly repeating it a few times.

- Read the passage again. As you do, this time listen carefully for a phrase that speaks to you. Just one simple phrase.

- Reflect on the chosen phrase, quietly repeating it a few times.

- Sit in quiet prayer and talk with God about what the phrase means for you at this time.

- Take some time to journal.

- Set all words, images, and feelings aside to spend a few minutes in contemplation—simply resting in God's loving arms.

- Conclude by offering a prayer of thanks to God.

> Lord and sustainer of all that is good,
> Thank you for your word, which is inspired and inspiring.
> You've spoken to me through your Sacred Scripture.
> May I carry that message with me as I strive to do your will.
> I ask this through Christ our Lord. Amen.

CHAPTER 3 REVIEW

TERMS

Use each of the following terms in a sentence that shows you know what the term means. You may include more than one term in a sentence.

Magisterium

Tradition

Deposit of Faith

biblical inspiration

biblical inerrancy

historical-critical approach

literary criticism

genre

metaphor

apocalyptic

New Testament

Old Testament

Septuagint

canon of Scripture

Palestinian Canon

deutero-canonical books

oral tradition

Gospels

synoptic Gospels

Epistles

Acts of the Apostles

Book of Revelation

PEOPLE

Regarding the Bible, tell what is significant about each person.

1. Saint Augustine

2. Saint Jerome

3. King James

4. Richard Challoner

5. Pius XII

6. Saint Paul

7. Theophilus

UNDERSTANDING

Answer each question and complete each exercise.

SECTION 1

1. **Discuss** What role did the Holy Spirit play in the composition of the Bible?

2. **Explain** Why must Tradition *and* Scripture be faithful to one another?

3. **Analyze** How does Tradition link members of the Church through time?

4. **Define** What is biblical inerrancy?

SECTION 2

5. **Analyze** Why is historical criticism valuable in reading the Bible?

6. **Explain** What does the following statement mean? "The authors wrapped the history and their message in many different packages."

7. **Infer** Why would the Bible contain so many different genres?

8. **Recall** Which biblical genre best describes the type of writing found in the Book of Revelation?

SECTION 3

9. **Infer** Large numbers of diaspora Jewish scholars worked for many years to translate the Septuagint from Hebrew to Greek. What does this tell us about their view of Scripture?

10. **Explain** Why is it necessary to have a canon for Scripture?

11. **Explain** Why can't recently discovered ancient writings be added to the canon?

12. **Recall** What is the other name for Saint Jerome's translation of the Bible?

13. **Interpret** Give two reasons why the following statement is true: "The New Testament is a much more compact set of writings than the Old Testament."

14. **Analyze** In what way is the Old Testament different from the New Testament?

15. **Infer** Why would letters have been so important to the early Christians?

16. **Examine** Why is the Book of Revelation considered to be a bookend to the Bible?

CONNECTING

Visual This is an illustration of one of the people who is mentioned in this chapter. Who is it? Which details in the artwork help you identify the person? What would you add to the image to make it more complete?

Question After working through this chapter, what advice would you give someone who wants to understand the different ways of studying the Bible?

Imagine You have a commission to make up an advertising campaign for the Bible. How will you "advertise" this book?

○ Design a print, radio, television, or Internet campaign.

○ You may want to consider which art, music, and spoken or written elements you want to include.

○ Another important consideration is the audience you want to attract. Be certain to aim your campaign at a specific age group.

Challenge You are talking about religion with a friend who is Christian, but not Catholic. Your friend asks:

    Friend: Do you believe what is in the Bible?

    You: What do you mean by "believe"?

    Friend: Every word is true.

    You: I believe that God's teachings in the Bible are true, but not all of the facts are true.

    Friend: What's the difference?

○ What is your next reply?

○ Continue the conversation, anticipating at least two more questions your friend might ask and how you would answer. Use information from the chapter to answer your friend.

SELF-ASSESS

On Your Own Make a list of the most important things you learned from this chapter. Select three things that represent your growth in understanding as you worked through this chapter. Write a paragraph explaining your choices.

With a Partner List what you found most helpful or interesting in this chapter, as well as any other questions that have surfaced.

What does this photo tell you about these young people? When has the Word of God brought you such joy?

CHAPTER **4**

The Church and Scripture

Go to the student site at
hs.osvcurriculum.com

DO

○ Describe the role the Bible plays in your life.

○ Explain how science, reason, and faith work together.

○ Study the Vatican II document on Scripture.

○ Write a report about Catholics who have listened closely to God's word.

○ Compare the four senses of Scripture.

○ Consider how you can live and pray the Scriptures.

○ Understand that Jesus embodies all of Scripture and what it means to be human.

○ Reflect on what "becoming like Christ" would look like in your life.

DEFINE

vernacular language
Council of Trent
Vatican Council II
Dei Verbum
Divino Afflante Spiritu
literal sense
allegory
moral sense
anagogy

A high school sophomore writes: Mary is 84, and she reads the Bible as if it were a novel. She wakes up in the morning around 5:30 and reads before Mass at 8:00 and probably more throughout the day when I'm in school. I know she reads before she goes to bed at night. Sometimes I catch her asleep with the Bible on her lap, hands folded, and reciting prayers. Mary is a very holy person. I don't think I can ever remember a day when I haven't seen her reading the Bible.

She has inspired me to read the Bible and pay close attention to what it says. It holds much wisdom that God wants us to cherish and remember.

Her Bible has bookmarks everywhere in it. She also keeps little pictures of family and friends inside. I believe she has read the whole thing. "So why go back and reread something that never changes?" I asked her once and she told me, "It keeps me alive." As simple as that, she reads it over and over because it keeps her alive. Her faith and love for God are all contained in that book and inside her heart.

WHAT ABOUT YOU?

Where Are You?				
Choose the response that best reflects where you are right now.				
I know how the Church interprets the Bible.	☐ A lot	☐ Quite a bit	☐ A little	☐ Not much
I can name Catholic practices and doctrines that come from the Bible.	☐ A lot	☐ Quite a bit	☐ A little	☐ Not much
I think that the Bible can be misinterpreted and misapplied.	☐ A lot	☐ Quite a bit	☐ A little	☐ Not much
I wish we would spend more time reading the Bible in religion class.	☐ A lot	☐ Quite a bit	☐ A little	☐ Not much

Scripture, Faith, and Modernity

What role has Scripture played in your life?

How can you understand what the Bible says?

How did the printing press change how people read the Bible?

What ancient biblical person serves as the best role model with a passion for God?

The Bible has shaped the Church's beliefs and our expressions of faith since the beginning. The hope is that the Bible has inspired you in some way, too. It may have helped form your sense of right and wrong, played an important role in shaping your understanding of God, or helped you believe that a connection with God is possible. Jesus, whom we meet in the Scriptures, has inspired so many people throughout history and today—to believe in his Father's great love, to hope, to sacrifice for the good of others, and to act with compassion.

The Bible has a lot to tell us about our world, our Church, and ourselves. The Bible is not just about the past. It inspires and shapes our lives today. This important belief underlies this course. As we said in the last chapter, the Bible cannot be separated from the living, growing Church of the past two thousand years. God's story—our story—contained in Sacred Scripture is carried within the heart of the Church, and within our hearts as well. In this chapter we'll look more closely at the Bible, alive today in the Church and in our lives. Let's start by looking at some historical developments that had a big impact on how we understand Scripture.

Introduction of Scientific Thinking

The early sixteenth century ushered in a time of upheaval, with the Protestant Reformation and the age of modernity. The Protestant Reformation will be studied in a later course, but it was a series of political and religious events beginning in the sixteenth century that resulted in the division of Western Christianity.

Soon after the Reformation, the Church and her members found themselves addressing modern ideas from Europe, such as the scientific method of observation, experimentation, and hypothesis testing. The development of the modern world challenged the way the Church approached Scripture. Since the sixteenth century, there has been an ongoing tension between scientific findings, based on rationality and provable facts, and religious teaching, based on faith. Both science and faith are supposed to point to the truth. When they disagree or seem to disagree, the conflict can be troubling.

Certain figures from history pop out when thinking about the relationship between faith and science, including Catholics Nicolaus Copernicus (1473–1543) and Galileo Galilei (1564–1642). And, later, the person most associated with the birth of modernity is the British scientist and mathematician Isaac Newton (1642–1727).

Describe

In small groups, take turns responding to the following:

○ Describe someone you admire and respect who loves the Bible.

PRIMARY SOURCES

I n 1543, Polish astronomer Nicolaus Copernicus published his findings that the Earth revolved around the sun. The Ptolemaic view of the universe, that the *sun* revolved around the *Earth*, influenced Catholic teaching at that time. However, contrary to popular belief, the Church did not object to Copernicus' teaching, as long as it was presented as a theory and not an irrefutable fact. A group of Jesuits in Rome and other Catholic scientists supported his work, and Copernicus even dedicated a major work on the topic to Pope Paul III.

In 1632, Italian physicist, mathematician, and astronomer Galileo Galilei published his findings supporting the Copernican theory. Years earlier Galileo had begun publishing his theories, and Church officials declared that he was free to hold the Copernican Theory as a working hypothesis. However, Galileo appeared to want more of an acknowledgment and pushed the discussion from the arena of science to that of theology. With his 1632 publication, Galileo broke a prior injunction not to speak or write about this particular topic. Galileo could offer no firm proof of his hypothesis, it appeared to contradict certain statements in the Bible, and it could present a danger to the faith of the common people if it circulated beyond the scientific community itself.

Galileo spent the rest of his life under house arrest, where he continued significant research among friends in Rome, but was not permitted to speak or write about on certain topics. In the centuries that followed, scholars developed a greater understanding of how to read and interpret Scripture. And, in 1992, the Church retracted its condemnation of Galileo, and again acknowledged that his viewpoints were neither contrary nor threatening to the faith.

These two men lived in a transition period of history when the relationship between faith and science was being debated in new ways. On this page are a couple of quotations that demonstrate their thoughts on the subject of faith and reason.

Copernicus

Galileo

I am aware that a philosopher's ideas are not subject to the judgment of ordinary persons, because it is his endeavor to seek the truth in all things, to the extent permitted to human reason by God.

—Nicolaus Copernicus

I do not feel obliged to believe that the same God who has endowed us with sense, reason, and intellect has intended us to forgo their use.

—Galileo Galilei

>> **Make a list of the points made by Copernicus and Galileo in their statements.**

According to Copernicus and Galileo, what is the relationship between faith and reason?

Mt. Graham International Observatory in Arizona

One change in perspective coinciding with the beginning of what historians call "the modern world" is its emphasis on science as a source of truth.

This shift in perspective resulted in conflicting views of science and religion. Some people embraced science as a way to help us understand the Bible. They said statements in the Bible should be held up to the scrutiny of science. Others saw science as a threat to the Bible. For example, they would ask whether modern science's theory that the Earth evolved over billions of years contradicted the Bible. They would say that scientific theories should be held up to the scrutiny of the Bible, not the other way around.

At the beginning of this course, we discussed the relationship between human reason, faith, and truth. The Church has a high regard for the human capacity to arrive at truth. Human reason, following its God-given design, can lead to truth. The Church points out that research of any kind, as long as it follows scientific methods and is not immoral, cannot conflict with faith. The reason is that everything of this world and of faith comes from the same source: God.

However, people are hampered in many ways as they use their reasoning in search of truth.

Identify

God is the author of all creation, the source of both the things of the world and the things of faith. When science is used in morally responsible ways, we know that it does not contradict faith and in fact supports it.

○ With a partner, list three problems we face in the world today that science and faith can work together to address.

They are limited by language that always falls short of the mystery of God. Where people live (geography) and when they live (history) can influence their perceptions of the truth.

A system of checks and balances is required in the search for truth. This system is the teachings of the Catholic Church. Faith balances reason, since faith and reason have the same source and the same goal. They both come from God and are directed toward knowing God.

Recall What change in perspective marks the beginning of what historians call "the modern world"?

Conclude What can you learn about judging others from the controversy between the Church and Galileo?

Evolution

ANOTHER FIGURE IN THE DIALOGUE between science and religion was English naturalist Charles Darwin. In 1859, in his book *On the Origin of Species*, Darwin presented his theory of evolution by natural selection—that all living things evolved from a single organism by natural means.

What does the Church say about evolution? This truth of Scripture reveals the fact of creation and God's singular role as Creator. The faith of the Church does not describe *how* God carried out this creation, and

Catholics have always been free to explore and affirm scientific theories of evolution that describe how the world developed over time. The theories of evolution are compatible with faith when they acknowledge that the creator and agent of that movement is God.

Explain how evolution theories are compatible with our faith.

➤➤ **Compare a Church document about creation with Darwin's theory.**

Response to the Reformation

vernacular language the language commonly spoken by people in a particular country or region, such as German, Spanish, or Mandarin Chinese

Council of Trent meeting of Catholic bishops from 1545 to 1563 that clarified and defined Catholic teaching, especially in contrast to Protestantism

During and after the Reformation period, scholars translated the Bible into the common languages, or **vernacular language,** of Western Europe. Recall from Chapter 3, for example, the discussion describing the development of the English translation known as the King James Bible. Martin Luther, a German monk whose criticisms of certain Church practices led to the Protestant Reformation, was also a Scripture professor. He translated the New Testament into German. The Dutch scholar Erasmus, who remained Catholic, greatly advanced the knowledge of Scripture through his translations using various ancient resources.

Until the Protestant split from the Catholic Church, "the Bible" essentially referred to the Vulgate—Saint Jerome's Latin version. Only highly educated members of society knew and spoke Latin, and only a few people—typically religious scholars and monks living in monasteries—had access to Bibles. That changed, thanks to Johannes Gutenberg's invention of the printing press in the middle of the fifteenth century, which meant that Bibles could be made available on a wide basis. In fact, one of the first books printed was Saint Jerome's Latin version of the Bible.

In the mid-sixteenth century, the Catholic Church and Pope Paul III responded to the Protestant Reformation and called an ecumenical council—a meeting of all the world's Catholic bishops. It was held in Trent, a city in German territory that is now part of Italy. The council lasted off and on for eighteen years, from 1545 to 1563. The Catholic Church clarified her own principles of belief and established her own agenda for reform.

More Bibles meant increased scholarly research into Scripture. The **Council of Trent** addressed issues that came about as a result of this research. The council also dealt with issues raised by the Protestant Reformation. Among the issues addressed by the world's bishops in union with the bishop of Rome, the Pope, were:

- The Council of Trent reconfirmed which writings make up Sacred Scripture. Specifically, it reaffirmed that all of the Old Testament writings found in the Septuagint are to be regarded as Scripture.

- The Vulgate Latin translation of the Bible was the only version to be used. This was in response to scholars having proposed using Greek or Hebrew versions.

- The bishops reminded Catholics that they should read the Bible as members of the Church and under her guidance. Individuals cannot decide on their own what is or is not Scripture. And, while the interpretation of Scripture rests with the Magisterium and is not up to individuals to determine, each person is called to make a personal application of Scripture.

Name Who was Martin Luther?

Recall What increased and resulted in the need for the Council of Trent?

The Gutenberg Bible

AROUND 1450 JOHANNES GUTENBERG (1400–1467) invented the printing press and moveable type. One of his crowning achievements was printing, in 1454–1455, 180 copies of the Bible. Before this time, it could take a year or more for someone to make one handwritten copy of a Bible. By the end of the fifteenth century, at least one thousand printing shops existed in Europe.

Today, forty-eight copies of Gutenberg's Bible still exist, a little less than half of them in perfect condition. Nine copies can be found in the United States. In 1974, the University of Texas at Austin bought a copy of Gutenberg's Bible for $2.4

million. It is one of just five complete copies in the United States of the first major book produced with moveable type. The Bible is on display at the university, but has also been reproduced digitally and is available online. The digital version allows anyone, for the first time, to view all the pages of the Texas copy.

>> Say you invented the printing press today. What book would you want to print first, and why?

If you could only print one book of the Bible today, which one would you choose? Why?

The Council of Trent took place in what is now the city of Trento, Italy.

○ The city dates back to the first century B.C. Roman Empire. Located on a bend in the Adige River, Trento takes its name from surrounding mountain peaks that resemble a trident.

○ Trade between Germany and Italy in the Middle Ages boosted the importance of Trento. In 1514, the city began preparing for the Council of Trent, which actually took place from 1545 to 1563. Today Trento, also called Trentino, is a communications center. Farming and manufacturing are also important economic sectors.

Faith & Culture

↗ Go to the student site at **hs.osvcurriculum.com**

Vatican Council II

Despite the Council of Trent's call for Catholics to read the Bible, most Catholics at the time could not read, and even more could not read Latin. Many continued to turn to the Sacraments for spiritual nourishment, especially the Sacraments of Reconciliation and the Eucharist. Nearly four hundred years after the Council of Trent, **Vatican Council II** was called by Pope John XXIII. His call for a council was by itself a sign of the Holy Spirit's continued presence in the Church, guiding her to be faithful to Christ's mandate to make and nuture disciples in the ever-changing circumstances of the world around her. Among the many influences of the Second Vatican Council, its teachings led to a renewed and increased emphasis on Scripture among Catholics.

In 1965, the bishops at Vatican Council II approved the "Dogmatic Constitution on Divine Revelation"—in Latin titled ***Dei Verbum***, "the Word of God."

Dei Verbum emphasized the importance of Scripture and the use of vernacular language at liturgies. Scripture would be more accessible and all Catholics were encouraged to become familiar with it. The document from the council, which started in 1962, ushered in a renewal in the Church, especially for preaching, religious education, theology, and spirituality.

"The Church and the Word of God are inseparably linked. The Church lives on the Word of God and the Word of God echoes through the Church, in her teaching and throughout her life" (cf. *Dei Verbum*, n. 8), said Pope Benedict XVI as he spoke on the fortieth anniversary of *Dei Verbum*.

> *It pleased God, in his goodness and wisdom, to reveal himself and to make known the mystery of his will (see Eph 1:9), which was that people can draw near to the Father, through Christ, the Word made flesh, in the holy Spirit, and thus become sharers in the divine nature (see Eph 2:18; 2 Pet 1:4). By this revelation, then, the invisible God (see Col 1:15; 1 Tim 1:17), from the fullness of his love, addresses men and women as his friends (see Ex 33:11; Jn 15:14-15), and lives among them (see Bar 3:38), in order to invite and receive them into his own company.*
>
> —*DV, 2*

Dei Verbum Literally "the Word of God." Latin title for the "Dogmatic Constitution on Divine Revelation" of Vatican Council II (1965)

Vatican Council II an ecumenical council of the Catholic Church. It was a meeting in Rome of the world's Catholic bishops from 1962–1965, called for by Pope John XXIII to "open wide the doors" and let "fresh air" into the Church

Explain How did Catholic worship and spiritual life shift focus after Vatican II?

Infer What do you think Pope John XXIII meant when he referred to Vatican Council II as letting "fresh air" into the Church?

The Church and Scripture **97**

Describe

Part of the Protestant Reformation involved separation from community and development of individuality.

○ Describe a time when something happened that made you glad you were part of a group or community.

○ Write a paragraph about whether you think most people in our country emphasize individuality or whether most people emphasize being part of a community.

○ How do you balance individuality and group membership in your own life, and what are the benefits of each?

GO TO THE SOURCE

Throughout the first few lines from *Dei Verbum,* there are numerous references to Scripture. Look up the Scripture references from *Dei Verbum* listed below.

Describe how each passage is reflected in the document.

○ Ephesians 1:9

○ Ephesians 2:18

○ 2 Peter 1:4

○ Colossians 1:15

○ 1 Timothy 1:17

○ Exodus 33:11

○ John 15:14-15

○ Baruch 3:38

Modern Discoveries

Thanks to advances in technology and an increased awareness of the relationship between faith and science, over the past one hundred years or so, Scripture scholars have gained information that had been lost for centuries. Along with historical-critical methods, and the criteria for interpretation that the Magisterium provides, this new information helps us better understand the Bible and its time. Below are a few of these discoveries.

Rosetta Stone French archaeologists during Napoleon's conquest of Egypt discovered the Rosetta Stone, a stone column written in three different languages from a few centuries before the time of Christ. Ancient monuments and proclamations were often written in three languages so that different groups of people could read them.

In 1822, a French scholar who knew two of the languages, classical Greek and Egyptian Coptic, was able to decipher the third language. It was a type of picture writing called hieroglyphics, used in ancient Egypt. Once this language was deciphered, scholars

could read writings from the ancient world that no one had understood for centuries. Soon other ancient languages were deciphered, such as Babylonian Cuneiform.

This type of language comparison has only been available for about 150 years. In fact, the ancient Ugaritic language, which was used in Canaan—the site of Jesus' first miracle—wasn't understood until 1928. The Rosetta Stone and the modern deciphering of ancient languages enabled Scripture scholars to compare the Hebrew language and biblical stories with those of the closest neighbors of the Israelites.

Gospel of Thomas In 1945, two brothers digging for limestone unearthed a collection of ancient Christian writings that had been buried in the Egyptian desert near Nag Hammadi. Among the writings was a collection of sayings by and about Jesus given the name "the Gospel according to Thomas." Evidence suggests that its origin may be from early in the Christian era. The Gospel according to Thomas is not included in our Bibles today, as discussed in the last chapter. Yet it offers interesting points of comparison and contrast with the four Gospels of the New Testament.

Research

Find out the connection that one of the following topics has to the Bible and its time, and then prepare a report for the class about it.

○ Nag Hammadi library

○ Gospel according to Thomas

○ Gospel of Judas

○ the Essenes

○ the library of Ashurbanipal

○ Enuma Elish (Babylonian creation myth)

Try to obtain a photo of the Rosetta Stone or other ancient hieroglyphics.

Dead Sea Scrolls Between 1947 and 1956, approximately nine hundred documents were found in caves near the Dead Sea in Israel. They are known as "the Dead Sea Scrolls." They include writings of a Jewish sect, called the Essenes, who some historians believe lived in the area before A.D. 100. Among the writings found are portions of the Hebrew Bible. These early copies of biblical texts show us that the Bible as we have it today has, for the most part, been copied accurately down through the ages. Remember, up until the mid-1400s and the invention of the printing press, books were copied by hand or passed on by word of mouth.

Recall Where did French archaeologists discover the Rosetta Stone?

Infer How can the materials discovered with the Rosetta Stone, the Gospel according to Thomas, and the Dead Sea Scrolls help us to understand Scripture?

GLOBAL PERSPECTIVES

In 1947, Bedouin shepherds discovered the first of the Dead Sea Scrolls. They had been hidden in caves near Qumran in Israel for two thousand years. Excavations have revealed long scrolls and thousands of fragments. Discovered in the find were copies of the Septuagint; the oldest written record of the Old Testament, including a complete copy of the Book of Isaiah; and rules for the Jewish community who lived in Qumran, which was destroyed by the Romans in A.D. 68. The Israel Antiquities Authority is in charge of preserving the scrolls, including a project to place images of the scrolls on the Internet.

○ What does this discovery tell us about the Old Testament?

○ Discuss why such a discovery as the Dead Sea Scrolls is important to us today.

Go to the student site at **hs.osvcurriculum.com**

SECTION 1 REVIEW

QUICK REVIEW

1a. Summarize What does the Church say about evolution?

b. Recall What does the Church always look to as the source of her teachings?

2a. List Which three pronouncements resulted from the Council of Trent?

b. Explain What did Dutch scholar Erasmus do?

c. Summarize Which version of the Bible was used before the Reformation, and what problems were involved in using it?

3a. Recall About how many years passed between the Council of Trent and Vatican II?

b. Analyze How did the publication of *Dei Verbum* cause a renewal in the Church?

c. Recall Which document from the Second Vatican Council encouraged the reading of Scripture?

Listen and Discuss Meet in small groups to discuss these questions:

○ Do you think that we take the Bible for granted? Why or why not?

○ Would we prize the Bible more if it were more rare? Explain your answer.

○ How can we increase our appreciation for it?

Pray Compose a short prayer expressing the role you would like the Bible to play in your life.

SELF-ASSESS

Which statement best reflects where you are now?

☐ I'm confident enough about the material in this section to be able to explain it to someone else.

☐ I have a good grasp of the material in this section, but I could use more review.

☐ I'm lost. I need help catching up before moving on.

Putting the Bible in Context

As you know, the Bible is a collection of writings composed over a thousand-year period. To put that time span into perspective, imagine a collection of writings in English that would include:

- Geoffrey Chaucer's *The Canterbury Tales*—written in what is called "Middle English" and barely intelligible to us today;

- William Shakespeare's plays—filled with words that we don't use or use differently today;

- the U.S. *Declaration of Independence*—which includes words such as usurpations, sufferance, and hither;

- President Abraham Lincoln's *Gettysburg Address*—which begins with the word "fourscore" and marks a turning point in America's bloodiest conflict;

- the song lyrics of Bob Dylan and the Beatles—which reflect a particular time period; and

- today's media articles from newspapers, magazines, websites, and blogs.

All of these works were written within a thousand years of one another. Some people may try to compare Shakespeare's sonnets composed in the late sixteenth century with hip-hop music composed in recent decades. However, most people would agree that we need to know something about Shakespearean England to understand his writings, just as we need to know something about urban-American culture to understand hip-hop lyrics. To read any of these writings out of context, or without examining the circumstances in which they were written, can result in misinterpreting them.

The Magisterium is a sure guide for Catholics in the proper interpretation of Scripture. As we learned in the last chapter, finding out about the cultures in which biblical writings were produced helps us better understand the writings and ultimately the inspired truths that they contain. It's essential to remember that God is communicating something to us in the Scriptures. So, we need to turn to God the Holy Spirit—and the Church that he guides—to help us study and apply Scripture.

Family viewing the Declaration of Independence at the National Archives Rotunda in Washington, D.C.

Scientific Study of Scripture

In 1943, Pope Pius XII issued an encyclical, **Divino Afflante Spiritu**, "Inspired by the Divine Spirit," that urged Catholic scholars to use modern methods of biblical criticism in the study of Scripture. Vatican Council II also encouraged biblical scholars to use solid rules of scholarship to bring about "a better understanding and explanation of the meaning of Sacred Scripture" (CCC, 119). Within Catholicism, human reasoning, science, and faith work together in the pursuit of truth.

In 1993, the Pontifical Biblical Commission published *Interpretation of the Bible in the Church*. It offers a summary of the various approaches to Scripture used by scholars thirty years after Vatican II. It describes methods of biblical scholarship as they developed over the past two hundred years. It also cautions that the danger of following a strictly "scientific" approach to the Bible or treating it merely as a historical document can make Scripture sterile. The goal of the study of Scripture is always to help us understand the meaning of the text better.

In October 2008 the Pope called together bishops from across the world for a Synod on Scripture, The Word of God in the Life and Mission of the Church. During this meeting, Pope Benedict XVI said the historical approach to biblical interpretation is not complete without including the theological or divine aspect. The Second Vatican Council, he indicated, lists three points to help interpreters find the theological sense of the Scripture.

- First, the interpretation of the text should consider the unity of the Old and New Testaments as the whole of Scripture.

- Second, the interpreter needs to take into account the living Tradition of the entire Church.

- Lastly, the interpretation must be consistent with the truths of faith made known to us by God.

Church Documents on Biblical Scholarship

Divino Afflante Spiritu (1943 encyclical by Pope Pius XII)—invited Catholic scholars to use modern methods of biblical criticism

Dei Verbum (1965 Vatican Council II "Constitution on Divine Revelation")—called for greater emphasis on Scripture in Church life

Interpretation of the Bible in the Church (1993 statement by Pontifical Biblical Commission)—reviewed and identified positives and negatives of various approaches to interpreting and studying the Bible

Address of His Holiness Benedict XVI during the 14th General Congregation of the Synod of Bishops (October 2008 address to the synod on the Word of God)—affirms that the three dimensions of theological methodology noted in *Dei Verbum* must be included in proper biblical interpretation

Recall What is the danger of following a strictly "scientific" approach to the Bible or treating it merely as a historical document?

Connect How did *Divino Afflante Spiritu* and Vatican II affect the study of Scripture?

Divino Afflante Spiritu 1943 encyclical by Pope Pius XII that urged scholars to use modern methods of biblical criticism in the study of Scripture

Biblical Interpretation

To correctly understand the Scriptures, we must refer to the Magisterium for its guidance and interpretation. In this way the Church seeks to discover what God wished to communicate, and what the human authors intended by how they conveyed God's message.

God is the author of Scripture. The human writers were people like us. They wrote in the expressions and phrasing of their times, under the guidance of the Holy Spirit. To help interpret a passage and discover its meaning, we have to consider the situation at the time the author wrote, the style or form of language used, and the ways things were narrated and spoken at that time. This alone, however, is not sufficient. We must call on the help of the Holy Spirit, under whose inspiration the writing was composed, and consider the Scripture in light of Magisterial teaching.

To do this, Vatican II instructed us to:

1. *"Be especially attentive 'to the content and unity of the whole Scripture'"* (CCC, 112).

Jesus explained this to his followers:

> Then he said to them, "These are my words that I spoke to you while I was still with you— that everything written about me in the law of Moses, the prophets, and the psalms must be fulfilled." Then he opened their minds to understand the scriptures, and he said to them, "Thus it is written, that the Messiah is to suffer and to rise from the dead on the third day."
>
> —Luke 24:44-46

2. *"Read the Scripture within 'the living Tradition of the whole Church'"* (CCC, 113).

One of the marks of the Church is that she is one. We are not alone in interpreting the Bible. We rely on the teaching of the bishops in union with the Pope as a sure guide and call upon the scholarship of Catholic biblical experts to assist us.

> There is one body and one Spirit, just as you were called to the one hope of your calling, one Lord, one faith, one baptism, one God and Father of all, who is above all and through all and in all.
>
> —Ephesians 4:4-6

3. *"Be attentive to the analogy of faith"*[9] (CCC, 114).

The truths of the faith have coherence among them and to the whole plan of Revelation:

> We have gifts that differ according to the grace given to us: prophecy, in proportion to faith; ministry, in ministering; the teacher, in teaching; the exhorter, in exhortation; the giver, in generosity; the leader, in diligence; the compassionate, in cheerfulness.
>
> —Romans 12:6-8

PRIMARY SOURCES

The Bible contains the story of God's People and their journey to know him. It can be a confusing concept to understand that God inspired human authors to write the truth contained in the Bible. Here is an excerpt from *Reading God's Word Today* by George Martin (page 118) in which he explains how the Bible was written.

➔ Go to the student site at
hs.osvcurriculum.com

We shouldn't imagine that God's voice came to the writers of Scripture in an audible way, giving them the exact words that they were to set down in writing. A voice from the heavens would have been heard, but wouldn't necessarily have led to human understanding and receptivity to insight. Rather, the Spirit worked by inspiration—by giving insights, by endowing human beings with wisdom, by enabling them to understand the significance of God's dealings with his people, by prompting them to write.

>> How does this help you understand how the Bible was written?

How does this compare to how you thought the Bible was written?

How does this explanation differ from others you may have heard?

To better appreciate these three criteria for interpreting a biblical passage, it helps to consider the senses of Scripture.

Recall Who is the author of Sacred Scripture?

Explain What does it mean to "Be especially attentive 'to the content and unity of the whole Scripture'"?

A Literal Example

From Scripture we gain an understanding of God's laws and will, and the direction he wants us to take in our lives. We've talked about how we get to know the Triune God in Scripture, learn about Christ's teachings, the work of the Holy Spirit, the nature of God. Scripture also informs and forms our conscience, gives us insight into life's great moments and challenging times, and shows us models of faith from whom we can learn.

> All scripture is inspired by God and is useful for teaching, for reproof, for correction, and for training in righteousness, so that everyone who belongs to God may be proficient, equipped for every good work.
>
> —2 Timothy 3:16-17

But for Scripture to be a light for our path and a guide for our lives, it's very important to have a correct interpretation of and approach to Scripture. Here is an example of a passage that can be misinterpreted if we look only at the words of the text and not its context and fail to consider the teachings of the Church. Read carefully these words from Saint Paul's Letter to the Romans:

> Let every person be subject to the governing authorities; for there is no authority except from God, and those authorities that exist have been instituted by God. Therefore whoever resists authority resists what God has appointed, and those who resist will incur judgment.
>
> —Romans 13:1-2

Identify
- Name circumstances today in which Catholics are called upon to question or resist governing authorities, a boss, or an owner of a company for which someone might work.
- Name other people who have challenged governing authorities when in conscience they believed it was their duty to do so.

If taken literally, what should Christians living under Nazi rule have done? Clearly the passage states that all authority comes from God and should be obeyed. One Austrian Catholic, Franz Jägerstätter, received notice that he was drafted into the Nazi army. Was it his duty as a Christian to obey this command? Some of his local religious leaders counseled him that indeed it was his duty to obey authority. Franz, however, believed that the Nazi cause was wrong and that in good conscience he could not and should not join their army. He was arrested and executed for holding to his stand. In October 2007, Jägerstätter was beatified, or proclaimed "blessed," by the Catholic Church.

Saint Paul offered his message about obeying authority to Christians in Rome who were trying to figure out how to be "Christian" and "Roman" at a particular time and in particular circumstances. He was providing them practical advice that was not meant to violate their consciences. Quoting this text out of context could lead Christians to be a very passive group in the face of civil authority. In fact, many Christians throughout history have stood up to injustice even when they had to resist civil authorities to do so. Some have even been declared saints for doing so.

Recall How did Franz Jägerstätter stand up for his beliefs?

Analyze What do the actions of some local Austrian religious leaders who counseled Franz Jägerstätter say about their interpretation of the passage from Romans?

MY✝FAITH

Spend a few days privately keeping the following questions in your head and heart.

What situation might the Holy Spirit be asking you to pay more attention to, question, or challenge, *for God's sake?*

○ Is it something local or is it global?

○ Is it a social, political, or job-related situation?

○ Is it about you personally or about someone else?

Write down what comes to mind and continue to make some notes as you act upon it in the next few weeks.

At the end of this course, you may want to include this information in describing some of your key experiences, lessons, discoveries, or spiritual goods.

🢅 Go to the student site at
hs.osvcurriculum.com

Discipleship . . . within the Body of Christ . . . for the glory of God and the good of the world

---

SECTION **2 REVIEW**

QUICK REVIEW

1a. **Analyze** Why is it important to know the context of a piece of writing?

b. **Name** Within Catholicism, what three things work together to help us discover truth?

c. **List** What three points did the Second Vatican Council say help interpreters find the theological sense of Scripture?

2. **Explain** How do we discover what the human authors of Scripture intended, and why is this not sufficient?

3a. **Debate** Did Franz Jägerstätter defy Scripture? Explain your answer.

b. **Infer** What is the problem with interpreting the Bible too literally?

Listen and Discuss With a partner work on the following:

○ Research a Catholic who has stood up to injustice and make a class presentation on that person.

SELF-ASSESS

Which statement best reflects where you are now?

☐ I'm confident enough about the material in this section to be able to explain it to someone else.

☐ I have a good grasp of the material in this section, but I could use more review.

☐ I'm lost. I need help catching up before moving on.

Four Senses of Scripture

Daniel in the Lions' Den, Briton Riviere

In the previous section we noted the need to look at the senses of Scripture when interpreting and applying a biblical passage to our lives. Let's look at what we mean by *senses of Scripture*.

Ancient Christian tradition identified two senses of Scripture, namely, the literal and the spiritual. The spiritual sense was further divided into the allegorical, moral, and anagogical senses. From this we have four ways in which Scripture can be understood and interpreted:

- the *literal* sense
- the *allegorical* sense, which represents a deeper spiritual meaning
- the *moral* sense
- the *anagogical* sense, which represents Heaven or the afterlife

Let your Scriptures be my chaste delight . . . O Lord, perfect me and reveal those pages to me! See, your voice is my joy. Give me what I love . . . May the inner secrets of your words be laid open to me when I knock. This I beg by our Lord Jesus Christ 'in whom are hidden all the treasures of wisdom and knowledge' (Colossians 2:3). These are the treasures I seek in your books.

—Saint Augustine, *The Confessions*

Once understood, these approaches to Scripture can help us appreciate what Saint Augustine meant by discovering "the treasures of wisdom and knowledge" in the sacred books. The Scripture contains layers of meaning, which these senses of Scripture can help us better understand.

literal sense the historical and cultural meaning of the words of Scripture intended by the human author

Literal sense "is the meaning conveyed by the words of Scripture . . ., following the rules of sound interpretation" (CCC, 116). The literal sense requires a knowledge of the historical and cultural setting in which the Scriptures were written and an appreciation for the styles of writing chosen by the author. The other senses of Scripture are rooted in this literal sense. When the author of Genesis writes that Cain killed his brother Abel, the words mean that Cain actually killed his brother. We have to understand the literal level of biblical stories before probing their possible deeper meanings.

Early Christians understood that the writings in the Bible were more than literal recordings. They discovered spiritual truths behind their literal meaning. This spiritual approach to Scripture sheds light on how it can speak to us today. If we never went beyond the literal level, the Bible primarily would be about past events. Old Testament prophecies and other passages were fulfilled in Jesus. New Testament passages can be applied to the future life of the Church and to our lives as well. Let's look at these four spiritual senses as found in Scripture.

> *The profound concordance of the four senses guarantees all its richness to the living reading of Scripture in the Church.*
>
> *A medieval couplet summarizes the significance of the four senses:*
> *The Letter speaks of deeds; Allegory to faith;*
> *The Moral how to act; Anagogy our destiny.*[10]
>
> —CCC 115, 118

allegory a story or image that contains an implicit hidden or spiritual meaning

The allegorical sense relates to **allegory** itself. Allegory has both a literal meaning and a deeper, implied meaning. The deeper meaning often is the main focus. An allegorical story or poem can be interpreted to uncover a hidden meaning. A number of movies are regarded as allegories. In 1999, some critics hailed *The Matrix* as an allegory of modern life. The same could be said of 1998's *The Truman Show*. It can be said that Aslan the lion in *The Lion, the Witch, and the Wardrobe* from *The Chronicles of Narnia* is an allegorical "Christ figure" in that he suffers and dies for his friends, only to rise again.

The *Catechism* points out that allegory in Scripture can give us a deeper understanding of the event by recognizing a connection with Christ. The crossing of the Red Sea, for example, is a sign of Christ's victory over death and of Baptism (see CCC, 117).

Early Christians found the Old Testament filled with allegories. It is important to remember that the allegorical sense is a tool that helps us gain deeper insight from Scripture. We can draw connections between the Old and New Testaments in this way.

The brief story about a man named Jonah, for instance, includes a detail about spending three days inside a fish. This can be viewed as a sign for the three days Jesus spent in the tomb. In the Book of Exodus, the blood of the lamb saves firstborn Israelites from the tenth plague. Christians regard this as a sign for Jesus' shedding his blood on the cross.

Parallel Themes Between Joseph and Jesus

1) *The Chosen One.* **Joseph** is his father's favorite son. He even wears a princely robe to prove it. A voice from Heaven speaks at **Jesus'** baptism: "This is my Son, the Beloved, with whom I am well pleased" (Matthew 3:17).

2) *A Compassionate God.* **Joseph's** father sends his beloved son into harm's way to make sure that his brothers are fine. God the Father sends **Jesus** to take on human flesh and to take away our human sinfulness.

3) *Human Sinfulness.* **Joseph's** brothers mistreat him, causing their father great sorrow. **Jesus** is mistreated and misunderstood: "Now the men who were holding Jesus began to mock him and beat him" (Luke 22:63).

4) *God Triumphs.* **Joseph** suffers, but lives to forgive his brothers and provide them new life. **Jesus** suffers and dies on the cross, giving all of us the chance to have life forever with God.

Christians also find the allegorical sense in the story of Joseph in the Book of Genesis. Christ's life resembles Joseph's. Parallel themes between Joseph and Jesus (see accompanying chart) are summed up in Joseph's words to his brothers in Egypt when they realize that their fate is in his hands. They presented themselves before Joseph as his slaves, but Joseph says instead: "Do not be afraid! . . . Even though you intended to do harm to me, God intended it for good . . . So have no fear; I myself will provide for you and your little ones" (Genesis 50:19-21). Think of Jesus forgiving those who have put him to death, or his being the Good Shepherd providing for us, his sheep, or offering himself to be our Bread of Life. All that happened to Jesus, including his suffering and death, his Father intended for good,

and ultimately Jesus provided for all his little ones by the gift of new life. However, while we can make these connections, the Old Testament passages still hold their original meanings for the Jewish readers.

The **moral sense** of Scripture means that the stories of Scripture can teach us how to live and act. After Cain kills his brother Abel, God questions Cain: "Where is your brother Abel?" Cain replies, "I do not know; am I my brother's keeper?" (Genesis 4:9) When we read that story, we may want to shout: "Yes, you are, Cain, and so are we!" We take from the story that we are all indeed caretakers of one another, responsible for one another's well-being, and called to be aware and attentive to one another. We all need help at one time or another, and God tells us we need to look out for one another. The story definitely has a moral message for us today.

moral sense reading Scripture as a source of guidance for right behavior and leading us to just actions

GO TO THE SOURCE

Sometimes Jesus used allegory in trying to get his message across to his listeners. One example comes in the Gospel according to John.

Read John 2:13-22, then work in pairs to answer the following questions:

○ How does Jesus use allegory in this passage?

○ How did it help his disciples understand what happened to him?

○ How does this passage help you understand who Jesus is?

Choose

Cain asks God: "Am I my brother's keeper?" But suppose that instead he said: "I do not want to be my brother's keeper" or asked, "Why am I my brother's keeper?"

○ Choose either the statement or the question, and respond to it as you think God would have. Then take it a step further: When is society not very good at being our "brother's keeper"?

The anagogical sense means a story contains a more profound sense that points us toward Christ and our true home in

Read the story of the Tower of Babel (Genesis 11:1-19)

Here is what Pope Benedict XVI wrote about it:

[In the story] sin is understood as the destruction of the unity of the human race, as fragmentation and division. Babel, the place where languages were confused, the place of separation, is seen to be an expression of what sin fundamentally is.
—Pope Benedict XVI, *Spe Salvi*

Interpret
○ Explain how this story illustrates Pope Benedict's view of sin.

○ How does this understanding of sin apply to our world today?

anagogy a story or image that represents a future, eternal reality

Heaven. **Anagogy** means that a story leads us to a future, eternal reality. For instance, the Bible speaks of the glory and greatness of the city of Jerusalem. From a Christian viewpoint, Jerusalem represents eternal life—the heavenly city, not a place but the perfect, everlasting life and love found from communion with the Trinity.

At one point, Hebrew leaders spend fifty years in exile in Babylon. A number of psalms (Psalm 137, for example) describe the Israelites longing to return to their home in Jerusalem on Mount Zion. Again, early Christians understood these songs and images about Mount Zion as referring to their own longing for Heaven. The anagogical sense, then, allows us to see the Church on Earth as a sign of the heavenly Jerusalem (see CCC, 117).

If I forget you, O Jerusalem,
*   let my right hand wither!*
Let my tongue cling to the roof
*   of my mouth,*
*   if I do not remember you,*
*   if I do not set Jerusalem*
*   above my highest joy.*

—Psalm 137:5-6

Psalm 137 was composed when the Israelites were in captivity in a foreign land—Babylon. Their homeland and its capital city, Jerusalem, take on special significance for them. For the Israelites, Jerusalem is a spiritual home—a spiritual experience where God's promise is fulfilled and his presence is felt—which has an actual physical, geographical location. A key theme of Psalm 137 is that we are strangers in a strange land, and we long for home.

As Catholics, we can relate to this anagogy. We long to return to our home with the Father, who dwells in Heaven, but at the same time is present in his majesty. "Heaven, the Father's house, is the true homeland toward which we are heading and to which, already, we belong" (CCC, 2802). Our belief in Christ brings us new life in the Holy Spirit and compels us to become more like Christ in how we relate to God the Father, ourselves, and others. This moral life grows stronger and matures through grace, not with the end goal of living a good life on Earth, but of finding completeness and fulfillment in Heaven.

Identify How does Cain respond when God asks him about his brother Abel?

Analyze How can the moral sense as well as the anagogical sense of Scripture be applied to Psalm 137?

REFLECT

Become more like Christ. List five things that you think are a must in order to be like Christ.

>> In looking at your life—the people in it, the priorities you have, your faith, what's most important to your family—what would you do the same, but more of, to be like Christ? What would you change to be like Christ?

The Psalter

The Psalter is the Book of Psalms arranged for liturgy. The *Catechism* puts it this way: "The Psalter is the book in which The Word of God becomes man's prayer" (CCC, 2587). It explains that other books in the Old Testament proclaim God's works and help us understand the mystery they reveal. The Psalmist, however, used words to sing for God. They praise his saving works. The same Holy Spirit inspires God's work and our response. Through Christ, "the psalms continue to teach us how to pray" (CCC, 2587).

The Fathers of the Church saw the whole psalter as a prophecy of Christ and the Church and explained it in this sense; for the same reason the psalms have been chosen for use in the sacred liturgy.
—General Instruction of the Liturgy of the Hours, 109

The psalms are arranged to be read at certain hours of the day, on particular days, and during particular seasons.

The 150 psalms are the prayer book of the Church. When we pray the psalms, we often see images of Jesus and the Church in them. Keep in mind that the psalms are the prayers of the Jewish people and the Christian interpretation of a given psalm is not the first or only interpretation. We reread the psalms with Christ in mind, as well as his death and Resurrection.

Catholics have always heard the voice of Christ crying out to the Father, or the Father talking with the Son, in the singing of the psalms. "They also recognized in the psalms the voice of the Church, the apostles and the martyrs" (GILH, 109).

The Church has an interest in praying the whole Psalter regularly. In the Psalter, the psalms are scheduled in a four-week cycle so that very few are omitted while a few traditionally more important psalms are repeated. Early in the twentieth century, Pope Pius X prepared the Psalter of Mary. It restored the ancient custom of praying the 150 psalms each week.

>> What is your favorite psalm? If you're not sure, take a look at the Book of Psalms and see if one speaks to you in particular.

Why do you think it's important to pray the psalms regularly?

Missionary Preacher

SAINT FRANCISCO COLL Y GUITART (1812–1875)

Saint Francisco Coll y Guitart possessed a passion for preaching at a time in Spain when rulers abolished religious order convents and monasteries. Father Coll was the youngest of ten children born in the tiny town of Gombreny, Spain, located in Catalonia. He entered the seminary at a young age and at seventeen entered the Convent of the Order of Preachers. This took place in 1830, but in 1835, before he could be ordained a priest, he and many others were forced by the government to leave their convent. He became a secularized Dominican and despite the dangers was ordained a priest on May 28, 1836.

Anti-clerical laws forbade Father Coll to live in his convent or to wear his habit, but he lived as a Dominican his whole life. For forty years, he ministered as a missionary traveling to parishes in northeast Spain. He was known as "the apostle of modern times" because of his preaching.

Father Coll led a life of prayer and dedicated untold hours to preparing homilies for his message to the missions. He also helped found a group called the "Apostolic Fellowship" for evangelization in 1846. It was a collaboration with diocesan and religious order priests meant to support each other spiritually and in their mission to spread God's Word. He also preached to cloistered nuns, prisoners, and the sick. He taught religious education to children and founded orders to help with the Christian formation of girls, whose education was lacking compared to that offered to young men. The Congregation of the Dominican Sisters of the Anunciata that he founded has more than one thousand members serving in Europe, the Americas, Africa, and Asia.

Father Coll was giving one of his famed homilies in 1869 when he became blind. He refused to retire, however, and continued preaching despite health problems. The government suppression of religious orders ended in 1872. Because Father Coll vigilantly kept his Dominican order in line, they were able to officially return without any major problems.

At Father Coll's beatification in 1979, Pope John Paul II, himself beatified in 2011, called the Spanish priest "a transmitter of faith, a sower of hope, a preacher of love, peace and reconciliation among those whom passions, war and hatred keep divided."

Pope Benedict XVI canonized Father Coll on October 11, 2009. Pope Benedict noted that Saint Coll y Guitart's preaching proclaimed and revived the Word of God in the various villages and towns of Catalonia "thus leading people to the profound encounter with the Lord. . . . His evangelizing activity included great devotion to the Sacrament of Penance, an outstanding emphasis on the Eucharist, and a constant insistence on prayer."

> **Think About It** How can Saint Coll y Guitart's life be an example for you?
> What can we learn about reconciliation from Saint Coll y Guitart's life?
> How has God called you to reconcile differences in your life or among others?

Go to the student site at
hs.osvcurriculum.com

QUICK REVIEW

1a. **Analyze** What is meant by "layers" of meaning in Scripture?

b. **Recall** Which level of understanding comes first when analyzing Scripture?

c. **Infer** How does interpreting on only the literal level change a reader's view of Scripture?

2a. **Recall** What is the allegorical sense of Scripture?

b. **List** Who are some of the allegorical figures in the Bible and whom do they represent other than themselves?

c. **Interpret** What does the moral sense of biblical interpretation imply?

3a. **Restate** What does an anagogical story represent?

b. **Interpret** What moral lesson can be learned from the story of Cain and Abel?

c. **Name** Which city does the speaker in Psalm 137 yearn for, and what does that city represent?

ACT

With a small group, design an allegorical story.

○ Share your story with the class, and see if they can interpret it.

SELF-ASSESS

Which statement best reflects where you are now?

☐ I'm confident enough about the material in this section to be able to explain it to someone else.

☐ I have a good grasp of the material in this section, but I could use more review.

☐ I'm lost. I need help catching up before moving on.

Going Deeper into Scripture

A model of passion for God appears early in the Bible. In the Book of Genesis, the account of Abraham serves as an analogy for all people of faith.

Abraham undergoes test after test. Leaving the security of home is a test. Being childless into old age is a test, particularly at that time, when a father depended on a son to take charge of the household when he dies.

Abraham's greatest test comes when God tells him to sacrifice his son, Isaac. The *allegorical sense* of Scripture helps us to see Abraham's test as a sign of God's willingness to sacrifice his only Son, Jesus, on the cross.

> "By faith, Abraham obeyed when he was called to go out to a place which he was to receive as an inheritance; and he went out, not knowing where he was to go."[11] By faith, he lived as a stranger and pilgrim in the promised land.[12] By faith, Sarah was given to conceive the son of the promise. And by faith Abraham offered his only son in sacrifice.[13]
>
> —CCC, 145

Abraham "lives by faith" in two ways. He obeys God, *and* he also trusts in God. Abraham undergoes hardships. His hopes appear to be dashed, yet he remains faithful to the God of his promise and trusts that God will provide.

This message sustained those who chronicled the stories about him, just as it has sustained Hebrew, Christian, and Muslim communities ever since. All three consider Abraham the father of their faith.

> Where the conditions are right, that is, where a heart is open in faith, the seed of God's word takes root and has a sure effect. . . . It is "the word of God, which is now at work in you who believe."
>
> —Jerome Kodell, OSB, *The Catholic Bible Study Handbook*, page 26

Abraham is said to be the father of our faith; as followers, we are his descendants. A literal interpretation would assert that we are genealogically linked to Abraham. Catholics have always found a spiritual, analogical meaning in the story of Abraham.

GLOBAL PERSPECTIVES

All-time bestselling book lists often include the Qur'an, *Quotations from Chairman Mao Tse-Tung, The Lord of the Rings, The Catcher in the Rye*, and several editions of the Harry Potter series. However, one title leads them all not by millions, but by billions of copies sold—the Bible. At least six billion copies of the Bible have been sold since Gutenberg invented his printing press in the fifteenth century, or we should say since records have been kept. Eleven complete copies of Gutenberg's Bible remain on vellum paper.

○ What translation of the Bible do you have, and who gave it to you?

○ When did you receive your Bible, and when was the last time you opened it?

➔ Go to the student site at **hs.osvcurriculum.com**

Abraham offers us a model of faith in the midst of ongoing challenges. "Because he was 'strong in his faith,' Abraham became the 'father of all who believe'" (CCC, 146).

Understanding how to interpret any biblical text helps us to realize its importance in our lives. Biblical truth is conveyed through multiple means. In stories like that of Abraham, God reveals his message to us through human authors who were products of particular times and places.

One of the points of this chapter is to help us be more thoughtful readers of Scripture. We've talked about history and culture, techniques and senses, correct interpretation. These insights give us perspective. They help us understand the bigger picture or context. But they can come across as technical or detached if we lose sight of their purpose: to get closer to Christ by better understanding and applying Scripture's divine message to our lives. To learn about God's commands and his will for us so that we can live as he made us to, so that we can find a true happiness that would not be possible otherwise. Yes, you could say the Bible is a story like no other, but it's far more than a piece of literature. The following contrast between two of your classes may help you appreciate a truth revealed to us in Scripture that we would otherwise lack.

Say you have biology class, followed by religion class. Your biology textbook has a series of diagrams in it. The first diagram depicts a human skeleton. A second shows the various organs of the body. Subsequent ones illustrate the muscular system, circulatory system, and so forth.

Does this series of diagrams give us "the truth" about being human? In one sense, the answer is yes. But don't we wonder if there is more to being human than many semesters of biology classes could tell us? Is there a "beyond" to the human condition that science can't reveal to us?

Discuss
○ What wisdom from Scripture have you written on your heart and made your own?
○ What biblical truth brings you the greatest amount of comfort, hope, or strength?

So now make your way to religion class. There you open up another book, quite different from your biology book—the Bible. Near the beginning it states that human beings are created in God's image (Genesis 1:26). That's a very powerful statement. It holds many implications for how we view ourselves, how we treat one another, and how we understand our relationship to the ultimate mystery, God.

The information we get from biology class can give us a *literal sense* of who we are. Yet there is more to us than a set of transparencies can show. The inspired writers of the Bible tell us there is indeed more to reality than what meets the eye.

The Bible gives us the *spiritual sense* (allegorical, moral, and anagogical). There is a spiritual side to our existence. This is the deep wisdom of the Scriptures. The source of this wisdom is the ultimate source of all truth, God.

The biblical writers chronicle the struggles of the Israelite people. In the *anagogical sense*, the Israelites try to understand what it means to be human in light of their relationship with God. What does it hold for their future and eternal reality? Then, in the fullness of time, what it means to be made in the image of God is revealed most completely in the Person of Jesus Christ.

All Sacred Scripture is but one book, and that one book is Christ, "because all divine Scripture speaks of Christ, and all divine Scripture is fulfilled in Christ" (Hugh of St. Victor, De arca Noe 2, 8: PL 176, 642 cf.ibid.2, 9: PL 176, 642-643).

—CCC, 134

Everyday life challenges you to think about right and wrong, to sort out the good from the bad, and to inform and form your conscience. Here's an example . . .

Muslims who take their faith seriously pray five times a day. A devout group of Muslims working at a factory asked their supervisor to give them additional break time every day so they could fulfill their religious prayers. Other workers objected because they would not be given the additional break times allotted to the Muslim employees.

The Muslim workers were clear: **"No pray, no work."**

Tell them to forget about it and get back to work.

Give them a place to pray because they are taking faith seriously.

Fire the workers for causing problems.

I don't know. I'm glad it's not my decision.

Keep religion out of the workplace.

The First Amendment gives people the right to practice their religion.

All parties should meet and settle their differences.

How do you respond?

Going Moral

REFLECT

Looking back on this course so far and what you already knew about the Bible, answer the following:

» **What have you learned about the Bible?**

How has your attitude toward the Bible changed?

Words can be empty or filled with meaning, or they can confuse or inspire us. Above all, words are vehicles that point to something else. For example, the word "driver" conjures up an image of particular realities: one behind the wheel of a car and the other hitting a golf ball off the tee. The Bible is the Sacred Scripture, the Holy Book. It is holy because:

- its principal author, God, is holy

- the truths it reveals are holy

- the way God wants us to live is holy

- its words are holy

Recall The story of Abraham and Isaac is an allegory for what?

Elaborate How do your religion classes relate to the other classes on your schedule?

SECTION 4 REVIEW

QUICK REVIEW

1a. Recall Who is Abraham's son Isaac said to represent allegorically? Why?

b. Interpret How did Abraham live by faith?

c. Analyze Why is Abraham worthy to be called "the father of all who believe"?

2a. Analyze In the Bible, how is "truth conveyed through multiple means"?

b. Recall Who is the central character in the Bible?

c. Interpret What is the point of reading and interpreting the Bible?

ACT

Do some research about Abraham. These questions can help you get started:

○ What is his role in the Jewish religion?

○ How is he viewed by Muslims?

○ Trace his travels through the Middle East. His travels and life took him through which modern-day nations?

Pray Compose a short prayer thanking God for a specific piece of wisdom you have received from Scripture.

SELF-ASSESS

Which statement best reflects where you are now?

☐ I'm confident enough about the material in this section to be able to explain it to someone else.

☐ I have a good grasp of the material in this section, but I could use more review.

☐ I'm lost. I need help catching up before moving on.

PRAYER

Litany to Old Testament Saints

Lord, have mercy on us. Christ, have mercy on us.
Lord, have mercy on us. Christ, hear us.
Christ, graciously hear us.

      God the Father of Heaven . . . have mercy on us
      God the Son, Redeemer of the world . . . have mercy on us
      God the Holy Spirit . . . have mercy on us
      Holy Trinity, One God . . . have mercy on us
      God of Abraham . . . have mercy on us
      God of Bethel . . . have mercy on us
      Mighty One of Jacob . . . have mercy on us
      God of Isaac . . . have mercy on us
      God of Hagar . . . have mercy on us
      God Almighty . . . have mercy on us
      God the Most High . . . have mercy on us

All you holy people before the flood . . . pray for us
Abraham and Isaac . . . pray for us
Esau, Jacob, and Joseph . . . pray for us
All you holy men . . . pray for us
Hagar, Sarah, and Rebekah . . . pray for us
All you holy women . . . pray for us
Old Testament saints of God . . . pray for us
Make intercession for us.

      Be merciful . . . Graciously hear us, O Lord.
      From all evil . . . O Lord, deliver us.
      From all sin . . . O Lord, deliver us.
      From falling away from the Faith . . . O Lord, deliver us.
      From doubting Your Word . . . O Lord, deliver us.
      From denying Your Name . . . O Lord, deliver us.
      From losing hope . . . O Lord, deliver us.
      We implore You . . . hear us.
      That we continue to walk by faith . . . hear us.
      That we grow in love for Your Holy Word . . . hear us.
      Amen.

CHAPTER 4 REVIEW

TERMS

Use each of the following terms in a sentence that shows you know what the term means. You may include more than one term in a sentence.

vernacular language

Council of Trent

Vatican Council II

Dei Verbum

Divino Afflante Spiritu

literal sense

allegory

moral sense

anagogy

PEOPLE

Tell what is significant about each person.

1. Erasmus

2. Saint Jerome

3. Johannes Gutenberg

4. Benedict XVI

5. Franz Jägerstätter

6. Saint Francisco Coll y Guitart

7. Joseph

8. Abraham

9. Isaac

UNDERSTANDING

Answer each question and complete each exercise.

SECTION 1

1. **Explain** When are the theories of evolution compatible with faith?

2. **Analyze** What effect did the invention of the printing press have on how people read Scripture?

3. **Summarize** What three pronouncements came out of the Council of Trent?

4. **Recall** Which council that started in 1962 encouraged the reading of Scripture?

SECTION 2

5. **Contrast** Is literal or contextual criticism of Scripture more complete? Explain your answer.

6. **Analyze** What view of the Bible does a literal interpretation lead to?

7. **Tell** To correctly interpret Scriptures, what must we do?

8. **Elaborate** What was Paul trying to say in Romans 13:1-2?

SECTION 3

9. **Sequence** Why does it help to become familiar with the literal meaning of a Scripture passage before looking for a deeper meaning?

10. **Recall** What two kinds of meaning are within an allegory?

11. **Infer** Why are moral interpretations useful?

12. **Explain** What does anagogical writing represent?

SECTION 4

13. **Explain** Why do Christians, Muslims, and Jews all honor Abraham?

14. **Summarize** How can we become more thoughtful readers of the Bible?

15. **Analyze** What does it mean to be created in God's image?

16. **Elaborate** How does Jesus reveal most completely what it means to be made in the image of God?

CONNECTING

Visual This is an illustration of the story of Joseph from the Old Testament. How does the artist use the image to reinforce the idea that an allegorical interpretation of the story makes Joseph a Christ figure?

Joseph Cast into the Pit by His Bretheren, Victorian Book Illustration

Challenge You are visiting with a Protestant friend and notice a Bible on his desk at home.

You: So what are you reading in the Bible?

Friend: We just finished reading the story of Jonah in Sunday school.

You: Really? We were talking about that same story in religion class the other day. What did you think?

Friend: Well, I think it's hard to believe it, but if it's in the Bible, it must be true.

You: But do you think that it really happened?

Friend: I don't have to decide whether it really happened; in my Church, we believe that the Bible is literally true.

○ What is your next reply?

○ Continue the conversation, being mindful that you should respect other people's religions. Anticipate questions you would have for your friend, as well as what he would ask you. Continue the conversation for at least three responses from each of you.

Question After working through this chapter, what advice would you give someone who wants to interpret the Bible correctly?

Imagine You are in a group of screenwriters who are assigned to write a screenplay for an allegorical film. The group is to emphasize the allegorical aspect of the original story, to highlight the similarities between the main character and a biblical character.

○ Select an allegorical story from the Bible or another source.

○ List examples of ways in which you can draw parallels between the story character and the biblical character, such as in words, songs, and gestures.

○ Write a short scene incorporating your ideas.

○ Share the scene with classmates, either in writing or as a performed piece.

SELF-ASSESS

On Your Own Make a list of the most important things you learned from this chapter. Select three things that represent your growth in understanding as you worked through the chapter. Write a paragraph explaining your choices.

With a Partner List what you found most helpful or interesting in this chapter, as well as any other questions that have surfaced.

What does this photo tell you about journeys?

What journey are you making?

CHAPTER **5**

The Old Testament

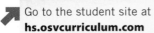

Go to the student site at
hs.osvcurriculum.com

DO

- ○ Explore the nature of story.
- ○ Find out what God wants us to know about creation.
- ○ Compare the stories of creation.
- ○ Tell a story that had an impact on your life.
- ○ Identify key themes that run throughout Genesis.

- ○ Describe your own spiritual exodus.
- ○ Learn about how the prophets communicate God's will.
- ○ Consider the spiritual practice of testimony in your life.
- ○ Recollect the ways God speaks to you.

DEFINE

Original Sin	Passover
covenant	Paschal Mystery
Promised Land	Decalogue
Pharaohs	monotheism
YHWH	prophet
Seder	

Students at a Catholic high school were asked: **"What's wisdom? And what does it mean to have wisdom?"** Here are some responses:

Wisdom is to have knowledge and use it for good.

Wisdom is knowing about Jesus.

To have wisdom means that you know and understand what's going on.

Wisdom is knowing what's right and wrong. People who make the right decisions have wisdom.

Wisdom is the knowledge that you are perfect the way you are and knowing that God loves you.

To have wisdom is to finally be at peace with yourself and the world.

Wisdom is knowing wrong from right. To have wisdom is being able to handle different situations like peer pressure.

Now it's your turn. How do you define wisdom? What does it mean to have wisdom?

WHAT ABOUT YOU?

Where Are You?

Choose the response that best reflects where you are right now.

I know that evolution cannot explain the "why" of creation.	☐ Quite a bit	☐ Somewhat	☐ A little	☐ Not at all
I understand how we are all children of Abraham.	☐ Quite a bit	☐ Somewhat	☐ A little	☐ Not at all
I can recite the Ten Commandments.	☐ Quite a bit	☐ Somewhat	☐ A little	☐ Not at all
I recognize the modern prophets of today.	☐ Quite a bit	☐ Somewhat	☐ A little	☐ Not at all
I have a good sense of what God expects of me.	☐ Quite a bit	☐ Somewhat	☐ A little	☐ Not at all
I make time to see the Holy Spirit working in my life.	☐ Quite a bit	☐ Somewhat	☐ A little	☐ Not at all

The Power of Story

"In the beginning when God created the heavens and the earth. . . ." (Genesis 1:1) Those first words of the Bible tell us of God's act of creating the world. After God breathed life into Adam and Eve, he began to reveal to them, and to their descendants, who he is. He therefore makes it possible for us to respond to him, to know him, and to love him beyond our natural capability (see *Catechism of the Catholic Church*, 52).

What we find in the Old Testament are truths God has made known to us about things that really matter. The Old Testament records what God reveals about himself, addresses some of the greatest questions ever asked, and includes the most enduring written works in history. It contains much of the sacred writings of our ancestors in faith, the Israelites. And its books set the stage for the great culminating event of our faith—the life, death, Resurrection, and Ascension of Jesus.

In this chapter you are invited to explore the nature of "story." You will be introduced to biblical figures whose stories show us something about who God is, and how he relates to us. They give us insights into who we are as people created by God. And, they point to Jesus in some way. As you read about the people and events, ask yourself what the major themes are and how they apply to Jesus and to your own life. What do they say about the journey of faith that these Old Testament figures were on? How do they relate to where you are on your own journey? And know that many Old Testament themes and events will be discussed in later courses that address salvation history.

Every page of the Old Testament addresses the questions of "'Who is God?' 'What does God do?' 'Why does God do it?'" While the Old Testament is the story of the people of Israel, "it is not primarily the story of God and Israel *alone*. Although the people remembered what God had done for them, they also spoke about what God does for the *whole* world and all its nations. The Bible testifies to the universal greatness and love of God" (*Reading the Old Testament*, Father Lawrence Boadt).

So we begin at the beginning with the Book of Genesis, in which we learn much about God, creation, and humans. In those divinely inspired words, we learn about "the first and universal witness to God's all-powerful love" (CCC, 288). The creation of the world and humans is the first communication of God's plan and his desire to be in relationship with us.

Throughout history, scientists have wrestled with the origins of the universe. You have heard of the big bang theory, credited to Edwin Hubble more than fifty years ago. And we previously commented on Charles Darwin's theory of evolution. It outlines the stages in the development of life on Earth. His theory has been around for more than 150 years.

Planetary Nebula NGC 2818

Discover

Read the quotation on the left about the importance of stories.

○ Identify three "stories" in life in which you play a role.

○ How does God's "story" continue today and where do you fit into that story?

Why does anybody tell a story? It does indeed have something to do with faith, faith that the universe has meaning, that our little human lives are not irrelevant; that what we choose or say or do matters, matters cosmically.

—Madeleine L'Engle, in Frederic and Mary Ann Brussat, eds., *Spiritual Literacy*

Those scientific theories deal with *how* things came to be. But, what does the Book of Genesis say about *why* the universe and humans came to be? The biblical account of creation includes two accounts. The first is a step-by-step description of how God created the world in seven days. The second focuses on the account of Adam and Eve in the Garden of Eden.

The Church doesn't debate whether creation actually happened as written in Genesis. Instead the Church looks at what is written for the religious truth that God wanted his people to know.

There is a recurring theme found in the opening chapters of the Bible: "And God saw that it was good." Blessed Pope John Paul II noted in his World Day of Peace message on January 1, 1990, that there is a significant change in that theme once God creates man and woman. "At this point the refrain changes markedly: 'And God saw everything that he had made, and behold, it was very good' (Genesis 1:31). God entrusted the whole of creation to the man and woman, and only then—as we read—could he rest 'from all his work'" (Genesis 2:3).

Scientific studies and all that come from them give us an even greater respect and appreciation for the innate goodness of our Creator. The research and findings invite us to praise God and give him thanks for all that he has created and made possible, including knowledge and wisdom of researchers (see CCC, 283).

In the Beginning

Storytelling serves a very important purpose. Human beings have always used stories to express themselves. The Israelites did. We know that Jesus did, drawing listeners and readers alike into the profound mystery of God through his words and actions. We still do today. Just think about how many movies you have seen in the last year, the books read, TV programs watched, and Internet websites surfed. Many music videos tell stories or at least offer images that make a good point or send a message. Family members and friends are always good for stories, too.

Some stories passed from generation to generation address a community or group of people's most important questions:

• What are our origins?

• Where are we going?

• Does our existence have meaning?

• What is our place in the universe?

The first eleven chapters of Genesis—often using figurative language—address these questions in ways that God wants us to contemplate. In these accounts, we see Adam and Eve and their interaction with God and other creatures. Here we meet the brothers Cain and Abel as well as people bent on building a tower to the heavens, and Noah facing the great flood.

These stories are not to be interpreted as strict, literal historical facts, whereas some later biblical stories are indeed rooted in historical fact.

Was flooding commonplace in parts of the biblical world? Yes. Is it likely that we will ever find the remains of a large boat called "Noah's ark"? Not likely. Did some ancient civilizations build towering structures and boast of their greatness because of them? Yes. Is that the reason people speak different languages? Not likely.

We don't read these stories of creation and destruction and the consequences of human pride as reflecting scientific, historical facts. They are different kinds of narratives meant to convey God's truth about who we are and who we are intended to be; their messages are not confined to one time and place.

On top of presenting such fundamental truths, these stories lay the foundation for the coming of Jesus. Throughout this course and subsequent ones, you will see how these accounts are connected with the coming of Jesus. This is how God chose to reveal himself to humankind. This is also how he prepared us for meeting God face to face.

A genealogy starting in Chapter 11, Verse 10 of the Book of Genesis lists names of the descendants of a man named Shem. In the list, which includes some biographical information about the descendants, we arrive at a

Storytelling
○ Tell a story about someone who had an impact on your life.
○ Tell a story about an incident in your life that helped shape who you are.
○ Tell a story about how you learned a truth you could take with you forever.

person named Abram, who the world will come to know as Abraham. This is where Genesis turns to the account of the patriarch Abraham and his succeeding generations, including Isaac and Jacob. These chapters contain an actual historical basis as well.

Abraham came from a real place that we can find on a map. He traveled through lands that we can visit today. He drank from wells that quite possibly are still there. And he lived a life of faith that we can learn from today; the choices he made, the joys and struggles he experienced, the trust and belief he displayed in God show us something about God's love and faithfulness, and the human ability to respond to it.

Faith & Culture

During the Jubilee year 2000, Pope John Paul II wanted to visit places linked to the Bible, starting with Abraham's home city of Ur of the Chaldees. Today, Ur is called Tell el-Moqayyar and is located in southern Iraq. The city once sat at the mouth of the Euphrates River where it met the Persian Gulf. Today, it is south of the river, well inland from the gulf. The Pope was not able to travel to the great patriarch's home in the Jubilee year 2000 because of political and safety concerns, but the Bible tells us the words God said to Abraham: "Go from your country and your kindred and your father's house to the land that I will show you. I will make of you a great nation, and I will bless you, and make your name great, so that you will be a blessing . . . in you all the families of the earth shall be blessed" (Genesis 12:1-3). "With these words," Pope John Paul II said, "the great journey of the People of God began."

Pope John Paul II on his trip to the Middle East during the Jubilee year 2000

↗ Go to the student site at **hs.osvcurriculum.com**

The stories of his travels and encounters give us snapshots of the various groups living at the time in lands we know today as Iraq in the north to Egypt in the south.

Describe What do we learn about God and humans from the creation accounts?

Explain What important purpose do these stories serve?

> *Reading is a matter of getting hold of a text and making it tell us something for today, something that will make us live.*
>
> —Etienne Charpentier,
> *How to Read the Old Testament*

Themes in Genesis

At times Genesis might read like a *New York Times* best seller, complete with family conflicts, deceptions, and petty jealousies. At other times it reads like an adventure tale. But we know this is not simply a story. This is the revealed word of God. This is what God wants us to know about Abraham and his descendants as they lead an entourage through many lands. When encountering other people, sometimes they use their wits to get by; sometimes they use their muscle. In other words, they react just like most people do today. The power of Genesis lies in what it says, how it says it, and, most important, in the fact that God wants us to know what it says. We need to go to Scripture itself

Major Themes in Genesis
Creation
The Fall and the Promise
Devastation Caused by Sin
The Covenant
Origins of God's Chosen People
The Struggles of God's People
The Dream of Salvation

to get all the details, but we can explore some themes that run through the book.

Over the past few centuries, biblical literalists and those who use context to interpret the Bible have debated the seven-day creation account and the existence of Adam and Eve. Whether interpreted literally or allegorically, we can identify at least three key themes in the initial account of creation. The Church teaches us that this is the *truth* that God wanted communicated and the Genesis writers passed on:

- Ultimately, God alone creates everything, freely and with no help, to share and make known his glory.

- All creation is good and a gift from God.

- Human beings are unique, made in God's image and likeness, and responsible for all other creatures.

Research

The truth and beauty of the Bible's creation accounts shine through when compared to accounts of creation from other ancient cultures. For instance, the ancient Babylonian creation myth tells of a battle between the god Marduk and the goddess Tiamat. Marduk wins the battle, crushes Tiamat's skull, and then splits her body in two to form the Earth and the sky.

Find a creation story from a different culture and compare its worldview to Genesis. Pose the following questions to the Genesis account and to the other creation myths:

○ Is the creation story optimistic or pessimistic?

○ What characteristics does God (or the gods) possess?

○ What does the story tell you about how the creator views humans?

As the inspired Word of God, we know that the Genesis accounts teach us fundamental religious truths. Describe those truths in your own words.

The Fall and the Promise

This second account of creation begins in paradise. Adam and Eve—in their original, God-given state—share a garden with all other creatures. They live without fear and feel at home with each other and with God. They live in what can be called an original state of holiness and justice. However, trouble lurks in the garden. Enticed by a serpent, Eve eats from the fruit of the forbidden tree, the tree of knowledge of good and evil. Adam quickly joins her. They give in to temptation by the evil one, and abuse the freedom that God gave them.

For the first time, the pair realizes that they are naked and feel ashamed to be so exposed. They hide from God, who banishes them from the garden. Now they must work, and they will be subject to pain, suffering, and death. This story is not exclusively about the first human beings. It applies to all human beings. Adam and Eve damaged human nature because of their first sin. They handed on to every human, except Mary and Jesus, a weakened nature deprived of the original holiness and justice created by God. This lack of original holiness and justice is what the Church calls **Original Sin** (see CCC, 417). Original Sin led to the universal human condition of alienation from God, of being subject to suffering and death, of having an inclination toward sin and hurtful behavior.

Throughout the books of the Old Testament, we see how humanity struggled due to the effects of Original Sin. We see the human tendency to take what is good and misuse it. It records some of the ways we seek happiness in material and physical ways instead of spiritual ways. It also shows the happiness that comes when we maintain a right relationship with God. Original Sin points to the need for redemption that ultimately comes from the love of our Father, who sent his only Son to take away and make up for human sin, and from Jesus' free choice to offer himself for our salvation.

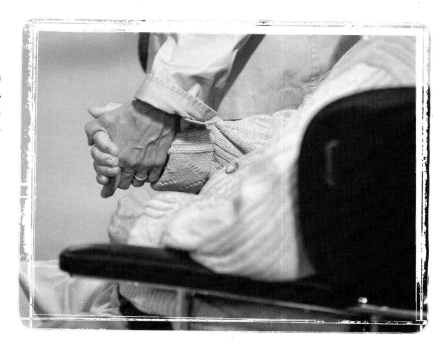

Jesus restored us to our original state of union with God. He took our fractured existence and restored it to wholeness. Without Jesus we experience a disconnect between ourselves and God, between ourselves and one another. In Jesus, we once again realize that we are all children of God. Jesus conquers Original Sin and makes possible the fulfillment of our deep-down yearning for happiness.

Another image that we can ponder when trying to understand Adam and Eve's Fall is "homesickness." The two of them, representing all of us, are banished from paradise—our true home—where we are fully one with God. When we choose a path that does not lead us to live according to God's commandments and Jesus' teachings, we wander around, constantly seeking material, physical, or social substitutes for our true home.

Even with God's grace, the homesickness never fully goes away. Jesus, the Son of the Father, calls us—his sisters and brothers—back to the Father. In him we are home; his Spirit dwells within us. Baptism welcomes us back into God's family by forgiving Original Sin and all personal sins.

Original Sin the lack of original holiness and justice in human nature, handed down from the first sin of Adam and Eve

covenant a solemn promise or agreement between humans or between God and his People that involves agreed-upon commitments or guarantees

One way to think about receiving Holy Communion at Mass is as food for the journey of discipleship, a gift from God that helps fill our needs during our deep-seated homesickness. In 2008, Pope Benedict XVI explained that in the Sacrament of the Eucharist we receive the Body and Blood of Christ, and we also become Christ's body, the Church. Unlike regular food that simply becomes part of our body, Holy Communion makes us part of Christ's body. In a spiritual way we are filled with God's loving grace, and in a practical way we are filled by being part of Christ's community. Each of us is personally united with Jesus in the Eucharist, and, as he is also united with others, so we are, too. "Thus Christ unites all of us with himself and all of us with one another. In communion we receive Christ. But Christ is likewise united with my neighbor: Christ and my neighbor are inseparable

in the Eucharist. And thus we are all one bread and one body" (Pope Benedict XVI, General Audience, December 10, 2008).

List What are two of the major themes of the Book of Genesis?

Explain How does Original Sin create the need for Jesus' life, death, and Resurrection?

God Makes Two Covenants

After Noah and his ark full of animals survived the flood, God made a covenant with Noah and all living things to allow them to be fruitful and fill the Earth. This was a renewed blessing of what God had given to all living things during the creation. The rainbow is a sign of that promise and his covenant. The **covenant**, or solemn agreement, with Noah remains in effect as long as the world lasts.

Abraham later wholeheartedly accepts this blessing and becomes integral to the history of salvation (see CCC, 1080). With Abraham and his descendants, God makes a covenant and a new understanding of what a relationship with him is meant to be. In biblical times, covenants often spelled out the rules and responsibilities between a ruler and his subjects. In this covenant, God forms his People. He promises to be faithful to Abraham and his family. God assures Abraham that he will look after him and his many descendants, no matter what.

The Bible, both Old and New Testaments, centers around the covenant and the one true God who remains faithful to it. In his Son, Jesus, God establishes his covenant forever. Listen for words about this the next time you take part in Mass. We, too, are covenant people, invited to be friends with the one true God who promised to look after Abraham and his descendants. Because of Jesus, God's words are for us as much as they were for the first generations of God's People: "Do not fear, for I am with you, do not be afraid, for I am your God" (Isaiah 41:10). We are called to be faithful to God and our relationship with him. What does this really mean? Some synonyms for faithfulness include loyal, true, constant, and steadfast.

"Do you not know that your body is a temple of the Holy Spirit within you, which you have from God, and that you are not your own? ... Therefore glorify God in your body."

—(1 Corinthians 6:19-20)

Perfect Body

WE ALL WISH we could fix something about our body. We may have too much here, and not enough there. Maybe our lips are a little thin, our teeth aren't straight enough, or our ears aren't shaped right.

Ever wonder where our dissatisfaction with our bodies comes from in the first place? Do you think our great-grandparents were as worried about their bodies as we are?

Could it be from the media? Could it be that when we are barraged by unattainable images of digitally edited perfection, we feel inadequate? Is it possible that advertisers *want* you to feel inadequate because then you'll be more apt to buy their product to feel better about yourself?

Sometimes influential people in our lives have given us mixed messages. Perhaps you've received positive messages about your body; perhaps you haven't. Think about the examples you've been given. What are your parents' attitudes toward their own bodies? Do they model self-acceptance or self-loathing? How about the messages given to athletes— do they focus on healthy choices or enhancing performance through body weight or muscle mass?

In the human body, there are "unpresentable members," not by reason of their...nature...but only and exclusively because in man himself there exists the shame that perceives some members of the body as "unpresentable" and leads to considering them as such.

—Blessed Pope John Paul II, *Theology of the Body*, 55

Wherever you got the notion that your body is "unpresentable," it certainly wasn't from God. It's not like God didn't know the answer when he asked Adam and Eve, "Who told you that you were naked?" (Genesis 3:11). Rather, we need to emphatically and thoroughly understand that this sense of "shame" is not something of God. It's a lie. It's *manufactured*.

Honoring the body means accepting it more than hating it. Honoring the body includes honoring the way it was built. It means becoming friends with your body instead of seeing it as something you are stuck with.

>> On a scale of 1-10 how much are you *honoring* the body God made for you?

What effect do you think media messages have on our body image?

Who or what reminds you that "you are fine, just the way you are"?

What truth do you most need to hear when it comes to your own body?

Identify

Old Testament Scriptures, especially the Psalms and Wisdom literature, frequently use the adjective *faithful* when speaking of friendship and one's relationship with God as one of his children. What do you think it means to be a faithful friend? A faithful disciple of Christ and member of the Church? Make two lists, one of characteristics you expect in a faithful friend, and another of characteristics found in a faithful disciple of Christ.

○ What's similar between your lists? What's different?

○ What faithful friends do you have in your life? How can you learn to be a better follower of God and friend from them?

Being faithful to God means remaining true and loyal to God and his laws, being honest and constant in the things we say and do. It involves making sure we honor his commands and all that his Son teaches us.

Identify How long will the solemn agreement with Noah remain in effect?

Explain What is God's part of the covenant with Abraham?

SECTION 1 REVIEW

QUICK REVIEW

1a. Explain Why is the Old Testament more than a story?

b. Analyze Must we choose between believing scientific theories about how the world began and believing the creation story?

c. Analyze What is the purpose of telling stories?

2a. Explain In what ways do the first eleven chapters of Genesis use figurative language to get at some of the most important questions people address?

b. Analyze What is the purpose of the accounts in the beginning of Genesis?

3a. Contrast What is the major difference between the first eleven chapters in Genesis and the story of Abraham?

b. Analyze How would the story of Abraham and his descendants be useful to historians?

c. List Which truths are conveyed in the story of creation?

4a. Recall When does Original Sin enter the world, according to Genesis?

b. Apply How does the Genesis story of the Fall apply to all people?

c. Explain How is Original Sin overcome?

ACT

On your own, think about creation. Here are some questions to guide you.

○ Is there a time of day or a season of the year when creation is especially beautiful to you?

○ What can you do to increase appreciation for all that God created?

Pray Compose a short prayer thanking God for the intellectual challenges that Scripture presents.

SELF-ASSESS

Which statement best reflects where you are now?

☐ I'm confident enough about the material in this section to be able to explain it to someone else.

☐ I have a good grasp of the material in this section, but I could use more review.

☐ I'm lost. I need help catching up before moving on.

A Light to the Nations

Several scholars and writers rank Moses as the most influential Jewish person in history. One reason is that God works through Moses to fashion a group of slaves into a people who became "a light to the nations" (Isaiah 42:6).

The second book of the Old Testament—Exodus—follows Moses' life from his birth through the release of God's Chosen People on their journey to the **Promised Land**, which God had earlier promised to Abraham and his descendants.

God reveals to Moses from the burning bush that he is "the God of your father, the God of Abraham, the God of Isaac, and the God of Jacob" (Exodus 3:6). God tells Moses that he hears the cries of his people enslaved in Egypt. He intends to set them free and lead them to "a land flowing with milk and honey" (Exodus 3:8). God wants Moses to represent him before **Pharaoh** to make it happen.

Moses does all that he can to convince God that he's not the right person for the work:

> *O my Lord, I have never been eloquent, neither in the past nor even now that you have spoken to your servant; but I am slow of speech and slow of tongue.*
>
> —Exodus 4:10

This response echoes a recurring theme throughout the Bible: *the one whom God chooses* is not the likely choice people would make.

For instance, the prophet Micah speaks about the important role for the small village of Bethlehem. "But you, O Bethlehem . . . who are one of the little clans of Judah, from you shall come forth for me one who is to rule in Israel" (Micah 5:2). The Messiah, the Savior, would come from a least likely place.

Or another example is the choice of David to become king of the Israelites. When a warrior is needed to fight Goliath, David volunteers. He is the youngest of the eight sons of Jesse. He still tends sheep even though his eldest brothers are warriors. Through a set of circumstances, however, David ends up facing the giant Philistine. His faith in God is strong, so he says to Goliath, "This very day, the Lord will deliver you into my hand, and I will strike you down" (1 Samuel 17:46). The truth is that even though we are all flawed, the Holy Spirit still works through us to bring the Good News where he wants it to go.

Back to the story of Moses. Before departing from the burning bush, Moses presses God to reveal his name. The answer he receives is the Hebrew letters for **YHWH**. The following comes closest to what scholars believe YHWH means: "I am who I am," or "I will be who I will be." In Hebrew, this word is the holy and personal name for God, who delivered the Israelites from slavery in Egypt and gave them the Ten Commandments.

Promised Land the land (from the River of Egypt to the Euphrates, known as Canaan) promised to Abraham and his descendants in Genesis Chapter 12

YHWH name for God revealed to Moses; "I am who I am" or "I will be who I will be"

Pharaohs rulers of ancient Egypt who were in power when the Israelites were slaves

GO TO THE SOURCE

- Read Exodus Chapter 2 about Moses' youth. What surprises you?
- Read Exodus Chapter 3. How would you describe God in this situation?
- Read Exodus Chapter 4:1-17. How would you describe Moses' attitude?

1. What do these three chapters tell you about vocation, callings, and serving God?

2. What other questions do you have about serving God?

3. What was the most recent thing you did to serve God?

THINKING THEOLOGICALLY

Shiphrah and Puah: Unknown Heroes

Most people know about Moses and Pharaoh. They know that Moses is the hero who responds to God's call and leads the Hebrews from slavery to the Promised Land. But many fewer people have heard of Shiphrah and Puah.

Shiphrah (SHIF•ruh) and Puah (POO•uh) are heroes, too. They stand up to the power of Pharaoh and make it possible for the entire Exodus story to unfold. And they are part of God's inspired word to us.

Read Exodus 1:15–22

1. Who are Shiphrah and Puah?
2. What heroic thing did they do?
3. Why don't we hear more about Shiphrah and Puah?

>> This raises theological questions:

Have the women depicted in this passage been diminished or overlooked?

Has the cultural status of women impacted how their stories have been told?

What do you think God wants to reveal through these women?

What do you think? How important is it to investigate these kinds of theological questions?

The *Catechism* addresses this: In revealing his mysterious name, "God says who he is and by what name he is to be called. This divine name is mysterious just as God is mystery. It is at once a name revealed and something like the refusal of a name, and hence it better expresses God as what he is—infinitely above everything that we can understand or say . . ." (CCC, 206).

Moses agrees to return to Egypt. With the help of his brother Aaron to speak for him, Moses goes before Pharaoh and demands, in God's name, that the Hebrew slaves be freed to worship their God. Eventually, the Israelites are released. They wander in the desert for decades before finally reaching the Promised Land. Moses and the people of Israel build a strong but tested relationship with God during the events recounted in the Book of Exodus. This God is the one who brings them out of their misery in Egypt and into the Promised Land.

Identify What is YHWH?

Elaborate Moses at first balks at God's request to go to Pharaoh. What biblical theme does Moses' response echo?

GO TO **THE SOURCE**

Read about Moses and Aaron before Pharaoh in the following passages: Exodus 5:1–6:13 and Exodus 7:1–12:32.

○ Why do you think Moses and Aaron became uncomfortable with God's demands?

○ Like the Pharaoh, in what way do we or the world make it harder for others to follow God's will?

○ What was the most recent demand God asked of you?

Everyday life challenges you to think about right and wrong, to sort out the good from the bad, and to inform and form your conscience. Here's an example . . .

}

The Bible says, "Eye for an eye. Tooth for a tooth." So people who've been betrayed, ridiculed, and lied about by a so-called friend have every right to—according to the Bible—payback.

Right?

Go for it. The Bible entitles you to get even.

Do what you gotta do. God understands your pain.

Revenge got changed by Jesus

Let it go. Two wrongs don't make a right.

The Bible also says, "You reap what you sow."

If you don't get even, he/she will do it to someone else.

Jesus told us to love one another, even our enemies.

What do you say?

Going Moral

Blessed Josephine Bakhita

A MODERN SLAVE SET FREE
(c.1869–1947)

In his encyclical on hope (*Spe Salvi*, 2007), Pope Benedict XVI tells the stories of a number of people who embodied hope in their lives. The very first person he writes about is a woman born around 1869 in the Darfur region of Sudan in Africa. Her life story mirrors the theme of Exodus, and thus is a good choice to illustrate hope. At the age of nine, she was kidnapped from her family and sold into slavery. Frequently beaten and abused, she was passed around from owner to owner, like any other commodity. Finally an Italian family bought her and brought her to Italy to take care of their house and children. In time Josephine accompanied one of the children to a school run by a religious order of nuns called the Daughters of Charity. There Josephine heard the Gospel message for the first time, and she realized that Jesus wanted all people—including her—to be free.

Then Josephine faced the challenge similar to the Israelites of old: being free does not simply mean a change in material circumstances; it also requires a change in attitude. When the family who owned her told her that they expected her to return with them to Sudan, Josephine understood that Italian law gave her an option. The law in Italy did not permit slavery. She didn't have to return to Sudan and continued slavery. The family pleaded with Josephine to be grateful and loyal for all that they had done for her. When that didn't work, the family sued to have their "property" returned. Despite their urgings, Josephine trusted in God and found the courage to say that she wanted to remain in Italy. She realized that Jesus knew and loved her and that gave her hope. She saw God in her life and, despite the tremendous suffering she had endured, remained hopeful, trusting in his care and will. She remained in Italy, was baptized, and entered the order of sisters who were so kind to her. She often served as the doorkeeper, greeting the sisters and all who entered. She was known for her gentleness, smile, and her holiness. Throughout her life, she responded to evil with goodness, and saw love when others may not have. She was canonized by Blessed Pope John Paul II on October 1, 2000.

Josephine Bakhita's story of enslavement is not ancient history; she lived until 1947. Unfortunately, there are still young people today who have similar tales to tell.

Talking with high school students in Leawood, Kansas, Salvatorian Sister Patrice Colletti gave several examples of slavery today, including a story about a 20-something-year-old woman who was first sold for $2,000 in China. Later she was taken to France and sold for $4,000. The woman was sold again, this time for $10,000, and sent to the United States. She worked in a sweatshop and came with her own immigration papers.

In 2009, *The Catholic Key* newspaper in the Diocese of Kansas City-St. Joseph, Missouri, reported that the woman was fed one package of noodles per day. She slept on the floor where she worked and was severely beaten twice while trying to escape.

The United States Conference of Catholic Bishops notes that, "The U.S. government estimates that approximately 800,000 people are trafficked across international borders each year, about 14,500-17,500 of them in the United States."

Think About It As we mentioned earlier, slavery exists in our world today—even in the United States.

- **Research modern-day slavery (sometimes called human trafficking), including the Church's teaching about and response to it, and report your findings to the class.**

- **Read about and report on one person's experience of slavery. Look to see how human dignity was preserved and/or was upheld in some way despite the horrific circumstances.**

- **Find out more about human trafficking and the "worst forms of child labor." What do they involve and what moral responsibilities do we have to respond?**

- **What statistic or piece of information about child labor or human trafficking left an impression on you? Describe your reaction.**

- **What can your school do to help raise awareness and bring an end to modern slavery?**

Go to the student site at
hs.osvcurriculum.com

Going Before Pharaoh

Starting in Exodus Chapter 5, we read about Moses and Aaron meeting with Pharaoh on a series of occasions. Pharaoh's initial response is to make life harder for the slaves. He tells the taskmasters to take away the straw the slaves use to make bricks but to require them to maintain the same production. God then unleashes plagues to afflict the Egyptians. After each plague, Pharaoh's heart is hardened and he refuses to let the Israelites go. The final plague is particularly harsh, but it sets in motion the pivotal turning point in the history of Israel. All the firstborn of the Egyptians (and even of their animals) die. God tells the Israelites to apply blood from the sacrificed Passover Lamb on the lintel and two doorposts of their homes, and they are spared.

GO TO THE SOURCE

When Pharaoh refuses to free the Israelites, God unleashes a series of plagues to convince the Egyptian leader to change his mind.

Read about each of the ten plagues in Exodus 7-12.

○ What stands out for you?

○ What insights or questions does it raise for you?

Passover Is About Today

Jews and Christians don't look upon what is recounted in Scripture as merely past events. Rather, we understand how those events speak to us today. When Jews partake of a **Seder** meal on **Passover**, they remember the past but also link the *past* to their *present* reality as well as to their *future* hope. Here's the *Catechism*'s explanation:

> *In the sense of Sacred Scripture, the* memorial *is not merely the recollection of past events but the proclamation of the mighty works wrought by God for men. In the liturgical celebration of these events, they become in a certain way present and real. This is how Israel understands its liberation from Egypt: every time Passover is celebrated, the Exodus events are made present to the memory of believers so that they may conform their lives to them.*
>
> —CCC, 1363

This is similar for Catholics during the celebration of the Eucharist, which is the memorial of the Passover of Christ. Jesus became the Passover or Paschal Lamb and the Exodus—the way out—for all humankind to be released from sin and death. By the divine action of the Holy Spirit, Christ's **Paschal Mystery**—the saving work brought about by his life, death, Resurrection, and Ascension—is made present in each celebration of the Eucharist. By our participation in the Sacrament of the Eucharist, and in all Sacraments, we take part in Christ's Paschal Mystery, personally dying to sin and rising to new life in the Holy Spirit.

Tell What is Pharaoh's initial response to God's request to let his People go?

Connect How are the celebration of the Passover and the Eucharist similar?

Seder the symbolic Jewish Passover meal ritual marking the start of Passover and celebrated each year near the beginning of spring

Passover Jewish holy day commemorating God's deliverance of the Chosen People from death by ordering the Jews to sprinkle the blood of the lamb on their doorposts in Egypt; also called Pesach or Pasch

Paschal Mystery Christ's work of redemption brought about by his Passion, death, Resurrection, and Ascension. We celebrate the Paschal Mystery in the liturgy of the Church, during which Christ's saving work is made present and communicated, most especially in the Sacrament of the Eucharist.

THE Eucharistic CELEBRATION

The faith of the Church has joined two distinct but inseparable understandings of the nature of the Mass—sacrificial memorial and sacred banquet. Christ linked them together from the beginning by his words at the Last Supper as he offered his Body and Blood to eat and drink. This revealed to his disciples that the deeper meaning of the meal was his sacrificial offering of himself to the Father.

The Eucharist is a sacrifice because it makes present Christ's sacrifice on the cross. It does this because it is the memorial of his Paschal Mystery and makes available the effects of Christ's redemptive sacrifice. We share in this sacrifice by joining in Christ's offering, both for our own sins and the entire Communion of Saints—all the faithful on Earth, in Heaven, and in Purgatory. Our participation truly is a "holy communion" since our prayers are joined with those of the entire Mystical Body, living and dead, with whom we are united in Christ through Baptism. It is a wondrous mystery that is called a "holy communion" because it unites us with Christ in Heaven, perpetually interceding with his Father on our behalf, as well as with the members of the Body of Christ, who join their earthly prayers to our own. To describe in words the scope of this mystery requires the skill of a poet, in addition to that of a theologian. This ancient prayer seems to be the work of both:

O sacred banquet in which Christ
is received as food,
The memory of his Passion is renewed,
The soul is filled with grace,
And a pledge of the life to come
is given to us!

>> How would you describe the Mass as both a memorial and a meal?

What words and actions during the Liturgy of the Eucharist make you think of "sacrificial memorial" and "sacred banquet"?

Pesach—Jews Celebrate the Exodus

PASSOVER, OR PESACH, is one of the holiest days in the Jewish year. It takes place at the beginning of spring. An important activity during Pesach is a meal called a Seder, which is celebrated at home. In fact, "being home" is an important theme of the holy day. *Home* is different from living under someone else's control (slavery in Egypt) or wandering about in the wilderness. It's customary to invite a stranger to partake of the meal. Hospitality, after all, is one more reminder that the people of Israel began as strangers in search of a home themselves.

The Seder meal provides an opportunity for Jews to remind themselves of God's saving action, setting them free from slavery and leading them to the Promised Land. Again, the point is not just that it happened to their ancestors; God's liberation is active and necessary today.

There are specific questions to be asked by the youngest member of the family to the oldest. Each question addresses the underlying question: *Why is this night different from all other nights?* Answers include:

- On other nights we eat leavened or unleavened bread, but this night we eat only matzoh.
- On other nights we eat vegetables, but on this night we eat bitter herbs.
- On all other nights we do not dip [our vegetables], but on this night we dip twice.
- On all other nights we eat either sitting up or reclining, but on this night we all recline.

(The translation of these questions and answers are from: George Robinson, *Essential Judaism*.)

Everything about the Seder is meant to keep alive the Exodus *experience*.

>> **Research and report on the foods served at a Seder. Explain the significance of each.**

The Seder commemorates the theme of Exodus— liberation from slavery and oppression. Create an artistic representation of this theme in a song, poem, story, or visual representation.

SECTION 2 REVIEW

QUICK REVIEW

1a. **Recall** Why is Moses considered the most influential Jewish person in history?

b. **Recall** How did God appear to Moses?

c. **Analyze** Why does Moses think he should not lead the slaves out of Egypt?

2a. **Infer** Why would the last plague have convinced the Pharaoh to free the slaves?

b. **Connect** Which modern Jewish holiday celebrates the Israelites leaving Egypt?

c. **Analyze** How does celebrating Passover today connect the past and the present?

3a. **Recall** What do Jews do at a Seder meal?

b. **Connect** How was Josephine Bakhita like the Hebrew people in Egypt?

c. **Explain** Is slavery a thing of the past?

Listen and Discuss In a small group, discuss these questions.

○ Why is it surprising to us that slavery still exists?

○ Can anything be done about slavery in today's world? Explain your answer.

SELF-ASSESS

Which statement best reflects where you are now?

☐ I'm confident enough about the material in this section to be able to explain it to someone else.

☐ I have a good grasp of the material in this section, but I could use more review.

☐ I'm lost. I need help catching up before moving on.

God Creates a People

f someone attempted to explain the Exodus "in a nutshell" it might go something like this: Slaves are suffering brutal oppression. They are treated like nobodies, considered good only for hard labor. The God of their ancestors, the almighty one, true God who has not forgotten them, steps in to set them free. He guides them and provides for them during a long and arduous journey through desert wasteland. He gives them laws through Moses and an identity as a people destined for greatness. With God's help they conquer a land where they can live and prosper as free people, so long as they remain faithful to their covenant with God and live up to what he expects of all people.

Those expectations were important, since moving from being slaves to being free is not easy. Even today people of oppressed countries struggle to figure out how to live when their nation becomes free or they relocate to a free nation. Every part of their being and behavior must be transformed. For instance, one of the directives for the Passover meal is that those present are to recline at the table while eating. This reminds everyone that free people relax while eating. Slaves, on the other hand, eat on the run, ready to drop everything at their master's beck and call.

Once the Israelites are free of the Egyptians and out in the wilderness, they are not alone. God accompanies them every step of the way. He guides them with a cloud by day and a pillar of fire by night. He provides food and water. Nonetheless, whenever anything goes wrong, the people grumble.

When Pharaoh and six hundred chariots pursue the Israelites, they chastise Moses: "What have you done to us, bringing us out of Egypt? . . . For it would have been better for us to serve the Egyptians than to die in the wilderness" (Exodus 14:11-12).

> *Identify times in your own life when you "grumble" about difficulties despite the fact that you are undoubtedly being cared for.*
>
> **>> What insight does this story from Exodus offer for your own grumblings?**
>
> REFLECT

The Exodus from Egypt to the Promised Land, from slavery to liberation, is a journey that takes forty years. The Israelites have much to ponder during their time in the desert.

- What are they supposed to do as a free people?

- How are they to treat one another? What should be their priorities?

- How can they sustain this precious but fragile gift called "freedom"?

Their questions are partially answered in an event that takes place on a mountain in the midst of the wilderness: God gives Moses a set of laws to guide the people's relationship with him and one another.

Recall How do the Israelites react when Pharaoh and his chariots pursue them after their release from slavery?

Summarize How does Passover help Jewish people recall the change from slavery to freedom?

MY FAITH

YOUR
EXODUS

Use this space to build your own faith portfolio.

Make some private notes about your own spiritual growth.

Keep track of your own faith journey—where are you with relying on the Father? What about Jesus is most inspiring? How aware are you of the Spirit's action?

Mark the spiritual commitments, questions, and actions that are important to you.

Here are some examples that may help you begin answering these important questions about your own spiritual exodus. You may have others.

You are on a spiritual journey a little like that of the ancient Israelites. They journeyed from slavery to the Promised Land. Even though they had their freedom, they wandered for forty years before they got to the Promised Land.

○ You are making a spiritual journey from childhood to the "promised land" of adult discipleship.

Spiritually speaking, what are the things still enslaving you? What will set you free?

○ It took the Israelites forty years, in part because they got distracted, worshipped false gods, wanted to be like God, argued, fought, etc.

What is distracting you? What do you need to avoid? What will it take for you to get to the promised land of adulthood and discipleship?

○ The Israelites followed a cloud by day and a burning flame at night all the way to the Promised Land.

What direction do you think God will send your way? Who or what will you trust to get you there?

Consider these questions thoughtfully and write your personal thoughts in the space provided.

Wrestle with these questions about your spiritual journey, make some notes, and remember that you may want to share some of this at the end of the course.

Need to be Free From	Need to be Free To
Unrealistic academic expectations	Do my best but accept my limits
Family tensions	Trust in God's help
Boredom	Invest in my own interests
Over-scheduling	Cut back
Anger	Let go
Fear	Take a shot

Go to the student site at
hs.osvcurriculum.com

Discipleship . . . within the Body of Christ . . . for the glory of God and the good of the world

PRIMARY SOURCES

There's a Great Camp Meeting, from *American Negro Songs* by John W. Work, 1940

Spirituals were sung when African American slaves in the United States called on God to hear their plight as he had once heard the Israelites' cries when they were slaves in Egypt. Read these lyrics to *There's a Great Camp Meeting*, from *American Negro Songs* by John W. Work, 1940.

Go to the student site at **hs.osvcurriculum.com**

O, Walk together children
Don't you get weary
Walk together children
Don't you get weary
Walk together children
Don't you get weary
There's a great camp meeting
 in the Promised Land

Talk together children
Don't you get weary
Talk together children
Don't you get weary
Talk together children
Don't you get weary
There's a great camp meeting
 in the Promised Land

Going to shout and never tire
Shout and never tire
Shout and never tire
There's a great camp meeting
 in the Promised Land

O, Get you ready children
Don't you get weary
Get you ready children
Don't you get weary
Get you ready children
Don't you get weary
There's a great camp meeting
 in the Promised Land

For Jesus is a-coming

Don't you get weary
Jesus is a-coming
Don't you get weary
Jesus is a-coming
Don't you get weary
There's a great camp meeting
 in the Promised Land

O, I feel the spirit. . . .

Now I'm getting happy

>> What might be the meaning of the line: "There's a great camp meeting in the Promised Land"?

Write a song or poem about your own experiences of feeling emotionally or spiritually enslaved, burdened, and/or your hope for freedom.

Gift of the Law

At first, laws might seem like a strange gift to give to people who just gained their freedom. Former slaves might reason: "We had rules imposed upon us when we were slaves. Now that we're free, we don't want any rules. Let us do whatever we want to do." However, the **Decalogue**, or Ten Commandments given by God on Mount Sinai, summarizes the entire "Law of Moses." They are the fundamental moral laws given by God to his Chosen People to help them live by the covenant—the solemn agreement he had made with the Israelites. In the covenant, God promised the Israelites to be their God, and they promised to be his people.

The Commandments are listed in two different places in the Bible. The first is in Exodus 20 and then again in Deuteronomy 5. They have served as one of the most important documents in all of human history. These laws articulate what the Israelites stand for. *We must never forget God or substitute anything else for God . . . We must set aside time every week to remember God and express our gratitude to him . . . We must take care of our old ones and treat with great reverence the life of everyone . . . We must always respect persons and all the goods of the Earth.* Jesus and the Church make it very clear—the laws of the Ten Commandments still apply to us today.

"There is no other" [God] . . . is a clear statement of **monotheism**, or belief that there is one God, even though some Israelites apparently continue to try their luck with other gods. Just before a listing of the Ten Commandments, Moses admonishes the people: "So acknowledge today and take to heart that the LORD is God in heaven above and on the earth beneath; there is no other" (Deuteronomy 4:39).

The liberated Israelites had a series of laws from God to govern themselves. These laws can be found in the books of Exodus, Leviticus, Numbers, and Deuteronomy. Many are interesting and reflective of the time, for example, the appropriate punishment when someone's bull gouges a neighbor. Free and God-fearing people run into many conflicts and controversies concerning proper behavior, so these laws would help them understand how to better live as God intends.

You might wonder about including a question such as "What is the most humane way to slaughter animals?" in the Bible. However, decisions like this connect to the essentials of society at the time and how they relate to living the law. Among these laws are forgiveness of debts, no interest charged on loans, payment for workers, and the right of the poor to pick from leftovers in the field. God looked out for the poor, and he wanted his people to do no less. Why did God make this part of his Law? In the Book of Deuteronomy, he says the poor will always be here. We should extend our hand to the poor, our brothers and sisters, he said. Jesus echoed these thoughts that we will always have the poor, but the Apostles would not always have him in their midst. Jesus invites us to recognize him in the poor. Saint Rose of Lima did when she said

GO TO **THE SOURCE**

Whether you ever study law or not, the laws of God have governed people for the millennia.

- Page through Leviticus, Numbers, and Deuteronomy. What particular concerns for a good society do you see expressed in the various laws found there?

- In these books, find five laws meant to clear up conflicts in the Israelite community.

- In these same books, find two laws that govern one's relationship with God, such as in worship or service to him.

- This section of the Bible teaches that belief in God is necessary for a good society. What role do you see God playing in American society? How can belief in the one true God be expressed in a society made up of many religions and beliefs?

Decalogue literally "ten words" or "ten teachings," referring to the Ten Commandments, given by God to Moses on Mount Sinai

monotheism belief that there is one God

to her mother: "When we serve the poor and the sick, we serve Jesus. We must not fail to help our neighbors, because in them we serve Jesus" (CCC, 2449).

The Jordan River and Beyond

At the end of the Book of Deuteronomy, the Israelites arrive near the land of Canaan and the Jordan River. The Jordan is both the real and the symbolic last barrier to cross before they enter the Promised Land. Moses again speaks on God's behalf, giving last minute instructions about how to keep the covenant. The words are Moses' farewell address, since he knows that he himself won't enter the Promised Land because he broke faith with God and didn't show God's holiness to the sons of Israel (Deuteronomy 32:51). God promises, however, to go before them and lead them to victory so that this land flowing with milk and honey will be theirs. Joshua, the hand-picked successor to Moses, takes over as leader of the Israelites during this crucial time.

God's Law guides the Israelites as they become a nation. Lest they forget, the Israelites are to read the Law aloud every seventh year. Following God's laws brings life and protection to everyone, including those who are poor.

While there are a variety of Hebrew terms for "poor," the one that appears most frequently in Scripture is *anawim*. *Anawim* refers to those who lack enough to provide for their basic material needs. Becoming poor through injustice, the *anawim* are without the means to protect themselves from oppression. In ancient Israel, the widow and the orphan were usually in need of protection since they had no adult male to provide financial support. Also, strangers (foreigners who traveled through Israel) were without protection. They were not poor due to laziness or carelessness, but because of oppression or the social structure. If the rest of the Israelites did not provide for the *anawim*, they would become homeless beggars. God foretells some of what will take place in the Promised Land. He gives a song to Moses who recites it for all the people. The Israelites become a nation in their own right. In fact, a few hundred years after the Exodus they became a kingdom rivaling other centers of power in the area. With increased power and wealth, however, came increased temptations to stray from being faithful to God. A good lens through which to view the next time period in Israel's story is provided by a group of inspired preachers called the prophets.

Identify What do the Ten Commandments summarize?

Evaluate Why do the Israelites read the Law out loud every seventh year?

Christian Orthodox clergy and pilgrims at the traditional ceremony of blessing the Jordan River on Epiphany Day

Moses' final message from God before the Israelites enter the Promised Land can be found in the Book of Deuteronomy.

○ Read Deuteronomy 30:8–31:4. What part of God's message stands out for you?

○ Read the *Song of Moses* in Deuteronomy 32:1-47. Summarize the change he made from his first encounter with God in the burning bush.

SECTION 3 REVIEW

QUICK REVIEW

1a. Explain How did God show himself to the Hebrews in the desert?

b. Recall How did the Hebrews react to problems in the desert?

c. Recall What is the primary content of the books of Leviticus, Deuteronomy, and Numbers?

2a. Define What is monotheism?

b. Summarize How do the Israelites come to dominate Israel?

Listen and Discuss Discuss these questions in a small group.

○ Who are the *anawim* in the Americas?

○ Who are the *anawim* in the world?

○ How are they treated in our country?

Pray Compose a short prayer for peace in the Holy Land.

SELF-ASSESS

Which statement best reflects where you are now?

☐ I'm confident enough about the material in this section to be able to explain it to someone else.

☐ I have a good grasp of the material in this section, but I could use more review.

☐ I'm lost. I need help catching up before moving on.

God Reassures His People

> I will raise up for them a prophet like you [Moses] from among their own people; I will put my words in the mouth of the prophet, who shall speak to them everything that I command.
>
> —Deuteronomy 18:18

prophet someone chosen by God to speak for him

Even though Moses was called a prophet, he was not the first one. The first person to be called a **prophet** in the Bible is Abraham (Genesis 20:7). In general, a biblical prophet is an intermediary between God and people, someone sent from God, and thus someone who speaks for God. In a more narrow sense, the prophets of Israel lived and preached around the same time that Israel had its kings and judges. One might think that after taking over Canaan and establishing kingship over the land, the Bible would focus on the kings who would rule the Israelites.

But focus during this time period is not on kings, but on prophets. The prophets speak for God. Other nations had "prophets" of sorts. For instance, when Moses went before Pharaoh, the Egyptians had their own priests or magicians who tried to match the power of their gods up against Moses and his God. Throughout the Middle East of the time, certain people claimed to have access to divine power or special knowledge that could come only from the gods. The prophets of Israel, however, are unique in a number of ways.

In other Middle Eastern countries, prophets worked for the king. They advised him and supported him in ruling the nation. The prophets of the Old Testament "worked" for the one, true God, and he worked through them. Through the prophets, God offers the hope of salvation for those who heed the radical redemption proclaimed by the prophets (see CCC, 64). In Israel, most prophets came from outside the political establishment. Many biblical prophets were strong critics of the kings and of the people, at times placing their lives in peril for doing so. The prophet Amos, for example, warned of God's judgment on Israel: "I will not revoke the punishment; because they sell the righteous for silver, and the needy for a pair of sandals—they who trample the head of the poor into the dust of the earth, and push the afflicted out of the way" (Amos 2:6-7).

Through the prophets, God calls Israel and all nations to turn to him, the source of salvation. The prophets helped people to see that God never stopped loving them. Because of that love, he would always forgive them and save his people, if they repented and turned to him (see CCC, 218).

The mission of the prophets included:

- Challenging the people to live by the covenant and stop behaving in ways that broke the law

- Teaching the faith

- Advocating for just treatment of those who were poor or suffering

- Preaching radical redemption and conversion of heart

- Interceding on behalf of the People when speaking to the LORD

(see CCC 716, 762, 2581, 2595).

Frequently in the Gospels Jesus refers to "the law and the prophets." By "law" he means the Torah, the first five books of the Bible. For Jesus and the prophets before him, there can never be a contradiction between the Torah and the prophetic message. The prophets constantly admonish people to repent and change their ways, to put God first in their lives, to praise and worship God in the words and actions. The way to do that is to be faithful to the Law as expressed in the Torah. People get into trouble when they stray from following God's way as expressed in the Law.

The prophets often criticize kings, queens, and the people for wanting to follow some other false god whom they believe can help them. For instance, in 1 Kings 16:31, it mentions that King Jeroboam and his wife, Jezebel, worship the god Baal. Purification, or cleansing, from such infidelities is a central message of the prophets.

As the *Catechism* points out, it is "the poor and humble of the Lord" for whom the prophets speak (CCC, 64). The prophets of Israel make the strongest possible case that worship of God cannot be separated from actions on behalf of poor, oppressed, and suffering people. So it's not surprising that some people who heard Jesus viewed him as a prophet, and that by our Baptism Catholics are called to share in Jesus' priestly, prophetic, and kingly mission.

Today people might associate prophecy with foretelling the future. That's not what the Hebrew prophets did. They were chosen by God to receive communications from him, which they transmitted to the people in his name. In other words, they were spokesmen or intermediaries for God. Often these communications included warnings. The prophets would warn the Hebrew people when they were headed down the wrong path and that if they continued harsh judgment would follow.

The Hebrew prophets speak out during dark times. Nevertheless, it is striking how hopeful they are. Their message of hope comes not from the way current events unfold for danger constantly looms on the horizon. It doesn't come from people changing their ways; nations and people are often misdirected in where they place their trust. Hope comes from only one source—the one, true God who revealed himself to the Hebrews through great leaders like Abraham, Moses, and David. Today we see the Hebrew prophets as pointing to a future hope that reaches its fulfillment in the one who is far more than a prophet—Jesus, Son of God himself. The prophets prepared for the coming of Christ by proclaiming the coming of the Messiah, thus leading to the expectation of the Messiah, and announcing a new Spirit (see CCC, 711).

Name Who is the first person in the Bible to be called a prophet?

Select What aspect of the biblical prophets' mission do you think is most important and why?

Research
Choose one of the prophetic books and summarize how that book demonstrates the seven characteristics of the prophets of Israel.

Words of the Prophets

The Hebrew prophets preached their message more than twenty-five hundred years ago. Throughout the centuries up to today, their words retain their power to challenge and inspire. Many phrases and images used by the prophets have become part of our common heritage. And their words on how to live faithfully are as alive and vibrant as ever. Their message is, indeed, as timely as today's headlines.

For instance, Isaiah calls us to set aside war-making for peace-making: "They shall beat their swords into plowshares, and their spears into pruning hooks; nation shall not lift up sword against nation, neither shall they learn war any more" (Isaiah 2:4).

We sing a version of the words of the prophet Isaiah in the midst of every Mass during the Liturgy of the Eucharist: "Holy, Holy, Holy Lord God of hosts. Heaven and earth are full of your glory" (see Isaiah 6:3).

Jesus chose the words of Isaiah when beginning his public ministry. He read aloud in his home synagogue:

The spirit of the Lord God is upon me, because the Lord has anointed me; he has sent me to bring good news to the oppressed, to bind up the brokenhearted, to proclaim liberty to the captives, and release to the prisoners; to proclaim the year of the Lord's favor . . .

—Isaiah 61:1-2 (see Luke 4:18-19)

From the very beginning, the followers of Jesus saw writings of the prophets as signs of future events surrounding the birth, life, death, and Resurrection of Jesus. Their message of faithfulness to the covenant and hope in the midst of difficult times mirrors that embodied in Jesus. Today, the Church proclaims the message of the prophets in the liturgy throughout the seasons, especially during the seasons of Advent and Lent. The following are some key insights from Old Testament prophets and how those insights relate to discipleship within the Church today.

Now there was a great wind, so strong that it was splitting mountains and breaking rocks in pieces before the LORD, but the LORD was not in the wind; and after the wind an earthquake, but the LORD was not in the earthquake; and after the earthquake a fire, but the LORD was not in the fire; and after the fire a sound of sheer silence. When Elijah heard it, he wrapped his face in his mantle and went out and stood at the entrance of the cave.

—1 Kings 19:11-13

The Still, Small Voice What can we make of this account? In a cave on a mountainside, Elijah learns that God is to pass by. We might expect God to be accompanied by thunder and lightning, earthquakes and fire. But in this story God is found in . . . sheer silence. Some translate the phrase as "a still, small voice" or "a gentle whisper." The story sets up a contrast as to how to find God. There is a subtle message here about how God often operates. A God of "sheer silence" is easily missed and not to be identified with any external show of power and might.

One wonders how many passersby on a road just outside of Jerusalem saw three men hanging on a cross two thousand years ago. Did anyone recognize one of these men as the Son of God himself? On the cross, Jesus did not show off his power; rather, he emptied himself of power and succumbed to

REFLECT

>> **How has the Spirit of God spoken to you most often?**

We started this chapter by giving you an opportunity to tell a story. Now, here at the end of the chapter, it's time to once again write down or tell a story of when you sense the Holy Spirit talking to you.

Was it in the still, small voice? A whisper? Or was it a loud, obvious, "can-I-please-have-your-attention" kind of thing?

Rate yourself on a scale of one to five (five being excellent). To what extent "Do you leave space to hear God's whisper, calling you forth into goodness"?

When God speaks to you, is it most often a voice within or through the voice of another person?

death. Without faith, we could easily miss his divine presence. Christians have referred to this passage from Kings many times to remind ourselves of how to listen for the gentle voice of God and to recognize God's quiet but true presence in our lives. When Pope Benedict XVI spoke to young people during his 2008 visit to the United States, he asked them: "Do you leave space to hear God's whisper, calling you forth into goodness? Friends, do not be afraid of silence or stillness, listen to God" ("Meeting with Young People and Seminarians," April 19, 2008).

Explain
- How would you describe the prophet's role in communicating God's will to the Israelites and to us?
- The Bible warns against "false prophets." How might we distinguish between true and false prophets?
- Who are the prophetic voices in your life calling you to live an authentic life?
- When you were baptized, you became a sharer in the prophetic voice of Jesus. How do you live out this role?

Hosea's Unfaithful Wife Often the prophets *act out* their message rather than simply using words. The beautiful, parental image of God caring for his dear children who have gone astray comes at a heavy price for the prophet Hosea. He is told by God to marry Gomer, a prostitute who continues to be unfaithful to Hosea. God tells Hosea to remain faithful to Gomer, even though she is being unfaithful with other men. This husband-wife relationship mirrors the relationship God has with his people. The people worship other gods, while the one true God remains faithful to these children whom he taught to walk and held close to his cheeks. Much of the Book of Hosea describes the horrible scenes of destruction that will befall the people of Israel. However, ever faithful, God ends on a note of reassurance: "I will heal their disloyalty; I will love them freely, for my anger has turned from them" (Hosea 14:4).

Throughout his ministry, Jesus echoes God's message of forgiveness that Hosea made known. In helping his followers understand the nature of sin, and God's merciful care, Jesus told the story of the Prodigal Son (Luke 15:11-32), a repentant sinner who is welcomed home. Even on the cross, Jesus accepts the remorse of a thief who is crucified next to him (Luke 23:43). Two Gospels record Jesus saying that he wants to be like a mother hen who gathers her chicks under her wings to protect them (Matthew 23:37, Luke 13:34).

Prophets of Social Justice The prophets Amos and Micah set up a contrast to explain what ails the people of Israel. The Israelites place their trust in burnt offerings. They're good at following prescribed rituals in worshipping the God of Israel—and perhaps other gods as well. Like all the prophets, Amos and Micah make it clear that God doesn't view these acts of worship as the test of their faithfulness. Giving alms to the poor and the needy as well as treating them justly are acts that are pleasing to God and are signs that people worship him.

Spiritual Practice of TESTIMONY

A spiritual practice for the life of discipleship

Testimony is the spiritual practice of speaking the truth about what's right, noble, or just. Testimony means pointing out with words or actions to one person or thirty-one people that something is not acceptable.

The prophets mentioned in this course were known for their practice of testimony. But a lot of people hated prophets because of it. The same can happen to you when you point out things like the following:

- that a racial slur is not right
- e-mailing that hurtful rumor is wrong
- pouting in practice is hurting the team
- making excuses so someone else does all the work is a cop-out

Testimony is a *spiritual* practice because it keeps asking you to pass the honesty test. And every time you practice it, you get stronger. You develop the habit of *standing up for the good*. You stand on the side of the angels.

>> When in the past have you practiced testimony?

What did it require of you?

What did you learn from the way you did it?

When have you reacted against testimony that confronted you?

What did that testimony help you see about yourself?

What might the Spirit be asking you to practice testimony on these days?

In the spirit of Amos and Micah, justice according to Jesus means the Kingdom of God belongs to the poor, hungry people will be satisfied, mercy is for the merciful, and God's children are peacemakers (see Matthew 5:3-11 and Luke 6:20-23). Like the prophets, Jesus encourages those who are poor and challenges people of means to share their good fortune with those in need.

> *With what shall I come before the LORD,*
> *and bow myself before God on high?*
> *Shall I come before him with burnt offerings,*
> *with calves a year old? . . .*
> *He has told you, O mortal, what is good;*
> *and what does the LORD require of you*
> *but to do justice, and to love kindness,*
> *and to walk humbly with your God?*
>
> —Micah 6:6, 8

> *I hate, I despise your festivals, and I take*
> *no delight in your solemn assemblies . . .*
> *But let justice roll down like waters,*
> *and righteousness like an ever-flowing stream.*
>
> —Amos 5:21, 24

Jesus also reflected the sentiments of Amos and Micah when he instructed people not to call attention to themselves when they pray, fast, or give alms to the poor (Matthew 6:1-18). Another strong parallel is the final judgment discourse told by Jesus in Matthew 25:31-46, in which he describes feeding the hungry and clothing the naked as prerequisites for entering Heaven.

Jeremiah and the New Covenant A true covenant relationship is rooted in our hearts, not based on externals alone. People can overlook and set aside laws written on stone tablets, as impressive as that image may be. Laws written on our hearts are not as easily dismissed.

Jeremiah uses the symbolism of marriage to describe the relationship that exists between God and his Chosen People. It's an appropriate image for a loving relationship, one that is found elsewhere in both the Old and New Testaments.

> *The days are surely coming, says the LORD,*
> *when I will make a new covenant with the*
> *house of Israel and the house of Judah. It will*
> *not be like the covenant that I made with*
> *their ancestors when I took them by the hand*
> *to bring them out of the land of Egypt—a*
> *covenant that they broke, though I was*
> *their husband, says the LORD. But this is the*
> *covenant that I will make with the house of*
> *Israel after those days, says the LORD: I will*
> *put my law within them, and I will write it on*
> *their hearts; and I will be their God, and they*
> *shall be my people.*
>
> —Jeremiah 31:31-33

Jeremiah's image of a covenant that we bear in our hearts sets the stage for the insight we receive from the First Letter of John mentioned earlier: "God is love" (1 John 4:8 and 4:16). Christians often refer to bearing Christ in their hearts. And since the time of Saint Paul, the Church has seen herself as the "bride of Christ," "so as to present the church to himself in splendor, without a spot or wrinkle or anything of the kind" (Ephesians 5:27).

Notice the feminine pronoun "herself" used for the Church. Once again, Christians affirm that "the days that are coming," foretold by Jeremiah, reach their fulfillment in Jesus and in his "bride," the Church.

Ezekiel and the Dry Bones Ezekiel prophesies during particularly dark times when the tribe of Judah lives in exile in Babylon. The holy city of Jerusalem itself is about to be overrun by invading armies. Ezekiel is handed a scroll filled with "words of lamentation and mourning and woe" (Ezekiel 2:10). He is told by God to eat the scroll, which he does, only to find that "it was as sweet as honey" (Ezekiel 3:3). The prophet receives a famous vision of great hope. The nation of Israel is seemingly as dead as dry bones—"very dry" bones. And yet God can and will breathe life into them.

> The hand of the LORD came upon me, and he brought me out by the spirit of the LORD and set me down in the middle of a valley; it was full of bones. He led me all around them; there were very many lying in the valley, and they were very dry. He said to me, "Mortal, can these bones live?" I answered, "O Lord GOD, you know." Then he said to me, "Prophesy to these bones, and say to them: O dry bones, hear the word of the LORD. Thus says the Lord GOD to these bones: I will cause breath to enter you, and you shall live.
>
> —Ezekiel 37:1-5

The Church applies this wonderful image of dry bones coming to life to the experience of resurrection and new life in Jesus. On the surface, our fate may seem to be ending up a heap of dry bones when we die. But through Christ we have our own resurrection, foretold in the Gospel according to Matthew after Jesus gave up his spirit: "The earth shook, and the rocks were split. The tombs also were opened, and many bodies of the saints who had fallen asleep were raised" (Matthew 27:51-52). We also refer to the Ezekiel vision of dry bones coming back to life when we experience God's grace moving in our lives, providing spiritual or emotional healing after situations that have left us feeling lifeless.

Isaiah's Peaceable Kingdom You may have seen the one of the many versions of the painting titled *The Peaceable Kingdom,* by the early nineteenth century artist Edward Hicks. He based some of his painting on a passage from Isaiah, in which the prophet gives us this image of lions and lambs living together without fear, with a child leading them. This child will be from the "root of Jesse," the father of David of Bethlehem, Isaiah says. He will be an advocate for the poor and the meek, dealing justly with them. In an earlier chapter, Isaiah prophesies that "the young woman is with child and shall bear a son, and shall name him Immanuel" (Isaiah 7:14).

Christians link Isaiah's prophecy of a child bringing about peace with the birth of Jesus. The Gospel according to Matthew quotes this passage: "'Look, the virgin shall conceive and bear a son, and they shall name him Emmanuel,' which means, 'God is with

Create

The prophets used rich concrete imagery to communicate God's message: different animals, honey, bones, streams, sky, storms, brides, husbands, hearts, body parts, etc.

○ Quietly open your mind and heart, saying a short prayer, focusing on a particular Scripture passage, meditating in whatever way you feel comfortable. What is God telling you? What message about God do you feel compelled to share? Write a poem or draw a picture using one or more vivid images to share this message as a prophetic statement.

us'" (Matthew 1:23). The angel's announcement of the birth of Jesus to the shepherds in the Gospel according to Luke brings glad tidings: "And suddenly there was with the angel a multitude of the heavenly host, praising God and saying, 'Glory to God in the highest heaven, and on earth peace among those whom he favors!'" (Luke 2:13-14). This peace is more than just the absence of violence and war, but peace in a deeper sense of well-being and security found in trusting God, relying on him, being faithful to his will. Peace is one of the fruits of the Holy Spirit, and one of the goals of Christian discipleship.

The wolf shall live with the lamb,
the leopard shall lie down with the kid,
the calf and the lion and the fatling together,
and a little child shall lead them. . . .
They will not hurt or destroy on all my holy mountain;
for the earth will be full of the knowledge of the LORD
as the waters cover the sea.

—Isaiah 11:6, 9

Identify What prophet did Jesus quote when starting his public ministry?

Conclude What connection can we make between Jesus and Ezekiel's image of the dry bones?

SECTION **4 REVIEW**

QUICK REVIEW

1a. Define What is a prophet?

b. List Give some examples of the mission of the prophets.

c. Analyze Why do warnings from prophets still challenge us today?

2a. Analyze Why did Jesus use words from Isaiah as he began his public ministry?

b. Recall Which prophet used images of maternal love to describe God?

3a. Explain Why were acts of worship less important to Micah and Amos?

b. Recall What image is associated with Jeremiah's covenant?

c. Analyze What does Ezekiel's image of dry bones prefigure?

ACT

Design a T-shirt that could be worn by one of the prophets listed in the book.

○ Read some of the prophecies in the Old Testament.

○ Draw pictures of some of the images you find.

○ Design a T-shirt that conveys the prophet's message.

Pray Compose a short prayer asking for help in hearing the voice of "God's whisper."

SELF-ASSESS

Which statement best reflects where you are now?

☐ I'm confident enough about the material in this section to be able to explain it to someone else.

☐ I have a good grasp of the material in this section, but I could use more review.

☐ I'm lost. I need help catching up before moving on.

PRAYER

Ant. Lead me, Lord, in the path of your commandments.

Psalm 119:33–40

Teach me the demands of your precepts
and I will keep them to the end.
Train me to observe your law,
to keep it with my heart.

Guide me in the path of your commands;
for there is my delight.
Bend my heart to your will
and not to love of gain.

Keep my eyes from what is false;
by your word, give me life.
Keep the promise you have made
to the servant who fears you.

Keep me from the scorn I dread,
for your decrees are good.
See, I long for your precepts:
then in your justice, give me life.

Psalm-prayer
In your justice give us life, Father. Do not allow greed to possess us but
incline our hearts to your commands. Give us understanding to know
your law and direct us according to your will.

Ant. Lead me, Lord, in the path of your commandments.

(From The Liturgy of the Hours IV)

CHAPTER 5 REVIEW

TERMS

Use each of the following terms in a sentence that shows you know what the term means. You may include more than one term in a sentence.

Original Sin

covenant

Promised Land

Pharaohs

YHWH

Seder

Passover

Paschal Mystery

Decalogue

monotheism

prophet

PEOPLE

Tell why each person or term is important.

1. Moses

2. Aaron

3. Abraham

4. Isaiah

5. Elijah

6. Hosea

7. Amos and Micah

8. Jeremiah

9. Ezekiel

UNDERSTANDING

Answer each question and complete each exercise.

SECTION 1

1. **Evaluate** How is learning from stories valuable?

2. **Analyze** Which qualities of a story do the creation accounts have?

3. **Discuss** Are the stories of Abraham and his descendants more real than those of Adam and his family? Why or why not?

4. **List** What are some of the religious truths God conveys in the book of Genesis?

SECTION 2

5. **Explain** Why is Moses considered the most influential Jewish person in history?

6. **Define** Who is YHWH? Why don't we know how to pronounce this word?

7. **Recall** How does God try to convince Pharaoh to free the Israelite slaves? What finally convinces him?

8. **Explain** What do the Jews celebrate during Passover, and how does that connect to what Catholics celebrate in the Eucharist?

SECTION 3

9. **Recall** How did God lead the Hebrews through the desert?

10. **Explain** Why are the Ten Commandments among the most important teachings?

11. **Tell** Why doesn't Moses enter the Promised Land?

12. **Define** What does the term *anawim* refer to?

13. **Define** Explain what a prophet is.

14. **Evaluate** Could there be prophets now? Why or why not?

15. **Analyze** Why was God a "still, small voice" when calling Elijah?

16. **List** Who are the main prophets? What messages are associated with them, and how do they prefigure Jesus' teachings?

CONNECTING

Visual This illustration shows Moses and the Israelites during a very famous event.

What event in Moses' life is this meant to illustrate? What do you think Moses and the Israelites are thinking at this time as illustrated by The Glue Society?

Challenge You are a reader for Sunday Mass, and you are preparing by reading aloud a passage from Isaiah about beating swords into plowshares. It's about twenty minutes before you all head to church. You read it aloud and notice your sister listening.

You: What do you think this means?

Your sister: I think it means that the people in the olden times were supposed to stop fighting.

You: That's right; that was the message when this was written.

Your sister: I don't understand why we read such old things at Mass. What's a plowshare anyway? We should read things that are about people today.

○ What can you say to her?

○ Continue writing the conversation, including at least two more questions your sister might ask and how you would answer. Use information from the chapter in the conversation.

Question After working through this chapter, what advice would you give someone who wants to know why the concept of faithfulness is so important to understanding the Old Testament?

Imagine You are in charge of inviting a prophet to speak at your school. You may invite any Old Testament prophet or someone who is living now.

○ Which prophet would you invite? Why?

○ How do you think people will react to the prophet's message?

○ What discussion or questions would they raise to what the prophet says?

SELF-ASSESS

On Your Own or With a Partner Make a list of the most important things you learned from this chapter. Write a paragraph explaining your choices.

Who do you think these people are?

On a scale of 1 to 10, how difficult is it to be a Christian today? Explain your rating.

CHAPTER 6

The New Testament

Go to the student site at
hs.osvcurriculum.com

DO

- Explore what it means to hear God.
- Recall memories that help shape your perspective on life.
- Describe some central themes of the New Testament.
- Identify the writings that make up the New Testament.
- Research the lives of the twelve Apostles.
- Identify people who have shared their faith in Christ with you.
- Discover key topics in the Letter of James and the first Letter of John.
- Debate who has a greater challenge to be Christian.
- Finish the statement: "Because I believe God is love, then . . ."

DEFINE

Marcionism
Pentecost
house churches
Gentiles
conversion
faith and good works

Students at a Catholic high school were asked: "What's your favorite Jesus story or quotation?" The following are some of their responses.

My favorite Jesus story or quotation is:

the multiplication of the five loaves and two fish.

the wedding when Jesus changed water into wine.

the birth of Jesus coming into the world.

when Jesus is on the cross in the middle of the two thieves.

when Jesus cries after hearing his friend Lazarus has died.

"Those who call on the name of the Lord shall be saved."

WHAT DO YOU SAY?

What's your favorite Jesus story or quotation?

Where Are You?			
Choose the response that best reflects where you are right now.			
I get the connection between the Old and New Testaments.	☐ Quite a bit	☐ Somewhat	☐ A little	☐ Not at all
I know what's in the New Testament.	☐ Quite a bit	☐ Somewhat	☐ A little	☐ Not at all
I understand why early Christians would die for their faith.	☐ Quite a bit	☐ Somewhat	☐ A little	☐ Not at all
I've had spiritual moments, insights, or discussions that have shaped me.	☐ Quite a lot	☐ Some	☐ A few	☐ Not at all
There are Bible verses that bring me hope.	☐ Quite a bit	☐ Somewhat	☐ A little	☐ Not at all
I understand what discipleship implies.	☐ Quite a bit	☐ Somewhat	☐ A little	☐ Not at all

Unity of Old and New Testaments

What can the New Testament tell us about the Holy Spirit?

Where did the courage and conviction of the first Christians come from?

Why are Paul's letters so important?

Why do we need the Old Testament when we have Jesus in the New Testament?

S ome Hollywood blockbuster movies have plots that involve unraveling a hidden mystery and discovering a long-lost source of knowledge. There's always a new destination where Indiana Jones can go to find an ancient artifact that holds a clue to forgotten knowledge and power. There's a "national treasure" out there that contains deep, hidden secrets from long ago. The ultimate knowledge may be found in a galaxy far, far away. And someone in Hollywood right now is probably planning a movie about stumbling upon a previously forgotten formula for achieving super powers.

[God's] revelation came in varied and partial ways, not because God wished to withhold himself from us, but because human beings had to grow their ability to hear God. All too often God spoke, but men and women did not listen; God acted, but humans failed to perceive what was happening.

—George Martin,
Reading God's Word Today, p. 129.

Write

○ What, in your opinion, are the core message and central truths of Jesus and the New Testament?

You search the scriptures because you think that in them you have eternal life; and it is they that testify on my behalf.

—Jesus in John 5:39

Popular culture keeps searching to satisfy the hunger for knowledge and understanding, but Catholics know that God has revealed himself as the only truth that can really fulfill our longing.

Throughout the Bible we discover God making himself known to us "by gradually communicating his own mystery in deeds and in words" (*Catechism of the Catholic Church,* 69). God did so, and continues to do so, because of his great love. We spend our lives trying to understand and respond to what God has made known. This is a gradual thing for us, too.

Discovering the Bible's message for obtaining true joy and wisdom is an ongoing process of study, but it's more than just that. It's an ability to hear, a willingness to listen, and openness to God's grace acting in our lives. It's recognizing the Holy Spirit's action in our parish and the Church everywhere, working through people we respect and some we don't even know by name.

The section of the Bible known as the New Testament continues God's Revelation in the Old Testament.

And the Church considers the Old and New Testaments to be one unified Scripture. This might seem obvious, but it stirred up a lot of questions early in Church history.

The central object of the New Testament is Jesus, the Word of God. He is in his very being what the Scriptures—both Old and New Testaments—seek to tell us. As you read this chapter and some of the New Testament along with it, think about what style of writing its authors chose to use and what insights they give us about Jesus.

> *The New Testament has to be read in the light of the Old. Early Christian catechesis made constant use of the Old Testament.[14] As an old saying put it, the New Testament lies hidden in the Old and the Old Testament is unveiled in the New.[15]*
>
> —CCC, 129

Marcionism a heresy that denied the unity of the two testaments and rejected the Old Testament based on the supposition that the New Testament has made it invalid

Something Old, Something New

A little more than one hundred years after Jesus, a Christian named Marcion (MAHR•see•uhn) created a controversy that caused quite a stir. At that time in the Church, priests in the West and East could be married. Marcion's father was actually a bishop, so Marcion had influence and was well-respected by those who knew him. When he read the New Testament next to the Old, he saw very different images of God. From Marcion's perspective, God in the Old Testament is a God of laws and vengeance. In the New Testament, God is loving and liberating.

Research
○ Look up "Marcionism" in an online Catholic encyclopedia to get more background. Restate Marcion's position in your own words and explain why Church leaders condemned his ideas.

○ How do you think the Old and New Testaments are similar and different?

Marcion concluded that the Old Testament should not be included in the Christian Bible because the New Testament had replaced the Old. He said that the Old Testament should be set aside as an outdated misrepresentation of God and the truth. We don't have any of Marcion's writings, but we have numerous writings from theologians and Church leaders who condemned Marcion's ideas. In A.D. 144, his position—called **Marcionism**—was condemned as heresy.

The New Testament has numerous references to the Old. Notice the constant references to Old Testament figures that Zechariah used in the first chapter of Luke. Now that we have studied some of the Old Testament, we may recognize what and who Zechariah is talking about when he speaks of:

• the Lord God of *Israel*,

• the hope for a *redeemer*,

• a savior from the *House of David*, and

• the promise God made in his *covenant* with Abraham.

GO TO THE SOURCE

Blessed be the Lord God of Israel,

for he has looked favorably on his people and redeemed them.

—Luke 1:68

The Gospel according to Luke begins with the birth of John the Baptist to an elderly couple named Zechariah and Elizabeth. Did you know that the Angel Gabriel actually appeared to this couple before appearing to Mary, their niece?

Read all of Luke Chapter 1.

○ What exactly did Gabriel tell Zechariah? (Luke 1:13-17)

○ How did Zechariah eventually show that he was willing to follow God's plan? (Luke 1:57-64)

○ Read the prophecy spoken by Zechariah in Luke 1:67-69.

○ Make a list of the references to the Old Testament made by Zechariah in his prophecy.

God's People, whom we meet in the Old Testament, underwent many trials and tribulations. During dark times, Old Testament prophets reminded God's People of his promise to always be with them. Zechariah knew that the coming of Jesus was the fulfillment of the promise of salvation, bringing light to those in darkness and offering a way to peace.

If we didn't know of the struggles that the Israelites underwent before this time, and if we didn't know the words and deeds by which God's mystery was shared in stages with his People in the Old Testament, then our understanding and appreciation for who Jesus is and what he has to offer would be very different.

Zechariah knew. His words read like a psalm, a song of praise. He could not sing this song if he didn't consider the Scriptures of the Hebrews to be the word of God. Marcion unfortunately didn't accept this view of the Old Testament.

Other Church leaders of Marcion's time knew that the God manifest in Jesus was also the God of Abraham, Moses, and the prophets. When we read the Old Testament along with the New, we discover what God is passionate about.

Recall What is the central object of the New Testament?

Contrast Name differences in how Marcion and Zechariah each viewed the Old Testament.

Old Testament Alive in New

The message of the New Testament lies hidden in the Old. Another account in the New Testament suggests how the Old sheds light on the New. In the Acts of the Apostles, an Apostle named Philip is traveling on a remote road near Jerusalem. There he has an interesting encounter.

In the account about Philip from Acts, it is clear that this Ethiopian official is an inquiring and probing person. He goes to the Temple in Jerusalem to pray and searches the Hebrew Scriptures for wisdom. The official runs across passages in Isaiah about who

Listen

○ What does it mean to listen to someone? To God?

○ How can you grow in your ability to hear God?

○ Name some people in your community who seem to be hearing God. What are the signs of their listening?

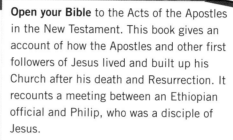

GO TO THE SOURCE

Open your Bible to the Acts of the Apostles in the New Testament. This book gives an account of how the Apostles and other first followers of Jesus lived and built up his Church after his death and Resurrection. It recounts a meeting between an Ethiopian official and Philip, who was a disciple of Jesus.

Read Acts 8:26-40 about Philip's encounter on a road near Jerusalem.

○ What's the significance of this event?

many Scripture scholars today call "the suffering servant." These passages speak of an innocent man who suffers and is humiliated and abused. Through his sacrifice he saves the People of God. How is someone unfamiliar with the Scriptures of the Hebrew people to understand these passages?

Philip obviously doesn't dismiss the message from the Old Testament. Images such as the suffering servant found in the Old Testament Books of Isaiah and Psalms come to life when read in light of Jesus. In other words, for Philip and other early Christians, the Old Testament is unveiled in the New.

Name What Old Testament book is the Ethiopian official reading from when he asks Philip to help explain?

Infer Why do you think the Ethiopian official wanted to be baptized right away?

Old Testament—New Testament Parallels

Adam—the first human being. Jesus—the "new Adam," humanity's fulfillment.

The Tower of Babel—disunity of people. Jesus—unity inviting all people to believe, and with the coming of the Holy Spirit at Pentecost, Apostles spoke different languages and everybody understood.

The great flood—destruction of a sinful world. Baptism—through the waters, dying and rising to new life with Jesus.

The covenant—people of Israel as God's People. Jesus—new covenant with God, meant for all.

The Exodus—slaves set free. Jesus—overcoming slavery of sin and death.

Passover meal—commemoration of the Exodus event. Eucharist—sacramental memorial that makes present the Paschal Mystery.

King David—the great king, one of God's anointed. Jesus—Messiah and Son of God.

Prophets—those called to be faithful to God's word. Jesus—the Word of God made flesh.

GO TO **THE SOURCE**

The Ethiopian official had read the well-known account from the prophet Isaiah about the suffering servant. The concept of the suffering servant of God appears to have come about during the Babylonian exile.

1. Read the entire section of the Book of Isaiah about the suffering servant that the Ethiopian official referenced (Isaiah 52:13–53:12). Identify passages that Christians would apply to Jesus. Explain why.

2. Then do the same with the three other "suffering servant" passages (Isaiah 42:1-7, 49:1-6, and 50:4-9).

SECTION 1 REVIEW

QUICK REVIEW

1. **Interpret** "The New Testament lies hidden in the Old and the Old Testament is unveiled in the New." What does this saying mean to you?

2a. **Recall** What did Marcion conclude about the Old Testament?

b. **Explain** How did the Church react to Marcionism?

c. **Analyze** How does Zechariah bridge the Old Testament and the New Testament?

3a. **Explain** How did Philip convert the Ethiopian official?

b. **Analyze** From the story of the Ethiopian official, what can we tell about Philip's attitude toward the Old Testament?

c. **List** Name some parallels between the Old Testament and the New Testament.

Listen and Discuss With a partner, discuss your attitude toward the Old Testament.

○ Which stories from the Old Testament are especially meaningful to you?

○ What would you want to learn that would help you better understand the Old Testament?

Pray Compose a short prayer that addresses the one God of both the Old and New Testaments. Try to indicate how you believe this.

SELF-ASSESS

Which statement best reflects where you are now?

☐ I'm confident enough about the material in this section to be able to explain it to someone else.

☐ I have a good grasp of the material in this section, but I could use more review.

☐ I'm lost. I need help catching up before moving on.

The Acts of the Apostles

The New Testament contains the ultimate truth of God's Revelation. We say ultimate truth because of its focus on Jesus—his actions, teachings, Passion, glory, and the early spread of the Church under the guidance of the Holy Spirit. The Word of God is offered in a "most wonderful way" in the New Testament (CCC, 124).

We mentioned in a previous chapter that the New Testament consists of twenty-seven books, including the four Gospels, the Acts of the Apostles, thirteen Letters attributed to Saint Paul, eight additional Letters to early Christians (seven of which are sometimes called catholic Letters, because they are written to the universal Church and not to a specific community), and the Book of Revelation. These books and Letters were written over a period of fifty years or so.

The four Gospels are central to all Scripture because they serve as our main source about the life, teaching, and redeeming work of Jesus. In the next two chapters we will see how the Gospels provide the Good News of Jesus from different points of view.

We'll begin here with the Acts of the Apostles, which tells of events that took place in the early days of the Church. It starts with a promise Jesus made before he returned to the Father: that he would always be with his followers. The coming of the Holy Spirit on Pentecost is the fulfillment of that promise.

> While staying with them, he ordered them not to leave Jerusalem, but to wait there for the promise of the Father. "This," he said, "is what you have heard from me; for John baptized with water, but you will be baptized with the Holy Spirit. . . ."
>
> —Acts 1:4-5

Pentecost—The Spirit Transforms

In the Acts of the Apostles, you will find accounts of people who went to unbelievable lengths to spread the message of Jesus. Many of his followers sacrificed their livelihoods and family life to continue the work begun by Jesus. They suffered greatly and risked horrible deaths to tell others about him. Why?

What would induce fishermen, tax collectors, and others among the Apostles to head out and spread the word to foreign lands? Most of the time this meant leaving families and friends as well as putting themselves in harm's way. The beginning of Acts describes Jesus appearing to his friends after the Resurrection and reminding them of his earlier teaching about the coming of God's

Research

○ According to reports from early Christian historians such as Eusebius (yoo•SEE•bee•uhs), all of the Apostles died as martyrs except for Saint John. Find out how and where tradition says each Apostle died.

>> Who or what do you feel so strongly about that you would be willing to put yourself in harm's way?

REFLECT

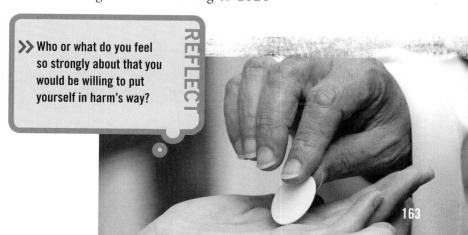

SYMBOL OF
Early Christians

After Jesus' death, Resurrection, and Ascension, many of his followers hid themselves for fear of persecution. It became necessary for these early Christians to be able to identify each other as fellow believers in Christ. They used secret symbols; the most well known of these is the symbol of the fish.

The Greek word for fish is *ichthus*. Early Christians used this word as an acronym, meaning each letter stood for a word. It is based on the Greek *Iesous* (Jesus) *Christos* (Christ) *Theou* (God) *Uios* (Son) *Soter* (Savior) and translated as "Jesus Christ, Son of God, Savior."

This symbol may have referred to the multiplication of the loaves and fishes (Matthew 13:14-21), the Risen Lord's breakfast of fish with the Apostles on the shore of the Sea of Galilee (John 21:9), or the fact that many of the Apostles were fishermen. Also in Mark 1:17, Jesus tells the Apostles that he would make them fishers of people.

In today's society, the fish symbol is often used in jewelry, bumper stickers, and on business signs, often with the word Jesus written inside the fish symbol. It still identifies the person as a follower of Christ.

History tells us that during the persecution of the early Church, when a Christian met someone new, he or she would draw the top outline of a fish in the sand.

Early Christians drew the symbol, as well as the word *ichthus*, on the walls of their homes and in the catacombs (underground Christian burial and meeting sites).

If the other person were a Christian, he or she would complete the outline of the fish. If the second person were not a Christian, the first symbol would not give the Christian away.

Catacombs of Saint Priscilla, Rome, Italy

↗ Go to the student site at
hs.osvcurriculum.com

When the day of Pentecost came, Jesus' Apostles and his Mother were gathered in one place. The second chapter in the Acts of the Apostles describes the coming of the Holy Spirit upon them.

Read Acts of the Apostles 2:1-42.

○ What happens after Peter addresses the crowd?

○ Choose one of Peter's specific points that appeals to you. Why do you think this passage has an impact on you?

Kingdom: "After his suffering he presented himself alive to them by many convincing proofs, appearing to them during forty days and speaking about the kingdom of God" (Acts 1:3). The book then immediately recounts an event that changes the course of history.

The Acts of the Apostles, Chapter 2, describes the coming of the Holy Spirit on **Pentecost**. Pentecost is a Jewish holy day commemorated fifty days after Passover. Christians regard it as a key event in the history of the Church.

Many people became followers of Jesus on that first Pentecost. The account describes the Holy Spirit—the third Person of the Trinity—filling, inspiring, and acting through Peter and the Apostles.

> *Day by day, as they spent much time together in the temple, they broke bread at home and ate their food with glad and generous hearts, praising God and having the goodwill of all the people.*
>
> —Acts 2:46-47

The new believers quickly devoted themselves to the Apostles' teachings on Jesus, to prayer, and to the communal breaking of the bread. They sold their possessions and distributed the money to those who needed it. With the continued presence of the Holy Spirit in the early Church community, their numbers grew every day.

Roman officials, however, did not consider these followers of Christ to be practicing a legal religion. These Jews who were now new believers in Christ distanced themselves from Jewish places of worship.

They had no physical building dedicated to worship, so first century Christians followed the example of Jesus, who had held the Last Supper in the upper room. They formed a system of **house churches** that actually sped up the spreading of the Gospel. In their private houses, they gathered, listened to the word of God, and broke bread. For the new disciples, this Eucharistic celebration was an encounter with Christ.

Christ had fulfilled his promises to send the Holy Spirit. The Apostles began to proclaim "the mighty works of God," and evangelizers spread out among the Jewish communities throughout the Roman Empire.

The witness of these first believers extended beyond the Jewish community to **Gentiles**, who were not Jewish. Peter and Paul assured the Jewish followers of Christ that they had not been rejected. The Jews continued as the root of the People of God, to which new branches, including the Gentiles, were added. "For from him and through him and to him are all things" (Romans 11:36). It showed that the Holy Spirit brought strength and united people who wanted to identify themselves with Christ, the Son of God who rose from the dead.

house churches small assemblies of early Christians who met in private homes to support one another, ponder Jesus' message, pray, and break bread

Pentecost the fiftieth day coming immediately after the seven weeks following Passover. On the fiftieth day after Jesus' Resurrection, Christians celebrate Pentecost, the day when the Holy Spirit came to the followers of Jesus, inspiring them to preach and carry on his message.

Gentiles designation for people who are not Jewish

Discuss

○ Why are wind and fire appropriate images for the power and presence of the Holy Spirit?

○ What are some ways in which the Holy Spirit continues to be present today? It might be helpful to recall from Chapter 4 the prophet Elijah's experience of God as "sheer silence," not just as a mighty wind and blazing fire.

○ When do we celebrate Pentecost every year?

○ What colors do we use for Pentecost liturgies? What is the symbolism of this color?

○ What is the Holy Spirit's role in the Sacrament of Confirmation?

Explain

The Acts of the Apostles gives us glimpses into the practices and way of life followed by the first Christians. Read the following passages from Acts. First, explain in your own words the activities each passage is describing. Then, describe ways in which members of the Church continue this activity today.

- 2:41-42
- 2:44-47
- 4:32-35
- 5:12-16
- 10:42-43
- 11:27-30
- 19:1-6

All who believed were together and had all things in common; they would sell their possessions and goods and distribute the proceeds to all, as any had need.

Acts 2:44-45

It was this identity that made people willing to suffer and even give their lives for the Gospel. Their suffering glorified God and became more important than any other power or even life itself. The Acts of the Apostles also tells us about the commitment of Saint Paul, who was both Jewish and Roman. He shared the Gospel message with more people than ever with a commitment to Christ that is still an example for us today. From the time of Paul, the Gospel moves from being embraced only by Jewish followers of Christ to being understood as the "Good News" for all people.

House churches remained in use for the first few centuries after Pentecost. The Acts of the Apostles describes some of these house church meetings. One passage says they met on the first day of the week to break bread. Paul held a discussion and kept speaking until midnight (Acts 20:7). Saint Justin Martyr mentioned a place for Baptism that was a private house. These meetings allowed followers of Jesus to grow spiritually in Christ's message, and as a result, the Church added many members through the Sacrament of Baptism.

Today, we celebrate the coming of the Holy Spirit every year on Pentecost Sunday. That day always signals the end of our Easter season and falls between late May and the first two weeks of June, depending on the date of Easter that year.

Recall What does the beginning of the Acts of the Apostles describe about Jesus?

Explain Why would people want to become Christians when they knew they might have to suffer for their beliefs?

Mighty Sermons

About one-fourth of Acts consists of speeches or sermons that show how the Apostles defended and explained the faith. The sermons follow a standard formula. They speak of:

- the *life of Jesus*, especially his Resurrection from the dead, as revealed in the *Scriptures* of the Hebrew People (what we know as the Old Testament),

- the *challenge* that Jesus poses to their audience.

For instance, in Acts 13:16-41, Paul is invited to speak in a synagogue in the city of Antioch. His sermon is filled with references to the Old Testament and to how Jesus fulfills the Scriptures. He challenges his listeners to accept the freedom and forgiveness offered by Jesus that keeping the Law of Moses has not provided them.

Most of Acts centers on the missionary activity of Paul, whom we will discuss in more detail in the next section. Its author may have accompanied Paul on some of his journeys. An interesting feature of Acts is that it begins in Jerusalem (center of Judaism) and ends with Paul in Rome (center of the Gentile, or non-Jewish world).

During the course of the book, the focus shifts from the Jewish roots of Christianity to an understanding that the Good News of Jesus is meant for everyone. Paul is called "the Apostle to the Gentiles" because of his missionary activity among non-Jews. Thus, the Acts of the Apostles expands and clarifies the message of God's Revelation in two ways:

1. Salvation comes not from following the Law of Moses, but from *faith in Jesus, who was raised from the dead.*

2. The covenant God originally made with Abraham and his descendants *now extends to all people, Gentiles as well as Jews.* Most Christians today are descendants of Gentile converts to Christianity.

Recall Where does the Acts of the Apostles begin and end?

Describe What is the standard formula for sermons that make up about a quarter of the Acts of the Apostles?

Compare and Contrast

Paul describes Jesus' call for breaking down barriers separating different groups, such as between Jews and Gentiles, in these words: "There is no longer Jew or Greek, there is no longer slave or free, there is no longer male and female; for all of you are one in Christ Jesus" (Galatians 3:28).

- ○ What is the difference between a nationalistic attitude and a global perspective?
- ○ Based on Paul, what is the Christian viewpoint on these two perspectives?
- ○ What divisions exist in the world that the Church overcomes through Christ and the Sacraments?

MY✝ FAITH

The coming of the Holy Spirit on Pentecost transformed the Apostles and disciples. The presence of the Holy Spirit made it possible for the early followers of Christ to carry on. Pentecost prompted them to share their belief. The movement of the Holy Spirit led them to pursue a life of discipleship. Many of them died because of it. Read Acts 7 to see who was the first disciple to be martyred.

What experiences have strengthened your faith?

What experiences of the Holy Spirit have shaped your spirituality?

How willing are you to travel the path of discipleship?

What do you need to do, remember, practice, or avoid?

What aspect of the Bible gives you real hope?

Once again make some notes in answer to these questions. And remember that you may choose to share or explain some of this at the end of the course.

Go to the student site at
hs.osvcurriculum.com

Discipleship . . . within the Body of Christ . . . for the glory of God and the good of the world

QUICK REVIEW

1a. Recall Who is the most frequently mentioned disciple in Acts?

b. Assess What effect did following Jesus have on the disciples?

c. Recall Which book of the Bible tells the story of Pentecost?

2a. Recall How was the Holy Spirit manifested at Pentecost?

b. Analyze Why is this description of Pentecost from Acts 2:43 appropriate: "Awe came upon everyone"?

3a. Explain How do the sermons in the Acts of the Apostles show the importance of the Old Testament?

b. Explain Why is Paul called the Apostle to the Gentiles?

ACT

Find a way to welcome, recognize, or support people who are being baptized into the Church. Consider doing one of the following:

○ attend a Baptism in your parish even if you don't know the person personally

○ design or write out a welcome card

○ offer a newly baptized person congratulations after a Mass in which he or she received the Sacrament or was recognized as a new member

SELF-ASSESS

Which statement best reflects where you are now?

☐ I'm confident enough about the material in this section to be able to explain it to someone else.

☐ I have a good grasp of the material in this section, but I could use more review.

☐ I'm lost. I need help catching up before moving on.

Paul's Letters

In this technological age, we sometimes don't appreciate the importance letters have in communicating with people. The *way* we share important messages with people may have changed over the years, but the *desire* to share thoughts, support, and some of ourselves through words hasn't. We can learn a lot about ourselves and our faith from the type of Letters included in the New Testament, sometimes called Epistles.

The Letters make up the greatest percentage of the New Testament; twenty-one of the twenty-seven books are Letters. Most of the Letters were written before the Gospels. In the Letters, we find the earliest description of what life was like for the first Christians. The authors of the letters wrote to instruct and encourage new Christians, and their work continues to be a source of guidance for us today.

Before the New Testament was formally put together, these Letters were read at different gatherings. We don't know for certain who wrote each and every Letter. Different people wrote the Letters to different groups of people living in different cities. Sometimes one person wrote a Letter using the name of another.

As we mentioned in the previous section, we do know that Paul wrote many of the New Testament Letters. Paul's story is an amazing one, and understanding a little more about him will give us insight into his remarkable travels and writings.

Paul, also known as Saul, was Jewish, specifically a Pharisee. In the Jewish community of the day, Pharisees were highly educated in the Hebrew Scriptures and extremely dedicated to them. Pharisees centered their lives on faithfully carrying out the dictates of the Law as laid out in the Torah, the first five books of Hebrew Scripture (and the Old Testament). Paul identified himself as one of the most zealous of this group.

Paul persecuted Jews who believed in Christ. He didn't know Jesus personally. Jews at the time didn't just live in Israel. Because of the Diaspora that was described in Chapter 3, there were Jewish communities scattered throughout the Roman Empire. Paul himself, while being a faithful Jew, was originally from a town named Tarsus, which is part of modern Turkey.

Name What is another name by which Paul was known?

Infer Given Paul's background, why might he persecute Jews who believed in Christ if he didn't even know Jesus?

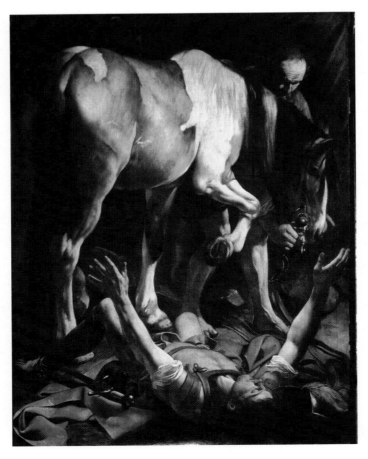

The Conversion of Saint Paul (c.1601),
Michelangelo Merisi da Caravaggio

Paul's Conversion

One time when Paul sought to punish Christian Jews who he believed were contaminating Judaism, he had an experience that transformed his life, and the world, forever. Paul was on his way to Damascus when:

A light from heaven flashed around him. He fell to the ground and heard a voice saying to him, "Saul, Saul, why do you persecute me?" He asked, "Who are you, Lord?" The reply came, "I am Jesus, whom you are persecuting. But get up and enter the city, and you will be told what you are to do." The men who were traveling with him stood speechless because they heard the voice but saw no one. Saul got up from the ground, and though his eyes were open, he could see nothing; so they led him by the hand and brought him into Damascus. For three days he was without sight, and neither ate nor drank.

—Acts 9:3-9

This passage describes how Paul has seen the Light, which is Jesus. The Jesus whom Paul has been persecuting is now revealed in all of his glory as light from Heaven. Paul realizes that Jesus was present in those whom Paul had persecuted, people who had placed their trust and belief in Jesus.

After his initial encounter with Jesus from on high, Paul is "blinded by the Light" and led into Damascus. After three days, a Christian man named Ananias is told by the Lord to go to Saul of Tarsus because Saul/Paul has been chosen to "spread the word" and to "suffer much"—two things that many Christians already experienced at the time.

So Ananias went and entered the house. He laid his hands on Saul and said, "Brother Saul, the Lord Jesus, who appeared to you on your way here, has sent me so that you may regain your sight and be filled with the Holy Spirit." And immediately something like scales fell from his eyes, and his sight was restored. Then he got up and was baptized, and after taking some food, he regained his strength.

—Acts 9:17-19

The Epistles

Scholars debate when the various Letters of the New Testament were written and even who wrote some of them. In the Bible, especially in the Pauline texts, the Letters are arranged more or less according to their length, longer followed by shorter. Here are approximate dates of composition and key themes of the Epistles.

Epistle	Approximate Date of Composition	Key Themes
Romans	57–58	We are saved ("justified") by Christ alone.
1 Corinthians	56	Avoid immorality and improper behavior at liturgies.
2 Corinthians	57	Paul explains ministry; calls people to holiness.
Galatians	54–55	Paul explains the nature of true faith.
Ephesians	80–100	Unity and mission of the Church.
Philippians	54–56	Instructions for living the Christian life.
Colossians	80–100	Beware of false teachers; stay true to Christ.
1 Thessalonians	50	Gives specific guidelines for leading a holy life.
2 Thessalonians	50s	Be ready for the end times.
1 Timothy	60 or 100	Describes duties of ministers and others in the community.
2 Timothy	60 or 100	Be strong and avoid disputes.
Titus	60 or 100	Advice for living under non-Christian authorities.
Philemon	55–56	Paul tells Philemon to treat his slave as a brother in Christ.
Hebrews	70–100	A reflection on the divine and human natures of Jesus.
James	70–100	Explains the importance of good works for faith.
1 Peter	70–90	How to be Christian in a hostile world.
2 Peter	100–125	Stay prepared for Jesus' Second Coming, even though it is delayed.
1 John	100	A meditation on the meaning of love.
2 John	100	Love one another by following Jesus' commands.
3 John	100	Welcome and show hospitality to strangers.
Jude	90–110	A plea to keep the faith.

NOTE: Dates included in the chart are A.D.

Letter Writing

A LONGSTANDING CHRISTIAN TRADITION

Letter writing among Christians did not end with the divinely revealed truths contained in the Letters in Scripture. We can learn much about the struggles, controversies, dedication, and successes of Christians throughout the ages by reading their letters.

Gregory Dalessio:
A Soldier's Letter

U.S. soldier Greg Dalessio of Cherry Hill, New Jersey, was stationed in Iraq. His unit worked with local community groups. After his first tour in Iraq, he had told his parish priest, "Nothing makes you a pacifist like being in combat." On June 23, 2008, his security detail was attacked and Dalessio was seriously wounded. As he lay dying, he said to his commander, "Tell me that I'm loved." His commander responded, "Greg, I love you." Dalessio died and was awarded the Purple Heart and the Bronze Star.

Years earlier while stationed in Iraq, Dalessio had written a letter as a Christmas gift to his family of eight siblings. Here are portions of a letter dated December 25, 2005, and printed with the permission of his family.

To my dear family,

Hello and Merry Christmas! It is now two days after Thanksgiving and we are enjoying a day off. I went to church this morning. It was an interesting experience in the sense that the congregation was full. It's amazing how being in a combat zone motivates people to develop a relationship with Jesus.

At any rate, I wanted to write you a letter for Christmas since I am unable to send you any presents. I figured it would be a good opportunity to let you know how you have been gifts in my life.

Where shall I begin, ah, with everybody's favorite . . . Nicky! In all seriousness, however, Nick's gift to me has been his sense of duty and responsibility. Nick, you have set an example for our family by striving to do the right thing in your daily actions.

Dan, you are an example of how to live a life full of compassion. I find it difficult to think of another human being as caring and thoughtful as yourself. I'm not sure what it is, but when I am around you I feel a tremendous sense of peace and security. This can probably be attributed to your gentle, caring nature—thanks for being a source of serenity in my life.

Tim, they called Elvis the King of Rock and Roll, well you my brother are the King of Love. There is no one—and I mean no one—on this earth as loving as you. I can think of very few people who, after having not seen them for a long time, can elicit an immediate smile upon my face at the moment of reunion—you are one of these people. Thanks for your love!

Alex, when thinking about you I am reminded of the Army values. While there are seven such values, you epitomize one in particular—loyalty. Whether it has been in supporting your siblings during the sometimes "dramatic" breakups with exes, or in your own relationships with your friends. Thanks for showing me what it means to be "in someone's corner."

Liz, you are always willing to lend a helping hand or offer your company for a trip to the store. Genuine kindness is a gift from God, and He has blessed you abundantly in this area, thanks for sharing. It is very difficult for me to think of a person more happy or kind than yourself.

Ana, you are an example of self-less service. In the civilian world, this attribute can be referred to as thoughtfulness. You are definitely one of the most thoughtful people I know, constantly considering the thoughts and feelings of those around you.

Abby, what else can I say but you're the best . . . ha . . . ha . . . now that everyone is through rioting let me be serious for a moment. Ab, your gift to the world is your love, specifically—your hugs. There is not one person in this world who gives better hugs than you.

Mom, you are my _favorite_ person in the world. There is no doubt in my mind that I can attribute all of my good traits to your patient love and kindness over the years. I hope I can be half the parent you are to us. Please know that your love has not gone unnoticed and that my love for you is immense.

Dad, I recently finished reading the book about Bono that you guys had sent earlier in the summer. In this book, the author asks Bono what makes him speechless. Bono's answer to this question was God's grace and forgiveness. I could not help but be reminded of you. Throughout the course of our lives your actions have served as examples of God's grace to His children. Your patience and love during the trying times—and your forgiveness during the turbulent times—have shown all of us what it truly means to be Christian. Thanks for your support all these years.

Merry Christmas and thank you all for your love.

Love,
Greg

Think About It In the last minutes of his life, and in his letter, Greg speaks of love lived out in many ways. What in this reminds you of Jesus' love and the way he lived his life? What can we learn from it about God's unconditional love?

The New Testament letters share the Good News and give witness to the faith of Christ's first followers. What witness does Greg and his family provide us?

If you were away from home and in harm's way, to whom would you want to express gratitude? What would you write?

Saint Paul's conversion to Christianity took place somewhere around the year A.D. 35. In the Acts of the Apostles, Paul retells in one of his numerous court hearings how he persecuted early Christians, and he describes what happened that day of his initial encounter with Christ.

Look up the following accounts of his conversion and identify the events that are described in all three versions.

- Acts 9:1-19
- Acts 22:3-21
- Acts 26:9-23

conversion "A radical reorientation of the whole life away from sin and evil, and toward God" (CCC, Glossary).

Thus, Paul comes to Christ. Paul and those he reached with the Gospel message experienced a **conversion**, or a reorientation of their lives away from sin and toward God. It is this kind of change of heart that is a central part of Christ's teaching and the Church's evangelization outreach. And it's a lifelong effort to learn and deepen within us the mystery of God's love.

Paul's conversion was strengthened through his time with Ananias, a member of the Christian community in Damascus. Paul becomes a "brother," a member of the Christian family, with the help of this man. Ananias is one of many Christians about whom we know very little, but who carried out the work and the message of Jesus. People like Ananias were included in Paul's contribution to the Scriptures in the form of Letters to various Christian communities that he had visited. These people reinforced Paul's faith as he spread that faith to them and others.

Several themes run through Paul's Letters, including the Trinity. In his Letters, and in

Identify
After his own conversion, Paul continually invites believers to a deeper conversion.

- Read Ephesians 4:17-32.
- Identify the kinds of conversion that Paul is calling for.
- What are the kinds of conversion you either have experienced or have seen in someone else?

all New Testament writings, we see the centrality of the mystery of the Trinity, fully revealed at Pentecost with the coming of the Holy Spirit. We learn a lot about the relationship among the Persons of the Trinity—Father, Son, and Holy Spirit—from Paul's Letters.

The Body of Christ

In his Letters, Paul speaks frequently of the Church as the Body of Christ: "For in the one Spirit we were all baptized into one body" (1 Corinthians 12:13). In fact, he is the only New Testament writer to use this phrase, but he did so prolifically. This image of the Church gets at the relationship of Christ with his Church and all her members. We read in Saint Paul's first Letter to the Corinthians that, like the body with many parts, the Church has members with many functions; the diversity of function makes the Church what she is. The analogy between the body and the Church rests on the fact that Jesus is the head of his Body, the Church. Through the Holy Spirit and

Paul saw himself as one of many instruments used by God to spread the faith; he recognized the role a man named Apollos played in his ministry as well as God's grace: "I planted, Apollos watered, but God gave the growth."

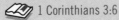 1 Corinthians 3:6

Express
- Name some people who have communicated the Gospel to you during your lifetime. Contact one of them and express to that person the role he/she played in your faith life.
- Paul realizes that to become Christian means that one will "suffer much." If you were in charge of a program initiating new members into the Church, how would you address this dimension of the Christian life?

○ Rome—Paul eventually goes to Rome as a prisoner and is martyred there around the year 67. The traditional location of his burial place is the Basilica of San Paolo.

Faith & Culture

Go to the student site at **hs.osvcurriculum.com**

---

the grace of the Sacraments, especially the Eucharist, Jesus constitutes the Church as his Body.

He typically begins his Letters by saying, "I give thanks to my God always for you" (for example, 1 Corinthians 1:4). He writes with such passion and conviction to these communities because he knows that Christ is present in and through them.

Identify Who was Ananias?

Explain What does Saint Paul mean by the term Body of Christ?

Jesus and the Law

As we have seen in our study of the Old Testament, the Law of Moses serves as the foundation for living out the covenant God made with his People. The Law is God's word; it pervades every aspect of life, turning the most mundane acts into acts of religious significance. It helps us know how to live a life characterized by love, one that challenges us to be and do for the good of God and others.

The *Catechism* explains that the Law in the Old Testament is holy, spiritual, and good. It is also completed and brought to perfection by the new Law of the Gospel. Jesus told us he did not come to abolish the Old Testament Law, but to fulfill it. Paul said the old Mosaic Law denounces and exposes sin, but it is only the beginning of our journey to the Kingdom. The Law prepares us for conversion and faith in God.

Paul also points out the difference between the old covenant based on the Law and the new covenant based on Jesus. Many of his fellow Jews questioned and challenged Paul on this point. Rather than *rejecting* the Law, Paul actually provides an explanation of how the Law is to be understood. He rejects a particular attitude toward the Law, but not the Law itself. We know Jesus gave his followers a deeper understanding of what it meant to follow the commandments: "You have heard that it was said to those of ancient times, 'You shall not murder'; and 'whoever murders shall be liable to judgment.' But I say to you that if you are angry with a brother or sister, you will be liable to judgment; and if you insult a brother or sister, you will be liable to the council . . ." (Matthew 5:21-22). And, from the earliest of times, Christians were called to live by not only Jesus' Beatitudes and his New Commandments, but by the Ten Commandments as well.

Yet, if it had not been for the law, I would not have known sin. I would not have known what it is to covet if the law had not said, "You shall not covet."

—Romans 7:7

In his Letter to the Romans, Paul says that the Law is good, but to approach it as a means of winning favor with God makes it an obstacle to God's love. To believe that we can *earn* God's care and concern is to deny the love of God; God then becomes a taskmaster, not a loving Father. The gift of God's Son is too great to be earned; it is given out of love. We *earn* wages, but we *receive* a gift. Isn't it true that love by definition is always a gift, not earned or purchased? The same is true of faith.

Focusing exclusively on the *letter* of the law—whether the Law of Moses (the Ten Commandments) or legitimate civil law—can prevent us from appreciating the *spirit* of the law, or perhaps we should say the *heart* of the law. Paul realizes that Jesus takes us to the very heart of the Ten Commandments. The ultimate goal we seek is a free gift from God, already bought and paid for by Jesus.

GLOBAL PERSPECTIVES

Like Paul, missionaries from the United States serve the Gospel all over the world. These include bishops, religious and diocesan priests, religious brothers and sisters, and lay people. According to the U.S. Catholic Mission Association's website, the missionaries work to transform society and proclaim the Kingdom of God. They also explore how to build relationships on a global scale. According to statistics from the *2010 Catholic Almanac*, missionaries from the United States serve in all regions of the world, except Antarctica. The nations with the largest numbers of missionaries by region are Kenya in Africa, the Philippines in Asia, Puerto Rico in the Caribbean, Russia in Eurasia, Italy in Europe, Peru in Latin America, Israel in the Middle East, the United States in North America, and Papua New Guinea in Oceania. This is just a sampling of where the more than 6,200 U.S. missionaries serve with hundreds of mission organizations.

○ Why do you think missionary work is so important from the Church's perspective?

○ If you could choose somewhere to serve as a missionary, where would you go, and why?

↗ Go to the student site at **hs.osvcurriculum.com**

PRIMARY SOURCES

Here are two quotations that reflect the theology of Saint Paul.

➔ Go to the student site at **hs.osvcurriculum.com**

Saint Paul preaching

"Amazed at being so loved, at being freely pardoned, the Christian, in Jesus, inspired by the Spirit, wants to be like his heavenly Father and to hand on to all the joy which Christians receive from him."

—Etienne Charpentier,
How to Read the New Testament

"The life of the church is about handing on the experience of knowing Jesus Christ. We enter the mystery of his saving life for us through the Sacred Scriptures and through the life of his living body, the church."

— Stephen Binz,
*Introduction to the Bible:
A Catholic Guide to Studying Scripture*

>> **Explain how each quotation can apply to discipleship today.**

Describe how the Church hands on the experience of Christ.

For this reason, Paul tells us: "For Christ is the end of the law so that there may be righteousness for everyone who believes" (Romans 10:4).

> *For there is no distinction between Jew and Greek; the same Lord is Lord of all and is generous to all who call on him. For, "Everyone who calls on the name of the Lord shall be saved."*
>
> —Romans 10:12-13

Paul tells us when we accept God's love in Christ Jesus as Paul experienced it, we "put on the Lord Jesus Christ" (Romans 13:14). As a result, we seek to act in the same spirit of freedom, love, hope, conviction, and dedication that Jesus demonstrated through his life, Passion, and death. The Holy Spirit guides and strengthens us as we try to learn the ways of Christ and live out our call to discipleship.

Recall What did Jesus tell us about the Old Testament Law?

Describe What is Paul's contribution to the discussion about the Law and salvation?

Explain

○ Make a case for the following statement: Paul does not reject the Law; rather, he rejects the way some people view the Law.

○ What does "success" mean according to the way Paul portrays the Law? What is "success" in light of the Gospel?

"Do you not know that your body is a temple of the Holy Spirit within you, which you have from God, and that you are not your own? ... Therefore glorify God in your body."

—(1 Corinthians 6:19-20)

Your Body

YOU'VE HEARD SAINT PAUL'S explanation that "your body is a temple of the Holy Spirit," and that you should "glorify God in your body" (1 Corinthians 6:19-20). So how are you doing with that, with taking care of your body?

God created you in his image and likeness. The image of God within you deserves respect and has dignity. Through our bodies, we show reverence and respect for God. Not just by what we do with our bodies physically, but also by what we choose to do *to* our bodies with health and hygiene. Life and health are gifts from God that we have the responsibility to care for, taking into account the needs of those around us.

> The reverence born in man for everything bodily and sexual, both in himself and in every other human being, male and female, turns out to be the most essential power for keeping the body "with holiness."
>
> —Pope John Paul II, *Theology of the Body*, 54

When we speak of the human person, we include our spiritual soul and our body. The entire person, the body and soul, is a temple of the Holy Spirit. This human body *is* a "human body precisely because it is animated by a spiritual soul . . . " (CCC, 364). "Spirit and matter, in man, are not two natures united, but rather their union forms a single nature" (CCC, 365). The whole person then is capable of becoming the Body of Christ. This is why we treat our bodies with honor and reverence by taking good care of ourselves.

Nutrition. What do you put into your body? How much do you eat and how often? Do you provide your body with proper nourishment—a balance of proteins, carbohydrates, fruits, and vegetables? How about those foods that fall into the "treats" category—do you enjoy those in *moderation*? Are your nutritional choices glorifying God in your body?

Fitness. Our bodies need exercise. It doesn't matter whether you play a sport or just run around and goof off. Athletes aren't the only ones who need to give their hearts, lungs, and muscles a proper workout. Get out and get some fresh air! Take a walk or even play on the playground like you're still a little kid. Your whole body benefits from exercise. Does your approach to exercise glorify God in your body?

Sleep. Our bodies need rest. Getting a good night's sleep makes a world of difference in a person's day, week, month, year. While we sleep, our bodies grow, heal, and rejuvenate. Sleep affects our immune system, concentration, and memory. Sleep even affects our life span. Do your sleep patterns glorify God in your body?

Hygiene. Our bodies need to be clean and cared for. Regular personal grooming is not just about appearance; it's about caring for the body's health and well-being through cleanliness. Brushing your teeth; showering; combing your hair; washing your hands after using the bathroom; washing your clothes; using deodorant; responsibly attending to wounds or injuries—do your personal hygiene habits glorify God in your body?

Having respect and reverence for your body is essential to recognizing and honoring the image of God within. And you know what? If you haven't been doing quite so well at glorifying God with your body, you can decide to change.

>> Evaluate your own personal practices of health and hygiene. How do you glorify God in your body?

What do you need to work on to better glorify God in your body?

SECTION 3 REVIEW

QUICK REVIEW

1a. Infer What would it mean to be a zealous Pharisee?

b. Summarize What are some key themes in the Epistles?

c. Explain How were Christian Jews treated in the early days of the Church?

2a. Summarize Tell how Saul met Jesus.

b. Interpret What role did Ananias play in Saul's conversion?

c. Analyze How is Ananias a model for us?

3a. Evaluate Does Saint Paul reject the Law? Explain your answer.

b. Explain What does it mean to "put on Christ"?

c. Interpret Why is it a problem to focus on the letter of the Law?

Listen and Discuss Meet in small groups to discuss the following.

○ Give examples of overemphasizing the letter of the law and minimizing the heart of the law.

○ Then give examples of the opposite: overemphasizing the heart of the law while minimizing the letter of the law.

○ Which extreme is worse?

○ Which extreme do you think is most common in our culture today?

SELF-ASSESS

Which statement best reflects where you are now?

☐ I'm confident enough about the material in this section to be able to explain it to someone else.

☐ I have a good grasp of the material in this section, but I could use more review.

☐ I'm lost. I need help catching up before moving on.

Letters of James and John

As we mentioned earlier, seven of the New Testament Epistles, including the Letters of James and John, are sometimes referred to as catholic, or universal, Letters. Unlike Paul's Letters, which are addressed to specific churches, these Letters were written for the entire Church. It's unlikely that James, Peter, John, or Jude wrote the Letters. Those who did probably knew these early Church leaders and the relationships they had with Jesus. Writing under another name, called pseudonymity, was common during this time. It was a way to thank or credit one's mentor or teacher for the knowledge one had received. Besides, using a known person's name gave the writing more credibility. We know that while the human authors may remain unknown, these Letters come from the work of the Holy Spirit and are God's inspired word to us.

The Christians who first received and read these Letters needed the encouragement, direction, and instruction to grow in faith and understanding. As we look at some of the fundamental themes of the Letters of James and John, we need to remember the original audience: new believers who sought to follow Jesus' teachings in a world that did not necessarily accept him.

The experiences of these men and women nearly two thousand years ago are not that different from our experiences today. Some would say that today's society creates challenges similar to those faced by the early Church communities. The values perpetuated by modern mainstream society often contrast with the Gospel virtues Jesus taught. However, Jesus did not dismiss the culture and lifestyle of those to whom he

preached, even if he called his followers to abandon both. He continually made reference to everyday occurrences and used images from the natural world to make his message understandable to his listeners. He seemed to understand that people's surroundings greatly influenced who they were and how they acted. The Letter writers addressed the needs of their readers in a similar fashion, pointing out that aspects of their previous lifestyle or practices might keep them from accepting and living the Gospel message.

James

> What good is it, my brothers and sisters, if you say you have faith but do not have works? Can faith save you? If a brother or sister is naked and lacks daily food, and one of you says to them, "Go in peace; keep warm and eat your fill," and yet you do not supply their bodily needs, what is the good of that? So faith by itself, if it has no works, is dead.
>
> —James 2:14-17

The Letter of James was intended for early Christians living outside of Israel. The author included references to Judaism and Jewish practices throughout the text. He was obviously aware of Jesus' sayings, and quoted them often. In some places, the book sounds like one of the prophets when James says: "Faith by itself, if it has no works, is dead." **Faith and good works** are necessary for eternal life, James is saying. He has harsh words and a warning for those who are rich, especially those who live in luxury without providing just wages for their workers.

faith and good works the belief that faith in Jesus and doing good works are both necessary for salvation

James reminds us that it's a sham when we "talk the talk" but don't "walk the walk." If people are in need of food and shelter and we do nothing about it, do we really have faith? What is the true test of faith?

> *Religion that is pure and undefiled before God, the Father, is this: to care for orphans and widows in their distress, and to keep oneself unstained by the world.*
>
> —James 1:27

In the Letter of James we get a sense that from the very beginning, Christian communities had to deal with some very real conflicts, similar to what takes place in society even today. Some people who joined a particular Christian community were undoubtedly rich; others were poor. How were they to get along in this new way of being together? In the first Christian community, people from all stations in life identified themselves as one family in Christ. Such a radical identity and lifestyle change would be easier said than done.

We also find in James the passage that gives witness to the earliest celebration of the Sacrament of the Anointing of the Sick:

"Are any among you suffering? They should pray. Are any cheerful? They should sing songs of praise. Are any among you sick? They should call for the elders of the church

GO TO THE SOURCE

Read through the Letter of James and focus on the passages addressed to people who possess wealth.

○ Give examples from the Letter of James that explain the meaning of the following statement from the *Catechism*: "The Lord grieves over the rich, because they find their consolation in the abundance of goods"[16] (CCC, 2547).

Empathize

Look at the first letter of the first word in each of the following statements. Find the one that comes closest in the alphabet to the last letter in your last name. That's the statement you must defend. It may require that you try to understand a perspective with which you don't actually agree.

○ Being humble, gentle, and nonjudgmental are not necessary for the Christian life.

○ In our society, people who are rich have a greater challenge being Christian than people who are poor.

○ God wants us to pray for those who are sick and seek his healing when we are ill.

○ Works of compassion cannot replace going to Mass.

and have them pray over them, anointing them with oil in the name of the Lord. The prayer of faith will save the sick, and the Lord will raise them up; and anyone who has committed sins will be forgiven" (James 5:13-15).

Explain What does the Letter of James say about faith?

Infer What does James mean when he reminds readers to be humble, gentle, and nonjudgmental? What is he asking them to reject?

Source of Love

The New Testament includes three short Letters attributed to John. Traditionally, this person has been identified as the Apostle John. The style and tone of the Letters are similar to the Gospel according to John, so it is possible that they were written by the same person. It is also possible that the writer is someone who knew him, possibly belonging to an early Christian community influenced by the Apostle John. John's first Letter contains a remarkable reflection on love—specifically God's love, the source of all love. It is love in the sense by which we love God above all things and our neighbors as ourselves. In this Letter, we find repeated at least twice the direct statement that "God is love" (1 John 4:8).

You can see how this simple statement transforms our understanding of everything. The author of 1 John assures us that "perfect love casts out fear" (1 John 4:18). That affirmation seems to fly in the face of our lived experience. If we live in Florida and discover an alligator camping in our kitchen one morning, we would be rightfully afraid. If we're stuck out in the middle of a field and thunder and lightning suddenly appear overhead, we would be afraid. But this Letter of John seems to be addressing fear on a much more spiritual level.

The kinds of fears 1 John 4:18 refers to include the daily anxieties and worries that most young people face in the course of growing up. This includes worries about:

- being different from everyone else and not fitting in;
- what others think of you and whether or not you're really accepted by your friends;
- your physical appearance (body size and shape, hair, face, skin);
- dating and relationships (or the lack thereof);
- school, grades, teachers, colleges, and the future; and
- family stress.

It's not a failure of faith to feel fearful and anxious. John is reminding us, however, that ultimately God's love supersedes everything else. For instance, what is more frightening than death? And yet if you've ever attended a Catholic funeral liturgy, you know that the message of Jesus to "be not afraid" is either said or sung. Moreover, John's passage on love is not simply a beautiful meditation. As God's love abides in us, the challenge before us is to truly love God and others.

GO TO THE SOURCE

Read 1 John 4:16-20 for a portion of the author's meditation on love.

- What does love "cast out"?
- Imagine beginning every discussion about God and religion with the words "Because I believe that God is love, then . . ."
- Imagine interrupting our thoughts about ourselves and the state of the world by completing the phrase "Because I believe that God is love, then . . ."
- Imagine what it could be like for a loved one who is dying or has died in light of the phrase "Because I believe that God is love, then . . ."

JUSTICE AND DISCIPLESHIP

PEOPLE ARE IN NEED OF FOOD around the world. Domestic hunger (within the United States) affects 35.5 million people; global hunger affects 923 million people across the world.

Every day, almost 16,000 children die from hunger-related causes—one child every five seconds. According to hunger relief organization Bread for the World, most of these deaths are not attributed to outright starvation, but to illnesses (such as diarrhea) and preventable diseases (such as malaria and measles) that become fatal because the children's bodies are so weakened by malnourishment.

Hunger is the most extreme form of poverty, in which individuals or families cannot afford to meet their most basic need for food. The United States Conference of Catholic Bishops has said:

"The right to a truly human life logically leads to the right to enough food to sustain a life with dignity. The poverty and hunger that diminish the lives of millions in our own land and in so many other countries are fundamental threats to human life and dignity and demand a response from believers."[17]

Hunger manifests itself in many ways other than starvation and famine: poor nutrition and calorie deficiencies cause nearly one in three people to die prematurely or have disabilities. Countries in which a large portion of the population battles hunger daily are usually poor and often lack the social safety nets people in our country benefit from, such as soup kitchens, food stamps, and job training programs. When a family that lives in a poor country cannot grow enough food or earn enough money to buy food, there is nowhere to turn for help.

Faith without works is dead (James 2:17). Yet how can we help people on the other side of the globe? Catholic Relief Services (CRS) assists impoverished and disadvantaged people overseas, working in the spirit of Catholic Social Teaching to promote the sacredness of human life and the dignity of the human person.

CRS invites each of us to make a difference in the lives of people who struggle in the midst of poverty, disease, war, and injustice.

Pray
Join CRS and the Church in praying for peace, healing, and hope in the world.

Learn
Read about issues that affect families and communities in the developing world and take the first step in combating hunger, disease, injustice—and our own impassivity.

Participate
Make a direct, positive impact on the lives of our brothers and sisters in need overseas.

Advocate
Support diocesan efforts to raise awareness. Write to elected officials in support of our brothers and sisters worldwide.

Go to the student site at
hs.osvcurriculum.com

You can be for justice without being a disciple, but you cannot be a disciple without being for justice.

THINKING THEOLOGICALLY

A Christian truth is that God jumps in first. Henri Nouwen writes about God's love relationship with us:

This sounds very simple and maybe even trite, but very few people know that they are loved without conditions or limits. This unconditional and unlimited love is what the evangelist John calls God's first love. ('Let us love,' he says, 'because God loved us first')

1 John 4:19
In the Name of Jesus, p. 25

When was the last time someone dared you to go first?

"I dare you to take that skateboarding jump" or "I dare you to try out for the play." Perhaps humans are simply more willing to jump in when someone else jumps first.

>> Another famous example of God jumping in first is John 3:16: God so loved the world that he sent Jesus. List two other examples of God jumping in first.

1. _____

2. _____

What do you think this "jumping in first" reveals about God?

Apply

Finish the following statement: "Because I believe God is love, then . . ." Compare your completed statement with others.

Explain the following concepts expressed in John's Letter:

○ Jesus reveals God's love.

○ When we love, God lives in us.

○ Perfect love casts out fear.

Throughout this chapter we have seen that the Holy Spirit, who inspired the authors of the Old Testament, also inspired the New Testament authors to tell us about Jesus and his message of salvation. Through the New Testament, God continues to make himself known, enlightening us and encouraging us. The New Testament comes out of the early Christian community—people who knew Jesus personally and in the flesh, or who were friends and companions of those who knew him in this way.

In these writings, we discover how the Christian message filtered into the Jewish and Gentile worlds. We learn how Saint Paul in particular expressed what faith in Jesus means, by his words and his actions. We get a glimpse into some of the issues these early Christians faced, and how the Holy Spirit continued to strengthen and guide the young Church as she grew. In the next chapter, we will turn our attention to the heart of the New Testament, and the heart of the Scriptures. The Gospels tell us most directly about Jesus, his message, and the gift of his life that he gave for us.

Recall What does love do with fear?

Evaluate How many times over the last week have you shown or said you do not love someone?

PRIMARY SOURCES

R ead or listen to the words from the following songs that address facing fear.

↗ Go to the student site at
hs.osvcurriculum.com

The Lord Is My Light
Refrain
The Lord is my light.
The Lord is my salvation.
Of whom should I be afraid?
Of whom should I be afraid?

1. You push the darkness,
   you push the darkness away, oh.
   The evildoers, well,
   they all stumble and fall.
   And if they try to wage war against me today, oh,
   still then my trust shall deepen in you, the Lord of all.

Here I Am
Refrain
Here I am, standing right
beside you.
Here I am; do not be afraid.
Here I am, waiting like a lover.
I am here; here I am.

3. I am here in the midst of ev'ry trial.
   I am here in the face of despair.
   I am here when pardoning
   your brother.
   Here I am, I am here.

>> Compare and contrast the styles of music and the lyrics in the two songs.

Write your own lyrics about not being afraid to do God's will instead of your own.

Now imagine, guess, or consider what words might appear in other stanzas of these songs.

Is it possible to not be afraid? Why or why not?

Find in the Bible three people who were told not to be afraid. Discuss with the class what they were afraid of, and what their responses were to that fear.

QUICK REVIEW

1a. Summarize What view of faith is shared in James?

b. Infer Why might it be necessary for the writer of James to warn early Christians that faith alone is not enough?

2a. Discuss Do you agree with John that people cannot love God if they do not love their sisters and brothers? What might this belief logically lead to?

b. Interpret What does it mean to say, "Perfect love casts out fear"?

c. Analyze How is John's message a challenge to Christians?

ACT

○ Talk about agencies that share Christ's love with everyone, such as food pantries or homeless shelters. Find out about such agencies in your community.

○ What do Saint Paul's Epistles and the Letters of James and John contribute to your understanding of Jesus?

○ How can their messages apply to current situations in your life or in the world? Be specific.

Pray Compose a short prayer asking God to help you find ways to show his love in the world.

SELF-ASSESS

Which statement best reflects where you are now?

○ I'm confident enough about the material in this section to be able to explain it to someone else.

○ I have a good grasp of the material in this section, but I could use more review.

○ I'm lost. I need help catching up before moving on.

PRAYER

God of my life,
I give you thanks that I have life,
and that my life is filled with touches of your love.

You have given me a heart that wants to be happy,
and You have placed in me a desire to make a difference.

Quiet the fears and distractions of my heart long enough
for me to listen to the movement of Your Spirit,
to hear your gentle invitation.

Reveal to me the choices that will make me happy.
Help me to discover my identity.

Let me understand how best to use the gifts
You have so lovingly lavished upon me
in preparation for our journey together.

And give me the courage to choose You
as You have chosen me.

Lord, let me know myself and let me know You.
In this is my happiness.

Augustinian Prayer for Discernment

Lord, Jesus, Christ, Good Shepherd of our souls, you who know your sheep and know how to reach our hearts, open the minds and hearts of those young people who search for and await a word of truth for their lives; let them understand that only in the mystery of your incarnation do they find full light; arouse the courage of those who know where to seek the truth, but fear that what you ask will be too demanding.

Stir in the hearts of those young people who would follow you, but who cannot overcome doubts and fears, and who in the end follow other voices and other paths which lead nowhere.

You who are the Word of the Father, the Word which creates and saves, the Word which enlightens and sustains hearts, conquer with your Spirit the resistance and delays of indecisive hearts; arouse in those whom you call the courage of love's answer: "Here I am, send me!"

Amen

—Blessed Pope John Paul II

CHAPTER 6 REVIEW

TERMS

Use each of the following terms in a sentence that shows you know what the term means. You may include more than one term in a sentence.

Marcionism

Pentecost

house churches

Gentile

conversion

faith and good works

PEOPLE

Use information from this chapter to tell why each person is important.

1. Zechariah

2. Philip

3. Ananias

4. Paul

5. James

6. John

UNDERSTANDING

Answer each question and complete each exercise.

SECTION 1

1. **Explain** Why was Marcionism a heresy?

2. **Connect** How did Zechariah's life and words connect the Old Testament and the New Testament?

3. **Summarize** Retell the story of Philip and the Ethiopian official.

4. **Connect** How does the story of Philip and the Ethiopian official show connections between the Old Testament and the New Testament?

SECTION 2

5. **Analyze** How is the growth of the Church reflected in Acts?

6. **Evaluate** Show how the structure of the sermons in Acts shows respect for the Old Testament.

7. **Explain** Summarize the events that occurred on Pentecost, and tell why they are important.

SECTION 3

8. **Summarize** What was Saul's life like before his conversion?

9. **Explain** How did Saul experience Jesus on the road to Damascus?

10. **Apply** How did Paul live out his duties of—in Ananias' terms—spreading the word and suffering much?

11. **Analyze** What is the difference between following the *letter* of the law and observing the *spirit* of the law?

12. **Recall** What does James see as the relationship between faith and works?

13. **Infer** What might have been the inspiration for James' writings on how Christians should behave toward one another?

14. **Discuss** How does John's belief about love change our view of God?

CONNECTING

Visual The painting *Pentecost* by El Greco shows the artist's concept of this holy event. El Greco was known for contrasting light and dark in his paintings. How does his painting style suit the subject of this painting? How would you describe the expressions on the faces of Jesus' followers?

Pentecost (c. 1596-1600), El Greco

Challenge You are exchanging instant messages with a friend who has a question:

>   **Friend:** Going to a movie Saturday afternoon. It's cheaper b4 6. OK?
>
>   **You:** Serving meals at homeless shelter.
>
>   **Friend:** They have 100s of volunteers they can call. People you're helping won't even know your name.
>
>   **You:** They do have a ton of help. Don't really care if they know who I am.
>
>   **Friend:** Why not?

○ What is your next reply?

○ Continue the conversation for at least two more lines from your friend and how you would respond. Use information from the chapter to answer your friend.

Question After working through this chapter, what advice would you give someone who thinks that faith is all you need to get into Heaven?

Imagine You want to start a campaign to encourage people to do good works in your community. This would be similar to the "Random Acts of Kindness" movement.

○ How might you target your campaign; that is, to whom should it be directed?

○ Which media might you use to promote your idea?

○ What kind of a slogan would you use to publicize the idea?

SELF-ASSESS

On Your Own or with a Partner Make a list of the most important things you learned from this chapter. Select three things that represent your growth in understanding as you worked through this chapter. Write a paragraph explaining your choices.

What does this
photograph symbolize?
Why do we use this symbol?

CHAPTER **7**

Introduction
to the
Gospels

Read these scenarios.

A sophomore in a Catholic high school, taking a required religion course, asks the teacher, "Did Jesus ever have a toothache? Seriously." Before the teacher can answer, students quickly raise more questions, "Do you think he ever got angry at his parents?" "Do you think he knew everything before it happened, like what people were about to say before they said it?" "Do you think he knew he was going to change history, or was he figuring it all out as he went—like most of us?"

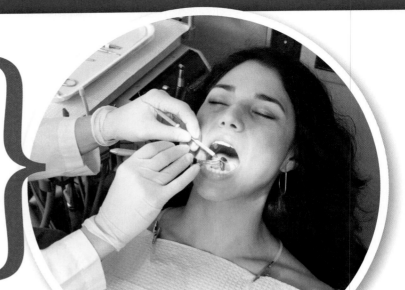

Every day, in every court in the United States, thousands of witnesses take an oath "to tell the whole truth and nothing but the truth, so help me God," by raising one hand and placing the other on the Bible before giving testimony. *Why the Bible?*

A junior tells a friend what really happened Friday night. Noticing disbelief in that person's face, the junior finally raises both hands up and says, "That's the gospel truth." *What's that about?*

HOW DO YOU RESPOND?

Where Are You?				
Choose the response that best reflects where you are right now.				
I know what's in the Gospels.	☐ Quite a bit	☐ Somewhat	☐ A little	☐ Not at all
I know that Jesus is both God and man.	☐ Quite a bit	☐ Somewhat	☐ A little	☐ Not at all
I understand what Synoptic Gospels means.	☐ Quite a bit	☐ Somewhat	☐ A little	☐ Not at all
I ask myself WWJD.	☐ Quite a bit	☐ Somewhat	☐ A little	☐ Not at all
I can explain the "Good News" of Jesus to someone else.	☐ Quite a bit	☐ Somewhat	☐ A little	☐ Not at all
I can name the central mysteries of Christ's life.	☐ Quite a bit	☐ Somewhat	☐ A little	☐ Not at all

Formation of the Good News

Where can we find the things that matter most in life?

What is the "Good News" that the Gospels contain?

What are the mysteries of Christ's life?

What are the differences and similarities contained in the Gospels?

"This just in!" "Special bulletin!" "Breaking news!" If you watch cable television news programs, you've heard or seen these words. Whether they are announced or scrolled on our TVs, or show up on our computer screens, these words and phrases are meant to alert us that something important is happening somewhere. The same thing happens with our faith. The word *gospel* means "good news" or "proclamation." Something important is happening; something that we need to know. We first encounter the term in the Gospel according to Mark: "The beginning of the good news [gospel] of Jesus Christ, the Son of God" (Mark 1:1). We have four such Gospels in which we can "read all about it!" The Son of God, foretold in the Old Testament, has come into our everyday, human existence in Jesus Christ.

The entire New Testament, including the Gospels, was most likely originally written in what is called Koine (coy•NAY) Greek. *Koine* means "common." It's not the language of scholars or the great classical Greek texts. It was the language of the streets and the marketplace. If you traveled around the Roman Empire during the first century, you spoke this form of popular Greek. Jesus himself

spoke Aramaic, but the Gospels were originally written for Jews as well as non-Jews.

From our understanding of the time, it appears that the Gospels were intended to be read and shared and talked about wherever people gathered. Their authors seemed less concerned about formalities of language than they were about getting out the message. What Jesus had to say was too important to be limited to scholars or those fortunate enough to be formally educated. Koine Greek was the appropriate language to spread the Gospel—a message to the people in the language of the people.

Recall Where do we first encounter the term "Gospel"?

Relate Koine Greek was the common language of the day in the Roman Empire of the first century. Can you think of some examples of "common language" in the English we speak today?

Write

○ The Gospels were written in Koine Greek. Choose one chapter from the Gospel according to Mark and, using everyday language, retell it in your own words.

Three Stages of Formation

Stop by the biography section of your local bookstore, and you'll find many books that aim to tell the life story of people. In some cases you might find multiple books on a person, each book with a unique point of view. As you page through a biography, it's important to remember that you are reading what the writer has gathered from many different sources, along with the author's own unavoidable biases, conscious or not. You don't have access to all of the author's oral interviews, written sources, or all the reasons why he or she included some information but not other information.

The intention of the Gospel writers was to tell the story of Jesus, the Son of God, but the Gospels are more than biographies. If you compare and contrast all four, you will notice that some of the details in the Gospels differ. The Gospels were not

> No one can read the Gospels without feeling the actual presence of Jesus. His personality pulsates in every word. No myth is filled with such life.
>
> —Albert Einstein

written following what we would consider the requirements of modern biography. Nevertheless, the core story and message are consistent in each one. This isn't a surprise since the Holy Spirit inspired the writers to convey the divine message in ways that communicate the heart and truth of our faith. Pope Benedict XVI tells us that: "Though the New Testament writings display a many-layered struggle to come to grips with the figure of Jesus, they exhibit a deep harmony despite all their differences" (*Jesus of Nazareth*, page xxiii).

Compare

Despite their differences, the Gospels share a deep harmony, Pope Benedict XVI wrote.

○ Work together to determine how the Gospels together exhibit "deep harmony" and give three examples.

The Gospels as we have them are the result of three distinct stages in their formation. The *Catechism* spells out these three stages in paragraph 126. The following pages provide a brief description of the three stages.

Symbols and Audience of the Evangelists

The cover of a book containing the four Gospels often has four images on it: a man, a lion, an ox, and an eagle. These images represent some quality found in each Gospel.

Evangelist	Symbol	Audience	Date
Matthew	Human being, since this Gospel traces Jesus' family roots beginning with Abraham.	Jewish	A.D. 75–90
Mark	Lion symbolizing the courage of John the Baptist and Jesus during his Passion.	Early Christians in Jerusalem facing persecution	A.D. 65–75
Luke	Ox (or bull), an animal used for lowly service, which is a key theme in this Gospel.	Gentile community	A.D. 75–90
John	Eagle, since this Gospel most powerfully takes us up where we are united with Jesus, the Father, and the Holy Spirit.	Jewish Christians facing persecution and internal strife	A.D. 90–100

GO TO **THE SOURCE**

One Gospel passage that reminds us that Jesus lived in a specific time and place is Luke 3:1-6. Read the passage.

○ Where and with whom does the passage begin? Where and with whom does it end?

○ Why do you think Luke presented geographical and historical information in this way?

○ What would be an equivalent way of identifying your own historical reality today?

1. Jesus' Life and Teaching First of all is the historical existence of Jesus. He was a real man who lived at a specific time and in specific places. He had to make provisions for food and drink, clothing and shelter, just like everyone else. He had to endure the hardships experienced by other people who came from his particular social and economic circumstances.

Second, Jesus addressed the concerns of actual people of his time and place. He was a Jew at a time when the Jewish nation was subject to Rome. The people from his area called Galilee were regarded as less sophisticated and more independent-minded—even by their fellow Jews.

Jesus, in his historical reality and divine Sonship, is the "gospel" proclaimed in the Gospels. His preaching and healing transformed the lives of those he encountered. Most importantly, his death and Resurrection—real actual events—brought his Apostles and other followers to an encounter with God that changed them forever. These disciples then answered the call to go out and proclaim who Jesus was. So the first layer in the development of the Gospels refers to the actual words and deeds of Jesus, the Son of God—truly divine and truly human—and his life and teaching.

2. The Oral Tradition Earlier in this book, we talked about "oral tradition" as it applies to the beginning sections of the Old Testament. Oral tradition, meaning stories passed on by word of mouth, is very important in the formation of the Gospels as well.

The Gospels were actually written down between forty and seventy years after Jesus' death, Resurrection, and Ascension, according to *The Scripture Source Book for Catholics* (Father Peter Klein, Our Sunday Visitor Curriculum Division). Up until that time, Jesus' Apostles and other disciples handed down verbal accounts of what they had heard him say, what they had seen him do, and the events that led up to and followed his death.

Perhaps they or people associated with them also wrote down some of these memories, just as a biographer today would jot down notes before writing up a definitive version. It's also likely that the Apostles and others in the earliest Christian communities added explanations for the teachings and actions of Jesus and the important events of his life.

Also taking place at this stage was the missionary activity of the Apostles, including Saint Paul. The previous chapter pointed out how they brought the Gospel to Greece, other parts of the Middle East and the Mediterranean region, and Rome.

The followers of Jesus were already coming together for years in house churches before the Gospels reached their final form. They celebrated Baptism and Eucharist, as Jesus had instructed them to do. The

The Garden of Olives, Jerusalem, Israel

proclamation during these liturgies included Jesus' vitally important message of salvation as well as the miracles and parables of his ministry. Preachers at these liturgies often used the Old Testament Scriptures to show how Jesus fulfilled the messianic prophecies. This instruction was shared with those who had not known Jesus as well as those who had accepted him. The celebration of the Eucharist and retelling stories of Jesus' life helped preserve the Scripture and Tradition of the Church. In fact, the "oral tradition" probably developed over the course of several decades. The Holy Spirit was definitely at work in this process of handing on accounts about Jesus. The written Gospels reflect this oral tradition.

Evangelists the authors of the Gospels

> *For, after the ascension of the Lord, the apostles handed on to their hearers what he had said and done, but with that fuller understanding which they, instructed by the glorious events of Christ and enlightened by the Spirit of truth, now enjoyed (DV 19).*
>
> —CCC, 126

There was a direct link between what the Apostles reported about Jesus, eyewitness accounts, and what is written in the Gospels. When the Church was discerning and determining the writings that would eventually make up the New Testament, or what we call the canon, this became a criterion to determine whether certain Christian writings were Scripture: Are they part of "Apostolic Tradition," connected directly to the Apostles? This early oral tradition is "gospel" in the sense that it represents the Good News that the Apostles themselves proclaimed about Jesus.

3. The Written Gospels The four Gospels present fundamental truths about Christ, his mission, and his saving actions for and among us. The Gospels may represent four different authors' perspectives, based on various sources, as well as on their own insights, but they were written by the promptings of the Holy Spirit. Each Gospel speaks to particular concerns of the communities *out of which* it was written and *for whom* it was written. Back in Chapter 3, we noted that God is

the true author of the Bible because the Holy Spirit inspired Scripture. That includes the Gospels, which the Church accept and hold sacred along with the other books of our canon. Any interpretation of Scripture, then, must involve the Spirit's action and a focus on what God wants us to know in order for us to be saved from our sins.

Notice how each Gospel has been named since early in Christian history: The Gospel *according* to Matthew, Mark, Luke, or John. Each written Gospel brings us closer to Christ, giving a unique account of the Good News of Jesus; it is the story of Jesus "according to" a particular author. The people who wrote the Gospels are called "**Evangelists**," a term derived from the Greek word for Gospel. One could describe the Gospel-writing process in this way: The Gospel writers included in their books specific material that had been handed on orally or in writing. Other parts they presented in a unique way to explain the Good News for the specific churches to which they were writing. They always wrote in a way that conveys to us the honest truth about Jesus' life and preaching (see CCC, 126).

> *The Gospels are the heart of all the Scriptures "because they are our principal source for the life and teaching of the Incarnate Word, our Savior" (DV 18).*
>
> —CCC, 125

List What are the three distinct stages of Gospel formation?

Summarize Describe the Holy Spirit's action in the writing of the Gospels.

When and Who?

Much scholarly discussion centers around exactly when each of the Gospels was written. We don't have any way of dating them definitively. We do have evidence that supports a general timeframe for when they were written and circulated for public use. For many centuries, most Christian scholars believed that the Gospel according to Matthew was the first one written. It's always placed first in the New Testament, and thus is called "the first Gospel." For a long time, the Gospel according to Matthew received greater attention in study and was used more frequently in liturgy. However, we now know that it was not the first Gospel.

The Gospel according to Mark was the first Gospel written, most likely between A.D. 65 and 75. Matthew and Luke were probably composed between A.D. 75 and 90. The Gospel according to John was written last, sometime between A.D. 90 and 100. However, when we remember the three-stage development of the Gospels, one of the things we learn is that the major sections of all four Gospels originate from similar sources.

List In what general order were the Gospels finished in written form?

Explain Why is the Gospel according to Matthew called "the first Gospel" when the Gospel according to Mark was written first?

Research
○ Choose one of the Gospels and research more about what scholars say about it.

○ What do scholars seem to agree on? What seems to be rather certain about the writing of that Gospel?

○ What are scholars still uncertain of—or disagree on—regarding that Gospel? How do your findings impact your understanding of who Jesus is and how you can follow him today?

○ Write up a two-page report.

The Four Evangelists
The Gospel writers didn't tell us who they were. Scholars have gone through the Gospels searching for hints about who wrote each one, along with when, where, and under what circumstances each was written. In addition, many Church Fathers and other Christian writers from the second century have commented on who the Evangelists were.

Traditionally, the Evangelists John and Matthew were considered to be the Apostles of those names. **Matthew** was believed to be a tax collector who became a follower of Jesus and wrote so stirringly about Jesus' teachings regarding the Law in his Gospel.

Scholarly opinion today indicates that the Gospel according to Matthew may have been written in the city of Antioch no earlier than the late seventies. At the time, Antioch had a large Jewish population, and the Gospel according to Matthew in particular addresses tensions between Jews and Gentiles. He wrote mainly for a Jewish audience, so he included many Old Testament references and prophecies, with which they would be familiar.

The Gospel according to **Mark** gives indications that the author was a close follower of Saint Peter and that the Gospel was written in Rome. He wrote approximately thirty years after the Ascension of Jesus and just before the fall of Jerusalem and the Temple. By then, Peter, Paul, and James had already died. Christians at this time had to decide whether to fight with the Jews to defend the Temple. Most chose not to because they believed the new temple was the Body of Christ. Mark wrote for Jewish Christians experiencing persecution as well as Gentile Christians. The Gospel contains an urgent message to model the life of Jesus. That meant serving others and very often also meant suffering for the faith.

Luke was traditionally considered to be a physician. The author of Luke had a Gentile background and was well-educated. The same author wrote both the Gospel and the Acts of the Apostles, but neither book mentions who wrote them. The name Luke does appear in other books of the New Testament. Colossians 4:14 refers to "Luke, the beloved physician"; Philemon 1:24 talks about a Luke as a "fellow worker"; and the Second Letter to Timothy 4:11 mentions Paul's companion Luke. The author of Luke knew Greek well, but shows signs of not being very familiar with Palestinian geography. It is likely that the author was writing from outside of Palestine for a non-Jewish audience.

John by tradition was the youngest Apostle and often receives credit for the Gospel that goes by his name, along with three Epistles and the Book of Revelation. No one knows for certain who wrote this Gospel (or any of the other three Gospels). This Gospel

What if three different people wrote stories about you (for example, a brother or sister, a friend, a teacher or coach)?

○ What symbol might they use to portray you? Why?

○ How would each tell the story of your life a little differently? What would be similar?

Discuss

○ How would you explain how the Gospels came into existence?

○ Describe an incident you are familiar with that underwent a similar progression of stages, from actual events to oral reports to written accounts.

and other works attributed to John may have been written by different authors or a group of Christians and put together in one of the great cosmopolitan cities of the time, such as Ephesus in modern-day Turkey or Alexandria in Egypt. The Gospel begins with a concise theology lesson on the Incarnation. The opening words echo the opening of Genesis. The light separated darkness in the creation, and in John, the light, which is Jesus, will confront the darkness. The author of this Gospel seems to use more mystical images than the others.

The Gospels represent well-established strains of thought, images, and even exact words from the Apostles. For that reason, we can say that the Gospels are the product of Apostolic Tradition. Whether or not the Evangelists were Apostles themselves, clearly they saw their task as presenting as accurately as possible:

• what the Apostles communicated about Jesus; and

• what was by then commonly accepted knowledge in their communities.

Explain What can hints found in the Gospels tell us about the four Evangelists?

Infer Why is it important to know something about who wrote the Gospels?

SECTION 1 REVIEW

QUICK REVIEW

1. **Explain** Tell why Koine Greek was a good choice for the language of the New Testament.

2a. **Recall** What was the first stage in the formation of the Gospels?

b. **Summarize** How did oral tradition contribute to the formation of the Gospels?

c. **Explain** Who participated in the third stage of Gospel formation, and what did they do?

3a. **Explain** How are the Gospels a product of Apostolic Tradition?

b. **Summarize** Tell who wrote each of the Gospels and when and where each was written.

Listen and Discuss Talk in small groups about these questions.

○ From the information in this section, what can you infer about biblical scholars?

○ What other occupations would allow you to study ancient peoples and the Bible?

Pray Compose a short prayer thanking God for the Gospels and the people who help us compile and understand them.

SELF-ASSESS

Which statement best reflects where you are now?

☐ I'm confident enough about the material in this section to be able to explain it to someone else.

☐ I have a good grasp of the material in this section, but I could use more review.

☐ I'm lost. I need help catching up before moving on.

Christ's Infancy and Hidden Years

No Gospels existed in fully written form during the earliest decades of Christianity. That doesn't mean that the early Christians didn't tell and hear Gospel stories. For the most part, Christians heard small portions of the Gospels read aloud during the liturgy. Christian gatherings, especially those centered around the celebration of the Eucharist, served to keep the Gospel accounts alive. And even after the four Gospels were written down, for centuries few people could actually read them.

Nonetheless, we can identify certain parts of the Gospels that Christians from early on must have heard over and over again. The rest of this chapter will focus on what we call the mysteries of Christ's life, starting with his infancy and what are sometimes known as the "hidden years."

The greatest gift from God the Father for all humanity is the **Incarnation**: that at the time appointed by God, the only Son of the Father became man and assumed human nature without losing his divine nature. He is the second Person of the Holy Trinity, one Person with two natures, human and divine. Our salvation flows from this initiative because Jesus, true God and true man, came to pay for our sins by dying on the cross. The sacrifice of the Father's Son on the cross leads to eternal life.

The authors of Matthew and Luke start with Jesus' birth. Perhaps these Evangelists simply wanted to say something about the birth of Jesus, or perhaps they knew stories of Jesus' birth that were already circulating around the Christian communities. For whatever reason, these two Gospels contain stories of events related to the birth of Jesus not found in the other two Gospels. We often call these stories the **Infancy Narratives**.

GO TO THE SOURCE

Many scholars say the Gospels according to Matthew and Luke were written after the Gospel according to Mark, and quote from Mark extensively. However, Mark includes nothing about Jesus' birth. Look up the Infancy Narratives in Matthew 1:18–2:23 and Luke 1:1–2:39.

○ Make a chart comparing the similarities and differences between the two accounts.

○ Why do you think Matthew makes a point of telling us about the homage given to the Infant Jesus by the three wise men?

○ Why do you think Matthew tells us about Jesus going to Egypt and then returning? Hint: Check out the Book of the prophet Hosea.

○ Why do you think Luke's account says that shepherds were the first to hear about Jesus' birth?

Infancy Narratives

The Infancy Narratives seem to have a more theological than historical purpose. They are more focused on explaining who Jesus is and what his mission is than about giving a complete description of historical events surrounding his birth. For this reason, the theological implications of the stories are what is most striking about them.

The two Infancy Narratives describe the coming of the Messiah, the Son of God, in lowly circumstances. His coming is good news for all, but especially the poor and outcasts, such as shepherds. He is the Savior of the World, and his message is for people of

Incarnation at the time appointed by God, the only Son of God the Father, while retaining his divine nature, assumed human nature and became man

Infancy Narratives accounts, found in the beginning of the Gospels according to Matthew and Luke, that contain the genealogy of Jesus and the events surrounding his conception and birth

all nations who seek truth and wisdom, such as the three Magi, or wise men, from the East (see Matthew 2:1-12). Circumstances surrounding his birth fulfill the predictions of the prophets. By his given name, we know he comes to save us from sins and restore our relationship with God. In other words, these Infancy Narratives tell us about Jesus and his message even before we hear about how his life and ministry unfold.

In the Gospel according to Luke, we find a description of the Annunciation. Mary does not understand why God has chosen her or how the events will take place, since she is not yet married and is a virgin. As Gabriel explains to her, "nothing will be impossible with God." Despite her fears, Mary responds with heartfelt faith to God's invitation. "Here am I, the servant of the Lord" (Luke 1:37).

In Luke we read that Jesus was born in a humble manger. His birth was announced to ordinary shepherds: "I am bringing you good news of great joy for all the people: to you is born this day in the city of David a Savior, who is the Messiah, the Lord" (Luke 2:10-11). Although he was descended from the royal family of King David, Jesus was born into a simple family (see Luke 2:1-20).

We know that Mary and Joseph were faithful Jews. They fulfilled the Jewish requirements of purification. Forty days after Jesus' birth, they presented him at the Temple in Jerusalem and offered sacrifices for the purification. There, as seen in the Gospel according to Luke, they met a man named Simeon (see Luke 2:22-38).

The Holy Family fled to Egypt to escape persecution. In the Gospel according to Matthew, the story of the flight into Egypt connects Jesus with the ancient Israelites who were persecuted in Egypt (see Matthew 2:13-23). Just as God chose Moses to liberate the ancient Israelites, so God chose his Son to liberate all his people from the slavery of sin.

Even in the Infancy Narratives, suffering had already entered into the story of his birth: there was no room for him in the inn. Mary and Joseph had to wrap him in bands of cloth and lay him in a manger—the feeding trough for animals. Poor shepherds first recognize him. Herod the Great slaughters innocent children as he tries to kill Jesus after his birth. Mary and Joseph flee with Jesus into exile in Egypt. At the Presentation in the Temple, Simeon says of Jesus, "This child is destined for the falling and the rising of many in Israel, and to be a sign that will be opposed . . ." and said to Mary, "and a sword will pierce your own soul too" (Luke 2:34-35).

Describe What is one account that the Gospels according to Matthew and Luke include that Mark and John do not?

Infer What do the Infancy Narratives tell us about Jesus?

Research

○ Some other early Christian writings were rejected as inaccurate representations of the teachings of the Apostles. Some of these "gospels" not included as Sacred Scripture are writings that reflect a movement known as Gnosticism. Gnosticism was highly dualistic. It held that some people had special knowledge that others lacked. There were people of the light and people of the darkness.

Spirit (good) and matter (bad) could never blend together into one. As a result, Gnosticism viewed Jesus as pure spirit—not being of human flesh and blood. The early Church rejected Gnosticism as heresy.

○ Research Gnosticism. What do you think was its appeal? Why did the Church reject it as a misrepresentation of the Christian message?

Marian Devotion

Mary, the Mother of the Son of God, loved Jesus with a mother's love. Mary is the Mother of the Son of God, and therefore we call her the Mother of God. She is also our mother and the Mother of the Church. She understands when we are confused and uncertain about the unexpected experiences of our lives. We can turn to her in prayer, for she understands our struggles. Mary was centered on doing God's will. Mary responds to God's call with self-surrender and trusting faith in him. Her life invites us to do the same.

The Church honors Mary as the most special and first saint. We celebrate many feast days throughout the Church, and we have numerous prayers to venerate her, most especially the Hail Mary. Many parish churches and family homes have statues of Mary, and some parishes honor Mary in a special way during the months of May and October. In future courses you will spend more time learning about Mary, what the Church teaches about her role in salvation, and how we venerate her as the perfect disciple and greatest saint.

Historical records do not give us a clear picture of when this practice began, but it seems that Saint Dominic, in the thirteenth century, preached a form of the Rosary in France. Evidence does point to the modern Rosary in conjunction with a Dominican priest in the late fourteenth century.

>> Do you know someone who has a devotion to Mary?

Tell about a time when you took part in a Marian devotion.

Praying the Rosary, with the accompanying blessed rosary beads, is perhaps one of the most popular Marian devotions.

The Rosary consists of praying decades of Hail Marys along with the Lord's Prayer and the Glory to the Father, while meditating on a different mystery of the Rosary.

See page 289 for a full description of how to pray the Rosary.

Blessing of the Fleet

Jesus' Childhood

Mary, Joseph, and Jesus returned from Egypt to live in Nazareth. We do not know much about those years of Jesus' life. We do learn from the Gospel according to Luke that the Holy Family traveled to Jerusalem each year for the feast of Passover. When Jesus was twelve, he followed the custom of traveling with relatives and friends to Jerusalem. When it was time to return to Nazareth, the boy Jesus stayed behind without Mary and Joseph knowing this. Upon discovering that Jesus was not in the caravan, Mary and Joseph returned to find him in the Temple talking with the teachers. Afterward, the Gospel tells us, "Then he went down with them and came to Nazareth, and was obedient to them" (Luke 2:49).

This story shows Jesus' continued love and obedience to Mary and Joseph. By loving and obeying Mary and Joseph, Jesus illustrates how to observe the Fourth Commandment to honor one's father and mother. Jesus began at an early age to show us the way to live with respect and dignity.

Identify Where did the Holy Family live after returning from exile in Egypt?

Imagine How would you and your family react if you were separated in a large city?

GO TO THE SOURCE

Read Luke 2:47-52 to find out how Jesus responded to his mother and Joseph when they found him in the Temple.

○ What does the story of Jesus in the Temple at age twelve say to you today?

○ How can people your age imitate Jesus in their attitudes and actions, especially toward their parents?

○ What can you do to show obedience to your parents or guardians? Give specific examples.

SECTION 2 REVIEW

QUICK REVIEW

1a. Describe What is the greatest gift from God for all of humankind?

b. Research Which Gospels include Infancy Narratives and where in Jesus' life do the other Gospels begin?

2a. Recall What is the purpose of the Infancy Narratives?

b. Name What events from Jesus' life are described in the Infancy Narratives?

c. Describe Tell about three examples of suffering from the Infancy Narratives.

3. Summarize What does the story of Jesus in the Temple tell us about his relationship with Mary and Joseph?

Pray Think about what Mary means to you, and write a prayer of devotion asking her intercession with her Son.

SELF-ASSESS

Which statement best reflects where you are now?

☐ I'm confident enough about the material in this section to be able to explain it to someone else.

☐ I have a good grasp of the material in this section, but I could use more review.

☐ I'm lost. I need help catching up before moving on.

The Mysteries of Christ's Public Years

Mark's Gospel begins with Jesus' public life, when around the age of thirty, Jesus began his ministry and gained a following of local people. This earliest Gospel begins with the baptism of Jesus by John the Baptist.

John believed that the messianic hopes of the Jews would soon be fulfilled. In spite of his insistence that he was not the Messiah, people continued to flock to John to be baptized and to hear him preach. Jesus came to John seeking a baptism of repentance, as did many other Jews. John knew from the moment he saw him that Jesus was truly the Messiah. As Jesus approached the banks of the Jordan River, John proclaimed to the crowds, "Here is the Lamb of God who takes away the sin of the world!" (John 1:29).

John the Baptist at first balked at baptizing Jesus. John knew that the baptisms he conferred using water in the Jordan amounted to very little compared to the Baptism the Messiah would grant through the Holy Spirit; in other words, it was not sacramental. Jesus, however, rebuked John and instructed him to proceed, saying that it must be done.

> And just as he [Jesus] was coming up out of the water, he saw the heavens torn apart and the Spirit descending like a dove on him. And a voice came from heaven, "You are my Son, the Beloved; with you I am well pleased."
>
> —Mark 1:10-11

The baptism given by John was a sign of a person's willingness to turn from sin and toward God. Even though Jesus was without sin, he sought to be baptized. This showed his connection with God's People who sought to strengthen their relationship with him. And the baptism of Jesus is the first of several New Testament events that reveal something of the nature of the Holy Trinity—Father, Son, and Holy Spirit.

Temptations

Immediately following Jesus' baptism, the Spirit led him into the wilderness, where he stayed for forty days (see Matthew 4:1-11). Here Jesus was tempted by the devil. Each temptation of Jesus was toward a different form of power. The first temptation was toward material power, the second to miraculous power, and the third to political power. They show the distortion between living by the powers of the world and living by the power of God. Jesus answered the devil by quoting Scripture.

The temptation narrative would have reminded Matthew's audience of the time their ancestors were in the desert. God tested the Israelites to see what was in their hearts and whether they would keep the

> [In Jesus] God's power is now revealed in his mildness, his greatness in his simplicity and closeness. And yet his power and greatness are no less profound.
>
> —Pope Benedict XVI, *Jesus of Nazareth*

Describe

Pope Benedict sees three qualities in Jesus that we may not normally associate with God: mildness, simplicity, and closeness.

- Which of these three qualities comes closest to what you experience in your relationship with Jesus?
- How could refocusing on these qualities improve your relationship with Jesus?
- Based on your own experience, what other qualities appropriately describe Jesus?

commandments (Deuteronomy 8:1-5). The Israelites often failed to follow God's commandments. Ultimately they realized that trusting God instead of turning from him was the only way they would complete their journey.

Jesus, however, trusted God the Father through all the temptations Satan presented, and Jesus refused to compromise with evil. He did not succumb to the false promises of Satan. He chose instead to trust in his Father's will and to believe in his Father's plan of salvation.

Explain How is the baptism administered by John the Baptist different from our own?

Elaborate With what kinds of power did Satan tempt Jesus?

Proclamation of the Kingdom and Call of Disciples

In the Synoptic Gospels, the coming of God's Kingdom is the central theme in Jesus' ministry and teaching, "The time is fulfilled, and the kingdom is at hand; repent and believe in the gospel" (Mark 1:15). Also called the Kingdom of Heaven and the reign of God, Jesus proclaims the **Kingdom of God** after his baptism and his forty days in the wilderness. Jesus teaches that the Kingdom of God is God's reign or rule in our lives, in this world, and in the eternal life to come. Jesus proclaimed that this saving intervention of God is close at hand, and in a certain sense is already present in him.

Jesus not only proclaimed the Kingdom with his words and his teachings such as parables; he also witnessed to it with his works and miracles. We'll spend more time on parables and miracles in the next chapter. The Kingdom is present and active in Jesus. The coming of the Kingdom of God is closely connected with the Person of Jesus. Jesus does not merely announce the coming of the Kingdom, as did the prophets of the Old Testament. He is the Person through whom God establishes his reign. The progress of the Kingdom coincides with the destiny of Jesus, whose triumph is the Kingdom's triumph and establishment. The full coming of the Kingdom is still in the future and an object of hope and prayer as reflected in the Our Father: "your kingdom come" (Matthew 6:10).

From the beginning, Jesus not only preached the Kingdom, he also called people to follow him. The Gospel according to Mark includes three call narratives, which describe how Jesus summoned others to hear and respond to the word and the power of God.

As Jesus began his ministry, he invited four ordinary people—Simon, Andrew, James, and John—to help him proclaim the message of the Kingdom of God. Jesus expected an immediate and total commitment to serve God. In similar ways, he invited others to follow him, too (see Mark 1:16-20).

For three years Jesus taught and preached the Good News, healed in the name of the Father, and called people to repent and believe. As we read the Gospels, we see glimpses into the future suffering and death that Jesus will endure before he is raised in glory.

Kingdom of God the reign of God ushered in by Jesus that makes God's grace present in the world, but reaches its fulfillment in Heaven

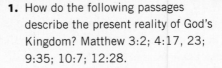

GO TO THE SOURCE

Compare and contrast the three call narratives from the Gospel according to Mark: Mark 1:16-20, Mark 3:13-19, and Mark 6:7-13.

○ Read all three narratives. Note the similarities and differences among them, particularly in what Jesus says and how he acts, how those he calls responds, what he is calling them to do, and so on.

○ If you had been there with the first followers, how would you have responded?

○ How does Jesus call people today? How do you respond?

GO TO THE SOURCE

1. How do the following passages describe the present reality of God's Kingdom? Matthew 3:2; 4:17, 23; 9:35; 10:7; 12:28.

2. How do the following describe the future reality of the Kingdom? Matthew 5:3, 10; 7:21; 8:11; 13:43; 18:3; 25:34.

3. How do the following relate to eternal life? Matthew 5:19 and 7:21.

Bible STUDY

A spiritual practice for the life of discipleship

> If you continue in my word, you are truly my disciples; and you will know the truth, and the truth will make you free.
>
> —John 8:31-32

Jesus himself told us that studying the Bible is essential for the life of discipleship.

Bible study is a spiritual practice that helps you to see how the word of God sheds light on the decisions you are dealing with, your heart's deepest longings, and your understanding of what the spiritual path of discipleship is all about.

Bible study is probably the most popular of all the spiritual practices associated with discipleship, and there are many ways to do it. Find the way that best suits how you learn and the schedule you keep.

You can block out a **set time**, such as every Sunday night for thirty minutes or every night for ten minutes before going to sleep.

Or you can do it **by the book**, by choosing one book at a time to go through in any order you wish.

You can also follow the **liturgical calendar** of Scripture readings. Either prepare for the upcoming Sunday Mass readings or follow up on the previous Sunday readings by studying the chapters from which the readings are taken.

And you can do so **with help**, such as a biblical reference or dictionary that explains terms and phrases that you want more information on, or with the help of soft music or contemporary Catholic/Christian artists playing in the background as you read.

However you decide to do a Bible study, keep in mind that Scripture teaches about:

- the nature of God—Father, Son, and Holy Spirit,
- conscience—knowing what is right and wrong, good and evil,
- character—the kind of person God wants you to be, and
- contribution—how we are to treat others.

> **Any time you read or hear the word of God and want to apply it to your life, ask yourself:**
>
> **What is God trying to tell me?**
>
> **What is this telling me about my understanding of who God is, conscience, character, contribution?**
>
> **Look up the following passages and decide which of the above four aspects the Scripture addresses:**
>
> | Matthew 5:36-37 | John 3:16-17 | John 14:6 |
> |---|---|---|
> | Galatians 6:9-10 | Colossians 3:12-16 | James 2:14-16 |

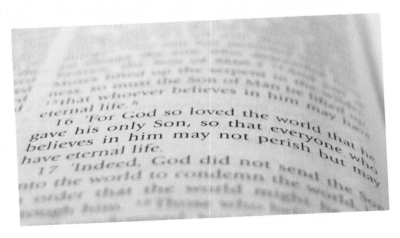

At his Transfiguration, Jesus takes Peter, James, and John up the mountain away from the crowds. While they are there, Jesus is transfigured, changed in appearance. A bright cloud comes over them, shining on Jesus, and a voice from the cloud says, "This is my Son, the Beloved, with him I am well pleased; listen to him!" (Matthew 17:5).

For a moment Jesus disclosed his divine glory, confirming what Peter had said—that Jesus was the Messiah.

Just as the baptism of Jesus began his public life, the Transfiguration of Jesus set the stage for his Passion, death, Resurrection, and Ascension. The cloud indicates the presence of the Holy Spirit, and the voice was that of God the Father. The Father and the Holy Spirit were with Jesus at the beginning and throughout his ministry.

Describe What is the Kingdom of God?

Explain What do we get a glimpse into at both the baptism and Transfiguration of Jesus?

Transfiguration the culminating moment in the public life of Jesus in which his appearance changed in the presence of the Apostles, and Elijah and Moses appeared beside him to reveal him as the true Messiah

Transfiguration

When we confess that Jesus is the Christ, we signify that God the Father has anointed him with the Holy Spirit for a divine mission. We see this at Jesus' baptism by John and something similar at Jesus' **Transfiguration**, as we get a glimpse into Jesus' divinity and the life of the Trinity.

SECTION 3 REVIEW

QUICK REVIEW

1a. Recall What does John the Baptist proclaim as Jesus approaches him at the Jordan River?

b. Elaborate What did Jesus' baptism show even though he was without sin?

2a. Identify What would the temptation narrative remind Matthew's audience of?

b. Summarize What role does trust play in the temptation narrative?

3a. Compare What is Jesus' role in the Kingdom of God?

b. Describe What are the call narratives of the Gospel according to Mark?

c. List Who did Jesus invite to help proclaim his message as he began his ministry?

4a. Explain What parallels are there between the baptism and Transfiguration of Jesus?

b. Tell What does Jesus disclose and confirm in the Transfiguration?

Listen and Discuss Describe the Transfiguration in your own words, then share your thoughts with a partner.

SELF-ASSESS

Which statement best reflects where you are now?

☐ I'm confident enough about the material in this section to be able to explain it to someone else.

☐ I have a good grasp of the material in this section, but I could use more review.

☐ I'm lost. I need help catching up before moving on.

Christ's Paschal Mystery

We know that the Gospels are not intended as biographical histories or detailed accounts of every aspect of Jesus' life. Each Gospel tells a unique story about Jesus and his teachings in order to give us unique insight into the mystery of God. A major focus of each one is the abandonment, suffering, agony, and cruel death that he endured. However, this total emptying of himself led to the clearest revelation of his divinity, his Resurrection from death, which is central to the Gospels and our faith.

No one can read the Gospels without feeling how petty are the books of the philosophers with all their pomp, compared with the Gospels!

—Jean Jacques Rousseau, quoted in
Tony Castle, *The New Book of
Christian Quotations*

Choose

Throughout the Bible, but especially in the Gospels, we find the authors refer to Jesus with various titles. Here is a list of some of the titles for Jesus found in Scripture: Alpha and Omega, Anointed One, Bridegroom, Comforter, Wonderful Counselor, Deliverer, Eternal God, God with Us, Good Shepherd, Intercessor, Judge of All, Just One, King of Kings, King of Peace, Lamb of God, Light of the World, Living Bread, Lord God Almighty, Morning Star, Prince of Peace, Redeemer, Resurrection and the Life, My Salvation, Savior of the World, Son of God, Son of Man, the Vine, the Way, the Word.

○ Select three titles that best reflect who Jesus is to you and find them in the Bible.

○ Explain why you are drawn to these titles.

Jesus' Last Supper and Passion

Before Jesus entered his Passion and willingly accepted death on the cross, he shared a meal with his Apostles. Many of the names we give to the Sacrament of Eucharist—the Lord's Supper, the Breaking of the Bread, the Memorial of the Lord's Passion and Resurrection—come from the account of this **Last Supper**, the last Passover meal that Jesus ate with his disciples the night before he died. We call the Sacrament The Lord's Supper because of its connection with the Last Supper.

Last Supper the final Passover meal which Jesus ate with his disciples before his crucifixion

Jesus' passing over to his Father by his death and Resurrection, the new Passover, is anticipated in the Last Supper and celebrated in the Eucharist, which fulfills the Jewish Passover and anticipates the final Passover of the Church in the glory of the kingdom. Hence the Eucharist is called "the Lord's Supper."

—CCC, 1329

We also refer to the Eucharist as the Breaking of Bread because that is what Jesus literally did. We call the Eucharistic celebration an assembly because the faithful are gathered together as the Church.

During the Last Supper, Jesus also washed the feet of the disciples and commanded them to love one another as he had loved them. He instituted the Eucharist as a pledge of his love to them and so the disciples could share in his Passover. The Eucharist is how we celebrate Jesus' death and Resurrection, which makes present his sacrifice of the cross. The Eucharist, then, is a Sacrament of love, a sign of unity, and bond of charity (see CCC, 1323).

Saint Joseph of Arimathea Society

A growing number of young Catholic people are taking Christ's sacrifice to heart in really practical ways. In recent years several Saint Joseph of Arimathea ministries have begun in Catholic schools and parishes. Joseph of Arimathea, you may recall from the Gospels, made sure Jesus had a place to be buried. Young people in these ministries make sure someone is available for those people in their community who have no one to care for them after they die.

Burying the dead is a Corporal Work of Mercy and has become an important ministry for students like those who volunteer from local Catholic high schools in Louisville, Kentucky. There are members of most communities who, for one reason or another, have no one to be with them at the time of their death and burial. These members of the community deserve a proper burial, one in which they are prayed for and given the respect they deserve. Students and faculty members in the Archdiocese of Louisville believe all people are born into this world with someone who loves them, and should leave their earthly life with someone who loves them. In some ways, the Catholic young people become "family" and serve these men, women, and children by praying for them and serving as pallbearers for them. It is a true act of mercy, a true act of compassion, and a true act of selfless love that these young people and adults share with the dead.

> **Think About It** How does this ministry serve God? What would it take to start such a society where you live? How does this society serve God?

↗ Go to the student site at **hs.osvcurriculum.com**

We consume Christ, which fills us with grace and the hope of glory.

Each Gospel gives an extensive and detailed account of the events leading up to and including the death of Jesus. These accounts are called **Passion Narratives** because of the intense suffering endured by Jesus out of love for us. Along with the Resurrection accounts, the Passion of Christ is the core message of each Gospel.

Elaborate Why is the Eucharist called the "Lord's Supper"?

Tell What are the Passion Narratives about?

Death and Resurrection

On the cross, we see Jesus in both his human and divine natures. The human part is easy to understand. People are never so weak and vulnerable as when they are dying. However, there is a Greek word that helps us understand how this same experience also reveals Jesus' divinity. *Kenosis* means "self-emptying." The Gospel according to John reports that a Roman soldier jabs Jesus with a spear to make sure he's dead. Blood and water flow out. Jesus gave his life to demonstrate the extent of God's love.

Here we have what the Gospel writers have been telling us all along—the fulfillment of the promises found in the Old Testament from Genesis to the prophets.

- Creation was the initial gift from God.

- The covenant with Noah and with Abraham and his descendants were gifts and promises of God's steadfast love.

- The Exodus told of God freeing his people from slavery and leading them to a good and prosperous land.

- The prophets, despite their angry words when the people went astray, also always included words of hope.

On the cross, we see *the ultimate act of God's self-emptying love.* Jesus takes on all the sins of the world and endures this gruesome suffering unto death to save all humankind from their sins, so that God's message of love and forgiveness would be manifest in one final, definitive act. Through his Passion, Jesus wins new life for us in the Holy Spirit. The grace we receive heals us from the damage that sin brings about.

But we can never separate Christ's death from his rising from the dead. This complete sacrifice leads to new life and the chance to be with God forever.

As Catholics, we revere the crucifix, wear a cross, place our faith in Christ on the cross, bless ourselves with the Sign of the Cross, and place crosses on top of our church buildings and in our homes. The crucifix symbolizes God's greatest gift. The sin of the world, and death itself, has been conquered through Jesus' dying and ultimate rising to new life. His Resurrection makes our own resurrection possible.

The Gospels don't end with Jesus' death. Each one has an account of his faithful followers encountering him after his death. Because Jesus was raised from the dead, all Christians have confidence that new life is offered them after death as well. The following passage from the *Catechism* describes how we are transformed by Christ's life, death, and Resurrection.

> All Christ's riches "are for every individual and are everybody's property."[18] Christ did not live his life for himself but *for us, from his Incarnation "for us men and for our salvation" to his death "for our sins" and Resurrection "for our justification."*[19]
>
> —CCC, 519

All four Gospels also address the historical event of the Resurrection. Each Evangelist addressed the particular need and background of his audience. However, they all profess the following beliefs:

- Jesus was crucified and was raised from the dead

- Jesus appeared to some women and other disciples

- Jesus' disciples were to share the Good News of Jesus with others.

Passion Narratives accounts of events leading up to the death of Jesus that show his love for humanity; found in all four Gospels

kenosis Greek word for "emptying"; in the New Testament, often it refers to "self-emptying"

GO TO THE SOURCE

Read Luke 24:1-12.

1. Who are the first people to enter the empty tomb?

2. What message do they recieve, from whom?

3. How do the Apostles initially react to the news?

4. Who confirms that the tomb is empty? Why might Luke have named him specifically?

The Resurrection is a fundamental truth of our faith. It is an unparalleled intervention of God into human history. In many of the New Testament letters, we read that Baptism unites believers not only with the death of Jesus, but also with his Resurrection. The Resurrection of Jesus is the source of new life we receive in Baptism that is strengthened in our celebration of the other Sacraments. The Church celebrates the Resurrection and the whole of the Paschal Mystery at every Mass.

People carry crosses every day. You carry burdens, anxieties, or problems, but we know that Jesus asked his disciples to take their cross and follow him. Through Jesus' Resurrection, however, we hold hope that our daily crosses will bring us new life. This is how the Good News can transform the lives of disciples. No matter how crazy, difficult, or desperate life becomes, Jesus offers something the world needs: **hope**. Hope is a theological virtue. The theological virtues are gifts from God that make possible a life of virtue. They do, however, call for a response on our part. By living faithfully, hopefully, and lovingly, we cooperate with God's gifts of faith, hope, and charity.

Define What is *kenosis*?

Explain What are three beliefs about the Resurrection professed in all four Gospels?

Ascension

On Easter Sunday night, the Risen Jesus appeared to the Apostles and told them not to be afraid. Slowly they began to realize the enormous truth. God the Father had raised up Jesus—the innocent one—from the darkness of death and "abolished death and brought life and immortality to light through the gospel" (2 Timothy 1:10).

As the Gospels bear witness, Jesus appeared to his Apostles in Galilee and in Jerusalem. During this final appearance, Jesus ascends into Heaven and is now seated at the right hand of the Father. "Then he led them out as far as Bethany, and, lifting up his hands, he blessed them. While he was blessing them, he withdrew from them and was carried up into heaven" (Luke 24:50-51).

This departure of Jesus is known as the Ascension. Ascending into Heaven is an image present in the Old Testament. Ancient holy figures, such as Enoch, Elijah, Moses, Baruch, and Ezra, were thought to have ascended to God in Heaven after their earthly lives. Indeed, ascension was a somewhat common literary device to show the greatness of certain individuals (Greco-Roman heroes, as well as Old Testament figures). Ascension to the heavens indicated divine approval or favor of the person, as well as his or her rise to heavenly power.

Like the Resurrection, the Ascension is a mystery of faith. From now on, until the end of the world, the Risen Lord is seated at the right hand of God the Father. Christ is "the King of kings and Lord of lords . . . and dwells in unapproachable light" (1 Timothy 6:15, 16). He exists as Son of God before all ages, one with the Father and the Holy Spirit.

Identify Where did Jesus appear to his Apostles after the Resurrection?

Explain What truth did the Apostles begin to realize on Easter Sunday night?

GO TO THE SOURCE

Read about what happened in Mark 16:19-20 and Luke 24:50-53.

○ Place yourself at the Ascension of Jesus. How might his Apostles feel about Jesus leaving?

○ How can a person remain close to Jesus today even though he isn't present in human form?

hope the theological virtue by which we trust in God the Father, in everything that Christ has promised, and in the help of the Holy Spirit. It is the desire to achieve eternal happiness in Heaven and to cooperate with the graces that make this desire come true.

JUSTICE AND DISCIPLESHIP

LEGALLY CONVICTED OF HIS "CRIME," Jesus was sentenced to death. Crucifixion was a painful, gruesome, and public form of execution. It would be hard to imagine Jesus receiving the lethal injection of today's capital punishment.

Catholic teaching is clear on capital punishment. All human life is sacred; the gift of life is given by God and is God's alone to take away. The late Cardinal Joseph Bernardin of Chicago explained that our respect for human life must be like the seamless garment, which Jesus wore on the cross (John 19:23-24): consistent, without exception, from the moment of conception to the moment of natural death.

The cases in which execution of an offender is necessary are very rare, if not practically non-existent (see CCC, 2267). In *Twelve Tough Issues*, Archbishop Daniel Pilarczyk of Cincinnati explains that society has the right to protect itself from violent criminals.

Present-day prison systems have enough security measures in place to ensure the safety of the public, making capital punishment unnecessary (see also CCC, 2267). Jesus calls for wrongdoers to repent, while admonishing would-be executioners: "Let anyone among you who is without sin be the first to throw a stone . . ." (John 8:7).

Consider your own stance on the death penalty—the legal, government-sanctioned killing of a person.

Learn more about capital punishment.

Advocate
Stand up for the "seamless garment" view on the sacredness of all life whenever you find yourself in the midst of discussions regarding birth and death issues. How you stand up each time may change depending on the situations.

Go to the student site at
hs.osvcurriculum.com

All human **life is sacred**; the gift of life is given by God

You can be for justice without being a disciple, but you cannot be a disciple without being for justice.

MY FAITH

What symbol or image would you use to portray your understanding of who Jesus is and what your relationship with him is like?

What specifically would you want the symbol to represent?

Take some time now and in the next week to work with this until you have an symbol or image in mind you think is an accurate representation.

Try drawing your symbol or image. If you can't decide on just one, no problem; go with two.

Remember that you may end up sharing this at the end of the course.

Consider these questions thoughtfully and write your personal thoughts in the space provided.

➜ Go to the student site at **hs.osvcurriculum.com**

Discipleship . . . within the Body of Christ . . . for the glory of God and the good of the world

SECTION **4 REVIEW**

QUICK REVIEW

1a. Identify What does each Gospel tell?

b. Recall What is the Paschal Mystery, and what does it mean for our faith?

2a. Explain What is the new Passover?

b. Elaborate Why are the events leading up to and including the death of Jesus called the Passion Narratives?

3a. Analyze Why is *kenosis* an appropriate word for Jesus on the cross?

b. Evaluate Why is the cross so important to Catholics?

c. Explain What message do the Gospels tell us about Jesus' Resurrection?

4a. Describe What happens to Jesus after he ascends to Heaven?

b. Explain What does Jesus' Ascension indicate?

ACT

With a group, write a play as if you were all there at the Ascension.

○ Be sure to describe the scene.

○ Describe what you all might have said and seen.

○ Then discuss what it means to believe even though you weren't there.

SELF-ASSESS

Which statement best reflects where you are now?

☐ I'm confident enough about the material in this section to be able to explain it to someone else.

☐ I have a good grasp of the material in this section, but I could use more review.

☐ I'm lost. I need help catching up before moving on.

PRAYER

Act of Love

O my Divine Jesus,
how shall I return thanks to you
for the goodness in giving yourself to me?
The only way I can repay your love
is by loving you in return.
Yes, my Lord, I love you,
and I desire to love you all my life.

My Jesus, you alone are sufficient for me.
Whom shall I love,
if I love not you, my Jesus?
You love me even when I neglect you.
Even when I fail to love you.
I love you.
Oh, do you also love me.
If I love you but little,
give me the love with which you love me.

O Mary, my good Mother,
and you, glorious Saint Joseph,
lend me your love wherewith to love my Jesus.
Amen.

Into the faithful hands of God
we commit ourselves now and always.
Lord, let us be yours forever;
through Jesus Christ your Son our Lord.
Amen.

CHAPTER 7 REVIEW

VOCABULARY

Use each of the following terms in a sentence that shows you know what the term means. You may include more than one term in a sentence.

Evangelists

Incarnation

Infancy Narratives

Kingdom of God

hope

Transfiguration

Last Supper

Passion Narratives

kenosis

PEOPLE AND TERMS

Use information from the chapter to tell why each person or term is significant.

1. oral tradition

2. Apostolic Tradition

3. Matthew

4. Mark

5. Luke

6. John

7. Gnosticism

8. Transfiguration

9. Crucifix

10. The Last Supper

UNDERSTANDING

Answer each question and complete each exercise.

SECTION 1

1. **Speculate** If you lived two thousand years ago, would you have recognized Jesus as God's Son? Why or why not?

2. **Describe** Explain each of the three stages of formation of the Gospel and why each one was important.

3. **Explain** List and explain the symbols of the Evangelists.

4. **Elaborate** What do the opening words of the Gospel according to John echo?

SECTION 2

5. **Connect** Why are Infancy Narratives important for understanding Jesus' life?

6. **Analyze** Why are genealogies included in the Gospels according to Matthew and Luke?

7. **Explain** How did suffering enter the story of Jesus' birth?

8. **Analyze** Why would Gnosticism be a heresy?

SECTION 3

9. **Explain** How would the temptation narrative have reminded Matthew's audience of their ancestors?

10. **Explain** After what significant event and time period did Jesus proclaim the Kingdom of God?

11. **Analyze** What does Jesus' Transfiguration give us a glimpse of?

12. **Describe** Who was present at Jesus' Transfiguration?

13. **Support** Along with the Resurrection accounts, why are they and the Passion Narratives the core of the Gospels?

14. **Explain** How do the Passion Narratives fulfill the promises found in the Old Testament from Genesis to the prophets?

15. **Recall** Name other figures who were thought to have also ascended into Heaven.

16. **Describe** Where is Jesus now seated?

CONNECTING

Visual This is an image of a well-known parable.

What parable does it illustrate? What details in the artwork help you identify it? Is there anything you would add to the image to make it more complete?

Challenge You are a teaching assistant in a sixth-grade religion class. The students have been reading the Bible. A student has a question.

> **Student:** Why are there four Gospels? Isn't one enough?
>
> **You:** Not really. Each of the Gospels teaches us something different about Jesus.
>
> **Student:** But isn't Jesus the same Jesus in all of them?
>
> **You:** Well, yeah, but it's like each writer draws a portrait instead of taking a picture.
>
> **Student:** I don't get it.

○ Explain what you mean as simply and as accurately as you can.

○ Continue the conversation, adding at least two more questions the student might ask and how you would answer. Use information from the chapter to frame your answers.

Question After working through this chapter, what advice would you give someone who wants to understand the Gospels better?

Imagine The Evangelists each wanted to have a social media page devoted to a Gospel. They would use these pages to summarize their Gospels. Design a page for one of the Evangelists. Consider these ideas as you design the page:

○ How might the author of your choice want his Gospel described?

○ What popular or religious songs would be linked to the page?

○ What kinds of images would be displayed on the page?

SELF-ASSESS

On Your Own Make a list of the most important things you learned from this chapter. Select three things that represent your growth in understanding as you worked through this chapter. Write a paragraph explaining your choices. Share your list and paragraph in small groups.

CHAPTER 8

How are these people living the Gospels?

What part of the Gospels could this commemorate?

Going Deeper into the Gospels

Go to the student site at
hs.osvcurriculum.com

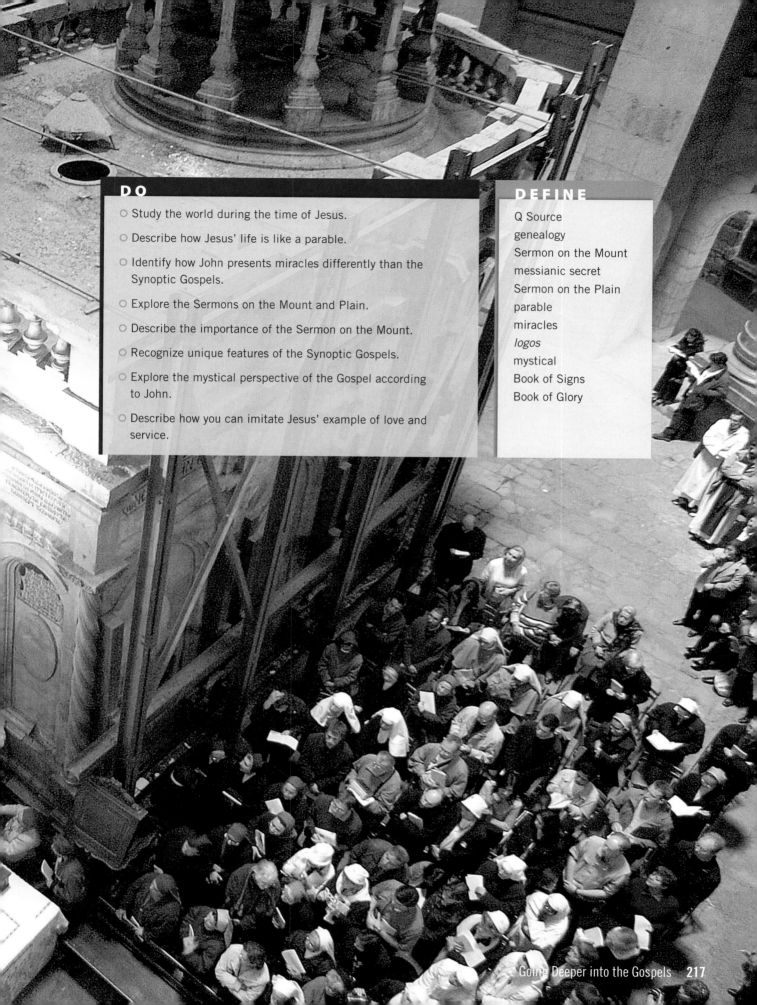

DO

○ Study the world during the time of Jesus.

○ Describe how Jesus' life is like a parable.

○ Identify how John presents miracles differently than the Synoptic Gospels.

○ Explore the Sermons on the Mount and Plain.

○ Describe the importance of the Sermon on the Mount.

○ Recognize unique features of the Synoptic Gospels.

○ Explore the mystical perspective of the Gospel according to John.

○ Describe how you can imitate Jesus' example of love and service.

DEFINE

Q Source
genealogy
Sermon on the Mount
messianic secret
Sermon on the Plain
parable
miracles
logos
mystical
Book of Signs
Book of Glory

Read this scenario.

Walking around their downtown park on a beautiful Sunday afternoon, four sophomores stroll pass several local artists painting portraits from people's photos. Paints, brushes, rags, canvas, frames, and art supplies hang everywhere. Artists are painting portraits based on the pictures of deceased parents, young children, or even pictures of themselves. Some people, including the owners of the pictures, stand and sit, studying the artists at work.

One conversation goes like this:

"Why would someone want a portrait painted when they already have a high resolution digital picture?"

"It'll never look as good as the picture."

"Plus, it's expensive."

"Yeah, but it's different."

"Stick with the picture. Even the old ones are better."

"And more accurate."

"You're missing the point."

WHAT DO YOU SAY?

Where Are You?				
Choose the response that best reflects where you are right now.				
I understand how each of the Gospels is different.	☐ Quite a bit	☐ Somewhat	☐ A little	☐ Not at all
I know how each of the Gospels are alike.	☐ Quite a bit	☐ Somewhat	☐ A little	☐ Not at all
I am familiar with the Sermon on the Mount.	☐ Quite a bit	☐ Somewhat	☐ A little	☐ Not at all
I understand the Beatitudes.	☐ Quite a bit	☐ Somewhat	☐ A little	☐ Not at all
I'm interested in reading one entire Gospel.	☐ Quite a bit	☐ Somewhat	☐ A little	☐ Not at all
The Gospel guides my life.	☐ Quite a bit	☐ Somewhat	☐ A little	☐ Not at all

In the Time of Jesus

What was the purpose of Jesus' miracles?
What sources did the Gospel writers use? What was it like where Jesus grew up?

Why did Jesus teach using parables?

How does the Gospel according to John differ from the Synoptic Gospels?

Popular images often portray Jesus with a halo of bright light surrounding his head. Or, if in a movie, angelic music sometimes plays in the background in case we miss that the divine presence is among us. What is most striking about Jesus, however, is that he is *God who is man*. God could manifest himself to us in any number of ways, in whatever way he chooses. The Son of God chose to be one of us, with all of the struggles and challenges that come with being human. Naturally we wonder what life was like for Jesus. Getting a sense of this is important as we study the Gospels.

One way to find out about Jesus and his time is to visit Israel and the Middle East, by actually going there or making a virtual visit. Read what one seminarian had to say after spending Holy Thursday 2009 at the Basilica of the Holy Sepulchre in Jerusalem.

I left the tomb struggling to process my incredible experience of the reality of Christ and of the Holy Land, the very land where He walked and taught, where He lived and died. This was the center of it all, the center of all time and space. That tomb, forever a monument to the Resurrection, had shown me Christ as I had never seen Him before.

—Joshua Allen, May 2009, *Why I Love the Holy Land*

Unfortunately today, the Holy Land can also be a dangerous place. Violence sometimes breaks out in this conflicted region. Life was unsettled during the days of Jesus as well. Israel was ruled by Herod under the Roman Emperor Augustus Caesar. Then Herod died and fights broke out in various parts of the territory. Jews hoped to be rid of the oppressive ruling family. Herod's sons, however, did gain seats of power. By the time Jesus began his public ministry around A.D. 27, Antipas, the Herod we read about in the Gospels, ruled the area under the new Roman Emperor, Tiberius.

Then in A.D. 26, Augustus appointed a Roman procurator to govern the city of Jerusalem. This man's name was Pontius Pilate. Most of the events of the Gospel take place during his rule of the holy city, from the ministry of John the Baptist to the death, Resurrection, and Ascension of Jesus.

Discuss

○ Name a historic place you once visited and describe what it was like.

○ How would knowing more about the time of Jesus on Earth help your relationship with God?

The Geography and Politics of Palestine

The land that Jesus traveled during his time on Earth stretched from the Mediterranean Sea in the west to the Jordan River in the east. That space spanned fifty miles and Israel stretched 150 miles north and south. It was an area about the size of New Jersey, according to Jerome Kodell, OSB, in *The Catholic Bible Study Handbook*. Most people of the era

Modern-day Tiberias, Israel, on the shores of the Sea of Galilee.

traveled by foot and could cover about 20 miles per day. There are three geographical areas in Israel:

- A plain borders the Mediterranean, with farming areas to the south. A ridge of hills bisects the region from north to south.
- The Jordan River and valley to the east are comprised of fertile and wilderness areas.
- A desert surrounds the Dead Sea.

The city of Jerusalem served as the political and religious center of Israel. Many of the residents of Jerusalem descended from Israelites who returned to their homeland following the Babylonian exile in the sixth century B.C. The land known as Samaria was located in the middle of the country. The Samaritans who lived there thought of themselves as fully Jewish. However, other Jews from the south, in Judea, considered the Samaritans as outsiders, and a mixed race, because they had intermarried with non-Jews.

Galilee, where Jesus grew up, was in the northern part of Israel. This farming area was the most fertile of the region, Kodell writes. The Sea of Galilee is a freshwater lake that covers twenty-four square miles. Many Gentiles, or non-Jewish people, lived in this area. "Galilean Jews made up for

their distance from the Jerusalem Temple by religious zeal and tenacity," Kodell reports. In fact, like any place, the political landscape was often contentious.

Analyze Why do you think the Son of God chose to be "one of us"?

Describe What types of geographical areas make up the Israel that Jesus traveled?

The Roman procurator Pontius Pilate, as leader of Samaria and Judea, controlled everything around Jerusalem, including tax collections for Rome, keeping the peace, and deciding capital punishment cases, Kodell writes. A number of Jews at the time supported Rome. They were known as the Herodians. On the other end of the spectrum were the Zealots, who wanted to rid Israel of Roman rule. Occasionally the Zealots staged acts of terrorism to fight for their cause. Heavy taxes boosted anti-Roman sentiment. You may recall that Matthew, one of the twelve Apostles, was a tax collector before answering Jesus' call.

The Bible also mentions many groups of religious people. These include the Pharisees and Sadducees, scribes, and the Sanhedrin.

- The Pharisees were a lay group of reformers who held a strict interpretation of the Old Testament Law. This brought them into conflict with Jesus.

The Gospels tell us the places where Jesus traveled. To get a perspective on walking distances, let's start in the holy city of Jerusalem that sits twenty-six hundred feet above sea level, equivalent to a 260-story building. Bethlehem, where Jesus was born, is six miles south of Jerusalem. Nazareth, where he grew up, is in the opposite direction, sixty-five miles north of Jerusalem. Close to Nazareth, the Sea of Galilee is about seventy miles north and east of Jerusalem. Heading south we find the Jordan River, which is twenty-one miles east of Jerusalem at its closest point. Jesus also visited the city of Jericho, at eight hundred feet below sea level and fifteen miles east of Jerusalem.

- How do you think Jesus' mode of transportation impacted his ministry?
- How much do you think he traveled in his ministry?

Faith & Culture

Go to the student site at **hs.osvcurriculum.com**

PRIMARY SOURCES

Saint Ambrose was a bishop from the fourth century (339–397) and Saint Alphonsus Liguori served as a bishop during the eighteenth century (1696–1787). Both were eventually named Doctors of the Church after living in two very different eras and writing many thoughts about God and the Church. Here are excerpts from each discussing Christ.

↗ Go to the student site at
hs.osvcurriculum.com

In Christ we are all things, He is everything to us. If you have wounds to heal, He is a physician; if fever scorches you, He is a fountain. Would you punish evil doing, He is justice. If you need help, He is strength; if you fear death, He is life; if you hunger, He is food.

—Saint Ambrose

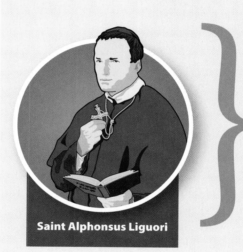

My Jesus, I believe that Thou art truly present in the Most Holy Sacrament. I love Thee above all things, and I desire to possess Thee within my soul. Since I am unable now to receive Thee sacramentally, come at least spiritually into my heart. I embrace Thee as being already there, and unite myself wholly to Thee; never permit me to be separated from Thee.

—Saint Alphonsus Liguori

>> **Compare and contrast these writings from two Doctors of the Church. What is the same and what is different about their thoughts?**

Which do you identify with more and why?

A Shared Land

GOD'S COVENANT with Abraham also included land. "To your descendants I give this land, from the river of Egypt to the great river, the river Euphrates . . ." (Genesis 15:18). Land was important because it was a symbol of power and a visible source of identity.

Generations of Abraham's children were blessed with land. In Israel, also called the Holy Land, the Temple was built, the one true God was worshipped, and many of the events recorded in the Old Testament took place. In fact, all three major religions that have emerged from Abraham's family tree claim the capital of Israel—Jerusalem—as their sacred city.

This land has not been shared without conflict. For centuries, among the descendants of Abraham, the ownership of land has been a source of hatred, violence, and murder.

- For the Jews, Jerusalem was the home of their most sacred site—the Temple. Built by King Solomon in 950 B.C. and destroyed by the Babylonians in c. 587–586, the Temple was the center of Jewish identity and religion. All that remains of the Temple is the western wall, sometimes known as the "Wailing Wall." Jews from all over the world go there to pray.

- For Christians, Jerusalem is the place of Jesus' Passion, death, and Resurrection. Christians from all over the world also go there on pilgrimages and to pray.

- Jerusalem is also the third holiest location for Muslims, after Mecca and Medina. Their mosque, the Dome of the Rock, enshrines the black rock on which Abraham is said to have almost offered Ishmael as a sacrifice to God. This story is similar to the story of Abraham and Isaac, except Muslims believe Ishmael was brought nearer to death than Isaac. Muslims believe that Muhammad ascended to Heaven from this site.

- The Sadducees were a ruling class of Jews who controlled the Temple in Jerusalem. Unlike the Pharisees, the Sadducees were often despised by the common people. They favored the rule of Rome because they themselves maintained power.

- Scribes were teachers of the Law. They set up schools and most were Pharisees during the time of Jesus' public ministry. A high priest presided over the official body, known as the Sanhedrin. It was a supreme council of seventy-one Jews modeled after Moses and the seventy elders written about in the Old Testament Book of Numbers.

Jewish life in the time of Jesus could be difficult, but it certainly centered on the Temple in Jerusalem and the many synagogues throughout the region. The Temple was the place where priests performed sacrifices. In the synagogues, Jews met for prayer, reading and interpretation of Scripture.

Describe What are the borders of God's covenant land?

Explain What two groups were on opposite sides when it came to Roman rule in Israel?

Jesus is the treasure the world has always dreamed about. Yet he was also like so many people of his time and culture.

- He didn't come from wealth or royalty or any of the centers of authority and influence at the time.

- He wasn't a scholar with years of schooling behind him.

- He didn't have any exceptional physical characteristics that we know of.

Jesus tells us that by the power of the Holy Spirit he lives within us. Through Jesus, the one who shared our humanity, we can be set free from our captivity. That's the treasure. Through him we can be free of the anxieties of life that distract us from following God the Father's will and experiencing his love. Through Jesus, our suffering is met with hope. It is a hope for ourselves and all others, that we may know God's love and mercy here on Earth and one day have eternal life with him. Why else would the saints of our faith sing the praises of God while they endured persecution or while they served others in the midst of human suffering? As you read more about Jesus in the Gospels, ask yourself:

- What message from Jesus is a treasure for you?

- How can you make the best use of this treasure?

- How is Jesus a treasure for today's world?

- What aspects of Jesus and his story do you want to explore more?

SECTION 1 REVIEW

QUICK REVIEW

1a. Recall From the ministry of John the Baptist to the death, Resurrection, and Ascension of Jesus, one man ruled Israel. Who was that?

b. Describe What type of land did Jesus know and travel?

c. Explain How many miles a day is it believed that Jesus traveled?

2a. Explain Why is Jerusalem important to Jews and Muslims as well as Christians? Why is it significant to each? Why is there conflict over this sacred city?

b. Describe What is the hope that Jesus gives us?

Listen and Discuss With a small group, discuss these questions.

○ What do you think it was like to walk Israel in the time of Jesus?

○ Do you think that Jesus was received well when he first entered a village or city?

Pray Offer a prayer for peace to those who suffer because of conflict in the holy city of Jerusalem.

SELF-ASSESS

Which statement best reflects where you are now?

☐ I'm confident enough about the material in this section to be able to explain it to someone else.

☐ I have a good grasp of the material in this section, but I could use more review.

☐ I'm lost. I need help catching up before moving on.

The Synoptic Gospels

As pointed out before, three Gospels in particular show a great deal of similarity—Mark, Matthew, and Luke. You may recall from earlier chapters that these three Gospels are labeled the Synoptic Gospels. "Synoptic" simply means "similar" or "to see together." The Gospel according to John, on the other hand, is quite different from the other three.

We already mentioned that biblical scholars generally agree that the Gospel according to Mark was the first one written. For instance, verses from Mark are found in the Gospels according to Matthew and Luke, sometimes using the same wording. It is clear that the writer of Matthew knew the Gospel according to Mark and built on it. Luke's author also used this Gospel as one of his sources.

Some time ago, scholars discovered another interesting feature in the Synoptic Gospels. Matthew and Luke share some passages in common that are not found in Mark. How can this be explained? The best explanation is that there was an additional written source that both Matthew and Luke had access to when composing their Gospels. We don't have an actual copy of this source, but its use is clearly evident within the two Gospels themselves. Since German scholars made this discovery, they labeled this earlier source *quelle*, German for "source." Scholars refer to this source as the **Q Source**. Thus, what we have in Matthew and Luke are: (1) material they both used from Mark; (2) material they both used from a common source, now called Q; and (3) material that is unique to either Matthew or Luke, not found in any other Gospel.

Q Source the term used for the apparent common source for passages found in both Matthew and Luke's Gospels but not in Mark's

GO TO **THE SOURCE**

Compare and contrast the similarities among the following passages from all three Synoptic Gospels:

- The Resurrection: Matthew 28:1-10; Mark 16:1-8; and Luke 24:1-12
- The Last Supper: Matthew 26:26-30; Mark 14:22-26; Luke 22:14-23
- Plucking Grain on the Sabbath: Matthew 12:1-8; Mark 2:23-28; Luke 6:1-5
- True Greatness: Matthew 18:1-5; Mark 9:42-48; Luke 9:46-48

Even with the common intention of giving an accurate account of the essentials of Jesus' life and teaching, and using other sources, the Gospel writers still display unique characteristics. The Gospels are more like portraits than photographs. Painted portraits reveal something about the artist and the "school" of art with which he or she is associated. Similarly, each Gospel, including John, tells us about its subject (Jesus) as well as about the author and the community to which the author belonged. For instance, why does Matthew change some of the wording about an incident that he clearly knew Mark described somewhat differently? He wasn't trying to "correct" Mark as much as he was trying to make a slightly different point about Jesus and the message in that passage.

Using these unique differences in each Gospel as background information, let's now look at the elements found in the portraits drawn by the synoptic authors.

Different Gospels may emphasize different elements of Jesus and his teaching. However, that doesn't mean other Gospels don't address those topics, too.

List What are the three Synoptic Gospels?

Categorize List the three sources of material for the Gospels according to Matthew and Luke.

> *I do not believe there is a problem in this country or the world which could not be settled if approached through the teaching of the Sermon on the Mount.*
>
> —Harry S Truman

Read through the Sermon on the Mount (Matthew 5–7).

>> **Name two statements of Jesus that you find most comforting, inspiring, or relevant to you.**

Which two do you find most challenging and why?

REFLECT

Matthew: Jesus the Teacher

Antioch was one of the largest cities in the Greco-Roman empire in the first century A.D., and it had a large mixed population of Jews and Gentiles. According to the Acts of the Apostles, Antioch was the first place where the disciples were called Christians and the first community that allowed uncircumcised Gentiles to join them. We also learn from Acts that Saint Paul began his missionary journeys from Antioch. Tradition states that Saint Peter served as the bishop of Antioch before he moved to Rome. So it's likely that the author of Matthew was writing to a mostly Jewish audience, but he also welcomed Gentiles into his accounts.

We mentioned earlier that the Gospel according to Matthew includes a story of Jesus' birth not found in Mark. Something else in the early section of Matthew is the **genealogy** of Jesus. The list of Jesus' ancestors begins with Abraham and works forward. Luke, Chapter 3, also has a genealogy, which starts with Joseph and works backward all the way to Adam and God. The Gospel according to Matthew contains a series of five long speeches given by Jesus, also not included in Mark. For this reason, some scholars consider Matthew to have the most Jewish influence of all the Gospels.

We can find many references in this Gospel to Jesus speaking of God as his Father. This corresponds to Matthew's presentation of Jesus as the "Son of God." In this Gospel,

Jesus also described himself as "servant of God," "Shepherd," "son of David," and "Son of Man." All of these descriptions have their biblical roots in the Scripture proclaimed and read by Jews.

Matthew's "portrait" of Jesus is very much the teacher. His **Sermon on the Mount**, beginning with Chapter 5 and running through Chapter 7, is the fullest presentation of Jesus' teaching. It's not really one long talk, but a collection of many of Jesus' teachings on moral living, prayer, and the Kingdom. At the end of the sermon, the Gospel notes, "the crowds were astounded at his teaching, for he taught them as one having authority, and not as their scribes" (Matthew 7:28-29). The beginning section of the Sermon on the Mount contains the Beatitudes, Jesus' teachings about the meaning and path to true happiness and description of the way to eternal holiness to which God calls all of us.

Sermon on the Mount a collection of teachings, including the Beatitudes and other moral teachings of Jesus, found in the Gospel according to Matthew, Chapters 5–7

genealogy a list of a person's ancestors

Matthew

AUTHOR: attributed to the Apostle who was a tax collector, probably a later Jewish convert to Christianity

PROBABLE PLACE OF ORIGIN: Antioch

HIGHLIGHTS:

○ includes Infancy Narrative and genealogy beginning with Abraham

○ Jesus portrayed as a great teacher who gives five long sermons

○ Jesus is the "new Moses" who fulfills the Law

○ emphasized that Jesus is the Christ, the Messiah

○ a key passage is the Sermon on the Mount, containing the Beatitudes

○ uses phrase "Kingdom of Heaven" when speaking of God's reign or rule

"They describe what might be called the actual condition of Jesus' disciples: They are poor, hungry, weeping . . . they are hated and despised," wrote Pope Benedict XVI in *Jesus of Nazareth*.

Jesus told us that the Beatitudes do not replace the old Law given by God to Moses on Mount Sinai. Instead Jesus' teachings fulfill the Law. In essence, Jesus is telling us how to live as God wants. The teachings of the Sermon on the Mount provide a path, guided by the Holy Spirit, that leads us to the Kingdom of Heaven.

The New Law, also known as the Law of the Gospel, clearly perfects all that God has revealed to us. "It is the work of Christ and is expressed particularly in the Sermon on the Mount" (CCC, 1965). The Holy Spirit is also at work here, as the New Law becomes our inner motivation to love. "The New Law is the *grace of the Holy Spirit* given to the faithful through faith in Christ" (CCC, 1966). The Sermon on the Mount teaches what we must do, and the Sacraments give us the grace to follow through.

The teachings of the Sermon on the Mount include three religious practices important to Jews at the time of Jesus—almsgiving, prayer, and fasting (Matthew 6:1-18). Jesus also cautions his followers to avoid public display of these spiritual disciplines.

> *If anyone should meditate . . . on the sermon our Lord gave on the mount . . . he will doubtless find there . . . the perfect way of the Christian life. . . . This sermon contains . . . all the precepts needed to shape one's life.*[20]
>
> —CCC, 1966

Prayer was integral to the religious life of a Jewish person. The Torah also gave guidelines for feeding the poor and for fasting. These three practices remain central to Jews and Christians alike. While these practices have an important role in the Catholic life year around, they take on special meaning during the season of Lent. We often refer to prayer, almsgiving, and fasting as Lenten practices or Lenten observances.

Jesus' teachings gathered into five long sermons would surely have reminded many Jewish readers of the five books of Moses, the great teacher of old. Also, since Matthew's genealogy begins with Abraham, the Gospel writer is clearly emphasizing Jesus' Jewish roots. Luke's genealogy, on the other hand, by beginning with Adam, is linking Jesus to all humanity, not just Judaism. In Matthew, then, Jesus is portrayed as something of the "new Moses," the new teacher. In Luke, Jesus is the "new Adam," the new image of what it means to be truly human.

Recall
- Without looking them up, see how many of the Beatitudes you can recite from memory.
- Then look them up in Matthew 5:1-12 and check your memory.

Identify Who is the "new Moses" and the "new Adam"?

Explain What is the significance of including the genealogies in the Gospels according to Matthew and Luke?

Mark: The "Messianic Secret"

The author of the Gospel according to Mark wrote about thirty years after the death and Resurrection of Jesus. The time was just before and during the fall of Jerusalem and the Temple. By then, Peter and Paul had been martyred, and the early Christians in Jerusalem were living in an occupied territory under the eye of Rome and the brutal Emperor Nero.

Under this situation, the author of Mark emphasized that following Jesus is a choice that leads to discipleship. Written to an audience that included Gentile Christians, this Gospel contains few references to the Old Testament, something to be expected if an audience did not have knowledge of the Scriptures.

Everyday life challenges you to think about right and wrong, to sort out the good from the bad, and to inform and form your conscience. Here's an example . . .

}

Your best friend from elementary school has gotten deep into some dangerous behavior ever since beginning high school.

We're not talking about one or two impulsive decisions; we are talking about a whole lifestyle change: hanging around the wrong people, getting drunk, selling drugs, lying about almost everything, and hooking up just because. Something inside you tells you to somehow let your friend's parents know.

But would that be betraying your friend?

It's a family matter. Mind your own business.

Maybe talk with your friend first.

Step up. Tell the parents. Help a friend.

Can't just sit back and do nothing.

Two words: Don't tell.

What happened to being your brother's keeper?

How do you respond?

Going Moral

Mark

AUTHOR: anonymously written (by an associate of Saint Peter) traditionally attributed to "John Mark"

PROBABLE PLACE OF ORIGIN: Rome

HIGHLIGHTS:

- this shortest Gospel gives us the term "gospel," a proclamation of good news
- this Gospel begins with Jesus' public life
- Jesus is constantly active, performing many miraculous deeds, with little commentary
- Jesus is an unrecognized, suffering Messiah who has come to serve
- key theme is "messianic secret"—Jesus' true glory revealed on the cross
- presents a very human portrait of Jesus during his Passion

The Gospel according to Mark has an urgent message to the community to model their lives after Jesus' life. This commitment required disciples who were willing to serve others as well as suffer for them. The author wrote that believing in Jesus wholeheartedly meant following in his footsteps.

Mark announces that the Kingdom of God is ushered in by Jesus, Messiah and King. However, whenever someone suggests in Jesus' presence that Jesus is the Messiah, or "Anointed One," Jesus warns that person not to speak publicly about it. His time has not come. His kingship is not the result of his teachings or his miraculous deeds; these are preliminary signs. His true message is shown in his suffering and death on the cross. Scholars call this delaying of the public proclaiming of Jesus as King the **messianic secret** (see Mark 8:27-30 and 1:43-44).

Mark's "portrait" of Jesus is one of action. Jesus goes about preaching and performing miracles and large numbers of people begin to follow him and his Way. When he speaks, his words are usually brief and to the point, calling his listeners to evaluate their actions and turn to God the Father.

messianic secret Jesus' command to his disciples not to tell others that he is the Messiah; it is found in some passages of the New Testament, especially in the Gospel according to Mark

Mark begins with Jesus' baptism when the voice of God from on high proclaims, "You are my Son, the Beloved; with you I am well pleased" (Mark 1:11). Jesus then makes his way south from Galilee to Jerusalem, performing miraculous deeds and making challenging, insightful, and sometimes confusing comments along the way. Mark goes into great detail about the events leading up to the crucifixion. He doesn't hold back from describing the human agony that Jesus underwent during this time.

Describe What is the messianic secret?

Conclude In the Gospel according to Mark, why does Jesus not want followers to identify him publicly as the Messiah?

Luke: Jesus of Compassion

The accompanying quotation begins the Gospel according to Luke. It probably also explains why the Evangelists were called and inspired to write *all* the Gospels, at least to some degree. Many accounts about the words and deeds of Jesus were handed down and passed around, beginning with eyewitnesses to them. Theophilus is not a Jewish name. It literally means "beloved of God," but it could be that Theophilus was a Gentile of high standing. Thus, it is thought that the Gospel is written for someone far removed from the Jewish people who first heard and spread the message of Jesus.

> *Since many have undertaken to set down an orderly account of the events that have been fulfilled among us, just as they were handed on to us by those who from the beginning were eyewitnesses and servants of the word, I too decided, after investigating everything carefully from the very first, to write an orderly account for you, most excellent Theophilus, so that you may know the truth concerning the things about which you have been instructed.*
>
> —Luke 1:1-4

The Gospel according to Luke is the first of a two-part work. The Acts of the Apostles, written by the same Evangelist, continues the story of what happened among the followers of Jesus after his Ascension. By the time that the four Gospels were written, the Christian message had already made great inroads into the Gentile world. In fact, by the end of the first century, many more Christians were of Gentile than Jewish descent. Luke chronicles this transition most thoroughly in the Acts of the Apostles.

At the time of Luke's writing, many believed that the Parousia was about to happen. The Parousia is the second coming of Christ at the end of time, when God's plan for salvation is accomplished and humanity is glorified. At this time the Last Judgment will take place. The Gospel according to Luke takes up this theme of the Parousia and cautions readers to be aware that the end is coming, but not as soon as some expected. The author tells readers to concentrate on the importance of living every day in this world in the manner of Jesus.

Luke's "portrait" of Jesus is someone who emphasizes compassion and care for the lowly, poor, and outcasts. We find many teachings on God's forgiveness and mercy, and the requirements of Christians to both repent and be forgiving themselves. Women play a more prominent role in this Gospel, even though every Gospel includes women among Jesus' earliest followers. Jesus' Mother, Mary, sings a powerful hymn in which she says that God "has looked with favor on the lowliness of his servant" and "has brought down the powerful from their thrones, and lifted up the lowly" (Luke 1:48, 52). Another example of this theme is Luke's story of the rich man and the poor man, Lazarus (Luke 16:19-31).

The Gospels of Luke and Matthew include a parallel account that, while told in different settings, proclaims some of the most profound teachings of Jesus' ministry. The Beatitudes are found in the **Sermon on**

Luke

AUTHOR: attributed to be a physician and companion of Saint Paul; a Gentile Christian writing to "Theophilus"
PROBABLE PLACE OF ORIGIN: Greece or Syria

HIGHLIGHTS:

○ includes Infancy Narrative and genealogy beginning with Adam

○ contains many parables, such as the Good Samaritan and the Prodigal Son

○ emphasizes Jesus' focus on prayer, mercy, forgiveness, compassion, and joy

○ frequently refers to the gift and the role of the Holy Spirit

○ women play a more prominent role than in other Gospels; Mary's *Magnificat*, for example

○ Acts of the Apostles is "Book Two" to this Gospel

the Plain (Luke 6:20-26) and the Sermon on the Mount (Matthew 5:1-12).

The name Sermon on the Plain comes from the beginning of this section of Luke, which says that Jesus "came down with them and stood on a level place . . ." (Luke 6:17). Luke's version of the Beatitudes shares the same message as Matthew's, but there are some interesting differences.

For instance, Luke says, "Blessed are you who are poor" (Luke 6:20). Matthew instead speaks of the "poor in spirit" (Matthew 5:3). Luke has four blessings and then follows them with four admonitions: "But woe to you who are rich, for you have received your consolation . . ." (Luke 6:24). Luke's Sermon on the Plain makes a strong statement about central themes of the Gospel: care and compassion for those in need are hallmarks of being Christian and the poor, the hungry, and the suffering are our guides in living the Christian life.

Recall What New Testament book is the second of two parts that starts with the Gospel according to Luke?

Analyze What does the opening of the Gospel according to Luke tell us about how the story of Jesus had been handed down?

Sermon on the Plain in the Gospel according to Luke, a collection of teachings by Jesus that includes a list of Beatitudes found in Luke 6:17-45

QUICK REVIEW

1a. **Recall** List two features of the Gospel according to Matthew.

b. **Recall** What is the Q Source?

c. **Explain** Why are the Gospels more like portraits than photographs?

2a. **Recall** Which Synoptic Gospel was the source for two others?

b. **Analyze** Why would Jesus want to keep his identity as the Messiah a secret?

c. **Describe** What is Jesus like in the Gospel according to Mark?

3a. **Evaluate** Why is Matthew considered the most Jewish of the Gospels?

b. **Summarize** What guidance does Jesus give in Mark?

4a. **Summarize** What are the main themes in Luke?

b. **Recall** Which passage in the Gospel according to Luke is similar to the Sermon on the Mount in Matthew?

Listen and Discuss With a small group, discuss these questions.

○ What do you think it was like to know about the messianic secret when Jesus was alive?

○ Do you think that you would be able to keep the messianic secret?

Pray Compose a short prayer thanking Jesus for whatever you appreciate most about who he is or what he said and did.

SELF-ASSESS

Which statement best reflects where you are now?

☐ I'm confident enough about the material in this section to be able to explain it to someone else.

☐ I have a good grasp of the material in this section, but I could use more review.

☐ I'm lost. I need help catching up before moving on.

Jesus' Parables and Miracles

Jesus' disciples often referred to him as "rabbi," or teacher. In fact, the image of teacher is used more frequently than any other in the Gospels to describe Jesus. The uniqueness of Jesus' teaching lay in its power. Jesus did not teach on his own authority, but on the authority he received from God the Father. In the Gospel according to John we read that Jesus said, "My teaching is not mine but his who sent me" (John 7:16).

We've discussed some of Jesus' teachings about prayer, love and dependence upon God, and just treatment of others. The Gospels contain many important understandings on virtue and how to live a moral life. Future courses will provide an in depth study of Jesus' teachings.

The authors of the Gospels capture Jesus' way of constantly reaching out to people through stories. He also often responds to questions with short stories. Many of his stories fall into the category of **parable**, a story that uses "simple images or comparisons which confront the hearer or reader with a radical choice about his [Jesus'] invitation to enter the Kingdom of God" (CCC, Glossary). Parables challenge a person to question commonly held perspectives.

Not every story told by Jesus is a parable. What characteristics make a particular story parabolic—that is, a parable? They are metaphors or similes drawn from common life experiences or nature to illustrate moral or spiritual truths. But that doesn't mean they're necessarily simple to understand or super obvious comparisons. You have to think about them. They are *not* an

parable a way Jesus taught with metaphors or similes drawn from common life experiences or nature to illustrate moral or spiritual truths that challenge people to make a radical choice about entering the Kingdom of God

GO TO **THE SOURCE**

Read the following parables. Name what you think is Jesus' main message in each. Explain how each message overturns a typical point of view held by people. Which message speaks the most to how you live your faith right now?

○ The Parable of the Mustard Seed (Luke 13:18-19)

○ The Parable of the Great Feast (Luke 14:16-24)

○ The Parable of the Pharisee and the Tax Collector (Luke 18:9-14)

○ The Parable of the Workers in the Vineyard (Matthew 20:1-16)

attempt to talk down to people, as if simple language were necessary for peasant folks who wouldn't understand more sophisticated statements.

In his parables, Jesus uses details, such as a feast or mustard seed, that could be easily recognized as a representation of something else. The mustard seed parable, for example, is found in the Gospels according to Matthew, Mark, and Luke. The original listeners knew the tiny size of a mustard seed. A great feast was something people could relate to, as was the dreaded collection of taxes. Workers working in the vineyard would be familiar as well.

Parables are stories that get us thinking and invite a personal response on our part. They disrupt and defy conventional wisdom. They overturn commonly held stereotypes and challenge popular presumptions. For instance, Jesus says, "the last will be first, and the first will be last" (Matthew 20:16). Is that the way the world typically operates? Let's look at two of the most famous parables, both from the Gospel according to Luke, to see how they evoke "parabolic thinking."

Recall What are parables *not*?

Infer Why do you think Jesus used parables?

> >> Who are some of the "Samaritans" from today's time?
>
> How does Jesus' parable speak to you about loving your neighbor?

REFLECT

GO TO THE SOURCE

Read Luke 10:25-37, then answer the following questions:

1. Who is the audience for the parable?

2. With whom would the listeners identify?

3. How would the listeners respond to the three passersby if they were in the victim's situation?

4. Who is the hero of the story?

5. Why is this person an unlikely hero from the perspective of the audience?

6. Why do you think Jesus chose this person to be the one to respond to the victim's needs?

The Good Samaritan

Jesus is speaking to a group of Jews in Jerusalem. A scribe puts the question to him: "Who is my neighbor?" Jesus answers with a parable. Keep in mind that Samaritans were looked down upon by the Jews. They were considered less than fully Jewish because their ancestors had mixed with other races.

> *But a Samaritan while traveling came near him; and when he saw him, he was moved with pity.*
>
> —Luke 10:33

Through parables, Jesus challenges people's usual ways of thinking and commonly held beliefs. Pope Benedict XVI equates parables with the teachings of the prophets whose messages went "against general opinion and the comfortable habits of life" (*Jesus of Nazareth*, page 189).

Jesus' Parables			
Parable	Matthew	Mark	Luke
New Patches on an Old Cloak	9:16	2:21	5:36
New Wine in Old Wineskins	9:17	2:22	5:37-38
The Sower and the Seeds	13:3-23	4:2-20	8:4-15
The Mustard Seed	13:31-32	4:30-32	13:18-19
The Wicked Tenants	21:33-45	12:1-12	20:9-19
The Budding Fig Tree	24:32-33	13:28-29	21:29-31
The Two Houses on Rock and Sand	7:24-27		6:47-49
The Yeast	13:33		13:20-21
The Lost Sheep	18:12-14		15:3-7
The Two Servants	24:45-51		12:42-48
The Weeds among the Wheat	13:24-30		
The Buried Treasure	13:44		
The Fine Pearl	13:45-46		
The Net Thrown into the Sea	13:47-50		
The Unforgiving Servant	18:23-35		
The Workers in the Vineyard	20:1-16		
The Two Sons	21:28-32		
The Wedding Feast	22:1-14		
The Ten Virgins	25:1-13		
The Talents	25:14-30		
The Sheep and the Goats	25:31-46		
The Seed that Sprouts		4:26-29	
The Watchful Servant		13:34-37	
The Good Samaritan			10:25-37
The Friend at Midnight			11:5-10
The Rich Fool			12:16-21
The Faithful Servants			12:35-38
The Barren Fig Tree			13:6-9
The Great Feast			14:16-24
The Lost Coin			15:8-10
The Prodigal Son			15:11-32
The Dishonest Steward			16:1-9
The Rich Man and Lazarus			16:19-31
The Master and the Servant			17:7-10
The Persistent Widow			18:1-8
The Pharisee and the Tax Collector			18:9-14
The Ten Gold Coins			19:11-27

PRIMARY SOURCES

The Ant and the Grasshopper

This is Aesop's famous fable titled "The Ant and the Grasshopper." Aesop was a Greek storyteller of more than six hundred fables who lived in the sixth century B.C. Many of the fables were written from oral tales handed down from Aesop's time. One of his more famous fables tells the story of the grasshopper and the ants. The ants work hard all summer preparing for winter, while the grasshopper fiddles the season away. When winter comes, the ants reap the rewards of their diligent work; the grasshopper pays the price for his lack of preparation. Read Aesop's fable "The Ant and the Grasshopper."

➤ Go to the student site at
hs.osvcurriculum.com

In a field one summer's day a Grasshopper was hopping about, chirping and singing to its heart's content. An Ant passed by, bearing along with great toil an ear of corn he was taking to the nest.

"Why not come and chat with me," said the Grasshopper, "instead of toiling and moiling in that way?"

"I am helping to lay up food for the winter," said the Ant, "and recommend you to do the same."

"Why bother about winter?" said the Grasshopper; "we have got plenty of food at present." But the Ant went on its way and continued its toil. When the winter came the Grasshopper had no food, and found itself dying of hunger, while it saw the ants distributing every day—corn and grain from the stores they had collected in the summer. Then the Grasshopper knew:

"It is Best to Prepare for the Days of Necessity."

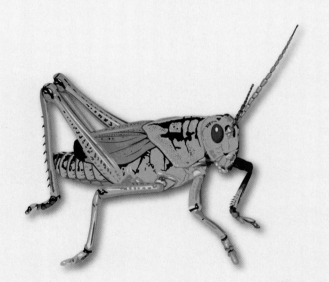

>> Compare that story to the Parable of the Laborers in the Vineyard (Matthew 20:1-16).

What would you say is the message of each?

Why do you think Jesus tells his story about the workers in the vineyard and not one like the grasshopper and the ants?

The Prodigal Son

Perhaps the most famous of Jesus' parables, this story is also called the Parable of the Prodigal and His Brother, the Parable of the Forgiving Father, the Parable of the Lost Son, and the Parable of the Two Sons.

Only the Gospel according to Luke includes the Parable of the Prodigal Son. This parable is part of a pattern of three stories: the lost sheep, the lost coin, and the lost son. All three share a theme in common: there is a loss, something is found, and there is a celebration.

Jesus told these parables to the scribes and Pharisees to give them valuable lessons about human life and God the Father's forgiveness, acceptance, and love. Each story expresses the joy of finding something or someone who is lost. God embraces the lost sinner with loving and forgiving arms. Jesus challenged the religious leaders to show great compassion and forgiveness to the people—their neighbors—whom they had not cared for, had rejected, and had been prejudiced toward.

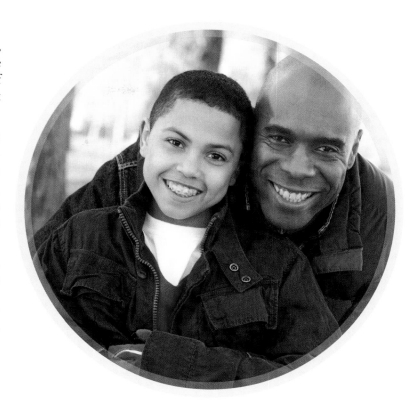

> Son, you are always with me, and all that is mine is yours. But we had to celebrate and rejoice, because this brother of yours was dead and has come to life; he was lost and has been found.
>
> —Luke 15:31-32

This parable once again overturns our normal way of perceiving what is right and expected. Shouldn't the father have at least required the Prodigal Son to work as a servant for many years to earn his way back into the family? Shouldn't the faithful son have been rewarded with a special celebration for all his devoted work?

Explain Why were the Samaritans looked down upon by the Jews?

Relate What does the father's reaction to seeing his son return signify?

GO TO **THE SOURCE**

Read Luke 15:11-32 and then answer the following questions.

- List the choices each son makes in the story.
- What does the father do when the one son asks for his inheritance? Why do you think the father does this?
- What does the father do after this son is gone?
- How does the other son react to his father's actions when his brother returns?
- What spiritual messages do you see in this parable?
- What insights does this story give you about Jesus' teaching?
- Which character in the story do you relate to the most? Why?

Blessed Pope John Paul II

During the over 26 years of his papacy (1978–2005), Pope John Paul II continually emphasized Christ as the one who fully reveals God's will for us. "It is he who opens up to the faithful the book of the Scriptures," Pope John Paul II wrote in his encyclical *Veritatis Splendor*, "The Splendor of Truth." John Paul issued the Third Edition of the *Roman Missal*, the book containing all the prayers, chants, and instructions for the celebration of Mass.

To give some history, the first book called the *Roman Missal* was printed in 1474, around the same time as the invention of the printing press. Then after the Council of Trent in 1570, Pope Pius V released the first *Roman Missal* to be used throughout the Latin Church. For the first time, the Church celebrated the Mass in a uniform way. After Vatican Council II, in 1969, the new *Roman Missal* was promulgated.

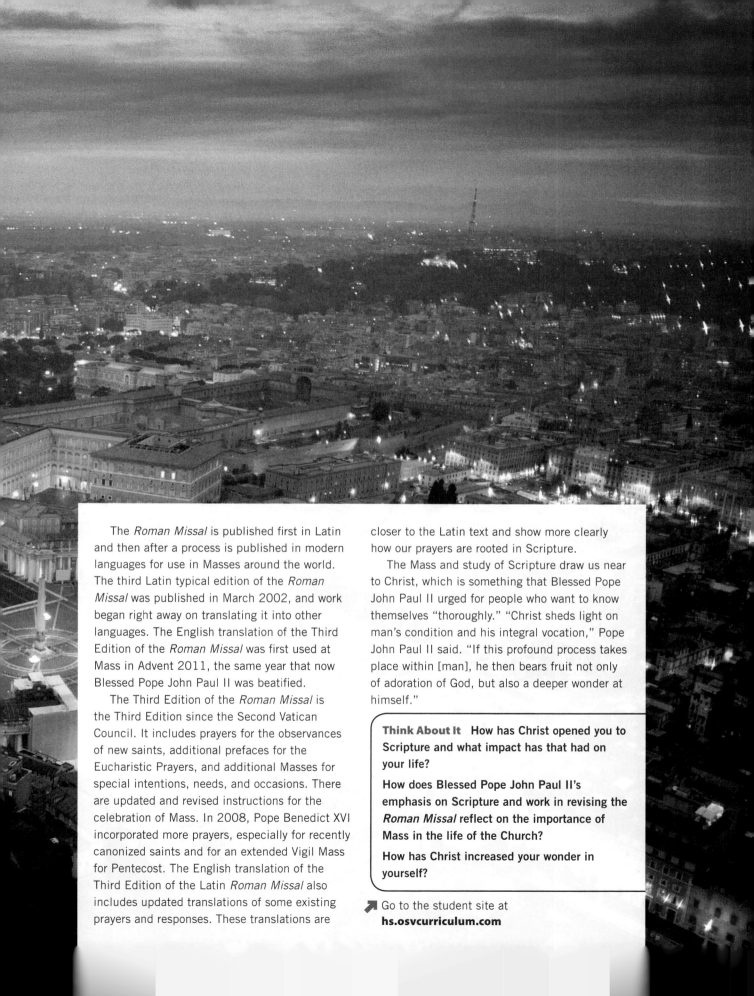

The *Roman Missal* is published first in Latin and then after a process is published in modern languages for use in Masses around the world. The third Latin typical edition of the *Roman Missal* was published in March 2002, and work began right away on translating it into other languages. The English translation of the Third Edition of the *Roman Missal* was first used at Mass in Advent 2011, the same year that now Blessed Pope John Paul II was beatified.

The Third Edition of the *Roman Missal* is the Third Edition since the Second Vatican Council. It includes prayers for the observances of new saints, additional prefaces for the Eucharistic Prayers, and additional Masses for special intentions, needs, and occasions. There are updated and revised instructions for the celebration of Mass. In 2008, Pope Benedict XVI incorporated more prayers, especially for recently canonized saints and for an extended Vigil Mass for Pentecost. The English translation of the Third Edition of the Latin *Roman Missal* also includes updated translations of some existing prayers and responses. These translations are closer to the Latin text and show more clearly how our prayers are rooted in Scripture.

The Mass and study of Scripture draw us near to Christ, which is something that Blessed Pope John Paul II urged for people who want to know themselves "thoroughly." "Christ sheds light on man's condition and his integral vocation," Pope John Paul II said. "If this profound process takes place within [man], he then bears fruit not only of adoration of God, but also a deeper wonder at himself."

Think About It How has Christ opened you to Scripture and what impact has that had on your life?

How does Blessed Pope John Paul II's emphasis on Scripture and work in revising the *Roman Missal* reflect on the importance of Mass in the life of the Church?

How has Christ increased your wonder in yourself?

↗ Go to the student site at
hs.osvcurriculum.com

Jesus' Divine Compassion

Accounts of Jesus' performing **miracles** run all through the Gospels, especially the Gospel according to Mark. The miracles Jesus performed invite belief in him. They are signs of the work of God the Father in Christ. They show that Jesus is the Son of God. Miracles can strengthen faith in the One who does the Father's works (see CCC, 548).

miracles wonders or signs attributed to divine power that show Jesus is the Messiah and that the Kingdom of God is present in him (see CCC, 547)

All four Gospels give accounts of miracles performed by Jesus. Why are so many included? They tell us that God's Kingdom is present and active in Jesus. The Gospels record four types of miracles, as indicted in the accompanying chart.

Interestingly, the Gospel according to John presents miracles differently than the Synoptic Gospels. John calls them "signs of wonder" and uses them to reveal Jesus' divinity. This Gospel includes seven such signs to show readers that Jesus is God's Son. The Synoptic Gospels, on the other hand, sometimes refer to the miracles as "deeds of power." The miracles included by Matthew, Mark, and Luke tend to emphasize Jesus' power over evil. In all the Gospels, we see Jesus' ability to heal people physically, emotionally, and spiritually, that is, from sin.

> *Everything in Jesus' life was a sign of his mystery.*[21] *His deeds, miracles, and words all revealed that "in him the whole fullness of deity dwells bodily."*[22]
>
> —CCC, 515

One time, the devil—the personification of evil—tempted Jesus to perform a miracle to display his divine powers. During his Temptations in the desert, the devil said to Jesus, "If you are the Son of God, command this stone to become a loaf of bread" (Luke 4:3). Jesus refused.

And again, at his crucifixion, the chief priests, scribes, and elders, seeing Jesus hanging on the cross, mocked him saying, "If you are the Son of God, come down from the cross" (Matthew 27:40). Scribes and elders who were there also mocked him: "He saved others; he cannot save himself" (Matthew 27:42). Even one of the men crucified along with him taunted him. Jesus performed miracles out of compassion for suffering people, or to heal those who showed faith, not to satisfy people's curiosity or to benefit himself.

Throughout the Gospels, we see accounts of miracles that illustrate the power and importance of faith. For instance, Peter was invited by Jesus to walk on water, which he did. When Peter's faith started to falter, he began sinking. The message seems clear: keep the faith—even when surrounded by fear, doubt, and troubled waters—otherwise you'll sink.

Jesus also associated physical healing with spiritual healing, or forgiveness from sin. This is back when it was commonly believed that illness and infirmities were caused by an act of God due to sin. Jesus assured people that God neither causes illness nor wants people to suffer. He wants their whole being to be healed, and by his words and his actions, especially his miracles, Jesus showed that he is divine, the Son of God. The miracles recorded in the Bible need to be viewed from the perspective of faith. Just as not everyone who heard Jesus' words believed in him, not everyone who witnessed Jesus' miraculous deeds understood them to be a sign of the glory of God.

Explain

Read one of the following passages: Mark 1:29-34, Matthew 8:23-27, Luke 9:37-43, or John 11:1-44.

○ Summarize the main point of the passage chosen and tell what type of miracle it is.

○ What miracles are you hoping for?

Jesus' Miracles

Miracles of Healing: Jesus cures people of various illnesses, including leprosy, paralysis, blindness, fever, and deafness.

Cleansing a leper	Matthew 8:2-4; Mark 1:40-45; Luke 5:12-14
Healing many at Peter's house	Matthew 8:14-17; Mark 1:29-34; Luke 4:38-41
Healing a crippled woman	Luke 13:11-13
Healing a paralytic	Matthew 9:1-8; Mark 2:3-12; Luke 5:18-26
Healing a sick man at Bethzatha	John 5:1-9
Restoring a man with a withered hand	Matthew 12:9-13; Mark 3:1-6; Luke 6:6-11
Healing a centurion's servant	Matthew 8:5-13; Luke 7:1-10
Healing of a blind and mute person	Matthew 12:22
Healing a woman with a hemorrhage	Matthew 9:20-22; Mark 5:25-34; Luke 8:43-48
Opening the eyes of two blind men; cure of a mute man	Matthew 9:27-31; Matthew 9:32-34
Healing a deaf and mute man	Mark 7:31-37
Opening the eyes of a blind person at Bethsaida	Mark 8:22-26
Opening the eyes of a person born blind	John 9:1-41
Healing of a man with dropsy	Luke 14:1
Cleansing the lepers	Luke 17:12-19
Opening the eyes of a blind man	Matthew 20:29-34; Mark 10:46-52; Luke 18:35-43
Healing Malchus' ear	Matthew 26:51-52; Mark 14:47; Luke 22:49-51; John 18:10-11

Miracles of Exorcism: Jesus has power over demons and evil spirits.

Curing a boy with a demon	Matthew 17:14-21; Mark 9:14-29; Luke 9:37-43
Healing those possessed with demons	Matthew 8:16-17; Mark 1:32-34; Luke 4:40-41
Healing a Canaanite woman's daughter	Matthew 15:21-28
Demoniac at Capernaum	Mark 1:23-28; Luke 4:33-37
Blind and mute demoniac	Matthew 12:22-29; Luke 11:14-15
Gadarene demoniac	Matthew 8:28-34; Mark 5:1-15; Luke 8:26-39
Infirm woman	Luke 13:10-17

Miracles over Nature: Jesus controls the forces of nature by stilling a storm, feeding multitudes, turning water into wine.

Calming the storm	Matthew 8:23-27; Mark 4:35-41; Luke 8:22-25
Walking on water	Matthew 14:22-33; Mark 6:45-52; John 6:16-21
The wedding at Cana	John 2:1-11
First miraculous catch of fish	Luke 5:1-11
Multiplication of loaves	Matthew 14:13-21; Mark 6:32-44; Luke 9:12-17; John 6:1-13
Walking on water	Matthew 14:22-33; Mark 6:45-52; John 6:16-21
Second multiplication of loaves	Matthew 15:32-38; Mark 8:1-9
Coin in the fish's mouth	Matthew 17:24-27
Cursing the fig tree	Matthew 21:8-19; Mark 11:12-14
Second miraculous catch of fish	John 21:1-4

Miracles over Death: Jesus restores the life of a person.

Jairus' daughter	Matthew 9:18-19, 23-26; Mark 5:21-24, 35-43; Luke 8:40-42, 49-56
The widow's son at Nain	Luke 7:11-17
Lazarus	John 11:1-44

MY FAITH

We have looked at how a portrait is different from a picture and how the Gospels are portraits of Jesus instead of pictures.

But what would a spiritual portrait of you look like?

In this My Faith, imagine painting your own spiritual self-portrait. If you are artistic, this your chance to do some introspective sketching. If not, simply describe your portrait in words. Use a couple of these questions to help you create it.

What characteristics of your spirituality would you want to highlight?

What are the obvious features of your spirituality? What are the features that are not so obvious to others?

How would you describe the dominant emotions of your spiritual self-portrait?

For example, would you have a peaceful portrait or would you have a serious tone? Would there be fear in your doubt, or confidence? A smile or a long face? Happiness or regret?

Do you have big eyes because you see so many spiritual things in the world, or would you have glasses?

Is your face kind of thin because you don't eat much spiritual food, or is it a well-fed face?

What other spiritual things about yourself can you portray?

This is meant to be a creative exercise. Play with it and pray with it. And see if you can nail down a few truths about your spiritual life.
Remember that you can use any of this as part of the final report you submit at the end of this course.

Go to the student site at
hs.osvcurriculum.com

Discipleship . . . within the Body of Christ . . .
for the glory of God and good of the world

EXAMINATION OF Conscience

Conscience is the act of judging based on one's knowledge of right and wrong, of what is morally good and morally bad. In order to use our conscience, we have to form it so that it's an informed conscience. Our conscience is formed in many ways. The Word of God is a light for our path, enlightening our conscience. The Gifts of the Holy Spirit helps us form our conscience:

- We read about Jesus and learn about his words and deeds.

- We develop the habit of prayer and study Church teaching on morality.

- We seek advice from good moral people whom we trust.

- We use our conscience and put what we've learned into practice.

- We also form our conscience by examining it.

In all of these efforts, the teaching of the Church guides us to develop our conscience and helps us become more informed moral decision makers. An important part of preparing for the Sacrament of Penance and Reconciliation is an examination of conscience. But that's not the only time we benefit from reflecting on our actions, thoughts, and words. Make a prayerful examination of conscience part of your regular routine.

How have I put my faith in God? When have I failed to trust in his ways? In what ways have I show gratitude and praise for all his gifts? When should I have done so?

How have I spoken God's name? Have I shown proper reverence for the name of others? Have I resorted to cursing and inappropriate language?

In what ways have I kept, or not kept, Sunday as a holy day? Have I actively participated in Mass?

How have I shown respect and obedience to my parents and others in authority? In what ways have I failed to do so? How can I change that?

When have I respected and protected life? When should I have done so?

How have I been faithful and loyal? Have I practiced the virtue of chastity?

Have I respected what belongs to others, avoided stealing, and shared with those in need?

How have I been honest and truthful, and when I have failed to be so? Have I avoided bragging and speaking negatively of others?

Have I practiced modesty in my thoughts, words, dress, and actions?

When have I been jealous of others' possessions and good fortune? How have I been genuinely happy for others and their success?

In paragraph 549, the *Catechism* says that Jesus freed *some* people from illness and infirmities. While not all people were healed of their physical ailments, they were ultimately released from the bondage that separated them from God. That gives us hope. Someone with great faith today may not be cured of illness. But that is not a sign of insufficient faith or abandonment by God. God offers the gifts of hope, love, and eternal life to all of us.

God's love and forgiveness heal us from sin and its effects. We can see God's loving presence not only in the miracles recorded in Bible but also in the events of the modern-day world. God does act in our lives in miraculous ways.

Recall How did the different Gospels refer to the miracles?

Explain What did the people who mocked Jesus on the cross not understand about the miracles he performed?

SECTION 3 REVIEW

QUICK REVIEW

1a. Explain What is something a person needs in order to understand Jesus' miracles?

b. Analyze Did Jesus heal all people with infirmities? Why or why not?

c. Clarify What did Jesus' miracles prove?

2a. Analyze Why would Jesus teach with parables and other stories?

b. Contrast How are parables and fables different?

c. Identify Which character from one of Jesus' parables are you most like? Why?

3a. Recall How many of the Gospels give accounts of Jesus' miracles? Why are so many included?

b. Explain What are the four types of miracles?

Listen and Discuss With a small group, discuss these questions.

○ What technique do you use to analyze and apply parables?

○ Do you think that most of Jesus' followers understood the meaning of the parables? What process did he use to help make himself clear?

Pray Compose a short prayer that expresses why a character from one of Jesus' parables is like you and how you find direction from Jesus' teaching because of the resemblance.

SELF-ASSESS

Which statement best reflects where you are now?

☐ I'm confident enough about the material in this section to be able to explain it to someone else.

☐ I have a good grasp of the material in this section, but I could use more review.

☐ I'm lost. I need help catching up before moving on.

The Gospel According to John

In the beginning was the Word, and the Word was with God, and the Word was God . . . And the Word became flesh and lived among us . . . No one has ever seen God. It is God the only Son, who is close to the Father's heart, who has made him known.

—John 1:1, 14, 18

The Gospel according to John has a very different style than the other Gospels. It doesn't include about ninety percent of the material found in the Synoptic Gospels. The beginning prologue (the quotation above) sends us into the timeless world of eternity and describes Jesus as the Word of God, or in Greek, *logos*. We previously discussed Jesus as the Word of God. John presents the Son of God as the Word of God who breaks through into the world bounded by time and space. The Son of God does this so that we can know God in the flesh, see him face to face in a way that not even Moses himself was able to do.

John's "portrait" of Jesus is of the true Light who enlightens all of us by becoming one with us; he is the Son of God and through him we become children of God ourselves. Because the Gospel according to John emphasizes the union of God the Father and Jesus the Son, and through Jesus our own union with God, it is sometimes considered the most **mystical** of the Gospels.

Contrast John's way of presenting Jesus with Mark's way of presenting Jesus. Mark starts out by telling us that Jesus is God's Son. However, he tells of Jesus making his way toward Jerusalem and undergoing many struggles that are not found in the Gospel according to John. Jesus is misunderstood by even his closest friends until his glory is finally revealed on the cross and in his Resurrection.

The Gospel according to John, on the other hand, starts out with Jesus glorified, the Word of God from the beginning—meaning before time even began. Jesus' divinity is the primary focus of this Gospel, whereas Mark seems to emphasize Jesus as the perfect man.

mystical an experience of union with God such as emphasized in the Gospel according to John

logos Greek for "word" used in the prologue of the Gospel according to John to refer to Jesus as "Word of God"

John

AUTHOR: traditionally attributed to the Apostle who was a son of Zebedee, but probably a Christian believer from a Jewish background

PROBABLE PLACE OF ORIGIN: Ephesus or another city in Asia Minor (today's Turkey)

HIGHLIGHTS:

- begins with prologue about the Word becoming flesh
- Jesus performs seven "signs" and uses images based on them to explain his oneness or mystical union with the Father
- Jesus refers to himself as "I am . . ." to express his human and divine natures in his one Divine Person
- filled with images and symbols that invite us into the light of God the Father's life and love, the Light who is Jesus
- two major sections: Book of Signs and Book of Glory
- Jesus washes the feet of the Apostles to demonstrate the message of service and love for one another

Describe

The Gospel according to John demonstrates that words—*logos*—have power.

- List five words that have power in your life.
- Choose the word that has the most power in your spiritual life. Describe the power that this word has had for your faith.
- Describe what would happen if those five words suddenly disappeared from your life.

Relate

○ Jesus refers to himself in a number of ways in the "Book of Signs" section of the Gospel according to John. Each image is rich in symbolism.

○ Explain how one of the following images from the Gospel of John would affect your relationship with Jesus: bread of life (John 6:35), light of the world (John 8:12), the gate (John 10:9).

These two different ways of presenting the mystery of Jesus as true God and true man help us better understand who Jesus is and what he calls us to.

The Gospel according to John was written around or after A.D. 90, which would make it the last Gospel composed in its final form. The Evangelist refers to himself as "the disciple whom Jesus loved" (John 21:20), but the identity of the writer is never given. The Gospel describes the "Beloved Disciple" leaning on the breast of Jesus at the Last Supper (John 13:23), standing at the foot of the cross (John 19:25-27), and entering the Empty Tomb of Jesus and believing in Jesus' Resurrection (John 20:3-10).

Identify Who or what is the Word at the beginning of the Gospel according to John?

Elaborate Why is the Gospel according to John described as the most mystical of the Gospels?

The Book of Signs

The Gospel according to John takes a formal, structured approach to the works and words of Jesus. Mark presents Jesus performing one healing or miraculous deed after another without much explanation. In contrast, John describes seven miraculous "signs" and uses them to explain Jesus in symbolic terms. Some scholars refer to this first half of the Gospel as the **Book of Signs**.

The Seven Signs in the Gospel according to John

1. Jesus changes water into wine (2:1-11)
2. Jesus heals an official's son (4:46-54)
3. Jesus heals a crippled man (5:2-9)
4. Jesus feeds five thousand (6:1-14)
5. Jesus walks on water (6:16-21)
6. Jesus gives sight to a blind man (9:1-7)
7. Jesus raises Lazarus from the dead (11:1-45)

In the Gospel according to John, Jesus makes a connection between himself and the Old Testament. He uses the phrase "I am . . ." a number of times during his explanations of the signs he performed. In later courses, we will address the "I am" statements in more detail. Here are a few examples.

- "I am the bread of life . . ." (John 6:35)

- "I am the good shepherd . . ." (John 10:11)

- "I am the way, and the truth, and the life . . ." (John 14:6)

As you recall, God referred to himself as "I AM" when he spoke to Moses from the burning bush. In other words, John makes it clear throughout the Gospel that Jesus says, "The Father and I are one" (John 10:30).

Tell Why do scholars refer to the first half of the Gospel according to John as the Book of Signs?

Conclude What is the purpose of Jesus' "I am" statements in this Gospel?

GO TO THE SOURCE

Read the following passages from John. What image of Jesus is depicted in each passage? What does each image reveal about who Jesus is, and what does Jesus reveal about God the Father?

○ John 5:19-29
○ John 6:35-40
○ John 8:12-20
○ John 10:7-18
○ John 11:25-27
○ John 14:6-14
○ John 15:5-17

Bread of Life

Chapter 6 is John's Eucharistic passage. It begins with Jesus feeding five thousand people with a few loaves of bread and some fish. This incident is described in the Synoptic Gospels as well. Typical of John's style, the miracle precedes a long talk by Jesus in which he explains what the miracle of the bread means. In this passage, Jesus says:

> Very truly, I tell you, unless you eat the flesh of the Son of Man and drink his blood, you have no life in you. Those who eat my flesh and drink my blood have eternal life, and I will raise them up on the last day.
>
> —John 6:53-54

Here Jesus not only explains the importance of participating in the Eucharist, but he also tells us who he is:

> I am the bread of life. Whoever comes to me will never be hungry, and whoever believes in me will never be thirsty. . . I am the living bread that came down from heaven. Whoever eats of this bread will live forever; and the bread that I will give for the life of the world is my flesh.
>
> —John 6:35, 51

The Book of Glory

The **Book of Glory**, the second major part of the Gospel according to John, includes the discourses of Jesus, the Last Supper, and the narrative of Jesus' suffering, death and Resurrection. Here we read that the last of the great miracles in the Gospel according to John was raising his friend Lazarus from death. This act gave the Jewish leaders cause to seek Jesus' death. They feared that Jesus was becoming too popular, which could upset the Romans, and thus reduce the power granted to them by the Romans (see John 11:45-53).

This section of the Gospel continues to reveal Jesus as the Son of God who is the one sent by God the Father. The author uses symbolism and irony to assist in our understanding that we, too, belong to God and must choose to follow the light rather than darkness.

When you participate in Mass, you hear the words said at the Consecration: "This is my body. . . . This is my blood. . . ." Each of the synoptic Gospels contains these words spoken by Jesus at the Last Supper. Bibles often place a heading before this section stating: "The Institution of the Lord's Supper," or "The Institution of the Eucharist." These words are absent from the Last Supper account in the Gospel according to John. Instead, in Chapter 13, John references the Passover meal, which the Apostles share with Jesus (John 13:3), and the washing of the feet.

Jesus says that this act (washing the disciples' feet), which is not recorded in the Synoptics, emphasizes an important part of discipleship and leadership. Jesus came to serve, not be served. He expects the same of his Apostles. We receive Christ in the Eucharist,

Book of Glory second part of the Gospel according to John beginning with Jesus' foot washing (John 13–21). This section contains Jesus' words of comfort to disciples and the proclamation of his glory.

GO TO **THE SOURCE**

Read John 13:1-15.

- How would you sum up what Jesus is trying to say to the Apostles through this act?

- On a personal level, to whom might Jesus be asking you to "do the same," and how can you do so?

Why does Jesus die at a different time in the Gospel according to John? What theological point is the writer making? In the Synoptic Gospels, Jesus dies on the day after he celebrates the Passover (Holy Thursday) and institutes the Eucharist with the words, "This is my body" and "This is my blood." But in the Gospel according to John, Jesus dies during the day of preparation, right before Passover begins.

To understand John's theology it's helpful to know what happened on the day of preparation.

Professor L. Michael White explains this "is the day when all the lambs are slaughtered and everyone goes to the temple to get their lamb for the Passover meal."[23] In the Gospel according to John, Jesus dies just when all the lambs for the Passover meal are being sacrificed.

> Since it was the day of Preparation, the Jews did not want the bodies left on the cross during the Sabbath.
>
> —John 19:31

>> What theological point is John making about Jesus by setting the time of his death exactly when the Passover lambs were being sacrificed?

and we grow as the body of Christ when we serve others. The ways we worship and participate in the Sacraments strengthen us to live a life of virtue. "Christians contribute to *building up the Church* by the constancy of their convictions and their moral lives" (CCC, 2045).

Name Which of Jesus' miracles is mentioned as being part of each of the four Gospels?

Explain How does the Gospel according to John address the Eucharist?

Write
Compose a short essay describing someone who has been a good role model of love and service to others. Note the kind of service he or she has done or is doing that makes him or her a good example of Jesus' command to love and serve others.

Following the washing of their feet, Jesus teaches the disciples the central principle of all of his teaching,

> I give you a new commandment, that you love one another. Just as I have loved you, you also should love one another. By this everyone will know that you are my disciples, if you have love for one another.
>
> —John 13:34-35

Jesus teaches that love is the heart of Christian service. Jesus' lesson in the washing of his disciples' feet illustrates that loving one another means being willing to serve one another. To love as Jesus loves means to love others without expecting anything in return.

From this section of the Gospel according to John we learn much about the relationship of Jesus to the Father and to the Holy Spirit, the third Person of the Blessed Trinity. In his discourses, Jesus teaches his Apostles the importance of the Holy Spirit, the unity that exists among the Trinity, and the necessity for the followers of Jesus to be united to the Trinity and to one another.

The Holy Spirit, the Advocate, would continue to lead the disciples. As Jesus tells them, "I have said these things to you while I am still with you. But the Advocate, the Holy Spirit, whom the Father will send in my name, will teach you everything, and remind you of all that I have said to you" (John 14:25-26). Now on the night before he dies, Jesus promises his followers that he will not leave them orphans.

The image of the vine and branches further emphasizes the unity of God and his people. We are united to God and to one another through the Church. And the Church is called to become one in God, to bear fruit in his name, and to be a sign of that oneness and the new everlasting life that comes through it (see John 15:1-8).

The Last Supper discourses end with Jesus offering a prayer to God the Father (John 17:1-25). The prayer, sometimes called Jesus' Priestly Prayer, begins with Jesus giving glory to the Father and asking for the Father to glorify him. Jesus continues his prayer by relating to the Father what he has done and how his followers belong to the Father. Finally, Jesus asks the Father to bless his disciples with the truth and to make them all be one.

The End or Beginning?

The climax of the Gospel according to John is the story of God the Father's self-giving act of friendship and love in allowing his Son, Jesus, to willingly lay his life down for others. The message of Jesus' ultimate return of love to God the Father is his pure self-sacrifice as illustrated in the glory of the cross in this Gospel. The glory of Christ crucified is the "hour" in which humanity is saved and God the Father is glorified in Jesus' sacrifice. This message was the one the author's community needed to hear. It is a message we need to hear as well. Like Jesus, we must be willing to lay down our lives for one another out of pure self-sacrificing love.

Who would want the Gospel story of Jesus to end? Can anyone ever say enough about what Jesus has done? The final words from the author of John indicate that Jesus said and did much more than has been recorded in books. His life and message live on through the Church. "But there are also many other things that Jesus did; if every one of them were written down, I suppose that the world itself could not contain the books that would be written" (John 21:25).

Telling anyone's life story is difficult. Trying to communicate in words why someone is the very Word of God in the flesh would not be possible without the inspiration of the Holy Spirit. Through these Gospels, we learn of the sacrifice Jesus made for us and for all. And we learn that through his death, Jesus rose to new life, and that he offers us this same gift. In Jesus, the Revelation of God is final and complete.

Describe What did leaders fear after Jesus raised Lazarus from the dead?

Infer What is said about the glory of God when Jesus washes his disciples' feet?

Write
○ If you were to design the way discipleship should actually be lived out, what are some Gospel practices and principles that you would include in it?
○ Write out your answer and be sure to include practices and principles that are based on the Gospels.

QUICK REVIEW

1a. Contrast How is the beginning of the Gospel according to John different from the beginnings of the Synoptic Gospels?

b. Analyze Why would John begin with a glorified Jesus?

c. Recall What is the Book of Signs?

d. Connect How do Jesus' "I am" statements link him with God the Father?

e. Analyze How does the Gospel according to John show the Eucharist to be important?

2a. Explain Why was the raising of Lazarus a problem for the Jewish leaders?

b. Analyze What is significant about Jesus washing his Apostles' feet in the Gospel according to John?

c. Speculate Why might someone want to add an ending to the Gospel according to John?

Listen and Discuss Write answers to the following questions and share them with a partner.

○ What do you think about the beginning of the Gospel according to John?

○ What sort of ideas does the beginning convey?

○ If you were an artist, how would you illustrate these ideas?

SELF-ASSESS

Which statement best reflects where you are now?

☐ I'm confident enough about the material in this section to be able to explain it to someone else.

☐ I have a good grasp of the material in this section, but I could use more review.

☐ I'm lost. I need help catching up before moving on.

PRAYER

Opening Prayer

We pray that, according to the riches of his glory, he may grant that we may be strengthened in our inner being with power through his Spirit, and that Christ may dwell in our hearts through faith, as we are being rooted and grounded in love. I pray that you may have the power to comprehend, with all the saints, what is the breadth and length and height and depth, and to know the love of Christ that surpasses knowledge, so that you may be filled with all the fullness of God.

Adapted from Ephesians 3:16-19

Closing Prayer

Peace be to the whole community, and love with faith, from God the Father and the Lord Jesus Christ. Grace be with all who have an undying love for our Lord Jesus Christ.

Ephesians 6:23

VOCABULARY

Use each of the following terms in a sentence that shows you know what the term means. You may include more than one term in a sentence.

Q Source

genealogy

Sermon on the Mount

messianic secret

Sermon on the Plain

parable

miracles

logos

mystical

Book of Signs

Book of Glory

PEOPLE AND TERMS

Use information from the chapter to tell why each person or term is significant.

1. Herod
2. Pontius Pilate
3. Pharisees
4. Sadducees
5. Scribes
6. Matthew
7. Mark
8. Luke
9. John
10. Prodigal Son
11. Good Samaritan
12. Acts of the Apostles

UNDERSTANDING

Answer each question and complete each exercise.

SECTION 1

1. **Name** Who was Pontius Pilate and who did he work for?

2. **Describe** Give a description of the land where Jesus traveled.

3. **Explain** How was Jesus like other people of his time and culture?

4. **Analyze** Why would the saints praise God while they were being persecuted?

SECTION 2

5. **Connect** Why do scholars agree that the Gospel according to Mark was written first?

6. **Identify** For which Gospels is the Q Source a source?

7. **Explain** What is the messianic secret? Why did Jesus want others to keep it?

8. **Analyze** Why are genealogies included in the Gospels according to Matthew and Luke?

SECTION 3

9. **Explain** What was the purpose of the parables that Jesus used?

10. **Explain** Why didn't Jesus show off his divinity by performing all kinds of miracles?

11. **Name** Tell one of the miracles from each category: miracles of healing, of exorcism, over nature, and over death.

12. **Compare** How does God act in miraculous ways in our lives today?

13. **Assess** Tell how the Gospel according to John begins, and explain why the writer used that approach.

14. **Explain** How is the Gospel according to John structured?

15. **Summarize** What is in the Book of Signs?

16. **Describe** What does Jesus teach in the Book of Glory?

CONNECTING

Visual Look closely at this French painting and interpret it. Use the questions below as a guide.

The Four Evangelists (oil on panel)
Musée National de la Renaissance, Ecouen, France
The Bridgeman Art Library

What are the people doing? Interpret the symbols by each person. What is unrealistic about this portrayal?

Challenge A friend says that the parables that Jesus uses to teach are sometimes confusing.

> **Friend:** I never quite understand what he's talking about.
>
> **You:** Well, that's their purpose, to get us thinking.
>
> **Friend:** OK, then pick one of the parables and explain it to me.

○ Answer your friend's challenge by choosing one of Jesus' parables and write an explanation using Scripture, Church teaching, and information that you learned in this chapter.

Question After working through this chapter, what would you say to someone who doesn't believe in miracles?

Imagine You have a daily Internet blog read by millions of high school students. You land an interview with the author of the Gospel according to John:

○ Make a list of five questions that you would ask the Evangelist.

○ What headline would you write for the blog page that includes the story about the interview?

○ How much of the article would you include about the Gospel's Book of Signs?

SELF-ASSESS

On Your Own Make a list of the most important things you learned from this chapter. Select three things that represent your growth in understanding as you worked through this chapter. Write a paragraph explaining your choices. Share your list and paragraph in small groups.

CHAPTER **9**

Scripture in Our Lives

Go to the student site at
hs.osvcurriculum.com

DO

○ Describe how you have experienced Scripture.

○ Reflect on the Liturgy of the Word.

○ Research our Jewish roots.

○ Look up the Liturgy of the Hours.

○ Review the contribution of Blessed Pope John XXIII.

○ Discuss your experiences using Scripture in prayer.

○ Identify a time and place that would help you pray.

DEFINE

liturgy
Sacraments
grace
Lectionary
Liturgy of the Word
Liturgy of the Hours
Breviary
lectio divina

Catholic high school students were asked to finish one of these sentences: "To me, the Bible is . . . " or "Most people think that the Bible is . . . " Here are some of their responses:

"Most people think that the Bible is . . .
• about spreading the good news of God."
• a group of parables or a long book."
• a book related to religious studies."
• a book on Catholic belief."
• something you can go to and learn about God."
• one of the most important and historical books."

"To me the Bible is . . .
• true, but sometimes confuses me."
• a guide for a good life in Christ."
• the story of Jesus' teachings."
• God's word that I should read more often."
• the word of God and a lesson on how to live."
• before, during, and after Jesus' life."
• a book you read for hope."

WHAT ABOUT YOU?

Where Are You?

Choose the response that best reflects where you are right now.

For me, the Bible is "a lamp to my feet and a light to my path."	☐ Quite a bit	☐ Somewhat	☐ A little	☐ Not at all
When I pray, I use the Bible.	☐ Quite a bit	☐ Somewhat	☐ A little	☐ Not at all
The last time I opened my Bible, what I read challenged me.	☐ Quite a bit	☐ Somewhat	☐ A little	☐ Not at all
I know where to find some specific stories, teachings, and quotes in the Bible.	☐ Quite a bit	☐ Somewhat	☐ A little	☐ Not at all
When I'm faced with an important decision, I look to the Bible for insight.	☐ Quite a bit	☐ Somewhat	☐ A little	☐ Not at all

The Centrality of Scripture

How is Scripture connected to the Sacraments and prayer?

Is it possible to pray without stopping?

What role does Scripture play in our lives?

How can you keep the message of Scripture vibrant within you and lived out through your life?

How are the Christian Scriptures rooted in the Jewish tradition?

Scripture is central to our liturgy and worship, theological study, in various ministries, and in our personal spirituality (see *Catechism of the Catholic Church*, 132–133). We read, study, and reflect on Scripture for many reasons, most especially

- to know Christ,

- to stay faithful,

- to have new life in Christ,

- to be strengthened for the work of justice, and

- to pray.

But we draw nourishment from *both* Scripture and Tradition of the Church. When Catholics pray, we turn to Scripture and the many prayers that have been handed down through the centuries. When we ponder how to live our lives, we go to Scripture for guidance. And when we search for meaning, we find it expressed in the panoramic story of the Bible that begins with creation and comes to fulfillment in Jesus.

Through the study of Scripture, we come to know Jesus. By praying with Scripture, we encounter him as one of us, as Savior, and as Son of God. Reading from Scripture is essential to the celebration of the Church's **liturgy**. Words of Scripture are spoken over Catholics at Baptism and at funerals.

Throughout this course, we have explored how Scripture came to be, what it reveals, and what the Church did to bring it from the Apostles, down through history, to the present time. In this chapter, we will focus on how we use Scripture today in ways that strengthen us.

There are many ways Catholics use the Bible, from daily Mass to adult faith formation and study groups. There are some unique ways as well, such as those practiced by the men from Our Lady of the Pillar Catholic Church in Half Moon Bay, California. This group gets together on Sunday mornings to discuss the Scripture readings for that day's Mass. They meet early so that it won't interfere with family time and so they can better concentrate on the Scripture readings during Mass.

liturgy the official public prayer of the Church, through which Christ continues the work of redemption through the Church's celebration of the Paschal Mystery; it includes the seven Sacraments and the Liturgy of the Hours

Here are more examples of how the Bible is integral to the life of Catholics:

- Programs designed to prepare young people for the Sacrament of Confirmation often include spending time reading, studying, and praying over the weekly Scripture readings for Sunday liturgy.

- Religious education in Catholic schools and parish programs typically give much time to the study of Scripture.

- The themes of our Church seasons, such as Lent and Advent, derive from Scripture, as do special feast days such as Pentecost, Ascension, and Corpus Christi.

- Many of the prayers in the Mass come straight from the Bible.

Modernize

"For everything there is a season, and a time for every matter under heaven" (Ecclesiastes 3:1). These well-known words begin a reflection that many people have used to find truth in their lives when they are faced with dilemmas.

- Read Ecclesiastes 3:1-15.
- Summarize the truth revealed in this passage.
- Write a modern version that upholds the same truth.
- Identify any verses that seem hard to accept.

The fact that we study, pray, and reflect on Scripture today is a given. As we've learned throughout this course, the Second Vatican Council (Vatican II) has had a lasting impact on how we relate to Scripture. Let's take a look at the man who called for the council in the first place.

A Pope and His Council

When Blessed Pope John XXIII was elected Pope in late 1958, he was already 76 years old. He was born November 25, 1881, and served as Pope until he died on June 3, 1963. Some did not expect him to have much impact in his remaining years. However, early in 1959, he announced to a group of cardinals of the Church that he was calling for a Church council to be held.

Pope John saw the council as an opportunity for the Holy Spirit to work through the give-and-take that a gathering of the world's bishops would create. He welcomed an exchange between what the Church and what the modern world had to offer. "Open wide the doors," he told the bishops as he began the council. This was to be his signature quote. It symbolized his desire for the Church to be open to fresh ideas about what the Spirit wanted from us.

Pope John addressed the opening of the council in 1962. He encouraged the bishops to look favorably upon the relationship between the Catholic faith and the modern world:

Our task is not merely to hoard this precious treasure, as though obsessed with the past, but to give ourselves eagerly and without fear to the task that the present age demands of us.

—*Pope John XXIII*, Peter Hebblethwaite

The Pope pointed out that modern methods of study can reinvigorate the way the Catholic faith is presented to the world:

> But [the Church's] authentic doctrine has to be studied and expounded in the light of the research methods and the language of modern thought. For the substance of the ancient deposit of faith is one thing, and the way in which it is presented is another.

—*Pope John XXIII*, Peter Hebblethwaite

The image of the Church as mother was expressed eloquently in Pope John XXIII's encouraging words to the bishops of Vatican II. He expressed great confidence that once the truths of Catholicism were exposed to the light, it would lead to greater understanding and foster growth and maturity for more and more people—Catholics and non-Catholics alike.

Blessed Pope John XXIII was beatified, or declared "blessed," by Pope John Paul II in 2000. Beatification is a step on the way toward being declared an official saint of the Church.

We've referenced *Dei Verbum*, the Vatican II *Dogmatic Constitution on Divine Revelation*, throughout this course. The opening lines from the document remind us that this emphasis on Scripture isn't something new. It's more of a recovery, or renewal.

> "The Church has always venerated the divine Scriptures as she venerated the Body of the Lord" (DV, 21): both nourish and govern the whole Christian life.

—CCC, 141

Church leaders at Vatican II recognized that increased study of the Bible would fill

Research
○ Identify the documents of Vatican II and the years in which they were written.
○ Read two commentaries on Vatican Council II. Write about the impact of the council on the Catholic Church. List some of the ways it impacted Catholic life.

Name
○ List two specific programs in which you have participated that incorporated Scripture in some way.
○ Name a time when the Scripture used in a program or event really spoke to you.

more hearts with God's Word. Emphasis on Sacred Scripture would build spirituality as Catholic worship centered on the Eucharist as the Body of Christ. The *Dogmatic Constitution on Divine Revelation*, while maintaining this devotion to the Eucharist, urged Catholics to renew their appreciation of Scripture as well. The document also advised that prayer accompany reading of the Bible. In this way it becomes a dialogue. We listen to God in the Sacred Scripture, then speak to him when we pray.

The constitution expresses the power of Scripture in simple language:

> In the sacred books the Father who is in heaven comes lovingly to meet his children, and talks with them.

—*DV*, 21

The constitution ends with the hope that increased attention to Scripture, combined with devotion to the Eucharist, will lead to a deeper spiritual life for Catholics:

> Just as from constant attendance at the Eucharistic mystery the life of the Church draws increase, so a new impulse of spiritual life may be expected from increased veneration of the word of God, which "stands forever."

—*DV*, 26

Because of Vatican Council II, Scripture has regained its rightful place in all areas of Church life.

Tell Why did Pope John XXIII want to hold a council?

Explain Why has the Church always venerated Scripture as well as the Eucharist?

Everyday life challenges you to think about right and wrong, to sort out the good from the bad, and to inform and form your conscience. Here's an example . . .

}

A young child is in need of medical treatment, but the parents say it is against their faith. They point out numerous Bible verses that urge us to place our trust in God alone for our healing. They believe that trusting doctors would be against trusting God for the natural healing of their child. They absolutely refuse to take their child to the hospital, saying, "We are called to prayer and faith, not doctors and medical science."

Killing a child isn't in the Bible.

Government should stay out of it.

This is a personal matter for the parents.

They are following their conscience. Respect their faith.

Gotta be child abuse. Illegal.

How do you respond?

Going Moral

MY FAITH

Pope John XXIII began the Second Vatican Council with the words, "Open wide the doors." The cardinals and bishops did exactly that, and it had a huge impact on Catholic life in modern times.

Spiritually speaking, how might God be making this same invitation to you?

What doors do you need to open?

What "fresh air" might come into your life, in order to help you develop spiritually?

What new openness to God are you being called to, and what changes would occur in the way you live?

This is a really good time to make some personal notes about these spiritual questions. As we near the end of the course, you'll be sharing some of your insights.

Go to the student site at
hs.osvcurriculum.com

*Discipleship . . . within the Body of Christ . . .
for the glory of God and the good of the world*

QUICK REVIEW

1a. **List** Give at least two reasons why we read, study, and reflect on Scripture.

2.a **Elaborate** What are some specific ways in which Catholics rely on the Bible directly or indirectly?

b. **Interpret** What did Pope John XXIII mean when he told the world's bishops to "Open wide the doors"?

c. **Explain** Why should prayer accompany reading and studying of the Bible?

Listen and Discuss With a partner, open the Bible, identify a passage randomly, read it, and discuss what it means.

Pray Compose a short prayer in which you quote a passage from the Bible and talk to God about it.

SELF-ASSESS

Which statement best reflects where you are now?

☐ I'm confident enough about the material in this section to be able to explain it to someone else.

☐ I have a good grasp of the material in this section, but I could use more review.

☐ I'm lost. I need help catching up before moving on.

Scripture and the Sacraments

One important element to our Catholic identity is the relationship with God we share in and celebrate in the seven **Sacraments**—effective signs of **grace**, instituted by Christ and entrusted to the Church, by which divine life is shared with us through the work of the Holy Spirit. In the Sacraments, Jesus continues his saving work. During his life, Jesus welcomed, fed, healed, and forgave people. Through the Sacraments, he continues to share God's life and love with his Church. Grace is our participation in the life of God.

Among many aspects, the Second Vatican Council:

- examined how the Sacraments, as practiced at that time, reflected the original intention of the Apostolic Church,

- ensured that each Sacrament expressed its connection to Scripture, and

- put a stronger emphasis on the communal dimension of each Sacrament.

Dei Verbum's message, which calls for increased emphasis on Scripture, is embodied in the way the Church celebrates the Sacraments.

As a result of decisions made at the council, the role of Scripture has been revitalized in how we celebrate each Sacrament. Hearing the Word of God proclaimed during the liturgy, especially at Sunday Eucharist, is particularly important. Jesus tells us, "Where two or three are gathered in my name, I am there among them" (Matthew 18:20). In the Mass, when we read from Scripture, the Living Word of God, Christ is present, as he is in the community gathered together in prayer, the priest celebrant, and most especially in his Body and Blood.

Celebrations of the Sacrament of Penance and Reconciliation, for example, call for reading from Scripture whether celebrated communally or individually. The Rite of Christian Initiation of Adults, or RCIA, is the process by which adults are initiated into the Church. The RCIA represents a renewal of an initiation process from the earliest days of the Church, known as the *catechumenate*, that had not been used for some time before Vatican Council II. Much as we would in a journey, the community travels with those coming into the Church, as they participate in some parts of

Sacraments effective signs of grace, instituted by Christ and entrusted to the Church, by which divine life is shared with us through the work of the Holy Spirit

grace our participation in the life of God; "grace is *favor*, the *free and undeserved help* that God gives us to respond to his call to become children of God, adoptive sons, partakers of the divine nature and of eternal life" (CCC, 1996)

the liturgy and then break open the Word, that is the Sunday reading, in order to learn more about Jesus, the Church's teachings, and Catholic practices and beliefs.

No Sacrament after Vatican II showed a greater renewed emphasis on Scripture than the Eucharist, or Mass. In celebrating the sacrifice of the Mass, the council said: "The treasures of the bible are to be opened up more lavishly so that a richer fare may be provided for the faithful at the table of God's word" (*Sacrosanctum Concilium*, 51). The readings in the Liturgy of the Word prior to the council were fewer, but now there are three readings, as Scripture is used in a more significant way at Mass. Psalms are sung or recited between readings, and homilists are urged to break open those Sunday readings in their preaching.

The *Catechism* calls Scripture "extremely important" in the celebration of Mass. "It is from the Scriptures that the prayers, collects, and hymns draw their inspiration and their force, and that actions and signs derive their meaning (*SC*, 24)" (CCC, 1100).

Recall What did Jesus say about when two or three are gathered in his name?

Elaborate What are three aspects of the Sacraments that Vatican Council II examined?

The Seven Sacraments

Because Jesus instituted the Sacraments and the early Church celebrated the foundational rituals of many of them, we can find biblical roots for the Sacraments.

Sacraments of Initiation Three Sacraments together complete initiation into the Church: Baptism, which begins new life in Christ; Confirmation, which strengthens that life; and Eucharist, which nourishes that life and transforms the recipient to become more Christ-like (see CCC, 1275).

Baptism	John 3:5; Matthew 28:19-20; Romans 6:3-11; Acts 19:1-7
Confirmation	Acts 8:14-17, 9:17-19, 19:5; Titus 3:4-8
Eucharist	John 6:1-15, 25-71; Matthew 26:26-28; Mark 14:22-25; Luke 22:7-20

Sacraments of Healing In these Sacraments, God's forgiveness of sins and healing are given to those suffering physical and spiritual sickness.

Penance and Reconciliation	John 20:19, 22-23; Mark 1:15, 2:5, 10; Luke 7:48, 15:18
Anointing of the Sick	Mark 6:12-13, 16:17-18; Matthew 10:8; James 5:14-15

Sacraments at the Service of Communion In these Sacraments, certain Catholics receive the grace to commit to and serve God and the community.

Holy Orders	John 10:36; Acts 1:8, 2:4; 1 Timothy 4:14; 2 Timothy 1:6-7
Matrimony	Matthew 19:6; John 2:1-11; 1 Corinthians 7:39; Ephesians 5:31-32

Choose one of the Sacraments, and read each of the passages.

○ Compare and contrast the passages for the Sacrament you chose.

○ What did you learn about the Sacrament you chose?

○ Get with a partner who chose a different Sacrament and share information you learned.

Scripture Readings and Liturgy

The Mass, also called the Eucharistic liturgy, was said in Latin before the renewals of Vatican Council II. This was the language of the Mass your grandparents experienced as children. This was the language used in the Mass everywhere in the world, since it's considered the universal language of the Church. Before the council, the priest celebrated the Mass in Latin while everyone in the pews read along from a translation of the Latin Mass. The translation book was called a Missal, or missalette. At the time, the same Gospel readings were used for specific Sundays each year. Most of those readings—more than eighty percent of them—came from the Gospel according to Matthew.

After the revisions initiated by the council, the Church adopted a three-year cycle for Sunday readings. Now, each year focuses on a different Synoptic Gospel. Passages from the Gospel according to John are proclaimed every year at certain times, such as the last Sunday of Lent, all of Holy Week, and during the Easter season. This new cycle helps people hear more of Jesus' preaching and life, his stories and teachings contained in the different Gospels.

As a result of Vatican II, liturgies also include a wider variety of readings from the Old Testament, the Epistles (Letters), and the Gospels. Psalms from the Bible are sung or recited between the first two readings. Now the readings and the entire Mass may be celebrated in Latin and in the vernacular

Observe

At next Sunday's Mass, pay particular attention to the first main part of the liturgy, up to and including the Prayer of the Faithful.

1. What would you say is most important from this part of the Mass?
2. What are the ways in which Scripture is present throughout this section?
3. What posture does the assembly take during the reading of the Gospel? Why do you think this is done?
4. If there was a homily, how did the priest make reference to Scripture readings?
5. How did he apply the readings to our lives as Catholics today?

(language of the people). The Mass in the extraordinary form is celebrated in Latin.

The **Lectionary**, the book containing all of the readings for Mass, also received greater attention, and a special Book of Gospels containing all the Gospel readings began to be used. We now proclaim the First and Second Readings from the Lectionary, and the priest or deacon proclaims the Gospel reading from the Book of Gospels. We show reverence for the Word of God by carrying the Book of Gospels in procession, incensing it, and kissing it or bowing before it. We also show reverence when we listen attentively to the Word proclaimed, apply the Word to our own lives, and act on the Word.

After the Introductory Rites, when we gather as an assembly to give thanks and praise, and prepare to hear the Word of God, the first main part of the Mass has always

Lectionary book that contains the Scripture readings for the liturgy throughout the year

Explain
○ Tell how the following themes from the Old Testament are expressed in the Eucharist: covenant, Exodus and Passover, and the Kingdom of God.

Liturgy of the Word The Word of God proclaimed as part of each sacramental ritual helps us to have the proper dispositions for each of the Sacraments

centered on Scripture. However, since Vatican II and the use of the people's language, we have been very intentional about calling this part of the Mass the **Liturgy of the Word**. "The Liturgy of the Word is an integral part of the celebration. The meaning of the celebration is expressed by the Word of God which is proclaimed and by the response of faith to it" (CCC, 1190).

The Word of God proclaimed in the Liturgy of the Word:

- helps form those gathered into a community,

- announces the Good News of our salvation, beginning in the Old Testament,

- teaches us how to live as followers of Jesus and as children of God, and

- opens us up to listen to God in our everyday lives.

Identify How do we show reverence for the Word of God?

Elaborate What happened to the readings at Mass following Vatican II?

The Jewish Roots

For both Jews and Christians Sacred Scripture is an essential part of their respective liturgies . . . In its characteristic structure the Liturgy of the Word originates in Jewish prayer.

—CCC, 1096

Because Jesus, the twelve Apostles, and many of his first followers were Jewish, it makes sense that there are Jewish roots throughout Christianity. If you were to attend a Jewish synagogue service, you would discover the Scripture readings are chanted. Psalms are sung and prayers of praise and intercession are offered, similar to what happens at a Catholic liturgy. There is also a sermon on the readings of the day. In other words, the essential elements of a Jewish Shabbat, or Sabbath service, are very similar to the Liturgy of the Word at a Catholic Mass, and evident in other Sacraments as well.

Early Christians who were Jews adapted the structure of the Jewish synagogue service and certain elements of their worship to their Christian Eucharistic celebrations. As Catholics, we refer to the great themes of the Old Testament in our worship. Other elements of Catholic worship originate with Judaism, especially reading the Old Testament and in the events fulfilled in the mystery of Christ, namely promise and covenant, Exodus and Passover, and exile and return. The relationship between Catholic and Jewish liturgy is also evident in the rituals of Passover and the Eucharist (see CCC, 1093, 1096).

For Jews, it is the Passover of history, tending toward the future; for Christians, it is the Passover fulfilled in the death and Resurrection of Christ, though always in expectation of its definitive consummation.

—CCC, 1096

Name What Old Testament prayers are often sung or recited during Catholic Masses?

Explain How is a Jewish synagogue service similar to the Catholic Liturgy of the Word?

QUICK REVIEW

1a. Identify How did the Sacraments change after Vatican II?

  b. Explain Why is Scripture important in the Mass?

2a. Summarize What changes occurred in the Mass readings as a result of Vatican II?

  b. Infer Why is the first part of the Mass called the Liturgy of the Word?

3a. Name What is the name of the Jewish service that is similar to the Liturgy of the Word at a Catholic Mass?

  b. Connect How is the Catholic Mass linked to Jewish worship?

ACT

Perform research or visit a Jewish temple or synagogue to learn more about Jewish worship.

Make an electronic presentation or a poster showing what you learned about Jewish worship and how elements are reflected in the Mass.

Pray Compose a short prayer incorporating an element of the Mass that comes from Scripture.

SELF-ASSESS

Which statement best reflects where you are now?

☐ I'm confident enough about the material in this section to be able to explain it to someone else.

☐ I have a good grasp of the material in this section, but I could use more review.

☐ I'm lost. I need help catching up before moving on.

Praying with Scripture

> *Rejoice always, pray without ceasing,*
> *give thanks in all circumstances; for this is*
> *the will of God in Christ Jesus for you.*
>
> —1 Thessalonians 5:16-18

Pray without ceasing. Is that possible? What would that look like? Does Saint Paul really mean all the time? It does make a lot of sense, when you think about it. Every day would definitely go better if we thanked God for all he has given us. Actually, we can use Scripture to pray without ceasing, expressing our joy and thanks to God. That's what the Liturgy of the Hours is all about.

The Liturgy of the Hours

The **Liturgy of the Hours** is the public prayer of the Church, in which the People of God participate in Christ's priestly work. It is also the cornerstone of monastic life, along with the Eucharistic Liturgy. Monks and nuns mark the day by gathering to chant and recite the prayers and readings established for particular hours. But monks and nuns aren't the only people who pray the Liturgy of the Hours. Clergy and lay people around the world join them because it is intended to be "the prayer of the whole People of God" (CCC, 1175).

The Liturgy of the Hours aims at consecrating and making holy the whole day and night. Praying at definite times of the day (the canonical hours) originated in Jewish practice. The canonical hours are the Church's cycle of daily prayer consisting of prayers, readings, hymns, and psalms.

In the early days of the Church, people gathered during three parts on the night before a feast day. These hours were called Vespers, Matins, and Lauds. The present hours of Evening Prayer, Office of Readings, and Morning Prayer correspond to these hours. The readings in the Liturgy of the Hours also include the daytime hours (midmorning, midday, and midafternoon), and night prayer.

In praying them throughout the day, the Church sanctifies the times of the entire day. The Liturgy of the Hours celebrates the mystery of Christ that "permeates and transfigures" every moment of every day. The structure of the Liturgy of the Hours makes the whole day holy in praising God (see CCC, 1174).

The **Breviary** is a prayer book of Psalms and readings used to more easily recite the Liturgy of the Hours. The Latin root of "Breviary" means "short or concise." The expressions "Breviary," "office," and "divine office" are sometimes used as synonyms.

Liturgy of the Hours the daily public prayer of the Church—divided up into segments—that celebrates the mystery of Christ, which permeates and transfigures the time of each day

Breviary the text of the divine office, including psalms, prayers, canticles, and readings to be prayed in the Liturgy of the Hours

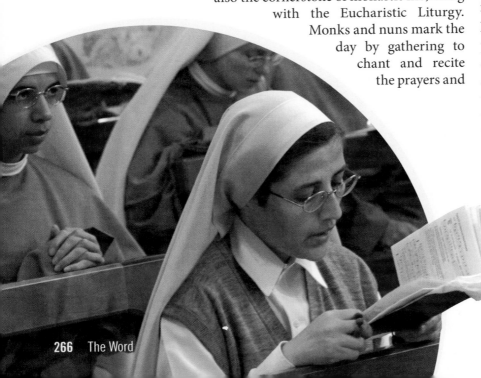

"O Antiphons"

The "O Antiphons" are a series of seven short verses recited or sung before the *Magnificat* during Vespers (evening prayer) of the Liturgy of the Hours. They cover the part of Advent known as the Octave Before Christmas (December 17–23). These antiphons were thought to be the inspiration for the Advent hymn, "O Come, O Come Emmanuel."

Composed and used by the Church as early as the seventh century, the antiphons were popular during the Middle Ages and used in liturgical celebrations in Rome. In some cities, church bells would ring each evening as they were sung.

Each antiphon begins with the invocation "O" followed by a title of Christ (Wisdom, Lord, Root of Jesse, Key of David, Rising Sun, King of Nations, Emmanuel) and includes an address, a description of what the Lord does, and finally a petition. They refer to the prophesies of Isaiah on the coming of Jesus, the Messiah. The antiphons ask God to come and save his people.

The "O Antiphons" are often used in parish and family Advent celebrations. Symbols reflecting the titles of Christ are used in banners and as decorations during the days prior to Christmas and are displayed as the antiphon is sung or recited.

For example, the "O Antiphon" for December 17 is: "O Wisdom, O holy Word of God, you govern all creation with your strong yet tender care. Come and show your people the way to salvation."

The related prophecy from Isaiah says, "The spirit of the LORD shall rest on him, the spirit of wisdom and understanding, the spirit of counsel and might, the spirit of knowledge and the fear of the LORD. His delight shall be in the fear of the LORD" (Isaiah 11:2-3).

Praying in Harmony

The Liturgy of the Hours is like "an extension of the Eucharistic celebration" (CCC, 1178). Besides psalms, it also includes readings from other parts of Scripture, especially the Gospels, and commentaries on the readings by various Fathers of the Church. By praying the Liturgy of the Hours, Catholics are participating in prayer that celebrates the holiness of each part of the day, reflects the seasons and times of the year, connects them to the whole Church, and reminds them of their connection to the mystery of Christ.

Because there are Catholics praying the Liturgy of the Hours according to every time zone throughout the world, praying is always going on. Wherever the sun is setting or rising, Catholics throughout the world are praising God and asking for his blessing. Thus, through the Liturgy of the Hours, the Church is one voice praying without ceasing, constantly praising God, and giving thanks for his gifts. From the perspective of the Church as the one People of God, this reminds us of Saint Paul's words to "pray without ceasing."

Describe What is the Liturgy of the Hours?

Conclude What does it mean to say the Liturgy of the Hours, along with the Eucharistic liturgy, is the cornerstone of monastic life in the Church?

> *Protect us, Lord, as we stay awake; watch over us as we sleep, that awake, we may keep watch with Christ, and asleep, rest in his peace.*
>
> —excerpt from the night prayer from the Liturgy of the Hours

Lectio Divina

One traditional way of reading Scripture in a meditative, prayerful way is called **lectio divina** (see CCC, 1177). This involves reading Scripture meditatively in order to tap into the power of the message and to link it to your own life. When beginning this type of prayer, start by praying for the help of the Holy Spirit. The approach calls upon you to engage all facets of your being. Here's how the *Catechism* describes this approach to Scripture:

> *Meditation engages thought, imagination, emotion, and desire. This mobilization of faculties is necessary in order to deepen our convictions of faith, prompt the conversion of our heart, and strengthen our will to follow Christ. Christian prayer tries above all to meditate on the mysteries of Christ, as in* lectio divina *or the rosary. This form of prayerful reflection is of great value.*
>
> —CCC, 2708

Saint Teresa of Ávila said prayer is a conversation with a friend. Saint Francis de Sales said prayer is talking to God and listening to God speaking to us in the depth of our heart. *Lectio divina*, or "holy reading," means approaching Scripture as if we are seeking to have a conversation with a friend. Conversations with even our best friends sometimes don't go well, or we might not even know what they're talking about. But we always know that our friends are there for us. A good way to read Scripture as prayerful conversation, or *lectio divina*, is to link its stories with our own story. Here are some steps to follow in such a process:

1. *lectio*—Read the passage slowly and attentively, several times.

2. *meditatio*—Focus on a word or phrase from the passage; memorize it and slowly repeat it to yourself.

3. *oratio*—Allow the meditation to lead you to a conversation with God.

4. *contemplatio*—Rest in the presence of God.

Friendship takes time. So does praying with Scripture. In a recent national survey, four out of five teenagers say they pray regularly, but only fifty percent say that they have ever read the Bible.

lectio divina literally "divine reading," "sacred reading," or "holy reading"; a meditative, prayerful reading of passages from the Bible

Discuss

○ What personal experiences have you had with using Scripture in prayer?

○ Which of those experiences did you find most beneficial?

○ What made them particularly beneficial?

> *The Church "forcefully and specially exhorts all the Christian faithful . . . to learn 'the surpassing knowledge of Jesus Christ' (Phil 3:8) by frequent reading of the divine Scriptures . . . Let them remember, however, that prayer should accompany the reading of Sacred Scripture, so that a dialogue takes place between God and man. For 'we speak to him when we pray; we listen to him when we read the divine oracles.'"[24]*
>
> —CCC, 2653

Create Space

Sure, we can read Scripture anywhere. "Sacred space" is everywhere because God is everywhere. However, our brains are hardwired to hold onto associations once they're formed. For instance, we become instantly happy when we hear the song we first slow danced to, or smell the roast that Grandma always cooks for family dinners. If there's a swimming pool where we almost drowned, we are likely to have that frightful memory come back to us every time we pass by it. It would be worthwhile, then, for us to create a space that we come to associate with prayerful reading of Scripture. Over time, when we enter that physical space, we are more likely to get to the place within us where we experience the presence of Jesus.

Some places are already created for us. For example, in the Catholic devotion of prayer in the presence of the Blessed Sacrament, we pray in a separate chapel or near the main altar, wherever the tabernacle is located. Sometimes we take part in Adoration, when the Blessed Sacrament is exposed in the Monstrance.

Along with the physical space where we pray, we also need to be attentive to creating a prayer space within ourselves. Do whatever helps you empty yourself of the busyness that you bring to prayer time. There might be a simple prayer that you say every time you begin your Scripture reading. (For example: "Come, Lord Jesus.") You might repeat the prayer while you take a few deep breaths. Then settle yourself into the posture that helps you stay relaxed but focused.

This is the ancient way of prayer that's been passed down from the early disciples. See how it works for you.

Write
- Describe the places you pray best.
- What makes them the best?
- When have you come out of a time of prayer feeling different from when you went in?

Trying *Lectio Divina*

What's the best way to select a Bible passage to read? Here are two ways:

- Follow the Lectionary, especially the readings for the upcoming Sunday liturgy.

- Choose a book of the Bible, or perhaps choose a section or chapter, to read from beginning to end.

Remember that *lectio divina* means "holy reading." It's not to be done the same way you would read one of your textbooks or a magazine article. Read slowly and reverently. Try to put yourself in the story or scene before trying to find a message for yourself. Some guidebooks on prayer suggest that you should try to visualize as concretely as possible the time, the place, and the people involved in the biblical story. Slow down. Savor the images. Pay attention whenever anything you read sparks a reaction from you. Read over that passage more than once, believing that it has something to say to you. Think more about savoring the reading than analyzing it. Perhaps one or a few words will strike you as worth pondering: "rest a while," "bread of life," "hope," "do the same."

Don't try to do too much with the reading, and especially don't be disappointed if little happens. There's a "Peanuts" cartoon in which Linus Van Pelt and Charlie Brown are looking at clouds in the sky. Linus says something profound and imaginative about what he visualizes in the cloud shapes. Charlie Brown answers that he was going to say that he saw a bunny and a duckie. Sometimes you'll be Charlie Brown and sometimes you'll be Linus.

Community of Sant'Egidio

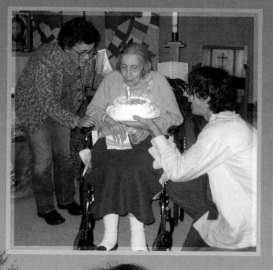

After Vatican II, a group of young adults living in Rome formed the Community of Sant'Egidio. Today, this movement of lay people has more than 50,000 members in more than seventy countries.

The community is known for its work to serve poor people and in peacemaking, especially through promoting exchanges among members of different religions.

The group's website describes this cornerstone of their good works. The starting point of the community has always been praying the Scriptures. By putting Scripture at the center of their lives, these young people are challenged to live a more authentic life: they discover the invitation to become Jesus' disciples, which Jesus addresses to all generations. It is a call to give up living just for oneself, and to begin to be instruments of a wider love for every man, woman, and child. They focus on the most vulnerable among us. Living the Word of God means following Christ's life, rather than their own, the organization says.

Prayer is the way to familiarize themselves with Jesus' words, with prayer from previous generations, such as the psalms. They present to the Lord the needs of the less fortunate, our own needs, and those of the world.

For this reason, the communities meet often to pray together. Many cities have common prayer open to all. Each member is also expected to find time and space for personal prayer and for reading the Scripture in his or her life, beginning with the Gospel reading.

Think About It On a scale of 1 to 10, with 10 being very important: How important is "prayer and action" to discipleship? Explain your rating. Choose another Catholic lay organization that you are unfamiliar with and write a summary about how members serve their communities.

↗ Go to the student site at
hs.osvcurriculum.com

Blessing *the* DAY
A spiritual practice for the life of discipleship

Blessing the Day is a prayerful practice that requires a little discipline before it becomes a habit. It involves asking God's guidance at the start of the day and giving God thanks at the end of the day.

Blessing the Day not only develops your relationship with God, it also helps you develop a grateful heart.

Some people discipline themselves to ask for God's guidance before getting out of bed every morning or while getting dressed. Others do so on the ride to school. Some do it at the start of homeroom, some as they open or close their lockers before school starts. No matter how you do it, Blessing the Day always begins with asking God's guidance at the start of a new day. You can make up your own short prayer—or what is called an *aspiration*—like "God, be with me this day," or "Lord, help me be more like you." Then use the same aspiration every morning. Or you can greet each day with a formal prayer, such as the Our Father, Hail Mary, Serenity Prayer, etc.

At night, Blessing the Day focuses on gratitude. It can mean offering God a simple prayer of thanksgiving. Some people develop the practice of doing this the moment they get under the covers. Others pray as they get undressed or wash up before going to bed. Some do so immediately after supper.

Some people take the evening prayer of gratitude a step further and mentally review the day's events to see how well they handled things that day, spiritually speaking. That's a prayer form called *examen*. Others develop a set of "night prayers" that "TAPP" into God's presence through:

- **T**hanksgiving
- **A**dmitting mistakes
- **P**ausing to hear what God might be trying to say
- **P**etitioning God for their needs and the needs of others

And you have already read how many Catholics worldwide join as one through the powerful prayer of the Liturgy of the Hours.

If you haven't already developed a way of Blessing the Day, give yourself the freedom to try several routines until you find one that feels most comfortable to you. Blessing the Day is guaranteed to strengthen your relationship with God and give you a grateful heart for as long as you live.

>> How do you want to practice Blessing the Day?

What will be your morning prayer, and when will you offer it?

What will be your evening prayer, and when will you offer it?

If you already practice Blessing the Day, describe the effect it has on you spiritually.

You don't need to explain what strikes you. You might simply respond, "That's interesting."

Identify What is *lectio divina*?

Name What does TAPP stand for?

Respond to God's Word

One more way in which reading Scripture is different from reading any other book is that it involves *active* reading. All reading is a conversation in which you take in what an author says, and then you mentally respond to it. After awhile, you might find that you want to say something to God in response to your reading and reflection on his Word. Sometimes a simple "Thank you, Jesus" is enough. At other times, you might find that you have more to say, such as, "Help me, Jesus, to be more . . . "

Some people find that keeping a prayer journal is also helpful. Some people doodle simple images that help them focus on the images in their head while praying.

Don't lose sight of the "big picture" message of Scripture. Some statements sound very harsh. (For instance, you might run across the incident when Jesus curses a fig tree for not bearing any figs. You might think, "Am I like that fig tree? Is Jesus cursing me too?") Remind yourself that Scripture is a love letter from God, not a judge's pronouncement of condemnation.

During your time with Scripture, when you experience God's presence in any way, that certainly is enough. If you sense that God actually has something to say to you personally during that time, that is a special blessing. You might also gain some insight into what you can do differently or how you can see yourself and others differently. If you don't experience God's presence in prayer, be persistent and do not stop praying. Don't get discouraged. God is present, even if you don't feel or experience his presence.

By spending time with Scripture, you are getting something of a "God's eye" view of yourself and what's happening around you. Come to Scripture with an open attitude that change is possible, and that God promises to share your burdens and wants peace for you.

Identify What is the "big picture" of Scripture?

Contrast How is reading Scripture different from any other reading you might do?

Study

Select one book from Scripture and practice prayerful Bible study. Select one of the following:

○ two Epistles from the New Testament

○ the Book of Proverbs

○ the Book of Sirach

Then, while prayerfully reading the Bible, write down the truths that speak to you most clearly, as well as any new thoughts you have about them.

QUICK REVIEW

1a. **Link** What is the connection between the Liturgy of the Hours and Jewish worship?

b. **Elaborate** Are monks and nuns the only people who pray the Liturgy of the Hours?

2a. **Explain** How does the Liturgy of the Hours extend the Eucharistic celebration?

b. **Connect** How does the Liturgy of the Hours fulfill Saint Paul's words to "pray without ceasing"?

3a. **Relate** Explain how to participate in *lectio divina*.

b. **Identify** When it comes to reading the Bible, what does active reading mean?

Listen and Discuss Talk with a partner about the following question.

○ How does it make you feel to know that there is praying without ceasing in the world?

SELF-ASSESS

Which statement best reflects where you are now?

☐ I'm confident enough about the material in this section to be able to explain it to someone else.

☐ I have a good grasp of the material in this section, but I could use more review.

☐ I'm lost. I need help catching up before moving on.

Living the Scriptures

The intent of this course has been to help you in your exploration of the meaning of Scripture. There is a personal invitation to continue reading, studying, and praying Scripture, which extends beyond this course. It is an invitation to continue engaging Scripture *for* yourself, but not *by* yourself.

> Your word is a lamp to my feet and a light to my path.
>
> —Psalm 119:105

There is much wisdom in the history of the Church and Church teaching today regarding how to make Scripture a living part of our lives. For Catholics, *how to read* Scripture can never be separated from *how to pray* Scripture and *how to live* the Scriptures.

> When you read God's Word, you must constantly be saying to yourself, "It is talking to me, and about me."
>
> —Søren Kierkegaard

Scripture can be a lamp that guides our path, if we spend time with it and are open to the Holy Spirit's work in it. Seeking guidance from Scripture, however, involves some critical thinking. If we keep searching, we *will* find wisdom there. That's why we rely on the Holy Spirit to help us understand and apply God's Word.

As we began this course, we discussed the role of virtue in faithful discipleship. In particular, we looked at the theological virtues

GO TO THE SOURCE

Read the following quotes from the New Testament. Describe how each one can be applied to your own living out of the Scriptures.

- Matthew 10:42
- Matthew 25:14-30
- Luke 9:46-48
- Luke 12:22-31
- Romans 12:9-21
- 1 Timothy 4:11-12

of faith, hope, and charity, which are the foundation for the moral or human virtues. Throughout the pages of the Old and New Testaments, the value and importance of a life of virtue are praised. "And if anyone loves righteousness, her labors are virtues; for she teaches self-control and prudence, justice and courage" (Wisdom 8:7).

Analyze Why is it important to read Scripture?

Tell Which theological virtues are the foundation for moral or human virtues?

Discuss
- Read Psalm 119:105, and discuss the metaphor for Scripture as a lamp that lights the way.
- What truth is the psalmist trying to point out?
- How can Scripture help us when we "get lost" or "make a wrong turn"?

PRIMARY SOURCES

"Your whole life should be a continual act of praise and prayer." That is how Sister Catherine McAuley described her ideal prayer life. She founded the Sisters of Mercy in Dublin, Ireland, in 1831, and her thoughts on prayer are echoed by many Catholics. Read these thoughts and prayers from prominent Catholics and answer the questions that follow.

➚ Go to the student site at
hs.osvcurriculum.com

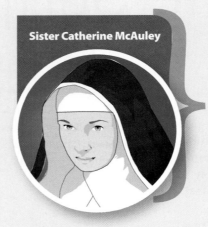

Sister Catherine McAuley

May I realize that whatever happens this day . . . we will do it together. Please take away any fears, anxieties or hurts that I might experience. And may I always be aware of your gift of hope delighting my heart and entire being. I pray all this, my God and my Lord until that great day we meet face to face . . . forevermore.

—Sister Catherine McAuley,
1778–1841

Saint Katharine Drexel

Saint Thomas More

*O Lord,
give us a mind
that is humble, quiet, peaceable,
patient and charitable,
and a taste of your Holy Spirit
in all our thoughts, words,
and deeds.*

—Saint Thomas More,
1478–1535, British
lord chancellor and
government official

The active life to be productive must have contemplation. When it gets to a certain height it overflows to active life and gets help and strength from the heart of God. This is the way the saints produced so much fruit, and we're all called to be saints.

—Saint Katharine Drexel, 1858–1955,
founder of the Sisters of the
Blessed Sacrament

Henri Nouwen

Although it is important and even indispensable for the spiritual life to set apart time for God and God alone, prayer can only become unceasing prayer when all our thoughts—beautiful or ugly, high or low, proud or shameful, sorrowful or joyful—can be thought in the presence of God.

—Henri Nouwen, 1932–1996, Dutch
Catholic writer and author

>> **What do each of these quotations or prayers have to say about separating our prayer life from the rest of our life?**

What should we talk about with God?

Which one of these quotations speaks to you?

JUSTICE AND DISCIPLESHIP

Jesus tells us that discipleship involves praying to the Father, studying his teachings and following his example, participating in the Eucharist, and living the virtues. He also calls us to act for justice.

DO YOU ENCOUNTER PEOPLE WHO BEG FOR MONEY IN PUBLIC PLACES like street corners and on public transit? What do you do when you are asked for money? Most of us see these people as the face of America's homeless population. They are often labeled by society as lazy and told to "just get a job."

Homelessness refers to people who "lack a fixed, regular, and adequate nighttime residence," be it in an apartment, house, or shelter.[25] This includes those "couch surfing" at friends' homes, families with children living in their cars, and those living in camping tents. Did you know that almost forty percent of the homeless population is made up of children, and more than a third of them are under the age of five?

The two main reasons why people are homeless are poverty and a lack of affordable housing. With new home construction primarily aimed at making higher profits, there has been a substantial decrease in the number of safe, affordable housing units available. Simultaneously, America has seen a significant increase in the number of people living in poverty. For someone living paycheck to paycheck, one crisis can mean having to choose either food, housing, or medical care. Or worse, for victims of domestic violence who must choose between being abused or being homeless.

Whether we encounter a panhandler asking for money or the "hidden homeless" families with children, our faith calls us to respect the dignity of every human person simply because they were created in the image and likeness of God (Genesis 1:26). The U.S. Conference of Catholic Bishops reminds us that "Christian love draws us to serve the weak and vulnerable among us. We are called to feed the hungry, to give drink to the thirsty, to clothe the naked, to shelter the homeless."[26]

This duty is not limited to one's own family, nation or state, but extends progressively to all humankind, since no one can consider himself extraneous or indifferent to the lot of another member of the human family. No one can say that he is not responsible for the well-being of his brother or sister (cf. *Gen* 4:9; *Lk* 10:29-37; *Mt* 25:31-46).[27]

As a matter of justice, you have the choice to act.

Tell about a time when you volunteered at a local homeless shelter, soup kitchen, or food bank.

How was the dignity of the people you served upheld?

Research homelessness in your city, county, or state and summarize the extent of the problem. Find out what initiatives the Catholic Campaign for Human Development has undertaken.

If you or someone you know is experiencing homelessness, consider describing for classmates the challenges that homeless families face.

↗ Go to the student site at **hs.osvcurriculum.com**

For someone living **paycheck to paycheck,** one crisis can mean having to choose either food, housing, or medical care.

You can be for justice without being a disciple, but you cannot be a disciple without being for justice.

Catholics live by the Scriptures and draw nourishment from them. Scripture is an essential element in all the Catholic Sacraments. Words of Scripture are breathed over Catholics at Baptism and over their bodies at funerals. When Catholics pray, they turn to Scripture. When Catholics ponder how to live their lives, they go to Scripture for guidance. And when they search for meaning, they find it expressed in the panoramic story of the Bible that begins with creation and comes to fulfillment in Jesus. Through our study of Scripture, we have come to know Jesus better. By praying with Scripture, we encounter him as friend, as Savior, and as Son of God.

SECTION 4 REVIEW

QUICK REVIEW

1a. **Elaborate** Explain Psalm 119:105: "Your word is a lamp to my feet and a light to my path."

  b. **Infer** Why can *how to read* Scripture never be separated from *how to pray* and *how to live* the Scriptures?

  c. **Identify** What comprises the foundation for the moral or human virtues?

ACT

Set up a personal prayer space. Build up a habit of using it several times a week, or daily if time permits.

Pray Compose a short prayer thanking God for something you have already learned from Scripture.

SELF-ASSESS

Which statement best reflects where you are now?

☐ I'm confident enough about the material in this section to be able to explain it to someone else.

☐ I have a good grasp of the material in this section, but I could use more review.

☐ I'm lost. I need help catching up before moving on.

PRAYER

Lord, Jesus, Christ, Good Shepherd of our souls, you who know your sheep and know how to reach our hearts, open the minds and hearts of those young people who search for and await a word of truth for their lives; let them understand that only in the mystery of your incarnation do they find full light; arouse the courage of those who know where to seek the truth, but fear that what you ask will be too demanding.

Stir in the hearts of those young people who would follow you, but who cannot overcome doubts and fears, and who in the end follow other voices and other paths which lead nowhere.

You who are the Word of the Father, the Word which creates and saves, the Word which enlightens and sustains hearts, conquer with your Spirit the resistance and delays of indecisive hearts; arouse in those whom you call the courage of love's answer: "Here I am, send me!"
Amen.

—Blessed Pope John Paul II

TERMS

Use each of the following terms in a sentence that shows you know what the term means. You may include more than one term in a sentence.

liturgy	Liturgy of the Word
Sacraments	Liturgy of the Hours
grace	Breviary
Lectionary	*lectio divina*

PEOPLE

Use information from the chapter to tell why each is significant.

1. Saint Paul
2. Blessed Pope John XXIII
3. Community of Sant'Egidio
4. Saint Teresa of Ávila
5. Saint Katharine Drexel
6. Sister Catherine McAuley
7. Saint Thomas More
8. Henri Nouwen

UNDERSTANDING

Answer each question and complete each exercise.

SECTION 1

1. **Recall** How does the Church use Scripture today?
2. **List** Why do we read, study, and reflect on Scripture?
3. **Expand** What did Pope John XXIII mean when he said, "Open wide the doors" at the beginning of Vatican II?
4. **Explain** What did the Church hope to do by increasing attention to Scripture?

SECTION 2

5. **Explain** Why would it be important to connect the Sacraments to Scripture?
6. **Link** What does the structure of the Mass show about the importance of Scripture?
7. **Explain** How is Catholic worship based on Jewish prayer?
8. **List** Name the seven Sacraments.

SECTION 3

9. **Recall** Where in the New Testament does one find the phrase "pray without ceasing"?
10. **Analyze** How does having a special prayer space aid in concentration?
11. **Elaborate** How did the Liturgy of the Hours develop?
12. **Explain** How is the Liturgy of the Hours literally one voice of prayer?

13. **Evaluate** What can you do to expand your use of Scripture?

14. **Explain** What does it mean to say, "For Catholics, *how to read* Scripture can never be separated from *how to pray* Scripture and *how to live* the Scriptures"?

15. **Evaluate** How can you improve your Scripture study habits?

CONNECTING

Visual This painting shows Jesus preparing to read from Scripture in the Temple.

How does this painting reflect the heritage shared by Catholics and Jews?

Challenge You are sitting in a quiet corner of your home when your younger sister asks a question.

> **Sister:** Can you help me with my homework?
>
> **You:** How about later? I'm doing something right now.
>
> **Sister:** But all you're doing is reading a book.
>
> **You:** I know that's what it looks like. But I'm praying, too.
>
> **Sister:** How can you be praying and reading at the same time?
>
> **You:** It's a special kind of reading called *lectio divina.*
>
> **Sister:** What does *that* mean?

○ What is your next reply?

○ Continue the conversation, including at least two more questions your sister might ask and how you would answer. Use information from the chapter in the conversation.

Question After working through this course, how would you say the Bible applies to people today?

Imagine You are part of a film crew that is recreating an incident from the Bible. You want to make it as realistic as possible as well as correctly interpret the story.

○ Which incident from the Bible would you want to recreate? Why?

○ What sources, in addition to Scripture itself, would you use to help you interpret the story?

○ What parts of the story would you have to interpret on your own, and how would you do so?

SELF-ASSESS

On Your Own Make a list of the most important things you learned from this chapter. Select three things that represent your growth in understanding as you worked through this chapter. Write a paragraph explaining your choices.

With a Partner List what you found most helpful or interesting in this chapter, as well as any other questions that have surfaced.

The Ecumenical (General) Councils

An ecumenical council is a gathering of the bishops of the world called together usually by the Pope to share the responsibility of teaching and guiding the Church. It has full authority over the entire Church. This authority cannot be exercised without the Pope's agreement (see *Catechism of the Catholic Church*, 337). There have been twenty-one such worldwide councils (see CCC, 884).

Council name	Date	Topic
1. **First Council of Nicea** in NW Asia Minor	325	Council of Nicea I condemned the heresy of Arius (a priest of Alexandria) who denied Jesus' divinity. It defined the consubstantiality of God the Son with God the Father. It declared Jesus, the Son of God, *homoousios* (coequal, consubstantial, and coeternal) with the Father; fixed the date for keeping Easter; and drafted the original form of the Nicene Creed.
2. **First Council of Constantinople** near Bosporus, a strait in today's Turkey	381	Council of Constantinople I confirmed the results of the Council of Nicea; affirmed the divinity of the Holy Spirit; added clauses referring to the Holy Spirit to the Nicene Creed; and condemned all forms of Arianism and Apollinarianism.
3. **Council of Ephesus** south of Smyrna in SW Asia Minor	431	The Council of Ephesus defined Jesus as one divine Person with two natures, divine and human. He is the second Person of the Trinity, true God and true man. This council emphasized the unity of the divine and human in the one divine Person. The divine *Logos*, while retaining his divine nature, assumed a human nature. The council declared Mary the Mother of God (*theotokos*); declared Nestorianism a heresy; and condemned Pelagianism.
4. **Council of Chalcedon** north of Constantinople	451	The Council of Chalcedon condemned Monophysitism (which claimed that there existed only one nature [the divine] in Christ). It declared Christ's two natures unmixed, unchanged, undivided, and inseparable.
5. **Second Council of Constantinople**	553	Council of Constantinople II condemned the errors of Origen and certain writings ("The Three Chapters") of Theodore, bishop of Mopsuestia, Theodoret, and Ibas, bishop of Edessa. It further confirmed the first four general councils, especially that of Chalcedon, whose authority was contested by some heretics.
6. **Third Council of Constantinople**	680–681	Council of Constantinople III put an end to Monothelitism (*Mono* [one] *thelema* [will]) by defining two natures in Christ, the human and the divine, as well as two wills in Christ, the divine and the human, which two are in perfect accord in the one divine Person, Jesus. It denounced and excommunicated Sergius (patriarch of Constantinople who originated Monothelitism), Pyrrhus, Paul, Macarius, and all their followers.
7. **Second Council of Nicea**	787	Nicea II condemned Iconoclasm and restored and regulated the veneration of holy images. Interesting fact: These first seven, "The Seven Great Councils of the Early Church," are the only ones on which many Eastern and Western Churches agree; they are the only test of orthodoxy among the Eastern Churches now separated from Rome.
8. **Fourth Council of Constantinople**	869	Council of Constantinople IV rejected the Acts of an irregular council (*conciliabulum*) brought together by Photius against Pope Nicholas and Ignatius the legitimate patriarch of Constantinople; it condemned Photius who had unlawfully seized the patriarchal dignity. The Photian Schism, however, triumphed in the Greek Church, and no other general council took place in the East.

ECUMENICAL COUNCILS continued

Council name	Date	Topic
9. **First Lateran Council** The Basilica of Saint John Lateran, Rome	1123	Lateran Council I, the first held in Rome, was concerned with the reform of the Church. It abolished the arbitrary conferring of ecclesiastical benefices by lay people, reestablished freedom from secular domination in the election of bishops and abbots, separated secular and Church affairs, reaffirmed that spiritual authority rests only in the Church, and did away with the emperor's claim to a right to interfere in a pope's election. This council also concerned itself with the recovery of the Holy Land from the Moslems.
10. **Second Lateran Council** Rome	1139	The object of Lateran Council II was to put an end to the errors of Arnold of Brescia, who contended that the Church was an "invisible body," not of this world, and should own no property. It also condemned the heresy of Peter Bruys (Bruis) and his Neo-Manicheans, who denounced the Mass as a "vain show," opposed the Eucharist, marriage, and the Baptism of children — all this leading to Albigensianism, which contended that all material things are evil in themselves. This council established rules for ecclesiastical conduct, morals, and discipline.
11. **Third Lateran Council** Rome	1179	Lateran Council III condemned the Albigenses and Waldenses and issued numerous decrees for the restoration of ecclesiastical discipline. It established that the election of a pope was to be conducted by the cardinals.
12. **Fourth Lateran Council** Rome	1215	Lateran Council IV issued an enlarged creed (symbol) against the Albigenses; condemned the Trinitarian errors of Abbot Joachim; made official the use of the word, "Transubstantiation;" and published seventy important reformatory decrees. This is the most important council of the Middle Ages, and it marks the culminating point of ecclesiastical life and papal power.
13. **First Council of Lyons** France	1245	Council of Lyons I excommunicated and deposed Emperor Frederick II for his attempt to make the Church merely a department of the state and directed a new crusade (the sixth), under the command of King St. Louis IX, against the Saracens and Mongols.
14. **Second Council of Lyons** France	1274	Council of Lyons II attempted a temporary reunion of the Greek Church with Rome; the word *filioque* (which expresses the procession of the Holy Spirit from both Father and Son as one principle) was added to the symbol of Constantinople; and means were sought for recovering Palestine from the Turks. It also laid down rules for papal elections.
15. **Council of Vienne** France	1311–1313	The Council of Vienne suppressed the Knights Templars; condemned the Beghards, and the Beguines who so stressed "inner union with God" (Quietism) that prayer and fasting became unimportant; and dealt with projects of a new crusade, the reformation of the clergy, and the teaching of Oriental languages in the universities.

Council name	Date	Topic
16. The Council of Constance Germany	1414–1418	The Council of Constance was held during the great Schism of the West. Its object was to end the divisions in the Church. The council became legitimate only when Pope Gregory XI formally convoked it. Owing to this circumstance it succeeded in putting an end to the schism by the election of Pope Martin V, which the Council of Pisa (1403) had failed to accomplish on account of its illegality. The rightful pope confirmed the former decrees of the synod against Wyclif and Hus. This council is ecumenical only in its last sessions (42–45 inclusive) and with respect to the decrees of earlier sessions approved by Pope Martin V.
17. Council of Basle (Switzerland)/ **Ferrara** (Italy)/ **Florence** (Italy)	1431–1439	The Council of Basle met first in that town. Its object was the religious pacification of Bohemia. Because of quarrels with the pope, the council was transferred first to Ferrara (1438), then to Florence (1439), where a short-lived union with the Greek Church was effected, the Greeks accepting the council's definition of controverted points. The Council of Basle is only ecumenical till the end of the twenty-fifth session. Pope Eugene IV approved only those decrees dealing with the elimination of heresy, the peace of Christendom, and the reform of the Church. Many Church historians and theologians do not recognize this Council in its entirety as an ecumenical council.
18. Fifth Lateran Council	1512–1517	The many decrees of Lateran Council V are disciplinary. A new crusade against the Turks was also advocated, but did not proceed because of the religious upheaval in Germany caused by Martin Luther.
19. Council of Trent Italy	1545–1563	The Council of Trent lasted eighteen years under five popes and was convoked to examine and condemn the errors promulgated by Martin Luther and other reformers, and to reform the discipline of the Church. Of all prior councils it lasted the longest, issued the largest number of dogmatic and reformatory decrees, such as those on the Eucharist, the Mass, the Sacraments (notably Baptism and Holy Orders), and teachings on marriage, Purgatory, indulgences, and the use of images. The Church officially designated all the writings of the Septuagint, along with all the books of the New Testament, as Sacred Scripture.
20. First Vatican Council	1869–1870	Vatican Council I was called by Pope Pius IX in December 1869, and lasted until July 1870, when it was adjourned. Besides important canons relating to the faith and the constitution of the Church, the council decreed the infallibility of the pope when speaking *ex cathedra* (the seat of Peter), i.e., when as shepherd and teacher of all Christians, he defines a doctrine concerning faith or morals to be held by the whole Church.
21. Second Vatican Council	1962–1965	Called by Blessed Pope John XXIII, the Vatican Council II had four principal aims: first, the Church must impart to herself and to the world a new awareness of her inner nature; second, there must be a renewal and reform of the Church; third, the Church should work to bring about Christian unity; and finally, the Church should be in dialogue with today's world.

CATHOLIC PRAYERS AND PRACTICES

Prayer and Christian life are inseparable, for they concern the same love and the same renunciation, proceeding from love; the same filial and loving conformity with the Father's plan of love; the same transforming union in the Holy Spirit who conforms us more and more to Christ Jesus; the same love for all men, the love with which Jesus has loved us

—*Catechism of the Catholic Church, 2745*

The following prayers and practices are based in Sacred Scripture and have evolved through Church Tradition. Some wording in these creeds changed when the Third Edition of the *Roman Missal* was introduced in November 2011.

Apostles' Creed

The Apostles' Creed contains a summary of the faith of the Apostles. It was developed from an early baptismal creed, and has existed since the second century. It was modified by early Church councils.

I believe in God,
the Father almighty,
Creator of heaven and earth,
and in Jesus Christ, his only Son, our Lord,

*At the words that follow, up to and including
the Virgin Mary, all bow.*

who was conceived by the Holy Spirit,
born of the Virgin Mary,
suffered under Pontius Pilate,
was crucified, died and was buried;
he descended into hell;
on the third day he rose again from the dead;
he ascended into heaven,
and is seated at the right hand of God the Father almighty;
from there he will come to judge the living and the dead.

I believe in the Holy Spirit,
the holy catholic Church,
the communion of saints,
the forgiveness of sins,
the resurrection of the body,
and life everlasting. Amen.

Nicene Creed

The Nicene Creed was formed as a response to the Arian heresy, which denied the divinity of Christ. It takes its name from the city of Nicea, site of the First Council of Nicea in A.D. 325. The original creed underwent modifications at ecumenical councils in Constantinople in A.D. 381 and Chalcedon in A.D. 451.

I believe in one God,
the Father almighty,
maker of heaven and earth,
of all things visible and invisible.
I believe in one Lord Jesus Christ,
the Only Begotten Son of God,
born of the Father before all ages.
God from God, Light from Light,
true God from true God,
begotten, not made, consubstantial with the Father;
through him all things were made.
For us men and for our salvation
he came down from heaven,
At the words that follow up to and including and became man,
all bow.
and by the Holy Spirit was incarnate of the Virgin Mary,
and became man.
For our sake he was crucified under Pontius Pilate,
he suffered death and was buried,
and rose again on the third day
in accordance with the Scriptures.
He ascended into heaven
and is seated at the right hand of the Father.
He will come again in glory
to judge the living and the dead
and his kingdom will have no end.
I believe in the Holy Spirit, the Lord, the giver of life,
who proceeds from the Father and the Son,
who with the Father and the Son is adored and glorified,
who has spoken through the prophets.
I believe in one, holy, catholic and apostolic Church.
I confess one Baptism for the forgiveness of sins
and I look forward to the resurrection of the dead
and the life of the world to come. Amen.

Athanasian Creed

This creed embodies Athanasius' theology of the Trinity and was composed by Hilary, bishop of Arles, in the fifth century.

Whosoever will be saved, before all things it is necessary that he hold the Catholic Faith. Which Faith except everyone do keep whole and undefiled, without doubt he shall perish everlastingly.

And the Catholic Faith is this, that we worship one God in Trinity and Trinity in Unity. Neither confounding the Persons, nor dividing the Substance.

For there is one Person of the Father, another of the Son, and another of the Holy Ghost. But the Godhead of the Father, of the Son, and of the Holy Ghost is all One, the Glory Equal, the Majesty Co-Eternal.

Such as the Father is, such is the Son, and such is the Holy Ghost.

The Father Uncreate, the Son Uncreate, and the Holy Ghost Uncreate.

The Father Incomprehensible, the Son Incomprehensible, and the Holy Ghost Incomprehensible.

The Father Eternal, the Son Eternal, and the Holy Ghost Eternal and yet they are not Three Eternals but One Eternal.

As also there are not Three Uncreated, nor Three Incomprehensibles, but One Uncreated, and One Uncomprehensible.

So likewise the Father is Almighty, the Son Almighty, and the Holy Ghost Almighty. And yet they are not Three Almighties but One Almighty.

So the Father is God, the Son is God, and the Holy Ghost is God.

And yet they are not Three Gods, but One God. So likewise the Father is Lord, the Son Lord, and the Holy Ghost Lord.

And yet not Three Lords but One Lord. For, like as we are compelled by the Christian verity to acknowledge every Person by Himself to be God and Lord, so are we forbidden by the Catholic Religion to say, there be Three Gods or Three Lords.

The Father is made of none, neither created, nor begotten. The Son is of the Father alone; not made, nor created, but begotten.

The Holy Ghost is of the Father, and of the Son neither made, nor created, nor begotten, but proceeding.

So there is One Father, not Three Fathers; One Son, not Three Sons; One Holy Ghost, not Three Holy Ghosts.

And in this Trinity none is afore or after Other, None is greater or less than Another, but the whole Three Persons are Co-eternal together, and Co-equal.

So that in all things, as is aforesaid, the Unity is Trinity, and the Trinity is Unity is to be worshipped.

He therefore that will be saved, must thus think of the Trinity.

Furthermore, it is necessary to everlasting Salvation, that he also believe rightly the Incarnation of our Lord Jesus Christ.

For the right Faith is, that we believe and confess, that our Lord Jesus Christ, the Son of God, is God and Man.

God, of the substance of the Father, begotten before the worlds; and Man, of the substance of His mother, born into the world.

Perfect God and Perfect Man, of a reasonable Soul and human Flesh subsisting.

Equal to the Father as touching His Godhead, and inferior to the Father as touching His Manhood.

Who, although He be God and Man, yet He is not two, but One Christ.

One, not by conversion of the Godhead into Flesh, but by taking of the Manhood into God.

One altogether, not by confusion of substance, but by Unity of Person.

For as the reasonable soul and flesh is one Man, so God and Man is one Christ.

Who suffered for our salvation, descended into Hell, rose again the third day from the dead.

He ascended into Heaven, He sitteth on the right hand of the Father, God Almighty, from whence he shall come to judge the quick and the dead.

At whose coming all men shall rise again with their bodies, and shall give account for their own works.

And they that have done good shall go into life everlasting, and they that have done evil into everlasting fire.

This is the Catholic Faith, which except a man believe faithfully and firmly, he cannot be saved.

The Lord's Prayer

Our Father, who art in heaven,
hallowed be thy name;
thy kingdom come,
thy will be done on earth as it is in heaven.
Give us this day our daily bread;
and forgive us our trespasses
as we forgive those who trespass against us;
and lead us not into temptation,
but deliver us from evil.
Amen.

Pater Noster

Pater noster, qui es in caelis:
sanctificetur nomen tuum;
adveniat regnum tuum;
fiat voluntas tua, sicut in caelo, et in terra.
Panem nostrum quotidianum da nobis hodie;
et dimitte nobis debita nostra,
sicut et nos dimittimus debitoribus nostris;
et ne nos inducas in tentationem;
sed libera nos a malo.
Amen.

Glory to the Father

Glory to the Father,
and to the Son,
and to the Holy Spirit,
as it was in the beginning
is now, and ever shall be
world without end.
Amen.

Gloria Patri

Glória Patri,
et Fílio
et Spíritui Sancto,
Sicut erat in princípio,
et nunc et semper
et in sáecula saeculórum.
Amen.

Prayer to the Holy Spirit

Come, Holy Spirit, fill the hearts of your faithful.
And kindle in them the fire of your love.
Send forth your Spirit and they shall be created.
And you shall renew the face of the earth.
Let us pray:
Lord, by the light of the Holy Spirit
you have taught the hearts of your faithful.
In the same Spirit, help us to choose what is right
and always rejoice in your consolation.
We ask this through Christ our Lord.
Amen.

Veni, Sancte Spiritus, reple tuorum corda fidelium,
et tui amoris in eis ignem accende.
Emitte Spiritum tuum et creabuntur;
Et renovabis faciem terrae.
Oremus:
Deus, qui corda fidelium Sancti Spiritus illustratione
docuisti.
Da nobis in eodem Spiritu recta sapere,
et de eius semper consolatione gaudere.
Per Christum Dominum nostrum.
Amen.

The Hail Mary

Hail, Mary, full of grace,
The Lord is with thee.
Blessed art thou among women
and blessed is the fruit of thy womb, Jesus.
Holy Mary, Mother of God,
pray for us sinners,
now and at the hour of our death.
Amen.

Ave Maria

Ave María, grátia plena,
Dóminus tecum.
Benedícta tu in muliéribus,
et benedíctus fructus ventris tui, Jesus.
Sancta María, Mater Dei,
ora pro nobis peccatóribus,
nunc et in hora mortis nostrae.
Amen.

The Magnificat

The Magnificat (also called the Canticle of Mary) is recorded in the Gospel according to Luke (1:46-55) and is Mary's joyous prayer in response to her cousin Elizabeth's greeting (Luke 1:41-45). This prayer forms part of the Church's prayer in the Liturgy of the Hours.

My soul proclaims the greatness of the Lord,
and my spirit rejoices in God my Savior,
for he has looked with favor on his lowly servant.
From this day all generations will call me blessed:
the Almighty has done great things for me,
and holy is his Name.
He has mercy on those who fear him in every generation.
He has shown the strength of his arm;
he has scattered the proud in their conceit.
He has cast down the mighty from their thrones,
and has lifted up the lowly.
He has filled the hungry with good things,
and the rich he has sent away empty.
He has come to the help of his servant Israel
for he has remembered his promise of mercy,
the promise he made to our fathers,
to Abraham and his children forever.
Glory to the Father and to the Son
    and to the Holy Spirit,
as it was in the beginning, is now,
    and will be forever.
Amen.

Magníficat ánima mea Dóminum,
et exsultávit spíritus meus in Deo
    salvatóre meo,
quia respéxit humilitátem
    ancíllæ suæ.
Ecce enim ex hoc beátam me dicent
    omnes generatiónes,
quia fecit mihi magna, qui potens est,
et sanctum nomen eius,
et misericórdia eius in progénies et
    progénies timéntibus eum.

Fecit poténtiam in bráchio suo,
dispérsit supérbos mente cordis sui;
depósuit poténtes de sede
et exaltávit húmiles.
Esuriéntes implévit bonis
et dívites dimísit inánes.
Suscépit Ísrael púerum suum,
recordátus misericórdiæ,
sicut locútus est ad patres nostros,
Ábraham et sémini eius in sæcula.
Glória Patri et Fílio
et Spirítui Sancto.
Sicut erat in princípio, et nunc
    et semper,
et in sæcula sæculórum.
Amen.

Act of Contrition (traditional)

O my God, I am heartily sorry for having offended you, and I detest all my sins, because of your just punishments, but most of all because they offend you, my God, who are all good and deserving of all my love. I firmly resolve, with the help of your grace, to sin no more and to avoid the near occasion of sin.

Act of Contrition (contemporary)

My God, I am sorry for my sins with all my heart. In choosing to do wrong and failing to do good, I have sinned against you whom I should love above all things. I firmly intend, with your help, to do penance, to sin no more, and to avoid whatever leads me to sin. Our Savior Jesus Christ suffered and died for us. In his name, my God, have mercy.

Prayer for Justice

Father, you have given all peoples one common origin.
It is your will that they be gathered together
as one family in yourself.
Fill the hearts of mankind with the fire of your love
and with the desire to ensure justice for all.
By sharing the good things you give us,
may we secure an equality for all
our brothers and sisters throughout the world.
May there be an end to division, strife, and war.
May there be a dawning of a truly human society
built on love and peace.
We ask this in the name of Jesus, our Lord.
Amen.

The Rosary

The Rosary is called the Psalter of Mary *because all fifteen of its mysteries, with their 150* Aves, *correspond to the number of Psalms. Saint Dominic popularized the fifteen-decade Rosary. He is so connected with this form of the Rosary that often it is referred to as the Dominican Rosary. Pope John Paul added five luminous mysteries to the previous fifteen glorious, joyful, and sorrowful mysteries.*

The Rosary is the most well-known and used form of chaplet (a devotion using beads; from a French word meaning "crown" or "wreath"). There are other chaplets, including Saint Bridget's Chaplet and the Chaplet of the Immaculate Conception.

1. Sign of the Cross and
   Apostles' Creed
2. Lord's Prayer
3. Three Hail Marys
4. Glory to the Father
5. Announce mystery
6. Lord's Prayer
7. Ten Hail Marys
8. Glory to the Father

Repeat last four steps, meditating on the other mysteries of the rosary.

The Mysteries of the Rosary and Recommended Scriptural Meditations

Joyful Mysteries
(Mondays and Saturdays)

1. The Annunciation (humility)
   Isaiah 7:10-14; Luke 1:26-38
2. Visitation (charity)
   Isaiah 40:1-11; Luke 1:39-45; John 1:19-23
3. The Nativity (poverty)
   Micah 5:1-4; Matthew 2:1-12; Luke 2:1-20; Galatians 4:4
4. The Presentation (obedience)
   Luke 2:22-35; Hebrews 9:6-14
5. The Finding of Jesus in the Temple (piety)
   Luke 2:41-52; John 12:44-50; 1 Corinthians 2:6-16

Sorrowful Mysteries
(Tuesdays and Fridays)

1. The Agony in the Garden (repentance)
   Matthew 26:36-46; Mark 14:26-42; Luke 22:39-53;
   John 18:1-12
2. The Scourging at the Pillar (purity)
   Isaiah 50:5-9; Matthew 27:15-26; Mark 15:1-15
3. The Crowning with Thorns (courage)
   Isaiah 52:13–53:10; Matthew 16:24-28, 27:27-31;
   Mark 15:16-19; Luke 23:6-11; John 19:1-7
4. The Carrying of the Cross (patience)
   Mark 8:31-38; Matthew 16:20-25; Luke 23:26-32;
   John 19:17-22; Philippians 2:6-11
5. The Crucifixion (self-renunciation)
   Mark 15:33-39; Luke 23:33-46; John 19:23-37;
   Acts 22:22-24; Hebrews 9:11-14

Glorious Mysteries
(Sundays and Wednesdays)

1. The Resurrection (faith)
   Matthew 28:1-10; Mark 16:1-18; Luke 24:1-12;
   John 20:1-10; Romans 6:1-14; 1 Corinthians 15:1-11
2. The Ascension (hope)
   Matthew 28:16-20; Luke 24:44-53; Acts 1:1-11;
   Ephesians 2:4-7
3. The Descent of the Holy Spirit Upon the Apostles (love)
   John 14:15-21; Acts 2:1-11; 4:23-31; 11:15-18
4. The Assumption (eternal happiness)
   John 11:17-27; 1 Corinthians 15:20-28, 42-57;
   Revelation 21:1-6
5. The Coronation of Mary (Marian devotion)
   Matthew 5:1-12; 2 Peter 3:10; Revelation 7:1-4, 9-12;
   21:1-6

Luminous Mysteries

(Thursdays)

1. Baptism in the Jordan (commitment)
   Matthew 3:13-17; Mark 1:9-11; Luke 3:21-22;
   John 1:29-34
2. The Wedding at Cana (fidelity)
   John 2:3-5, 7-10; John 13:14-15; Luke 6:27-28, 37;
   Luke 9:23; John 15:12
3. Proclamation of the Kingdom of God (conversion)
   Mark 1:14-15; Luke 4:18-19, 21; Matthew 5:38-39, 43-
   44; Matthew 6:19-21; Matthew 7:12; Matthew 10:8
4. The Transfiguration (promise)
   Matthew 5:14, 16; Matthew 17:1-2, 5, 7-8; Luke 9:30-33;
   John 1:4-5, 18; 2 Corinthians 3:18
5. Institution of the Eucharist (grace)
   John 13:1; Matthew 26:18; Luke 22:15-16, 19-20;
   Matthew 5:14, 19-20; 1 Corinthians 11:26; John 17:20-
   21; 1 Corinthians 12:13, 26-27

The Ten Commandments

The division and numbering of the commandments have varied in the course of history. The Catechism of the Catholic Church follows the division established by Saint Augustine which has become the Catholic (and Lutheran) tradition. The first three concern love of God and the other seven love of neighbor (see Exodus 20:1-17, Deuteronomy 5:1-21).

1. I am the Lord your God: you shall
   not have strange gods before me.
2. You shall not take the name of the
   Lord your God in vain.
3. Remember to keep holy the Lord's day.
4. Honor your father and your mother.
5. You shall not kill.
6. You shall not commit adultery.
7. You shall not steal.
8. You shall not bear false witness against your neighbor.
9. You shall not covet your neighbor's wife.
10. You shall not covet your neighbor's goods.

The Eight Beatitudes

The Gospels according to Luke and Matthew contain the Beatitudes. They are statements of praise, stressing the joy of those who participate in the Kingdom of God. The Beatitudes also tell us about what it means to be a member of the Church. (see Matthew 5:3-11; Luke 6:20-26).

1. Blessed are the poor in spirit, for theirs is the kingdom of heaven.
2. Blessed are those who mourn, for they will be comforted.
3. Blessed are the meek, for they will inherit the earth.
4. Blessed are those who hunger and thirst for righteousness, for they will be filled.
5. Blessed are the merciful, for they will receive mercy.
6. Blessed are the pure in heart, for they will see God.
7. Blessed are the peacemakers, for they will be called children of God.
8. Blessed are those who are persecuted for righteousness' sake, for theirs is the kingdom of heaven.

The Seven Corporal Works of Mercy

". . .Just as you did it to one of the least of these who are members of my family, you did it to me" (Matthew 25:31-46).

1. Feed the hungry.
2. Give drink to the thirsty.
3. Clothe the naked.
4. Shelter the homeless.
5. Visit the sick.
6. Visit the imprisoned.
7. Bury the dead.

The Seven Spiritual Works of Mercy

Based on Christ's teachings and Christian practice since the Apostles.

1. Counsel the doubtful.
2. Instruct the ignorant.
3. Admonish sinners.
4. Comfort the afflicted.
5. Forgive offenses.
6. Bear wrongs patiently.
7. Pray for the living and the dead.

VOICES OF TRADITION

Throughout this course you've read about many different people of faith. Below you'll find a prayer, a quote, or a biography of some of them.

Saint Augustine, bishop of Hippo (354–430)

Saint Augustine was the last bishop of Hippo in North Africa (390–430). After his death, the Vandals invaded and burned the city to the ground and its inhabitants dispersed. Saint Augustine's library was the only thing that escaped. Although he died with no will, Possidius, in his biography of Saint Augustine, says, "It was a standing order that the library of the church and all the books should be carefully preserved for posterity."

Saint Ignatius of Antioch (c. 50–98 to 117)

Saint Ignatius of Antioch, one of the Greek Fathers of the Church, is said to have been a convert of Saint John and consecrated as the third bishop of Antioch by Saint Peter. Legend has it that he was the child whom Jesus put in the midst of the disciples as an example. "Truly I tell you, unless you change and become like children, you will never enter the kingdom of heaven. Whoever becomes humble like this child is the greatest in the kingdom of heaven. Whoever welcomes one such child in my name welcomes me" (Matthew 18:3-5).

Saint Catherine of Siena (1347–1380)

In 1970, Saint Catherine of Siena was named as a Doctor of the Church. Doctor of the Church is a title given since the Middle Ages to authors of learning and holiness whose work has enhanced the cause of Christ and his Church. Other women named Doctors of the Church include Saint Teresa of Ávila (named in 1970) and Saint Thérèse of Lisieux (named in 1998).

Saint Anselm of Canterbury (d. 1109)

Saint Anselm, the first medieval theologian to attempt a rigorous study of Christian thought, defined theology as "faith seeking understanding." This approach to theology, using philosophical tools to understand and organize Christian teaching, came to be known as scholasticism, and Saint Anselm is called the Father of Scholasticism. Schools of theology grew into great universities, and the university system of education that exists throughout the world today can trace its origins back to this movement during the Middle Ages.

Saint Thomas Aquinas (1225–1274)

"Better to illuminate than merely to shine, to deliver to others contemplated truths than merely to contemplate."

—Saint Thomas Aquinas

Saint Thomas Aquinas was one of the greatest theological thinkers of the thirteenth century. His impact on Christianity was so immense that his writings are still at the core of Roman Catholic seminary education. He is the patron of Catholic universities, colleges, and schools.

Saint Francis of Assisi (1181–1226)

The Peace Prayer

Lord, make me an instrument of your peace;
where there is hatred, let me sow love;
where there is injury, pardon;
where there is doubt, faith;
where there is despair, hope;
where there is darkness, light;
and where there is sadness, joy.
Grant that I may not so much seek
to be consoled as to console,
to be understood as to understand,
to be loved as to love;
for it is in giving that we receive,
it is in pardoning that we are pardoned,
and it is in dying that we are born to eternal life.

This prayer is often attributed to Saint Francis. The Peace Prayer has been known in the United States since 1936. Cardinal Francis Spellman distributed millions of copies of the prayer during and just after World War II. A version of this prayer is found in *Twelve Steps and Twelve Traditions*, a book published by Alcoholics Anonymous World Services, Inc. Blessed Mother Teresa of Calcutta made it part of the daily prayers of the Missionaries of Charity, the order she founded. She attributed importance to it when receiving the Nobel Peace Prize in Oslo in 1979 and asked that it be recited. It has also been made into a hymn, "Make Me a Channel of Your Peace" (adapted by Sebastian Temple in 1928).

Saint Athanasius (296–373)

Because of his learning, spiritual insight, and zeal at the time of the first ecumenical council in Nicea, Saint Athanasius has been the subject of many icons. Popular in Eastern Christian heritage, icons are sacred images of Christ, Mary, and the saints, or of events in salvation history. The word "icon" comes from the Greek word for "image." Icons are more than decorative or educational. They have been called "theology in color." For example, an icon by Nicholas Papas, a liturgical artist from Greensburg, Pennsylvania, commemorates Saint Athanasius' life, which was spent defending Jesus' divine nature as the Son of God. In the icon the saint is pictured with a scroll, which reads "It is no temporal feast that we come to but an eternal heavenly feast."

Saint Macrina (330–379)

Saint Macrina, the sister of Saints Basil the Great and Gregory of Nyssa, devoted herself to a life of virginity and the pursuit of Christian perfection. On the death of their father, Basil took her and their mother to an estate on the River Iris, in Pontus (a region on the southern coast of the Black Sea, located in modern-day northeastern Turkey). Here, with their servants and other companions, they led a life consecrated to God. After her mother's death, Macrina became the head of this community. Many pious women joined the monastery, eventually following the rule that Basil had written for the monks. These women fed and clothed the poor and cared for many homeless and needy persons.

In 1933, the sisters of the Order of Saint Basil the Great, who have Saint Macrina as their patroness, bought the 1,000-acre property of Josiah Van Kirk Thompson, a bankrupt millionaire baron of the coal industry near Scranton, Pennsylvania. The sisters converted the mansion to a monastery and in 1934 named the area Mount St. Macrina in honor of their patroness. Today, the mansion serves as the House of Prayer (formerly the Retreat Center), a place of spiritual renewal and refreshment.

Saint Thérèse of Lisieux (1873–1897)

Saint Thérèse of Lisieux, who died at the age of twenty-four, often worried about how she could achieve holiness.

> I have always wanted to become a saint. Unfortunately when I have compared myself with the saints, I have always found that there is the same difference between the saints and me as there is between a mountain whose summit is lost in the clouds and a humble grain of sand trodden underfoot by passers-by. Instead of being discouraged, I told myself: God would not make me wish for something impossible and so, in spite of my littleness, I can aim at being a saint. It is impossible for me to grow bigger, so I put up with myself as I am, with all my countless faults. But I will look for some means of going to heaven by a little

way which is very short and very straight, a little way that is quite new. . . . I sought in holy Scripture some idea of what this life I wanted would be, and I read these words: "Whosoever is a little one, come to me." It is your arms, Jesus, that are the lift to carry me to heaven. And so there is no need for me to grow up: I must stay little and become less and less.

—Saint Thérèse of Lisieux

Saint Paul (c. 10)

Pope Benedict XVI declared June 2008–June 2009 a Year of Saint Paul to celebrate the 2000th anniversary of the Apostle's birth. Saint Paul is thought to have been born between A.D. 6–10. In his homily at First Vespers of the Solemnity of the Holy Apostles Peter and Paul in Rome, the Pope said, "The Apostle to the Gentiles, who was especially committed to taking the Good News to all peoples, left no stones unturned for unity and harmony among all Christians. May he deign to guide and protect us in this bimillenial celebration, helping us to progress in the humble and sincere search for the full unity of all the members of Christ's Mystical Body."

Saint Jerome (340-2–420) and Saint Paula (347–404)

Saint Jerome spent his last years in the Holy Land, where he lived and worked in a large cave near Jesus' birthplace. He opened a free school and also a hospice for pilgrims, "so that," as Saint Paula said, "should Mary and Joseph visit Bethlehem again, they would have a place to stay."

> ". . . Here bread and herbs, planted with our own hands, and milk, all country fare, furnish us plain and healthy food. In summer the trees give us shade. In autumn the air is cool and the falling leaves restful. In spring our psalmody is sweeter for the singing of the birds. We have plenty of wood when winter snow and cold are upon us. Let Rome keep its crowds, let its arenas run with blood, its circuses go mad, its theaters wallow in sensuality. . . ."

Saint Jerome died near Bethlehem and was buried under the church of the Nativity at Bethlehem. In the thirteenth century his body was moved to the Sistine Chapel of the basilica of Santa Maria Maggiore at Rome.

Saint Justin Martyr (130–165)

In this description by Saint Justin Martyr from his *First Apology*, 67, which was rediscovered in the sixteenth century, the saint describes what Mass was like in the year 152.

> On the day called Sunday there is a meeting in one place of those who live in cities or the country, and the memoirs of the apostles or the writings of the prophets are read as long as time permits. When the reader has finished, the president in a discourse urges and invites us to the imitation of these noble things. Then we all stand up together and offer prayers. . . . when we have finished

the prayer, bread is brought, and wine and water, and the president similarly sends up prayers and thanksgiving . . . and the congregation assents, saying the Amen; the distribution, and reception of the consecrated elements . . . takes place and they are sent to the absent by the deacons. Those who prosper, and who so wish, contribute, each one as much as he chooses to. What is collected is deposited with the president, and he takes care of orphans and widows, and those who are in want on account of sickness or any other cause, and those who are in bonds, and the strangers who are sojourners among us, and, briefly, he is the protector of all those in need.

The Catholic Source Book
Our Sunday Visitor Curriculum Division, 2007, page 282

Saint Francis de Sales (1567–1662)

Born in France, Saint Francis de Sales studied in Paris and received a doctorate in law. He pursued his dream of being a priest. Legend has it that God made his will clear to Francis while he was riding. Francis fell from his horse three times. Every time he fell his sword came out of its scabbard and both the sword and scabbard came to rest on the ground in the shape of the cross. Francis was appointed provost of his diocese, second in rank to the bishop, and in 1602 he was made bishop of the diocese of Geneva. Because of his outstanding writings on the spiritual life, Saint Francis de Sales is patron of writers and the press.

Saint Katharine Drexel (1858–1955)

If we wish to serve God and love our neighbor well, we must manifest our joy in the service we render to Him and them. Let us open wide our hearts. It is joy which invites us. Press forward and fear nothing.

—Saint Katharine Drexel

Saint Katharine Drexel was born in Philadelphia. Her parents impressed on her by word and example that their wealth was simply loaned to them and was to be shared with others. Early in life she became aware of the plight of the Native Americans and the Blacks, and when she inherited a vast fortune from her father and stepmother, she devoted her wealth to helping these disadvantaged people. In 1885 she established a school for Native Americans in Santa Fe, New Mexico. In 1891, with a few companions, Mother Katharine founded the Sisters of the Blessed Sacrament for Indians and Colored People. The title of the community summed up the two great driving forces in her

life—devotion to the Blessed Sacrament and love for the most deprived people in her country. She died at the age of 96 in 1955 and was canonized in 2000 by Pope John Paul II.

Saint Thomas More (1478–1535)

"A Man for All Seasons" is a 1966 film based on Robert Bolt's play of the same name about Saint Thomas More. The plot is based on the true story of Sir Thomas More, the sixteenth-century lawyer, author, and statesman, who became Lord Chancellor of England. More refused to sign a letter asking the Pope to annul King Henry VIII's marriage to Catherine of Aragon, and resigned in 1532 rather than take an Oath of Supremacy declaring the king the supreme head of the Church of England. He was indicted for high treason and sentenced to be hanged. Some days later King Henry changed this order to beheading on Tower Hill. The execution took place on Tower Hill "before nine of the clock" on July 6. His head was exposed on London Bridge for a month afterward. In 1935 he was canonized by Pope Pius XI.

Saint Anthony of Egypt (250–355)

Saint Anthony of Egypt contributed to the spread of monasticism, and his rule became the norm in Northern Egypt, from Lycopolis (Asyut) to the Mediterranean. His final resting place became the oldest inhabited monastery in the world. It is located in the Egyptian Sahara Desert of Egypt. It was built a few years after Saint Anthony's death. Because of attacks from the Berbers and Bedouins, the monks built fortress walls surrounding it. There are several agencies today restoring it and its remarkable paintings. Some of these works date back to the seventh and eighth centuries. Although the original library was plundered, more than seventeen hundred documents still remain in the hands of the monastery.

Saint Pachomius (292–348)

Saint Pachomius started the first monastery in A.D. 320 and is credited with writing the first communal rule for monks. This rule, called cenobitic, is characterized by life in common with regular worship, strict discipline, and manual labor. It signifies a change from the eremitic life, or life as a hermit. Eremitic monks or hermits lived alone in huts or caves, while cenobitic monks lived together in monasteries comprising one or a complex of several buildings. Pachomius is thought to have conceived the idea for living quarters like these from the time he spent in the Roman army, because the style is "reminiscent of army barracks."

Saint Basil the Great (329–379)
Prayer for a Deeper Sense of Fellowship with All Living Things

O God, grant us a deeper sense of fellowship with all living
   things, our little brothers and sisters to whom, in common
   with us,
   You have given this earth as home.

We recall with regret that in the past we have acted high-
   handedly and cruelly in exercising our domain over them.
Thus, the voice of the earth which should have risen to you
   in song has turned into a groan of travail.
May we realize that all these creatures also live for
   themselves and for You
   - not for us alone.
They too love the goodness of life, as we do, and
   serve you better in their way than we do in ours.

—Saint Basil the Great

Adapted from Catholic Community Forum

Saint Teresa of Ávila (1515–1582)
Born in Ávila, Spain, in 1515, Saint Teresa joined the Carmelite
Order in 1535. She had a severe illness that left her legs
paralyzed for three years, but then experienced a vision of "the
sorely wounded Christ" that changed her life forever. From
this point on, she moved into a period of increasingly ecstatic
experiences, in which she came to focus more on the passion
of Christ. She reformed her order and tried to create a more
primitive type of Carmelite called the Discalced, or "shoeless,"
Carmelites. Saint Teresa left a significant legacy of writings.
These works include *The Way of Perfection* and *The Interior
Castle*. She also wrote an autobiography, *The Life of Teresa of
Ávila*. In 1970 she was declared a Doctor of the Church for her
writing and teaching on prayer, and is one of three women to be
honored in this way. She is considered the patron of headache
sufferers and Spanish Catholic writers.

Blessed Hildegard von Bingen (1108–1179)
Blessed Hildegard von Bingen was a remarkable woman for
medieval times. Known as the "Sybil of the Rhine," she advised
bishops, popes, and kings. She traveled widely giving speeches,
something also unheard of at that time. She used the curative
powers of natural objects for healing, and wrote about natural
history and the medicinal uses of plants, animals, trees and
stones. She is the first composer whose biography is known.
She wrote music and texts to her songs, mostly liturgical
plainchant honoring saints and Mary for holidays and feast days.
Her musical plays were performed at the convent she founded.
Widely proclaimed a saint, she has not been canonized by the
Church. Her canonization process was officially applied, but the
process took so long that all four attempts at canonization were
not completed.

GLOSSARY

A

Acts of the Apostles New Testament book that gives an account of events in the early Church (p. 81)

allegory a story or image that contains an implicit hidden or spiritual meaning (p. 106)

anagogy a story or image that represents a future, eternal reality (p. 108)

apocalyptic Greek for "unveiling," a type of writing, often prophetic, that uses symbolic imagery to depict future events, often as a triumph of good over evil (p. 70)

B

biblical inerrancy the teaching that the Bible presents faithfully and without error the truths that God revealed for our salvation (p. 64)

biblical inspiration the gift of the Holy Spirit which assisted human authors in the writing of biblical books and which assured that the writing teaches without error God's saving truth (p. 63)

Book of Glory second part of the Gospel according to John beginning with Jesus' foot washing (John 13–21). This section contains Jesus' words of comfort to disciples and the proclamation of his glory. (p. 245)

Book of Revelation last book of the Bible; an account of highly symbolic visions of the future of the Church and the end times (p. 82)

Book of Signs first half of the Gospel according to John containing seven miracles performed by Jesus followed by his commentary explaining how each "sign" applies to him (p. 244)

Breviary the text of the divine office, including psalms, prayers, canticles, and readings to be prayed in the Liturgy of the Hours (p. 266)

C

canon of Scripture the list of writings officially recognized and accepted by the Catholic Church as inspired books of Sacred Scripture (p. 75)

contemplative prayer a solemn, silent expression of prayer that focuses on Jesus and the word of God (p. 47)

conversion "A radical reorientation of the whole life away from sin and evil, and toward God" (CCC, Glossary) (p. 174)

Council of Nicea first ecumenical council held in the year 325 in modern-day Turkey (p. 40)

Council of Trent meeting of Catholic bishops from 1545 to 1563 that clarified and defined Catholic teaching, especially in contrast to Protestantism (p. 96)

covenant a solemn promise or agreement between humans or between God and his People that involves agreed-upon commitments or guarantees (p. 128)

D

Decalogue literally "ten words" or "ten teachings," referring to the Ten Commandments, given by God to Moses on Mount Sinai (p. 142)

Dei Verbum literally "the Word of God." Latin title for the "Dogmatic Constitution on Divine Revelation" of Vatican Council II (1965). (p. 97)

Deposit of Faith the heritage of faith contained in Sacred Scripture and Tradition, handed on in the Church from the time of the Apostles, from which the Magisterium draws all that it proposes for belief as being divinely revealed (see *Catechism*, Glossary) (p. 60)

deutero-canonical books Catholic expression referring to those writings included in the Septuagint (Greek Old Testament) not found in the Palestinian canon of the Hebrew Bible; literally, "second canon" (p. 76)

discipleship accepting Jesus as our Lord and Savior and following him by studying and putting his ways into practice (p. 33)

Divine Revelation God's communication of himself, by which he makes known the mystery of his divine plan, a gift of self-communication which is realized by words and deed over time, and most fully by sending us his own divine Son, Jesus Christ (CCC, Glossary) (p. 31)

Divino Afflante Spiritu 1943 encyclical by Pope Pius XII that urged scholars to use modern methods of biblical criticism in the study of Scripture (p. 101)

doctrine general Church teachings (p. 39)

dogma fundamental truths of Revelation that have been defined by the Church as *"de fide"* and must be held by all Catholics (p. 39)

E

Epistles the twenty-one Letters included in the New Testament (p. 81)

Evangelists the authors of the Gospels (p. 196)

F

faith believing in God and all that he has revealed; faith is both a gift from God made possible by accepting and submitting to grace and a free, human choice (p. 32)

faith and good works the belief that faith in Jesus and doing good works are both necessary for salvation (p. 180)

G

genealogy a list of a person's ancestors (p. 225)

genre type of writing, such as history, parable, or poetry (p. 69)

Gentiles designation for people who are not Jewish (p. 165)

Gospels the Good News—the message of God's mercy and love, his Kingdom, and salvation revealed in Jesus. In particular, the four accounts of the life, teaching, death, and Resurrection of Jesus contained in the New Testament are the Gospels according to Matthew, Mark, Luke, and John (p. 80)

grace our participation in the life of God; "grace is *favor*, the *free and undeserved help* that God gives us to respond to his call to become children of God, adoptive sons, partakers of the divine nature and of eternal life" (CCC, 1996) (p. 261)

H

historical-critical approach analyzing a biblical text to try to learn the sources that influenced it, how people thought and expressed themselves at the time, and what the text meant to the audience for which it was written (p. 67)

hope the theological virtue by which we trust in God the Father, in everything that Christ has promised, and in the help of the Holy Spirit. It is the desire to achieve eternal happiness in Heaven and to cooperate with the graces that make this desire come true. (p. 210)

house churches small assemblies of early Christians who met in private homes to support one another, ponder Jesus' message, pray, and break bread (p. 165)

I

Incarnation at the time appointed by God, the only Son of God the Father, while retaining his divine nature, assumed human nature and became man (p. 199)

Infancy Narratives accounts, found in the beginning of the Gospels according to Matthew and Luke, that contain the genealogy of Jesus and the events surrounding his conception and birth (p. 199)

K

kenosis Greek word for "emptying;" in the New Testament, often it refers to "self-emptying" (p. 209)

Kingdom of God the reign of God ushered in by Jesus that makes God's grace present in the world, but reaches its fulfillment in Heaven (p. 204)

L

Last Supper the final Passover meal which Jesus ate with his disciples before his crucifixion (p. 207)

lectio divina literally "divine reading," "sacred reading," or "holy reading"; a meditative, prayerful reading of passages from the Bible (p. 268)

Lectionary book that contains the Scripture readings for the liturgy throughout the year (p. 263)

literal sense the historical and cultural meaning of the words of Scripture intended by the human author (p. 106)

literary criticism analyzing writing in terms of the literary form in which it is written (p. 69)

liturgy the official public prayer of the Church, through which Christ continues the work of redemption through the Church's celebration of the Paschal Mystery; it includes the seven Sacraments and the Liturgy of the Hours (p. 255)

Liturgy of the Hours the daily public prayer of the Church—divided up into segments—that celebrates the mystery of Christ, which permeates and transfigures the time of each day (p. 266)

Liturgy of the Word the Word of God proclaimed as part of each sacramental ritual helps us to have the proper dispositions for each of the Sacraments (p. 264)

logic specific method of forming an argument or a conclusion through the use of reason (p. 41)

logos Greek for "word" used in the prologue of the Gospel according to John to refer to Jesus as "Word of God" (p. 243)

M

Magisterium the official teaching office of the Church—the bishops in communion with the Pope—that interprets Scripture and Tradition and ensures faithfulness to the teachings of the Apostles (p. 60)

Marcionism a heresy that denied the unity of the two testaments and rejected the Old Testament based on the supposition that the New Testament has made it invalid (p. 160)

messianic secret Jesus' command to his disciples not to tell others that he is the Messiah; is found in some passages of the New Testament, especially in the Gospel according to Mark (p. 228)

metaphor a figure of speech comparing two things that are unlike but have certain similarities. The metaphor uses a concrete word to refer to something else to indicate a resemblance, for example, "God is my rock". (p. 69)

miracles wonders or signs attributed to divine power that show Jesus is the Messiah and that the Kingdom of God is present in him (see CCC, 547) (p. 238)

monotheism belief that there is one God (p. 142)

moral sense reading Scripture as a source of guidance for right behavior and leading us to just actions (p. 107)

mystical an experience of union with God such as emphasized in the Gospel according to John (p. 243)

mysticism an intense experience or direct communication of love of and union with God (p. 47)

N

New Testament the twenty-seven books of the Bible written by Christians during the first century that center on the life, teachings, and mission of Jesus and the early Church (p. 74)

Nicene Creed profession of Catholic faith, which came from the first ecumenical Councils of Nicea and Constantinople (p. 40)

O

objective not influenced by personal feelings or opinions when considering or representing facts (p. 43)

Old Testament the forty-six books of the Bible written before Jesus' time that deal with the time from the beginning of creation to shortly before the coming of Jesus and record the stories and events of God's relationship with his Chosen People (p. 74)

oral tradition stories, poems, songs, and proverbs that are passed down verbally from one generation to another without being fixed in written form (p. 77)

Original Sin the lack of original holiness and justice in human nature, handed down from the first sin of Adam and Eve (p. 127)

P

Palestinian Canon the books of Hebrew Scripture often used in Israel (Palestine) at the time of Jesus and declared the official Jewish Scriptures by rabbis around A.D. 100 (p. 76)

parable a way Jesus taught with metaphors or similes drawn from common life experiences or nature to illustrate moral or spiritual truths that challenge people to make a radical choice about entering the Kingdom of God (p. 231)

Paschal Mystery Christ's work of redemption brought about by his Passion, death, Resurrection, and Ascension. We celebrate the Paschal Mystery in the liturgy of the Church, during which Christ's saving work is made present and communicated, most especially in the Sacrament of the Eucharist. (p. 136)

Passion Narratives accounts of events leading up to the death of Jesus that show his love for humanity; found in all four Gospels (p. 209)

Passover Jewish holy day commemorating God's deliverance of the Chosen People from death by ordering the Jews to sprinkle the blood of the lamb on their doorposts in Egypt; also called Pesach or Pasch (p. 136)

Pentecost the fiftieth day coming immediately after the seven weeks following Passover. On the fiftieth day after Jesus' Resurrection, Christians celebrate Pentecost, the day when the Holy Spirit came to the followers of Jesus, inspiring them to preach and carry on his message (p. 165)

Pharaohs rulers of ancient Egypt who were in power when the Israelites were slaves (p. 131)

Promised Land the land (from the River of Egypt to the Euphrates, known as Canaan) promised to Abraham and his descendants in Genesis Chapter 12 (p. 131)

prophet someone chosen by God to speak for him (p. 145)

Q

Q Source the term used for the apparent common source for passages found in both Matthew and Luke's Gospels but not in Mark's (p. 224)

R

reason the ability to think, decide, and form conclusions in a logical way (p. 26)

S

Sacraments effective signs of grace, instituted by Christ and entrusted to the Church, by which divine life is shared with us through the work of the Holy Spirit (p. 261)

Seder the symbolic Jewish Passover meal ritual marking the start of Passover and celebrated each year near the beginning of spring (p. 136)

Septuagint Greek translation of the Hebrew Scriptures for Jews that no longer knew Hebrew, completed around 100 B.C., and eventually accepted by the Catholic Church as our version of the Old Testament (p. 74)

Sermon on the Mount a collection of teachings, including the Beatitudes and other moral teachings of Jesus, found in the Gospel according to Matthew, Chapters 5–7 (p. 225)

Sermon on the Plain in the Gospel according to Luke, a collection of teachings by Jesus that includes a list of Beatitudes found in Luke 6:17–45 (p. 229)

subjective an attitude or viewpoint arising from personal background, experience, bias, or reflection (p. 43)

Synoptic Gospels The Gospels according to Matthew, Mark, and Luke insofar as they display much similarity. Synoptic means "similar" or "to see together." (p. 80)

T

theology the study of God or of religious faith and practice. Saint Augustine described it as "reasoning or concerning the deity" (*City of God* VIII, i) (p. 41)

Tradition the living transmission, under the inspiration of the Holy Spirit, of the message of the Gospel in the Church (see *Catechism*, Glossary) (p. 60)

Transfiguration the culminating moment in the public life of Jesus in which his appearance changed in the presence of the Apostles, and Elijah and Moses appeared beside him to reveal him as the true Messiah (p. 206)

Trinity the mystery of one God in three divine Persons: Father, Son, and Holy Spirit (p. 25)

V

Vatican Council II an ecumenical council of the Catholic Church. It was a meeting in Rome of the world's Catholic bishops from 1962–1965, called for by Pope John XXIII to "open wide the doors" and let "fresh air" into the Church (p. 97)

vernacular language the language commonly spoken by people in a particular country or region, such as German, Spanish, or Mandarin Chinese (p. 96)

W

wisdom a spiritual gift that makes it possible for someone to know about the purpose and plan of God; one of the seven Gifts of the Holy Spirit (p. 26)

Y

YHWH name for God revealed to Moses; "I am who I am" or "I will be who I will be" (p. 131)

INDEX

ENDNOTES

1 (CCC, 294) AG 2; cf. I Cor 15:28.

2 (CCC, 32) St. Augustine, Sermo 241, 2: PL 38, 1134.

3 (CCC, 85) DV 10 § 2.

4 (CCC, 107) DV 11.

5 (CCC, 110) DV 12 § 2.

6 (CCC, 125) DV 18.

7 (CCC, 124) DV 17; cf. Rom 1:16.

8 (CCC, 124) Cf. DV 20.

9 (CCC, 114) Cf. Rom 12:6.

10 (CCC, 118) Lettera gesta docet, quid credas allegoria, moralis quid agas, quo tendas anagogia. Augustine of Dacia, Rotulus pugillaris, I: ed. A. Walz: Angelicum § (1929) 256;

Augustine of Dacia, Rotulus pugillaris, I: ed. A. Walz: Angelicum § (1929) 256.

11 (CCC, 145) Heb 11:8; cf. Gen 12:1-4.

12 (CCC, 145) Cf. Gen 23:4.

13 (CCC, 145) Cf. Heb 11:17.

14 (CCC, 129) Cf. I Cor 5:6-8; 10:1-11.

15 (CCC, 129) Cf. St. Augustine, Quaest. in Hept. 2, 73: PL 34, 623; Cf. DV 16.

16 (CCC, 2547) Lk 6:24.

17 USCCB J&D-Global Hunger

18 (CCC, 519) John Paul II, RH 11 [32].

19 (CCC, 519) I Cor 15:3; Rom 4:25.

20 (CCC, 1966) St. Augustine, De serm. Dom. 1, 1: PL 34, 1229-1230.

21 (CCC, 515) Cf. Lk 2:7; Mt 27:48; Jn 20:7.

22 (CCC, 515) Col 2:9.

23 Professor L. Michael White

24 (CCC, 2653) DV 25; cf. Phil 3:8; St. Ambrose, De officiis ministrorum 1, 20, 88: PL 16, 50.

25 According to the Stewart B. McKinney Act, 42 U.S.C. § 11301, et seq (1994).

26 Renewing the Earth, 11.

27 The Hundredth Year, #51, p. 99.

28 (CCC, 2759) Lk 11:1.

29 (CCC, 2759) Cf. Lk 11:2-4.

30 (CCC, 2759) Cf. Mt 6:9-13.

31 (CCC, 2675) Cf. Lk 1:46-55.

PHOTO CREDITS